Passion Before Me, My Fate Behind

Passion Before Me, My Fate Behind

Ibn al-Fāriḍ and the Poetry of Recollection

Th. Emil Homerin

SUNY PRESS

Cover illustration of a manuscript page featuring verses from Ibn al-Fāriḍ's *Wine Ode* together with verses from his poem *al-Dālīyah*, courtesy of the Memorial Art Gallery, University of Rochester, Rochester, NY. Used by permission.

Published by State University of New York Press, Albany

Printed in the United States of America

For information, contact State University of New York Press, Albany, NY
www.sunypress.edu

Production by Eileen Meehan
Marketing by Michael Campochiaro

Library of Congress Cataloging-in-Publication Data

Homerin, Th. Emil, 1955–
Passion before me, my fate behind : Ibn al-Farid and the poetry of recollection / Th. Emil Homerin.
p. cm.
Includes bibliographical references and index.
ISBN 978-1-4384-3901-3 (hc : alk. paper) 978-1-4384-3900-6 (pb : alk. paper)
1. Ibn al-Farid, 'Umar ibn 'Ali, 1181 or 2-1235—Criticism and interpretation. 2. Sufi poetry, Arabic—History and criticism. I. Title.

PJ7755.I18Z683 2011
892.7'134—dc22 2011003164

10 9 8 7 6 5 4 3 2 1

Contents

Preface vii
Acknowledgments xi
Plan of the Work xiii
On Translation, Transliteration, Pronunciation, and Time xv

INTRODUCTION 1
Life 1
On the Sufi Path 3
Words of Love and Longing 8
Luminaries 14

1. MYSTICAL IMPROVISATIONS 31
Master Poet 31
Homage to al-Mutanabbī 32
Transformations 49
Riddles & Rubāᶜīyāt 54

2. LOVE'S SECRETS 63
Tryst 63
Love Talk 65
Hymns of Devotion 69
Sun and Full Moon 77
"You Have Been Remembered" 84

3. JOINED AT THE CROSSROADS 103
The Changing Ode 103
Sacred Fire 108
Turn Aside at Ṭai 118
Holy Pilgrimage 128
"Greetings from Suᶜād" 136

4. THE BELOVED'S WINE 143
Blood-Red Wine 143
A Liberated Spirit 147
Two Intoxications 152
Drunk by a Glance 157
Immortal Wine 165
Wine of the Covenant 172

5. POEM OF THE SUFI WAY IN "T"–MAJOR 177
The Great Ode 177
Together Alone 178
Shifting Guises 191
Love's Sweet Season 203
Spirit and Matter 207
Yesterday's Tomorrow 212
Manifest Sites 215
Shadow Play 221
Poet & Guide 228
Covering Reality 231
Two Masters 239

CONCLUSION: THE POETRY OF RECOLLECTION 243
I but not "Me" 243
Content *and* Form 245
Beginning to End 246
Meditation and Recollection 249

Notes 253
Bibliography 293
Index 307

Preface

From the beginning, mystical perceptions of life have been part of the Islamic world, and by the ninth century CE, they began to appear in Arabic poetry. Many medieval and modern readers have viewed this poetry as verse accounts of Sufi doctrine reflecting a mystic's endeavors to describe an experience of great profundity and overwhelming emotion. Yet, too often, such explanations are based on romantic notions of poetry that focus on an individual's lonely self-struggle, and they isolate this poetry from its larger social, religious, and literary contexts. Certainly, some poets attempt to depict a religious experience or to evoke similar moods by aesthetic means. However, the words of a poem are meaningful only if they convey to others an experience of life that imaginatively involves and moves them. Mystical verse, then, is as much a collective as an individual vision of reality that interprets human existence in order to imbue life with sense and significance. Therefore, to understand and appreciate the depth and effect of Muslim mystical poetry, we must examine this verse not only in context of the life of a particular poet, but also in light of systems of religious belief and their expression within established literary traditions.

At the heart of the Arabic poetic heritage is the lyric ode (*qaṣīdah*) and the love poem (*ghazal*) that served as the primary vehicles for Arabic poetic expression beginning with their pre-Islamic usage. The formal and symbolic dimensions of this verse served as a foundation for Islamic mystical poetry providing a method of speculation and communication concerning things of collective importance. Nevertheless, many pre-Islamic beliefs were no longer acceptable in the Islamic milieu, and so they were recast in new forms, often humanized and assimilated by the symbolic and evocative nature of metaphor. Thus, the primary symbols of Arab culture were perceived and colored by Muslims and their concerns, receiving a specific complexion over time. The multiple, often subtle, meanings of these symbols lent themselves to religious and poetic usages whose function was to establish humanity's meaningful existence in a seemingly indifferent world. Many motifs and metaphors of Islamic mystical poetry reflect this process of mythopoesis, and poets used them to deepen the feeling and impact of their verse. The mystical character of this poetry was further enhanced by the use of rhetorical strategies (*badīᶜ*), including antithesis, alliteration, and paronomasia, which offered new and exciting opportunities for both abstraction and synthesis to the point of synesthesia.

Perhaps no one was more sensitive to this Arabic poetic legacy than ᶜUmar Ibn al-Fāriḍ. Born in Cairo in 576/1181, Ibn al-Fāriḍ became a respected religious scholar and poet, known for his mystical themes. One of Ibn al-Fāriḍ's sons, Kamāl al-Dīn Muhammad, apparently possessed a manuscript of poems written by Ibn al-Fāriḍ in his own hand prior to his death in 632/1235, and these poems became the core of a collection entitled the *Dīwān Ibn al-Fāriḍ* compiled and arranged by ᶜAlī, Ibn al-Fāriḍ's grandson. ᶜAlī prefaced the poems with stories of Ibn al-Fāriḍ's saintly life, and he ended his collection with an appendix of a few additional poems thought to be by his grandfather. ᶜAlī's collection was read and copied often over the centuries, and it has remained the standard edition of Ibn al-Fāriḍ's verse until today.[1]

In his poems, Ibn al-Fāriḍ persistently evoked and at times articulated a mystical view of existence suffused with divine love and light. Essential to this verse is *dhikr*, "recollection," in both its poetic and mystical aspects. Poetically, the act of recollection often initiates a poem on love, loss, and longing. Especially in religious poetry, the poet may project his reverie on to various poetic personas to enact an interior drama through which he voices his thoughts and feelings as he seeks a divine presence within. On occasion, meditative disciplines have informed the shape and content of such verse, leading to what has been referred to as meditative or contemplative poetry.[2] In Ibn al-Fāriḍ's case, the Sufi practice of *dhikr*, the "recollection" or meditation on God, is echoed in many of his poems, particularly the famous *al-Khamrīyah* wine ode and his Sufi classic the *Naẓm al-Sulūk*, "The Poem of the Sufi Way." In these and other poems, Ibn al-Fāriḍ drew from the Arabic poetic tradition and Islamic mysticism to evoke a view of existence in which the seeker might be transformed by an epiphany revealing his intimate relationship to the divine beloved.

In his verse, Ibn al-Fāriḍ expressed the spiritual concerns and longings of many Muslims, and the enormous popularity of his Arabic poetry led to his enduring reputation as the greatest Arab Sufi poet and, over the centuries, to his veneration as a saint. Although Ibn al-Fāriḍ's saintly status has declined over the past two hundred years, Arabs and Muslims continue to show unfailing esteem for his refined poetry. Significantly, Ibn al-Fāriḍ's own contemporaries viewed him primarily as a poet. This is not to deny the importance of Islamic mysticism to him and his verse for which he became so famous among later generations. However, the beauty of his poetry, its moods, meanings, and spiritual import can be more fully grasped and appreciated within the contexts of both Islamic mysticism and Arabic poetry where Ibn al-Fāriḍ remains the *sulṭān al-ᶜāshiqīn*, "the sultan of lovers."

Acknowledgments

This study has taken shape over a number of years, building on the efforts of many others. Earlier works on Ibn al-Fāriḍ, especially those by R.A. Nicholson, A.J. Arberry, C.A. Nallino, and H.H. Ḥilmī, are foundational, to which may be added a number of more recent studies, including those of Issa Boullata and Giuseppe Scattolin, particularly the latter's critical edition of the poet's *Dīwān*, which I have used throughout this study. Furthermore, many institutions and foundations have supported this project, and my thanks are due to the Mrs. Giles Whiting Foundation, the Fulbright Foundation, the National Endowment for the Humanities, and the University of Rochester. In Egypt, I was greatly assisted by Dār al-Kutub al-Miṣrīyah, Dār al-Wathā'iq, the Arab League Manuscript Institute, the Netherlands-Flemish Institute in Cairo, the American University in Cairo, and the American Research Center in Egypt and, in Turkey, by the Süleimaniye Kütüphanesi.

Friends and colleagues have graciously offered their advice, comments and corrections, as did the two anonymous readers for SUNY Press, and their insightful suggestions have made this a better book. In particular, I wish to thank Daniel Beaumont, Daniel Bisgaard, Mark Brandl, Douglas Brooks, the late and much missed William Cleveland, Vincent Cornell, Kenneth Cuno, Bruce Craig, Robert Dankoff, Ernest Dawn, Frederick De Jong, Frederick Denny, Frederick Donner, Carl Ernst, William Scott Green, Aḥmad Ḥarīdī, Evelyn Hartleben, the late and inspiring teacher Ronald Jennings, Barbara Jordan, Mahmud Erol Kilic, Blair Kling, Franklin Lewis, Paul Losensky, Sean Marmon, Heshmet Moayyad, Nancy Norwood, Séan O'Feahy, Ruth Ost, Rudolaph Peters, Carl Petry, the late, great scholar, Fazlur Rahman, Jerold Ramsey, Helga Rebhan, Iymān Fu'ād Sayyid, Giuseppe Scattolin, Michael Sells, Suzanne Stetkevych, John Swanson, Edward Wierenga, and, with love, Nora Walter.

Finally, I offer a special word of thanks to Jaroslav Stekevych. For a number of years under his guidance, I read Arabic verse, including that of Ibn al-Fāriḍ, and he patiently taught me how to read poetry in the first place. For that I am most grateful, and so I dedicate this book to Professor Jaroslav Stekevych, a true scholar, teacher, and friend.

Plan of the Work

This study begins with a concise biography of Ibn al-Fāriḍ based largely on accounts from his students and supplemented from the hagiography written on him by his grandson. This is followed by an overview of Islamic mysticism and a survey of early Sufi verse through the seventh/thirteenth century, which help to place Ibn al-Fāriḍ within the religious and poetic trends of his time. Chapter 1 then explores specific literary dimensions of Ibn al-Fāriḍ's poetry and the influence on him by earlier Arab poets. Particularly important was the verse by the famous fifth/tenth-century Arab poet al-Mutanabbī, as Ibn al-Fāriḍ consciously patterned two of his poems on poems by him. A careful comparison of these poems demonstrates how Ibn al-Fāriḍ used various rhetorical strategies and Sufi ideas and terms to transform al-Mutanabbī's poems in praise of his patrons into mystical poems on love and longing. Ibn al-Fāriḍ often employed such rhetorical elements to create a mystical paradox at the heart of his poems, including riddles and quatrains, which also reveal the poet to be erudite and, sometimes, funny.

Chapter 2 focuses on Ibn al-Fāriḍ's *ghazals* as the product of changing notions of love and the Sufis' use of the language of love to convey mystical themes. Ibn al-Fāriḍ's love poems are examined in terms of both style and content, with an inquiry into the possible identities of the beloved. In his *ghazals*, the beloved is sometimes male and other times, female, yet Ibn al-Fāriḍ leaves clues throughout his love poems that the beloved may be the prophet Muhammad, and occasionally, God. A close reading of Ibn al-Fāriḍ's *ghazal* rhyming in "J" brings a number of these elements into sharper focus. Chapter 3 traces a similar trajectory as chapter 2, save that its subject is Ibn al-Fāriḍ's *qasīḍahs*, or lyric odes. The pre-Islamic Arabic ode was adapted and transformed during the Umayyad and Abbasid periods and, in time, Sufis began to read the ode as a mystical allegory. Significantly, Ibn al-Fāriḍ's lyric odes revolve around the Hajj pilgrimage to Mecca as the paradigmatic quest for union with God. The chapter ends with a close reading of Ibn al-Fāriḍ's *qasīḍah* rhyming in "D," to illustrate and highlight important themes and elements in these odes.

Chapter 4 features Ibn al-Fāriḍ's wine verse. Formally, he composed at least three wine poems, one of them being his massive *Naẓm al-Sulūk*, which is the focus of chapter 5. Chapter 4 traces pre-Islamic Arabic wine poetry through its Christian and Muslim varieties until the sixth/twelfth century. During the Muslim period, Sufis often composed verses on wine and intoxication to speak of love and union, and Ibn al-Fāriḍ combined these and other elements in his *al-Khamrīyah*. A close reading of this poem suggests why it became the most famous wine ode in all of Islamic mysticism. Staying with mystical themes, chapter 5 is organized around a reading and analysis of Ibn al-Fāriḍ's longest and most famous poem on the Sufism. Entitled the *Naẓm al-Sulūk* ("Poem of the Sufi Way") or the *al-Tā'īyah al-Kubrā* ("The Longer Ode in T"), this poem spans 760 verses, and, here, the poem is divided into a number of discreet sections in order to examine prominent stylistic elements and Ibn al-Fāriḍ's views on mysticism, which were substantially influenced by thought of earlier Sufi masters, especially, al-Junayd, al-Tusturī, and Muhammad al-Ghazālī.

The conclusion returns to essential elements and themes in Ibn al-Fāriḍ's verse, including the lyrical persona and its range of tone and mood as the poetic "I" may be a lover, a student, a teacher, a mystic in union, the beloved, or the Light of Muhammad. Yet, whatever the poetic persona, Ibn al-Fāriḍ's verse stands as a clear example of contemplative poetry for meditation is a central feature. Ibn al-Fāriḍ frequently alludes to the Sufi practices of *dhikr* ("recollection') and *samā*ᶜ ("audition"), which were essential to his poetry and mystical life. As such, Ibn al-Fāriḍ's poems draw from his recollections—of the beloved, of the pilgrimage, and of his larger Sufi and Muslim heritage—in order to speak of love and life, and their spiritual transformation.

On Translation, Transliteration, Pronunciation, and Time

Most of the Arabic poems cited in this study have been regarded as classical works for centuries, and so they deserve a reasonable poetic counterpart in English. When translating this verse, I have been concerned not only with form and content, but also with a poem's tones, moods, and deeper meanings. Toward this end, my own method of translation generally follows that laid out by Robert Bly in *The Eight Stages of Translation*.[3] The final stages of a translation are particularly crucial, and here I have been greatly helped by my previous study of English poetry and its composition with two fine poets, Barbara Jordan and Jerry Ramsey. Michael Sells of the University of Chicago and Ruth Ost of Temple University also have read drafts of many of my translations over the years, and both have offered valuable suggestions in light of their deep knowledge and appreciation of poetry and mysticism.

Certain key Arabic terms and verses are cited in transliteration along with their translations in order to alert the reader to multiple meanings, word plays, and subtle relationships among important word clusters. The transliteration of these words follows the system used for Arabic by the Library of Congress. Well-known words and names, however, are generally cited in their common English forms (e.g., Sufi, not Ṣūfī; Cairo for al-Qāhirah; Moses, not Mūsā). When pronouncing these transliterations, the reader should be aware that Arabic vowels and consonants approximate those of English. There are three short Arabic vowels: (1) *a* as in "bat," (2) *i* as in "bit," (3) *u* as in "put," whereas long vowels are usually lengthened short vowels. There are two Arabic diphthongs: (1) *ay* as in the "i" of "bite," and (2) *aw* as in "cow." The majority of Arabic consonants sound like their English equivalents with the following additions: the *hamzah* (ʾ) is a glottal stop; the *ʿayn* (ʿ) is produced by "swallowing" the vowel immediately preceding or following it (e.g., ʿUmar); *kh* approximates the "ch" of "loch" or "Bach; "*ḥ*" resembles a breathy, whispered "ha!" Furthermore, there are four velarized or "emphatic" consonants: *ṣ*, *ḍ*, *ṭ*, *ẓ*, which give a "darker" quality to the surrounding vowels (e.g., Arabic *s* is pronounced like the English "sad," while *ṣ* approximates "sod." The emphatics are of special importance to this work since the poet's name is Ibn al-Fāriḍ; the emphatic *ḍ* gives the *ā* the sound of a prolonged "a" as in "father."

All dates are cited in their Islamic/Ḥijrī year followed by their Common Era equivalent: for example, 632/1235.

Introduction

ᶜUmar Ibn al-Fāriḍ is the most famous Arab poet within Islamic mysticism. He was a master of the Arabic poetic tradition, composing verse in a number of forms including the quatrain, the *ghazal*, the ode (*qaṣīdah*), and wine ode (*khamrīyah*). Ibn al-Fāriḍ's poetry is lyrical and complex, as he explores mystical feelings and themes relating to the quest of a devoted lover to regain union with his lost beloved. Ibn al-Fārid'ṣ poems, with their intricate style and elegant beauty, have moved generations of Muslims, and for centuries, he has been admired and imitated as an Arab poet and venerated as a Muslim saint.

Life

When ᶜUmar Ibn al-Fāriḍ died in 632/1235, he was an established poet and a respected teacher. Several of his students left brief biographical notices on him, and these earliest sources agree that ᶜUmar was born in Cairo on the 4th of Dhū al-Qaᶜdah 576/1181. He was the son of Abū al-Ḥasan ᶜAlī ibn al-Murshid ibn ᶜAlī, and a descendent of the Saᶜd tribe of Arabia. His father ᶜAlī ibn al-Murshid migrated to Cairo from Hama prior to ᶜUmar's birth, probably to serve in the judiciary of the Ayyubid dynasty, which had replaced the Shīᶜī Fatimids in 568/1171.[1] The Ayyubid sultan, Ṣalāḥ al-Dīn (Saladin, r. 566–89/1171–93) established several Sunni law schools in Cairo together with a *khānqāh*, a residence and chantry for as many as three hundred Sufis. In his attempts to promote Sunni Islam, Ṣalāḥ al-Dīn also appears to have favored non-Egyptian scholars to fill many legal positions, perhaps to ensure their loyalty to him, and this may have brought ᶜUmar's father to Cairo.[2] There, ᶜAlī ibn al-Murshid served as a women's advocate (*fāriḍ*) in legal proceedings, thus ᶜUmar's eventual title Ibn al-Fāriḍ, "son of the women's advocate." ᶜAlī ibn al-Murshid was a member of the Shāfiᶜī law school and was respected for his religious knowledge.[3]

ʿAlī ibn al-Murshid oversaw ʿUmar's education in the religious sciences and in Arabic language, literature, and poetry (*adab*). ʿUmar also studied the traditions of the prophet Muḥammad (*ḥadīth*) with the noted traditionalist of Damascus Abū Muḥammad al-Qāsim ibn ʿAlī Ibn al-ʿAsākir (d. 527/1203). Early sources also note that Ibn al-Fāriḍ was, like his father, a member of the Shāfiʿī law school, and that he undertook the study and practice of Islamic mysticism, or Sufism, composing poetry on the Sufi path (*ʿalā ṭarīqat al-taṣawwuf*). Unfortunately, his students do not record any information regarding Sufi masters or books that he may have consulted. Ibn al-Fāriḍ's earliest biographers add that he went on pilgrimage to Mecca, where he lived and studied for a time, after which he returned to Cairo. There, he supported himself by teaching *ḥadīth* and poetry at the Azhar congregational mosque. ʿUmar Ibn al-Fārid died on the 2nd of Jumādā I 632/1235, and was buried at the foot of Mt. Muqaṭṭam in the Qarāfah, the large cemetery north east of Cairo.[4]

The early, brief sketches of Ibn al-Fāriḍ by his students may be fleshed out by an influential later source, the *Dībājah* ("The Adorned Proem"). Composed by the poet's grandson ʿAlī (fl. 735/1334), this work is an introduction to the *Dīwān Ibn al-Fāriḍ*, ʿAlī's definitive collection of his grandfather's poetry. However, the *Dībājah* must be used with caution, for the work is clearly a hagiography of a saintly life, not a factual biography of a grandfather who had probably died before ʿAlī was born. Still, ʿAlī provides important information regarding Ibn al-Fāriḍ's family by noting that Ibn al-Fāriḍ was married and had at least two sons, Kamāl-Dīn Muḥammad (d. 689/1290) and ʿAbd al-Raḥmān, and an unnamed daughter, who was ʿAlī's mother. ʿAlī also relates many stories about his grandfather, ordering them in such a way as to portray Ibn al-Fāriḍ's progress along the mystic path from a religiously naive youth to a spiritually realized Sufi master and divinely inspired poet. Along the way, many miraculous events occur to his grandfather, including Ibn al-Fāriḍ's instantaneous travel over hundreds of miles, his conversation with a lion, and his frequent trances followed by automatic recitation of scores of verses.[5]

Despite such tales, ʿAlī may have based his narrative loosely on Ibn al-Fāriḍ's life as told to him by his uncle, Ibn al-Fāriḍ's son, Kamāl-Dīn Muḥammad. According to the *Dībājah*, in his youth ʿUmar would sit with his father during court cases and teaching sessions. But ʿUmar would grow restless, and so leave and wander in the Muqaṭṭam Hills for spiritual retreat. There, he met an old shaykh who instructed him to seek enlightenment in Mecca. Following this advice, ʿUmar went on pilgrimage to Mecca, where he lived and studied for about fifteen years. Ibn al-Fāriḍ then returned to Cairo as a mature religious scholar and an accomplished poet. In Cairo, Ibn al-Fāriḍ was a member of the religious and cultural elite of his day, teaching at the Azhar mosque, and discussing poetry with colleagues.[6] This last fact is corroborated by the literary scholar al-Ṣafadī (d. 764/1363), who recounted an instance of Ibn al-Fāriḍ adjudicating a dispute between two poets who claimed to have composed the same poem.[7]

ᶜAlī mentions that Ibn al-Fāriḍ composed some of his poems in Mecca, though ᶜAlī suggests that his grandfather composed much more of his verse in Cairo, including his famous poem the *Naẓm al-Sulūk* ("Poem of the Sufi Way"). In several stories, ᶜAlī highlights his grandfather's reputation as an acclaimed poet and venerated figure in Cairo, where one of his poems was recited before the Ayyubid sultan al-Malik al-Kāmil (r. 615–35/1218–38). The poem so impressed the sultan that he sent a gift of money to the poet, which Ibn al-Fāriḍ refused to accept. The sultan and one of his amirs made other offers on several later occasions, but Ibn al-Fāriḍ declined them all. The clear moral of such stories was that Ibn al-Fāriḍ would not be tainted by money or power.[8] Although we cannot verify the historical accuracy of these accounts, it is significant that Ibn al-Fāriḍ's collected poems do not contain any panegyrics for rulers or their retainers, who often were the patrons and subjects of professional poets of the time.

On the Sufi Path

ᶜAlī concludes his *Dībājah* with two different accounts of Ibn al-Fāriḍ's final hours of mystical rapture and eventual death, and the explicit signs that his grandfather should be recorded among God's saintly friends. In one account, the spirit of the prophet Muhammad suddenly appears to lead the prayers at Ibn al-Fāriḍ's funeral.[9] Although ᶜAlī's reverential account of his grandfather differs substantially from the earlier notices on the poet by Ibn al-Fāriḍ's students, all agree that Ibn al-Fāriḍ had studied and participated in the Islamic mystical tradition. Known in Arabic as *taṣawwuf*, "following the Sufi path," Islamic mysticism is commonly known in the West as Sufism. Islamic mysticism may be defined as the study of experiences within Islam characterized by ineffability and transience, and frequently by a positive sense of passivity, timelessness, and unity. Sufism also includes the methods to attain and refine these experiences, the theories and doctrines regarding their origin and significance, and the place of these experiences within the lives of individuals and their societies.[10]

Sufism shares much in common with other mystical traditions, and some similarities probably owe to the fact that Islam arose and flourished in an environment of religious diversity, which included Zoroastrianism, Gnosticism, Judaism, and Christianity. Islamic mystics clearly were influenced by Christian ascetic and mystical practices in the region, such as wearing a simple frock of wool (*ṣūf*), from which Sufism derives its name.[11]

The forefathers of the Sufi movement were the Muslim ascetics, who feared transgressing God's commandments and the divine punishment to follow. Some of these pious Muslims undertook asceticism as penance and as a means to restrain temptation. Their practices included fasting, late-night prayer vigils, and seclusion, as well as periods of celibacy, although lifelong celibacy generally was regarded as a violation of the Qur'ān and Muhammad's prophetic tradition. Although asceticism did not appeal to most Muslims, for some, including many Sufis, ascetic practices were essential tools for self-control, purification, and repentance.[12] Fear of the Judgment Day and divine chastisement were prime motives for an ascetic life, yet, Muslim mystics also sought solace in God's love and forgiveness as mentioned in the Qur'ān:

> Say [to them Muhammad]: "If you love God, then follow me, that He may love you and forgive your sins, for God is forgiving and merciful." (3:31)
>
> God loves those who depend on Him completely. (3:159)
>
> To God belongs the east and west; wherever you turn, there is the face of God. (2:115)
>
> If my servants inquire of you concerning Me, lo, I am near. (2:186)
>
> We are nearer [to the human being] than his jugular vein. (50:16)

In these and similar passages, the Qur'ān declares that God is ever-present with His creation and, in his mercy, He has sent down revelations to humanity. As such, the Qur'ān is the essential guide for all Muslims who seek to live in accordance with God's commandments. Moreover, Muslim mystics have been inspired by the Qur'ān's accounts of human and divine encounters. Stories of the prophets, including

Moses on Sinai, and his standing before the Burning Bush, Abraham's conversations with God, and Jesus' miracles, have served as patterns for a close personal relationship with God. Even more paradigmatic has been the life of the prophet Muhammad, and the Qur'ān's allusions to his moments of spiritual revelation:

> Blessed be He who took His servant [Muhammad] by night from the sacred mosque to the furthest mosque, whose precincts We have blessed, that We might show him Our signs . . . (17:1)

> Truly this is a revelation inspired, taught to him [Muhammad] by one powerful, possessing strength, who set himself on the farthest horizon and then drew close and descended to within two bows' lengths or nearer, and he revealed to His servant what he revealed. The heart did not lie about what it saw, so will you wrangle about what he saw? He saw him descend again, near the furthest lote tree where the Garden of Sanctuary is, where there enveloped the lote tree what enveloped it. His vision did not turn away or transgress, and truly, he saw one the greatest signs of his Lord! (53:4–18)

For Muslims, these accounts form the basis of Muhammad's miraculous night journey from Mecca to Jerusalem, from where he ascended to heaven (*al-isra' wa-al-miʿrāj*). According to tradition, Muhammad, accompanied by the archangel Gabriel, met with various prophets in heaven and, ultimately, with God. While the Qur'ān's enigmatic passages just cited do not mention ascension at all, later Muslim tradition gives detailed descriptions of these events based on prophetic *ḥadīth* (*al-ḥadīth al-nabawī*). The *ḥadīth* are accounts of Muhammad's sayings and actions and the second foundational source for Islam. They have been essential for elaborating on Muhammad's heavenly ascension and other archetypal aspects of his pious life, and when compiled together in a narrative form, they may resemble a Christian gospel. Still other *ḥadīth* collections serve as guides for religious ritual and legal matters, and offer aphorisms and advice for following the straight path to God:

> [Muhammad], the Apostle of God, God's blessings and peace be upon him, said: "Sincerity is that you worship God as if you see Him, and if you do not see Him, know that He sees you."

> The Prophet, God's blessings and peace be upon him, said: "Not one of you truly believes until you love for your brother what you love for yourself."
>
> The Messenger of God, God's blessings and peace be upon him, said: "Be in this world as if you were a stranger or wayfarer."[13]

Together with the prophetic *ḥadīth* is a smaller body of traditions known as "Divine Sayings" (*al-ḥadīth al-qudsī*), which are purported to be the words of God revealed to Muhammad but not found in the Qur'ān for various reasons. Among them is the famous "Tradition of Willing Devotions" full of mystical import:

> The Messenger of God, God's blessings and peace be upon him, said: "God said: 'My servant draws near to Me by nothing more dear to Me than by the religious obligations that I have imposed upon him, and My servant continues to draw near to Me by willing acts of devotion such that I love him. Then, when I love him, I become the ear with which he hears, the eye with which he sees, the hand with which he grasps, and the foot with which he walks. Surely if he were to request something of Me, I would give it, and if he were to seek My protection, I would shelter him . . .' "[14]

By the early third/ninth century, mystically inclined religious scholars cited the Qur'ān, prophetic traditions, and divine sayings in their Qur'ānic commentaries, guidebooks, and other works, including biographies, spiritual genealogies, mystical lexicons, and epistles containing explanations and instructions regarding Sufi thought and practice. These works explore some of the psychological states (*ḥāl*/*aḥwāl*), and ethical and cognitive stages (*maqām*/*maqāmāt*) on the mystic path leading toward the annihilation of selfishness (*fanā'*) and, subsequently, abiding in accord with the will and living presence of God (*baqā'*). Sincere love and humility are essential to achieving this ultimate goal, and for Sufis, this requires a physical and mental struggle against selfishness (*nafs*) in order to uncover the divine spirit (*rūḥ*) within. Therefore, one must continually check base tendencies by introspection and a strong conscience aligned with God's guidance, so that one may be at peace and pleasing to one's Lord:

> So be mindful of God as much as you can, and listen, obey, and spend (on charity) for your own good, for whoever

> is saved from his own selfishness will be among the prosperous. (Q. 64:16)

Throughout the Qur'an, God exhorts humanity to *dhikr*, to remember and be mindful of Him and His blessings, and Sufis developed *dhikr* into a meditative practice. *Dhikr* recollection entails the repetition of God's divine names and/or religious formulas including the witness to faith "There is no deity but God." This and other formula may be recited in silence or aloud, alone in seclusion or in unison with fellow seekers. Additionally, *dhikr* rituals developed by Sufi orders include procedures for posture, breath control, chant, song, music, movement, and dance.[15] But no matter the specific form, the Sufi *dhikr* aims to purify its practitioner of selfishness so that one may experience the divine presence in obedience to God, holding true to the covenant to worship Him alone, as attested in the Qur'ān:

> And when your Lord drew from the loins of the children of Adam their progeny and made them bear witness against themselves: "Am I not your Lord?" They said: "Indeed, yes! We so witness!" (7:172)

> Recall (*adhkurū*) the blessings upon you from your Lord and His covenant (*mīthāq*) that He confirmed with you when you said: "We hear and obey!" (5:7)

For many Sufis, this pledge was taken in pre-eternity on the Day of the Covenant (*yawm al-mīthāq*), which begins God's test of humanity and the human spirit's painful longing to return to its heavenly home. This tribulation, however, is the necessary spark for the Sufi's spiritual quest to rein in selfish tendencies so as to encounter exhilarating moments of illumination stabilized within a selfless spiritual life. Yet this enlightened life is only possible if God totally eradicates the Sufi's selfish will and graces him with the experience of mystical union. In this light, Sufis have asserted that the true meaning of God's oneness (*tawḥīd Allāh*) is not merely monotheism, but above all God's absolute oneness. Therefore, mystical union is not the joining of two separate and distinct essences or natures but, rather, the realization of the divine unity underlying all existence. Thus, this radical monotheism may lead to monism, where only God ultimately exists.[16]

Over the centuries, Sufi scholars have composed detailed accounts of their thought and practice, carefully noting the Qur'ānic and prophetic basis for Islamic mysticism. Additionally, their works attempt to systematize Sufism and to situate it within the larger Islamic tradition. Muslim scholars often have invoked Sufism's attention to personal experience in order to give spiritual relevance to the letter of the law, and to enliven the God of theology. Furthermore, during the fifth–sixth/eleventh–twelfth centuries, Muslim scholars worked to harmonize the various branches of Islam into a balanced and holistic faith where each aspect held its proper place and value. Law (*sharīᶜah*) was the foundation for any legitimate system, and accomplished Sufi masters have made adherence to it a requirement for spiritual development. A Muslim must master the rules and obligations regulating such important matters as the canonical prayers, fasting, and proper behavior, before entering the Sufi path (*ṭarīqah*), which necessitates additional regulations concerning mystical devotions, personal conduct, and communal life. Even then, however, the adept requires the divine grace of mystical union for a vision of creation in its relation to God (*ḥaqīqah*). Thus, belief, ritual, law, and mystical experience are all essential for those who seek the inner truth (*bāṭin*) beneath the world of exterior form (*ẓāhir*). From this perspective, all of creation when seen aright glows with God's supernal light, and here again, Sufis cite the Qur'ān as proof:

> God is the light of the heavens and the earth. The semblance of His light is like a niche in which is a lamp, the lamp in a glass. The glass is like a shining star lit from a blessed tree, an olive, of neither east nor west, whose oil would seem to shine even if not touched by fire. Light upon light, God guides to His light whom He wills, and God strikes parables for humanity, for God knows everything! (24:35)

Words of Love and Longing

Appearing in Sufi writings as early as the third/ninth century was verse ascribed to Muslim mystics. Some of the earliest Sufis poems may be classified as *zuhdīyāt*, or ascetic poetry, which is moralizing and didactic, and often tinged with a sense of impending doom:[17]

man lādha bi-llāhi najā bi-llāhi
  wa-sarrahu marru qaḍā'i-llāhi
in lam takun nafsī bi-kaffi-llāhi
  fa-kayfa anqādu li-ḥukmi-llāhi
li-llāhi anfāsun jarat li-llāhi
  lā ḥawla lī fīhā bi-ghayri-llāhi

He who seeks refuge in God is rescued by God,
  and pleasing to him is God's bitter decree.
If my soul is not in the hand of God,
  then how can I obey God's judgment?
To God are the souls who rush to God;
  I have no strength among them save God!

Arabic ascetic poetry echoes images and themes found in the elegy with its melancholy mood, and this resonates with the life of many ascetics and Sufis known for their life of material poverty and sincere piety based on trust in God. Yet, among the Sufis, there was an increasing emphasis on the reciprocal love between God and His devout worshippers:[18]

aḥibbuka ḥubbayni ḥubbu-l-hawā
  wa-ḥubban li-annaka ahlun li-dhākā
fa-ammā-l-ladhī huwa ḥubbu-l-hawā
  fa-shughlī bi-dhikrika ᶜamman siwākā
wa-ammā-l-ladhī anta ahlun lahu
  fa-kashfuka lī-l-ḥajba ḥattā arākā
fa-lā-l-ḥamda fī dhā wa-lā dāka lī
  wa-lakin laka-l-ḥamdu fī dhā wa dākā

I love you with two loves:
  passion's love and a love you deserve.
Passion's love is my constant recollection
  of you and no one else,
While the love you deserve
  is your raising the veil for me to see you.
But there is no praise in this or that for me,
  for in this and that the praise belongs to you!

From such a perspective, life's hardships and sorrow can be dispelled by God's compassion and mercy, which help the sincere believer to subdue selfishness in loving submission to God's will. Then, with God's blessing, the mystic may be given a brief premonition of the eternal life to come. The quest for such a mystical experience of loving union is central to Arabic Sufi poetry, and so, traditional love imagery and themes became favorite allegories for aspects of the mystic way. Like the verses above ascribed to Rābi ᶜah al-ᶜAdawīyah (d. 185/801), most early Sufi poems rarely exceed six or seven verses, and the surviving corpus of early Arabic Sufi poetry is quite modest. Undoubtedly, some Sufis recited poetry to highlight and reinforce mystical doctrines and beliefs. But much of this verse probably was composed by mystics who, like many other Muslims, participated in the popular Arab pastime of versification.[19]

In marked contrast to this occasional mystical verse was the contemporary Abbasid court poetry, which flourished as the ruling elite heavily patronized their poets. This helps to explain the rising popularity of poems of unified theme such as those on hunting, love, and wine. Not surprisingly, Sufis soon allegorized this wine imagery, too, as emblematic of mystical love and gnosis.[20] Some Abbasid poets also attempted to expand the expressive limits of Arabic poetry by the use of *badīᶜ*. *Badīᶜ* literally means "unprecedented" or "innovative," and the term has frequently been equated with rhetorical devices such as paronomasia (*tajnīs*), antithesis (*ṭibāq*), and metaphor (*istiᶜārah*). However, these are the means and not the ends of good *badīᶜ* poetry. To be more precise, *badīᶜ* is a method of abstraction, which uses rhetorical devices to personify and articulate complex and often abstruse concepts. The early Abbasid period was marked by rational inquiry and intense legal and theological disputation, which had an impact on all of the arts and sciences. Concomitantly, creative litterateurs viewed poetry in increasingly abstract and etymological terms, and they began to manipulate the metaphors and themes of traditional Arabic poetry in attempts to communicate their own ideas and concerns and take Arabic poetry in new directions.[21] Within this environment, the innovative poet Abū Tammām (d. 232/846) used paronomasia, alliteration, and punning for emphasis but also to establish logical and semantic links between words and concepts whose relationships might be only subliminally grasped:[22]

matā ya'tīka-l-miqdāru lā taku hālikan
wa-lākin zamānun ghāla mithlaka hāliku

When the fated time comes to you,
you will not perish,
but time—a destroyer like you—
will perish!

Here, Abū Tammām personifies his patron's appointed time of death as his foe on the battlefield in order to endow this abstraction with another, namely the finiteness of time. Thus, time and death itself must fall before some stronger entity, in this case, the immortality promised to this Muslim general for his defense of Islam.[23] The larger intent and range of *badīᶜ* poetry are well illustrated by Abū Tammām's celebrated "Ode to ᶜAmmūrīyah," where he employs antitheses—Arab caliph–Greek emperor, light–darkness, male–female—to repeat and accentuate his major theme of Islam's triumph over infidelity. *Badīᶜ* poetry at its finest, then, is not the mere presence of certain rhetorical devices, but their use as a mode of thought and expression, which is at once metaphorical, abstract, and dialectic.[24]

Badīᶜ dramatically enhanced the creative possibilities of Arabic verse as it freed the poet to abstract from the concrete poetic image, and this, naturally, expanded the range of symbolic mystical poetry. Among the first Sufi poets to compose *badīᶜ* verse was al-Ḥusayn ibn Manṣūr al-Ḥallāj (d. 309/922). One of the most controversial figures in the history of Islamic mysticism, al-Ḥallāj appears to have been an outspoken advocate for moral reform, which won him many followers. But this may have angered the increasingly unpopular Abbasid regime, which feared public unrest; al-Ḥallāj was arrested and, ultimately, executed on charges of fomenting rebellion. Al-Ḥallāj also aroused the suspicion of the religious establishment by his growing reputation as a holy man, and his public preaching on love and the possibility of union between the human and the divine. A number of religious leaders took exception to several statements ascribed to al-Ḥallāj, which strongly suggested unacceptable notions of divine incarnation within a human being.[25]

anā man ahwā wa-man ahwā anā
  naḥnu rūḥāni ḥalalnā badanā
fa-idhā abṣartanī abṣartahu
  wa-ithā abṣartahu abṣartanā

I am he whom I love,
  and he whom I love is me;
    we are two spirits
      dwelling in one body.

So, when you see me,
    you see him,
      and when you see him,
        you see us.[26]

Al-Ḥallāj often alludes to enigmatical mystical states and complex metaphysical ideas, and the abstract and often paradoxical nature of these subjects is reflected in his mature *badīᶜ* style. As in the verses just presented, al-Ḥallāj employs antithesis, paronomasia, the repetition of verbs, and the use of multiple and contrasting prepositions within a single verse to rupture the rational categories of space and time:[27]

al-ᶜishqu fī azali-l-āzāli min qidamin
fīhi bihi minhu yabdū fīhi ibdā'un

1) Eros in the eternity of eternities
from the primordial,
in it, by it, from it
appearance appears in it.

2) Eros before time
is an attribute
among the attributes
of him whose victims live.

3) His attributes are from him,
within him, without time,
while the temporal
depends on creation.

4) When creation appeared
he invoked eros,
an attribute in him who appeared,
and so a gleam glimmered there.

5) Then the *lām* is united
to the connected *alif,*
together one meaning
in priority.

6) But in separation,
they are two;
when together in disunion
they are slave and master.

7) Just so the true ones:
the fire of desire
rages from reality
whether they be far or near.

8) They were submissive, powerless
when driven mad by love!
Indeed, the mighty, excited by desire,
are humbled.

The opening verses of this poem conjure a timeless pre-eternity in which divine love has pride of place among God's eternal attributes. Alluding to the Qur'ān, al-Ḥallāj declares that those martyred by this love will be revived by God and live with Him in Paradise (cf. Q. 3:169–70). For divine love is the spark and energy of temporal creation. But this creation necessitates a distinction between creator and creature, and in verse 5, al-Ḥallāj symbolizes this duality by two connected letters: the bending *lām* for creation (*khalq*), and the straight *alif*, the first letter of the Arabic alphabet, for God, the Creator (*Allāh al-khāliq*)). Together, they spell *lā* or "no," which begins the first half of the Muslim profession of faith: *lā ilāha illā Allāh*, "There is no deity save God." Al-Ḥallāj's invocation of *lā*, which merges the two separate letters, appears to deny the absolute nature of creation's duality. Still, a state of separation continues to exist, if only temporarily, between the Lord and His worshippers. Thus, the true lovers of God burn for union with Him, as the spark of eros becomes a raging fire consuming their self-regard before the divine beloved.[28]

Although the content and meaning of this poem may be elusive, the explicit and frequent rhetorical plays within the verses are clearly aimed at inducing a shift in perspective in order to speak of nonrational spiritual matters. But, as a result, such *badīᶜ* mystical poetry often is quite complex, both in theme and syntax, and may verge on nonsense for the uninitiated.[29] This, in turn, led several medieval litterateurs to criticize the paradoxical "Sufi style" as inappropriate to good poetry. This was clearly the case when the literary scholar al-Thaᶜālibī (d. 427/1035) criticized al-Mutanabbī (d. 354/965) for "imitating the expressions of the Sufis and using their tangled words and abstruse meanings" in his verse.[30] One of the most famous poets of the Abbasid period, al-Mutanabbī spent much of his career as a panegyrist in the Hamdanid court of Sayf al-Dawlah (r. 336–56/947–67) in Syria, and al-Mutanabbī's elegant poems became a classical standard for later poets who imitated his verse for generations.[31] Although inclined more toward courtly than religious life, al-Mutanabbī nuanced his sophisticated poetry with formal elements associated with the Sufis, yet this hardly impressed critics, like al-Thaᶜālibī, who targeted many verses for criticism:[32]

wa-lakinnaka-d-dunya ilayya ḥabībatun
  fa-mā ᶜanka lī illā ilayka dhahābu

Beloved, you are the world to me,
  so leaving you is, to me, a return to you!

In this verse, al-Mutanabbī links the verbal noun *dhahāb* ("going") to three prepositions within a hemistich to give the word opposite meanings: "My leaving from you is my returning to you." This paradox is pivotal to the extraordinary image of the royal beloved as encompassing the entire globe so that wherever the poet begins, he ultimately ends still within his patron's domains. Al-Thaᶜālibī also took exception to al-Mutanabbī's use of some words that had become Sufi technical terms. The following verse contains the word *qurb*, which means "nearness" in general, but more specifically in Sufism, "spiritual proximity to God."[33] Al-Thaᶜālibi claimed that had this verse been ascribed to the famous third/ninth-century mystics al-Juanyd and al-Shiblī, "the Sufis would have argued endlessly over it:"[34]

naḥnu man ḍāyaqa-z-zamānu lahu fī-
ka wa-khānathu qurbaka-l-ayyāmu

For your sake, time crushed us;
the days made off with your nearness.

In his criticism of al-Mutanabbī, al-Thaᶜālibī obviously believed that he could distinguish clearly between proper poetic diction and style, and those types of speech appropriate to other forms of discourse, but not to poetry. For him, Islamic mystical language was distinguished by the presence of a paradox and/or technical mystical terminology.[35] However, many litterateurs were either unable or unwilling to make such distinctions. *Badīᶜ* was certainly not an exclusively mystical style, nor did all Sufis composing poetry use *badīᶜ*. Moreover, many poets, mystical or otherwise, drew from a common pool of philosophical, mystical, and related sources to speak of their loves and raptures.[36] For their part, Sufis continued to read and interpret the Arabic poetic tradition in terms of their spiritual concerns, as they expanded and enhanced their mystical allegories.

Luminaries

By the beginning of the sixth/twelfth century, mysticism was an integral and valued part of the Muslim tradition. Sufism's personal and devotional qualities were attracting an ever increasing following among all social strata, and Sufi orders (*ṭarīqah*/*ṭurūq*) with their own particular mystical beliefs and practices coalesced around spiritual masters. Among scholars, Sufism was regarded as one of the braches of the Islamic religious sciences, and a number of institutions, particularly the *zāwiyah* and the *khānqāh*, supported Muslim mystical life.[37] As a result, mystical ideas and practices were prominent in Muslim culture as is apparent in Muslim literatures at the time. In Persian poetry, Ṣanāᶜī (d.c. 525/1131) developed the didactic *mathnavī* form to spread his ascetic and mystical teachings, and he composed Persian *qaṣīdahs* as homilies.[38] Later, Farīd al-Dīn ᶜAṭṭār (d.c. 617/1220) masterfully refined the mystical *mathnavī*, composing several compelling allegories, most notably, the *Manṭiq al-Ṭayr*, or "Conference of the Birds"; ᶜAṭṭār also contributed to the Persian tradition of mystical *ghazals* or love poems.[39] In Arabic poetry, too, we begin to see more Sufi verse around this time. In earlier centuries, an anthologist might quote a verse or two by a given Sufi, but there does not appear to have been Sufi poets, per se, although a substantial amount of poetry has been ascribed to al-Ḥallāj and, a smaller amount to the Egyptian Sufi Dhū al-Nūn (d. 246/861).[40] Nevertheless, the amount of Arabic mystical verse was still small in comparison to the poetry composed under state sponsorship. Official ministries of documents (*dīwān al-inshā'*) were established by the Abbasids, in the courts in Spain and, later, by the Fatimids and Ayyubids in Egypt and Syria, which often set the topics appropriate for poetic compositions, such as Muslim military victories or the fine qualities of the ruler.[41]

A fair appraiser of this situation may be Ibn Khallikān (608–81/1211–82), a younger contemporary of Ibn al-Fāriḍ and a respected legal scholar in Damascus and Cairo. Ibn Khallikān is most famous for his biographical work *Wafayāt al-Aᶜyān*, which contains more than eight hundred biographies of notable men and women living in the Arabic speaking world from the rise of Islam until the middle of the seventh/thirteenth century. Ibn Khallikān did not include entries on the prophet Muḥammad, his companions, or on caliphs about whom much had already been written, and he choose instead to compile biographies of officials, scholars, and litterateurs whose date of death was know with some certainty.[42] Ibn Khallikān was extremely well read in Arabic poetry, citing from the works of a number of important literary scholars including Ibn Qutaybah (d. 276/889),[43] Ibn ᶜAbd Rabbih (d. 328/940),[44] Abū al-Faraj al-Iṣfahānī (d. c. 363/972),[45] Ibn Rashīq (d. c. 463/1071),[46] Ibn Bassām (d. 542/1147),[47] and ᶜImād al-Dīn al-Iṣfahānī (d. 597/1201).[48] He also gives the biographies of a number of classical poets including Dhū al-Rummah (d.c. 117/735),[49] ᶜUmar Ibn Abī Rabīᶜah (d. ca. 103/720),[50] Abū Nuwās (d.c. 198/813),[51] Abū Tammām, al-Buḥturī (d. 284/897),[52] and al-Mutanabbī, one of his favorites. Additionally, Ibn Khallikān offers entries on scores of other lesser known and later poets, citing examples of their verse, which often are rhetorically complex and usually composed for learned friends and patrons. For example, the Egyptian Ẓāfir al-Ḥaddād (d. 529/1134) was a poet and a blacksmith, who was called one day to the residence of Amīr al-Saᶜīd, the governor of Alexandria, to cut off a ring that had become too tight for the governor's fat little finger. Ẓāfir carefully removed the ring and then recited these verses:[53]

qaṣṣara ᶜan awṣāfika-l-ᶜālamu
wa-kathura-n-nāthiru wa-n-nāẓimu
man yakuna-l-baḥru lahu rāḥatan
yaḍīqu ᶜan khinṣirihi-l-khātimu

Humanity fell short of describing your qualities
though their writers and poets be many.
He whose palm is ample as the ocean,
the signet ring must surely squeeze his pinky!

The governor then gave Ẓāfir the gold ring in appreciation for his praise.[54] Ibn Khallikān quotes hundreds of such verses in his *Wafayāt*, including a number by contemporary poets whom he knew. Ibn Khallikān regarded Ibn Sanā' al-Mulk (d. 608/1211),[55] Ibn ᶜUnayn (d. 630/1233),[56] Ibn Maṭrūḥ (d. 649/1251),[57] and Bahā' al-Dīn Zuhayr (d. 656/1258),[58] to be excellent poets.[59] All of them had served as administrators or secretaries to the Ayyubid dynasty, whose princes they praised. Generally, these poets composed their panegyrics in the *badīᶜ* style, as in the following verses by Ibn ᶜUnayn on the noble sons of the sultan al-Malik al-ᶜĀdil:[60]

wa-lahu-l-banūna bi-kulli arḍin minhumu
mulkun yaqūdu ilā-l-aᶜādī ᶜaskarā
min kulli waḍḍāḥi-l-jabīni tukhāluhu
badran wa-in shahada-l-waghā fa-ghaaḍnfarā
mutaqaddimun ḥattā idhā-n-naqᶜu-njalā
bi-l-bayḍi ᶜan sabiyi-l-ḥarīmi ta'akhkharā
qaumun zakū aṣlan wa-ṭābū muḥtadan
wa-tadaffaqū jūdan wa-rāqū munẓarā
wa-taᶜāfu khayluhumu-l-warūda bi-manhalin
mā lam yakun bi-dami-l-waqā'iᶜi aḥmarā
yaᶜshū ilā nāri-l-waghā shaghfan bi-hā
wa-yajillu an yaᶜshū ilā nāri-l-qirā

He has sons,
each a prince in every land,
leading an army
against the foes.

Each with a bright brow
making him seem a full moon,
but when battle appears
a fierce lion!

He leads the charge until the dark dust
is dispelled by shining swords
revealing the captive women,
then he lags behind.

A family, pure of lineage,
pleasant, harmonious,
brimming with generosity,
and a delight to see.

Their steeds loathe
to drink from a pool
that was not turned red
from the blood of battles.

By night they travel with passion
toward the fire of war,
too exalted to seek out
the fire of hospitality!

In addition to panegyrics, these Ayyubid poets also composed love poems, riddles and quatrains, some in simpler, more direct styles, particularly when musing on old age and death, as did Ibn Khallikān's good friend Ibn Maṭrūḥ:[61]

aṣbaḥtu bi-qaᶜri jufratin murtahanā
lā amlaku min dunyāī illā-l-kafanā
yā man wasaᶜat ᶜubbādahu raḥmatuhu
min baᶜḍi ᶜibādika-l-musī'īna anā

I was deposited in the bottom of a pit,
owning nothing of my world save a shroud.

O, One whose mercy holds His servants,
  among Your wayward worshipers am I!

In addition to biographical notices to government officials and professional poets, Ibn Khallikān gives accounts of many Muslims noted for their piety and scholarship, including a number of Sufis. Ibn Khallikān was well informed on Islamic mysticism, too, having read al-Qushayrī's (d. 465/1072) popular Sufi compendium, the *Risālah*, and his commentary on the Qur'ān,[62] along with the saints' lives recorded in the *Ḥilyat al-Awliyā'* by Abū al-Nuʿaym al-Iṣfahānī (d. 430/1038).[63] Ibn Khallikān also had studied a number of works by Muḥammad al-Ghazālī (d. 505/1111), including his *Iḥyā' ʿUlūm al-Dīn* and the *Mishkāt al-Anwār*,[64] and the more recent and popular Sufi guide book the *ʿAwārif al-Maʿārif* by ʿUmar al-Suhrawardī (d. 632/1235).[65] Ibn Khallikān gives a notice to each of these important mystical authors, as well as to a number of other earlier Sufis, including Dhū al-Nūn, Rābiʿah al-ʿAdawīyah, al-Junayd (d. 297/910), and al-Hallāj. Ibn Khallikān also made entries for the North African mystical theologian Ibn al-ʿArīf (d. 536/1141),[66] and for Abū Najīb al-Suhrawardī (d. 563/1168)[67] and Aḥmad al-Rifāʿī (d. 578/1182),[68] both of whom founded Sufi orders that bear their respective names.

As was the case with earlier Sufi biographers, Ibn Khallikān offers a verse or two in some of his entries, such as this verse by ʿUmar al-Suhrawardī:[69]

in ta'ammaltukumu fa-kullī ʿuyūnun
  aw tadhakkartukumu fa-kullī qulūbun

When I contemplate you,
  I'm all eyes,
    and when I recollect you,
  I'm all heart!

Significantly, however, Ibn Khallikān identifies several poets as composing verse specifically on mystical topics. One of them, al-Murtaḍā Ibn al-Shahrazūrī (465–511/1073–1117), was from a respected scholarly family in Iraq, and held positions as an *ḥadīth* scholar, judge, and preacher in Mosul. Like other educated Muslims of the period, Ibn al-Shahrazūrī was at once a religious official, a mystic, and a litterateur. Reflecting these concerns, his poetry is often homiletic in tone, mystical in content, and classical in form, as in the following quatrain:[70]

yā qalbu ilāma lā yufīdu-n-naṣḥu
daᶜ mazḥaka kam janā ᶜalayka-l-mazḥu
mā jāriḥatun fīka ᶜadāhā jurḥu
mā tashᶜuru bi-l-khummāri ḥattā taṣḥū

O heart, how long will you ignore advice?
Stop kidding around; how often it has led to vice.
You're all banged up, but until you're sober,
you won't know the wine's price!

Ibn al- Shahrazūrī's mystical proclivities are discernable in several poems cited by Ibn Khallikān, which address Sufi themes in traditional poetic contexts. The following poem combines love themes with well-known Sufi technical terms (v. 1: *qalb*/ "heart;" v. 5: *waṣl*/ "union;" v. 7: *baqā'*/ "staying," "abiding;" v. 8: *fanā'*/ "passing away") to portray the purging of the lover prior to mystical annihilation in the beloved.[71]

bi-qalbī minhumu ᶜulaqu wa-damᶜī fīhumu ᶜalaqu

1) My heart is bound to them;
my tears are blood

2) I burn for them;
my insides blaze.

3) We huddle at their door,
fear melting our hearts.

4) But they left nothing, just a spark;
if only they cared.

5) There is no union, no parting,
no sleep, no sleeplessness,

6) No hopelessness, no hope,
no patience or disquiet.

7) They were cruel and did not spare me;
if only they had stayed,

8) That I might have passed away,
 while the fragrance of my love lingered,

9) Like a candle, delighting its companions,
 while consuming itself.

Ibn al-Shahrazūrī composed a number of short mystical love poems, in addition to several on wine.[72] However, Ibn al-Shahrazūrī's fame does not rest on these short, if elegant pieces, but rather on a long allegorical ode of forty-four verses recounting a quest for mystical illumination. Ibn Khallikān rarely cited long poems in full, but he did so in this case because the ode was hard to find, although much sought after. In fact, this ode, entitled the *al-Mawṣlīyah* because Ibn al-Shahrazūrī composed it in Mosul, is one of the earliest surviving formal Arabic *qaṣīdahs* on Sufism, and, as such, it represents an important development in the history of Arabic poetry.[73]

Such mystical odes would become quite popular late in the sixth/twelfth century, although much Sufi verse continued to be short modest love poems, like those by the Egyptian Sufi, Muḥammad Ibn al-Kīzānī (d. 560/1166).[74] In his brief biography of him, Ibn Khallikān noted that Ibn al-Kīzānī was a pious ascetic, scholar, and Qur'ān reader famous in Egypt, with his own Sufi order. Further, he had a collection of poetry, and although Ibn Khallikān had not seen the collection himself, he had heard one of the poet's verses:[75]

wa-idhā lāqa bi-l-muḥibbi gharāmun
 fa-kadhā-l-waṣlu bi-l-ḥabībi yalīqu

If passion is proper for a lover,
 then union befits the beloved.

Although Ibn al-Kīzānī's collection of poems is now lost, nearly seventy of his poems were preserved by later biographers and anthologists.[76] Several of these sources note that Ibn al-Kīzānī was also a preacher and that his collection of poetry was widely read and admired in Egypt. Most of these poems rarely exceed ten verses, and in a number of them, Ibn al-Kīzānī assumes the role of the spiritual guide to instruct his audience on leading a righteous life:[77]

qif ᶜalā-l-bābi ṭāliban
 wa-daᶜi-d-damᶜa sākiban

Stand at the door as a seeker
  and pour out your tears.
Implore Him with them
  and turn away from sin.
Accept from His gracious blessings
  such wondrous things.
But fear Him who sees you
  riding hell-bent to sin.
Yet He rewards with ease
  and bestows what is desired.
Piety is the worshipper's garb,
  so be the companion of truth.

Quite often, Ibn al-Kīzānī's verse contains a pronounced devotional element, and he frequently mentions *dhikr*, the Sufi practice of recollection:[78]

wa-llāhu law lā anna dhikraka mu'nisī
  mā kāna ʿayshī bi-ḥayāti yaṭību

Oh God,
  were recollection of you
    not my constant companion,
  my life would not be sweet.

When my eyes cry
  longing for you,
    then every limb
  weeps for you.

Do you think distance
  will loosen my love?
    Though you are far away,
  your phantom is near.

How can I find solace
  when rapture is within
    spying
  on what is in the heart.

Passion has set out for you
with my last breaths;
the sickness is all-consuming,
yet you are the doctor!

In this poem, Ibn al-Kīzānī mentions two characters common to classical Arabic poetry, the *raqīb*, or "spy," who seeks to protect the beloved, and the *khayāl*, or "phantom" of the beloved who may visit the lover in a dream.[79] Here, in light of the term *dhikr*, "recollection" in verse 1, both figures have become metaphors for the mystic's meditation and rapture that are wholly focused on God. In many other poems, as well, Ibn al-Kīzānī draws on the Arabic *ghazal* tradition to allude to the love of God and the trials on the mystical quest for union:[80]

laysa ḥaẓẓī mina-l-ḥabā'ibi illā
lauᶜatun aw ta'assufun aw gharāmu

My lot with lovers is but torment,
and regrets and desire.
They decreed separation, while passion was within me,
though they knew I was mad for them.
But I am satisfied; let them do as they will,
for impatience with them is forbidden me.
They are my hope and my farthest wish;
they are balm for my heart and peace!

Without knowing that a Sufi composed this poem, there is little to suggest a mystical meaning. However, in other poems, Ibn al-Kīzānī employs Sufi technical terms and themes, as in the following verses that refer to the Day of the Covenant alluded to in the Qur'ān 7:172:[81]

anā bi-ṣ-ṣabri fīhi lā-ṣ-ṣabri ᶜanhu
taḥta ḥukmi-l-hawā bi-mā jā'a minhu
qad ṣafat lī maḥabbatun lam ukaddir-
hā wa-ᶜahdun muqaddamun lam akhunhu

I bear him patiently,
never impatient with him,
under passion's decree
that came from him.

For a pure love was meant for me
  that I did not taint
    and an earlier covenant
  that I did not break.

Ibn al-Kīzānī also takes up themes common to the traditional *qaṣīdah*, especially the beloved's departure and the abandoned campsite,[82] and occasionally he refers to the wine of love.[83] Again, these poems generally consist of only a few verses, quite in contrast to the long mystical wine ode that Ibn Khallikān quotes in his entry for the famous Sufi and philosopher, Yaḥyā al-Suhrawardī (d. 587/1191).[84] Ibn Khallikān notes that al-Suhrawardī ended his career prematurely at the age of thirty-six in Aleppo, where he was executed on charges of heresy by order of the sultan Ṣalāḥ al-Dīn. As was the case with al-Ḥallāj, a number of religious authorities were suspicious of al-Suhrawardī's mystical doctrines, which he derived from a theology of light. However, Ibn Khallikān quotes sources contemporary with al-Suhrawardī suggesting that his downfall may have resulted more from his abrasive personality and grandiose claims to spiritual authority; as one source noted: "his knowledge was greater than his sense."[85] Whatever the case against al-Suhrawardī's character and beliefs, his mystical writings display erudition in both content and form, and Ibn Khallikān lists a number of his writings, including the *Ḥikmat al-Ishrāq* ("The Wisdom of Illumination"). Some of al-Suhrawardī's finest works are his allegorical tales composed in a lucid and elegant Persian prose, but he also composed Arabic verse in the *badīᶜ* style, and in addition to the wine ode, Ibn Khallikān quotes the following enigma:[86]

fa-khafaytu ḥattā qultu lastu bi-ẓāhirin
  wa-ẓahartu min saᶜatī ᶜalā-l-akwāni

I was hidden, so I said: "I've disappeared!"
  Then I appeared to all beings from my capacity.

The term *saᶜatī*, "my capacity," is derived from the verb *wasuᶜa*, "to encompass, to hold." Here, it may refer to the mystic's heart, *saᶜatu-l-qalb*, and so be an allusion to a divine saying often quoted by the Sufis, in which God says:[87]

mā wasuᶜanī arḍī wa-samā'ī wa-wasuᶜanī qalbu
  ᶜabdī-l-mu'mini

"My earth and My heaven do not hold Me, but the heart of My believing servant holds Me."

A similar transformation occurs to the mystic in the following poem by al-Suhrawardī preserved by another anthologist:[88]

khalīliya inna-al-unsa fī furqati-l-insi
fa-kun abadan mā ᶜishta fī ḥaḍrati-l-qudsi

1) Friend, intimacy is in separation from humanity,
so as long as you live, be in the presence divine.

2) You will live without death, abide without passing,
you will reach the meaning and leave the senses.

3) The planets will envy you for what you've achieved,
as a light from you illuminates the orb of the sun.

4) For you are the meaning, it exists in you;
all creation is in you, the throne and the stool!

The central theme of this poem is the enlightened gnostic who becomes a microcosm of all existence; even the heavenly throne and footstool may be found in him, suggesting the encompassing nature of the realized gnostic and his great spiritual authority. The religious nature of the poem is suggested in the first verse by the word play between *uns* ("intimacy") and *ins* ("humanity"), and the opposition between separation (*furqah*) from the world and presence (*ḥaḍrah*) with God. The second verse builds on this dichotomy with references to life and death, and mystical elements are apparent in the common Sufi pairings of abiding (*tabqā*) and passing away (*fanā*), and spiritual essence (*maᶜnā*) versus sensate matter (*ḥiss*). The gnostic's transcendence rises to cosmic proportions in verses 3 and 4, which probably reflect al-Suhrawardī's metaphysics of light, although one could also read them as exuberant declarations of mystical exhilaration.[89]

As al-Suhrawardī's short poem demonstrates, Sufis sometimes composed poems on mystical subjects without recourse to traditional love or wine themes, which is the case with a number of poems ascribed to a contemporary of al-Suhrawardī, the North African Sufi master Abū Madyan (d. 594/1198). His poems often take the form of prayers for forgiveness or meditations on God and His power:[90]

Allāhu rabbī lā urīdu siwāhu
hal fī-l-wujūdi-l-ḥayyu illā-llāhu
dhātu-l-ilāhi bi-hā qiwāmu dhawātinā
hal kāna yūjadu ghayruhu law lāhu

God, my lord, I want nothing but Him.
Is anything in existence alive save Him?
Divinity's essence sustains our being.
Could anything else be found without Him?

Abū Madyan also composed Sufi love poems and *muwashshaḥ*, a strophic poetic form popular in Spain and North Africa. He is also credited with several wine odes and a poem in praise of the Sufis and their exalted spiritual path.[91] Despite, Abū Madyan's great reputation as a religious scholar among his many followers in North Africa, Ibn Khallikān makes no mention of him or his poetry in the *Wafayāt*. Perhaps, Abū Madyān's teachings, which were passed on orally in the Maghrib, were not yet well known farther east in Egypt and Syria.[92] Stranger still is the omission of any word on the writings of another famous Sufi author, Muḥyī al-Dīn Ibn al-ᶜArabī (d. 638/1240). Although Ibn al-ᶜArabī had been born in Spain and educated there and in North Africa, he traveled to the eastern Muslim lands and eventually settled and died in Damascus.[93] Ibn Khallikān mentions that he had met him there, and that Ibn al-ᶜArabī was one of several North African jurists who did not rely on past legal traditions, but came to their own conclusions in their cases based on the Qur'ān, the prophetic traditions, consensus (*ijmāᶜ*), and analogical reasoning (*qiyās*).[94]

Despite Ibn Khallikān's omission of a biography on this Sufi master, Ibn alᶜArabī was a pivotal figure in Islam, and his numerous writings and personal charisma made a tremendous impact on the Sufi tradition.[95] Of particular importance was his mystical philosophy, which dominated Islamic metaphysical thought for centuries. Commonly referred to as *waḥdat al-wujūd*, or "the unity of being," this doctrine asserts that the existence of anything is identical to its relation to necessary being. Contingent existence, then, is relational to the Absolute, which it must reflect if only in a limited and transient way. Therefore, the spiritual seeker must grasp the relativity of himself and all other things. Then he will find and witness the permanent ground of all being within its ever changing self-disclosure in the guises of the divine names and attributes.[96] Ibn al-ᶜArabī developed these and related ideas in a number of books and epistles, most notably in his *al-Futūḥāt al-Makkīyah* ("The Meccan Revelations") and the *Fuṣūṣ al-Ḥikam* ("The Bezels of Wisdom"). Scattered throughout these works are verses composed by him to accentuate complex and often abstruse teachings. Not surprisingly, much of this poetry is in the *badī*ᶜ style:[97]

fa-yaḥmadunī wa-aḥmaduhu
*wa-ya*ᶜ*budunī wa-a*ᶜ*buduhu*

1) So he praises me while I praise him,
and he worships me while I worship him.

2) In a state, I confirm him
while in essence, deny him.

3) So he knows me while I know him not,
while I know him and so witness him.

4) So where is self-sufficiency,
while I help and assist him?

5) For this truth, he created me,
so I know him and find him.

6) So did the *ḥadīth* come to us,
its meaning realized in me.

Brevity and paradox lend a creed like quality to this poem, which concludes Ibn al-ᶜArabī's chapter on Abraham in the *Fuṣūṣ al-Ḥikam*. The poem highlights the chapter's main theme of the interdependence of creator and creation, of the worshipped and the worshipper. In a style reminiscent of verse by al-Ḥallāj, Ibn al-ᶜArabī repeats verbs with different subjects, at times negating them for antithesis. Furthermore, the pronominal suffix *hu*, found in every verse, becomes a sliding referent with three possible meanings—him/Him/it—grammatically reinforcing Ibn al-ᶜArabī's ideas on interdependence.[98] According to a divine saying popular among the Sufis, God was a hidden treasure who desired to be known and, so, initiated creation. God's self-knowledge, therefore, is dependent on His being known in and by creation. Thus, although enlightened believers praise and worship God, it could be said, relatively speaking, that He praises and worships them for helping to manifest Him (vv. 1–2). This creation, then, confirms a creator, who cannot be known otherwise, for the unmanifest Absolute is necessarily without predicate (vv. 2–3). However, within the realm of creation, God, as creator, is dependent on His creations who manifest His names and attributes and so witness to His existence (vv. 4–5). The realized mystic discovers this reality within and so lives not according to his own selfish will, but according to the divine will, which he finds throughout existence (vv. 3, 5–6). As God says in the "Tradition of Willing Devotions" referred to in the final verse of the poem:

> And My servant continues to draw near Me through willing acts of devotion until I love him, and when I love him, I become his ear with which he hears, I become his eye with which he sees . . .

Ibn al-ᶜArabī composed a great deal of poetry, which may be found throughout his many doctrinal works and in his *Dīwān*, a substantial collection of poetry filled with verse in various forms on a variety of subjects. The poems include several *qaṣīdahs* and elegies along with numerous shorter poems on such topics as astral phenomena, dreams, the spiritual significance of the alphabet, the ninety-nine names of God, and the chapters of the Qur'ān. The majority of this verse has few rhetorical devices, and its religious and pious intent is usually unambiguous. Additionally, a few of the poems reflect newer poetic forms such as the five-hemistich *takhmīs*, and the Andalusian *muwashshaḥ*, which was becoming popular in Ayyubid Egypt and Syria.[99] Ibn al-ᶜArabī also compiled a second collection of poems consisting of *qaṣīdahs* and *ghazals*, and entitled the *Turjumān al-Ashwāq* ("The Interpreter of Desires"), to which he added a mystical commentary to each poem.[100] Ibn al-ᶜArabī's commentary may have been the first such work on Sufi poetry, and it appears to have set a trend within Islamic mysticism as several of his students and a number of later Sufi scholars began to expound their mystical doctrines in commentaries by reading verse by others as embodying specific Sufi doctrines and experiences. Ironically, for the next five centuries, the focus for the overwhelming majority of these commentaries would not be Ibn al-ᶜArabī's verse, but that by his Egyptian contemporary, ᶜUmar Ibn al-Fāriḍ.[101] Ibn Khallikān might have appreciated this fact, since one of his longest entries for any Sufi poet in the *Wafayāt al-Aᶜyān* was that on Ibn al-Fāriḍ:[102]

> Abū Ḥafṣ and Abū al-Qāsim, ᶜUmar ibn Abū al-Ḥasan ᶜAlī ibn al-Murshid ibn ᶜAlī, of Hama by origin, Egyptian by

birth, residence, and death, known as Ibn al-Fāriḍ, having the title al-Sharaf [i.e., Sharaf al-Dīn].

He has a volume of fine (*laṭīf*) poetry in which his style is pure and elegant, following the mystics' way (*ṭarīqat al-fuqarā'*). He has an ode of about six hundred verses in accordance with their technical terminology and method.[103] How fine is his statement in one of the long odes:[104]

How welcome the words
I was unworthy to receive
from the bearer of glad tidings,
proclaiming relief after despair:

"Good news for you,
so strip off what is on you,
for you have been remembered
despite your crooked ways!"

And his saying from another ode:[105]

Because of you,
I am never free of envy.
So do not waste my night vigil
with the shocking phantom's disgrace.

Ask the night's stars
if sleep ever visited my eyes,
for how can it visit
one it does not know?

And from it:[106]

And despite the skill
of those who describe his loveliness,
time will pass away with things in him
yet to be described!

He has rhymed couplets (*dūbayt*), colloquial verses (*mawāliyā*), and riddles (*alghāz*). I have heard that he was a pious, virtuous, and abstemious man. He lived for a time in Mecca; may God add to its honor! He made a fine companion and was praiseworthy. One of his companions told me that one day in solitude (*khalwah*), (Ibn al-Fāriḍ) was humming a line of al-Ḥarīrī, the author of the *al-Maqāmāt*:[107]

Who is the one who never sinned,
  who is he who has only the best?

(The companion) said: "He heard a speaker—but saw no one—recite:

Muhammad, the guide,
  to whom was Gabriel's descent!"

A group of his companions recited his colloquial verses to me about a young man who was a butcher by profession. They are clever, but I have not seen them in his *Dīwān*:

I said to a butcher: "I love you,
  but oh how you cut and kill me!
He said: "That's my business,
  so you scold me?"
He bent and kissed my foot to win me,
  but he wanted my slaughter,
So he breathed on me to skin me.[108]

I have written it according to their usage though they do not observe the final vowels or voweling. Rather, they allow grammatical error; indeed, most of it is ungrammatical. So, let him who comes upon it not censure it.

(Ibn al-Fāriḍ) used to say: "I learned two verses in my sleep, and they are:

By the life of my longing for you,
  by the sanctity of dignified patience,
My eyes have never held other than you,
  nor have I desired another friend."[109]

His birthday was on the fourth of Dhū al-Qaᶜdah, in the year 576 [1181] in Cairo, and he died there on Tuesday, the second of Jumādā I, in the year 632 [1235]. He was buried

> the next day at the foot of Mt. Muqaṭṭam. May God most high have mercy upon him! The *fāriḍ* is one who draws up the legal shares (*furūḍ*) that men must pay to women.

Ibn Khallikān's biography of Ibn al-Fāriḍ echoes accounts by the poet's students but it is much more substantial regarding Ibn al-Fāriḍ's verse. Ibn Khallikān did not state that he personally knew Ibn al-Fāriḍ, who had died when Ibn Khallikān was still a young man of about twenty-five. However, Ibn Khallikān had spoken to some of the poet's companions, and he described Ibn al-Fāriḍ as pious, of good company, and good-natured; he also noted Ibn al-Fāriḍ's interest in Sufism and his long mystical poem the *al-Tāʾīyah al-Kubrā*. Ibn Khallikān was clearly familiar with a collection of Ibn al-Fāriḍ's poetry, which included rhymed couplets, colloquial verse, and riddles, and he cited verses from several long poems and some colloquial verses, not included in early editions of the *Dīwān*, which he found to be a delightful example of Ibn al-Fāriḍ's literary wit.[110] Moreover, Ibn Khallikān mentioned that Ibn al-Fāriḍ once reflected on a verse by al-Harīrī regarding a sinless person, and while the story has a rather miraculous ending, Ibn al-Fāriḍ's familiarity with al-Harīrī was yet another sign of being an accomplished man of letters.[111] Unlike his biographies of Ibn al-Shahrazūrī and Yaḥyā al-Suhrawardī, Ibn Khallikān did not include a full poem by Ibn al-Fāriḍ, save a short couplet. Yet, this was not because he did not admire Ibn al-Fāriḍ and his verse. Rather, Ibn Khallikān regarded such long quotation as unnecessary since Ibn al-Fāriḍ's verse was well known and easily accessible. In fact, when Ibn Khallikān compiled his biographical dictionary, Ibn al-Fāriḍ's poetic reputation was already secure, to such a degree that later scholars would refer to other Sufi poets as composing verse "in the way of Ibn al-Fārid."[112]

1

Mystical Improvisations

> In most of his moments of inspiration, the Shaykh was always perplexed, eyes fixed, hearing no one who spoke, nor even seeing them. Sometimes he would be standing, sometimes sitting, sometimes he would lie down on his side, and sometimes he would throw himself down on his back wrapped in a shroud like a dead man. Ten days, more or less, would pass while he was in this state, he neither eating, drinking, speaking, or moving. . . . Then he would regain consciousness and come to, and his first words would be a dictation of what God had enlightened him with of the ode *Naẓm al-Sulūk*.[1]

Master Poet

This account of Ibn al-Fāriḍ's trance and verse reflects several medieval Muslim notions regarding poetic and religious inspiration. First, the trance confirms the inspired quality of the poet's verse that, then, should not be confused with the contrived poetry of academic artifice. Like the pre-Islamic poets and soothsayers, and the legendary Muslim poets driven mad by love, Ibn al-Fāriḍ has tapped deep spiritual sources. Yet his inspiration is not from a jinni or Satan, but from God, and this attests to the profound truth of the poet's religious message. After being lost in divine love, Ibn al-Fāriḍ recovers to spontaneously recite verse, which would later compose his most famous mystical poem. Such miraculous tales of Ibn al-Fāriḍ were popularized and passed on by generations of his admirers, and they form an important chapter in the story of the poet's posthumous sanctification.[2] But this image of Ibn al-Fāriḍ as an ecstatic Sufi obscures important literary dimensions of his work, especially questions regarding his literary benefactors and their influence. For Ibn al-Fāriḍ's polished and highly mannered poetry challenges persistent views of him as a manic oracle reciting from the depths of mystical trance. His poems are carefully crafted works replete with intricate rhetorical displays, and Ibn al-Fāriḍ's learned poetic skill is also evident in his conscious references to verse by earlier Arab poets.[3]

In an eleventh/seventeenth-century grammatical commentary on Ibn al-Fāriḍ's *Dīwān*, Ḥasan al-Būrīnī (d. 1024/1619), occasionally noted the poet's direct dependence on amorous verses by his predecessors, including al-Buḥturī.[4] More recently, A.J. Arberry believed that Ibn al-Fāriḍ was indebted in several places to Imru' al-Qays and ᶜUmar Ibn Abī Rabīᶜah. Furthermore, Ibn al-Fāriḍ was clearly influenced by several of his older contemporaries including Yaḥyā al-Suhrawardī, as Yūsuf Sāmī al-Yūsuf has argued persuasively.[5] Ibn al-Fāriḍ also improvised on a *ghazal* by an earlier Egyptian Sufi poet Ibn al-Kīzānī.[6] However, the poet who may have exerted the strongest influence on Ibn al-Fāriḍ was al-Mutanabbī.

Homage to al-Mutanabbī

Every competent Arab poet and litterateur of the sixth/twelfth century was well acquainted with al-Mutanabbī's esteemed poetry. Al-Būrīnī often cited verses by al-Mutanabbī in commenting on Ibn al-Fāriḍ's *Dīwān*, and he recorded several examples of direct borrowing. Arberry pursued al-Būrīnī's leads and discovered that Ibn al-Fāriḍ had gone so far as to pattern two of his poems, the *al-Lāmīyah* and the *al-Dhālīyah*, after two poems by al-Mutanabbī. Arberry charted the rhyme words and a few of the themes and images common to the poems, and further analysis will reveal the extent to which Ibn al-Fāriḍ mystically improvised on this master poet.[7] Ibn al-Fāriḍ's *al-Lāmīyah* is a beautiful love poem of sixty verses, in the meter *ṭawīl*, rhyming in the letter *lām*, or "L," and modeled on a panegyric by al-Mutanabbī that begins:[8]

ᶜazīzun asan man dā'uhu-l-ḥadaqu-n-nujlu
ᶜayā'un bihi māta-l-muḥibbūna min qablu

How a man hurts afflicted by beautiful eyes;
so many lovers died, victims of this incurable disease.
If you want, look at me; the sight of me
should warn you: passion is not easy.
It is nothing, just a glance after a glance,
but it snares the heart, and sets loose reason.

Love for her flowed like blood in my veins,
and I was obsessed by her alone.

Al-Mutanabbī begins this ode with the familiar *ghazal* themes of an overpowering love and the sorrow it brings on the lover. He then goes on to recount how love has left him emaciated and the object of ridicule. Still, he is deaf to his blamer, and sleeplessly passes his night in hopes of meeting his beloved, who is as beautiful as the moon (vv. 5–10):

I love one like the full moon,
but I complain to one who has no peer,
To one unique in all the world, Shujāᶜ Ibn Muhammad,
the valiant, benefit to God and himself!

Here, al-Mutanabbī makes his transition from the opening section on love (*nasīb*) by beseeching his patron to rectify this sorry state (v. 9), and this initiates a long description of his liege lord. Al-Mutanabbī lauds Shujāᶜ's noble Arab lineage to the prophet Muhammad and, indeed, had God wished to send other messengers, it would have been by means of this worthy descendent (vv. 11–12). Next, al-Mutanabbī celebrates his master's swift blade and daunting courage in battle; though his worthy foes eye his fall, they only see his spear points, which blind and kill them (vv. 13–21). With the obvious metaphor of blinding as death, al-Mutanabbī again refers to eyes and vision to draw attention to key themes. For in Arabic, the word *ᶜayn* may mean "spring," "eye," or one's "inner self," and so, *ᶜayn* and related terms for eyes often have the double meaning "eye/self-I." Eyes and glances, then, dominate the opening verses of this panegyric where the emotional and psychological tumult of love is apparent; the poet's love began with a glance, and the beloved's wide eyes have since afflicted him with sleeplessness (vv. 1, 3, 8). Furthermore, in this panegyric, al-Mutanabbī depicts others as looking at this powerful knight, particularly during battle (v. 18), and he calls his listeners to do the same (vv. 15–16). In this way, al-Mutanabbī progressively adds to his iconic image of his noble master and builds toward a conclusion proclaiming his lord's boundless, life-giving generosity (22–29):[9]

Grieve for a soul blind to you for a moment,
and bless the eye beholding you every hour!
So the poor need not worry, watching for your flash,
for there is no barren land when you are its pouring rain!

Ibn al-Fāriḍ begins his *al-Lāmīyah* with an elaboration of al-Mutanabbī's warning to those who think love is an easy affair:[10]

huwa-l-ḥubbu fa-slam bi-l-ḥashā mā-l-hawā sahlu
fa-mā-khtārahu muḍnan bihi wa-lahu ᶜaqlu

It is love, so guard your heart, passion is not easy;
wasted by it, would you choose it, if you had reason?
Live free of love, for love's ease is hard;
it begins in sickness, and ends in death.
But to me, death in love by drowning desire,
is life revived by my beloved.
I have warned you, knowing passion and my enemy,
so choose for yourself what is sweet.
But if you want to live well, then die love's martyr,
and if not, well, love has its worthy ones.
Not to die in love is not to live by love;
before you harvest honey you must surely face the bees.

Ibn al-Fāriḍ borrowed the maxim of the honey and the bees from another poem by al-Mutanabbī, and there is a reference to yet a third poem by al-Mutanabbī in verse 8 where Ibn al-Fāriḍ says:[11]

wa-qul li-qatīli-l-ḥubbi waffayta ḥaqqahu
wa-lil-muddaᶜī hayhāta mā-l-kaḥalu-l-kuḥlu

Say to love's victim: "You paid the price,"
but to the pretender: "Coal black eyes are not of kohl."

Al-Mutanabbī had used a similar image to acclaim a patron's genuine forbearance:[12]

li-anna ḥilmaka ḥilmun lā takallafuhu
laysa-t-takaḥḥulu fī-l-ᶜaynayni ka-l-kaḥali

Your forbearance is never feigned;
kohl-made eyes are not coal-black.

In addition to these borrowed motifs, Ibn al-Fāriḍ reused all but six of the twenty-nine rhyme words from the model poem.[13] Yet, despite formal similarities, there remains an obvious difference between the poets' concerns and subjects. Al-Mutanabbī's opening sketch of the beloved and the pains of love forms a lyrical introduction meant to convey his love and loyalty toward his patron who will rectify the poet's complaints. Unquestionably, al-Mutanabbī hoped to be rewarded for his exaltation of his lord and his public allegiance to him, the poem's main subjects (vv. 9–29). By contrast, Ibn al-Fāriḍ begins his *ghazal* with what might be termed a "creed of love," which sets the poem's tone and mood as the poet traces the effects of love on the lover. The antitheses of his opening verses—ease and hardship, sickness and health, life and death—send spiritual vibrations resonating throughout the poem where love is eternal (vv. 30–31):

> Ancient is my tale of love for her;
> it has, she knows, no beginning, no end,
> And there is none like me in passion for her,
> while her enchanting beauty has no equal!

This "ancient tale" (*ḥadīthī qadīmun*) alludes to the primordial covenant made between God and humanity in pre-eternity. Some Arab love poets in the second/eighth century, known as ʿUdhrī poets, claimed that their loves were foreordained then, whereas Ibn al-Fāriḍ and other Sufis looked to the covenant as a sign of the everlasting love between God and His worshipers.[14]

Perhaps following al-Mutanabbī, Ibn al-Fāriḍ also refers to eyes and vision; those who envy are blind (v. 12), whereas the true lover is sleepless, crying bloody tears (vv. 22–23, 28). But Ibn al-Fāriḍ often makes a subtle contrast between the eye and the heart, the locus of spiritual manifestations (vv. 1, 13, 20, 44, 56, 59). There, the lover holds and beholds his dear beloved as he seeks to eradicate any lingering trace of selfishness (vv. 34–36):

> Wasting away, I disappeared; my visitor could not find me.
> How can those visiting the sick see one without a shadow?
> No eye ever stumbled across my track,
> for those wide eyes left no trace of me in love.
> Yet, when I remember her, a resolve rises within me,
> and when she is mentioned, my cheap spirit grows rich.

Ibn al-Fāriḍ's mystical intent is further distinguished from al-Mutanabbī's more earthly and political concerns, by the direct reference to the martyrdom required for the sweet life of love (vv.

36–60). This difference is seen clearly at the ends of their poems. Anticipating his patron's munificence, al-Mutanabbī addresses him in the penultimate verse (v. 28):

wa-waylun li-nafsin ḥāwalat minka ghirratan
wa-ṭūbā li-ᶜaynin sāᶜatan minka lā takhlū

Grieve for a soul blind to you for a moment,
and bless the eye beholding you every hour!

Ibn al-Fāriḍ alters this verse to declare a more spiritual fealty as he concludes an oath to his love (v. 58):

la-anti ᶜalā ghayẓi-n-nawā wa-riḍā-l-hawā
ladayyā wa-qalbī sāᶜatan minki mā yakhlū

Whether in parting's anger or passion's acceptance,
you are with me, my heart holding you every hour.

Here, Ibn al-Fāriḍ substitutes the word *qalb* ("heart") for *ᶜayn* ("eye"), and so transforms al-Mutanabbī's courtly image of the poet humbly beholding his patron into one of the lover devoutly recollecting his beloved within the heart. Thus, Ibn al-Fāriḍ returns to his opening image of the heart emptied of selfishness and filled with the beloved. This, in turn, evokes images of the popular Sufi exercise of *dhikr*, "recollection" or meditation on the presence of God within oneself, a practice supported by the divine saying: "My heavens and earth do not embrace Me, but the heart of My faithful servant does embrace Me!"[15]

In his *al-Dhālīyah*, Ibn al-Fāriḍ performs a similar transformation from panegyric to mystical *ghazal*. In this case, Ibn al-Fāriḍ followed al-Mutanabbī's poem more closely, and he openly acknowledges his debt to the great poet. Composing a poem rhyming with the letter *dhāl* is difficult owing to the small number of words ending with this letter, and both poets appear to have composed only one poem with this rhyme. Al-Mutanabbī dedicated his *al-Dhālīyah* to Musāwir ibn Muhammad al-Rūmī, a vizier and early patron of the poet. Al-Mutanabbī opens his panegyric with a rhetorical question meant to underscore the striking royal depiction of the lion walking before the equally majestic vizier.[16]

a-musāwirun am qarnu shamsin hādhā
am laythu ghābin yaqdumu-l-ustādhā

1) Is this Musāwir
   or the sun's first rays,
      or a lion of the jungle
   leading the master?

2) Sheath the sword
   you drew in haste,
      its sharp edge
   hacking men to bits.

3) Suppose you break
   Ibn Yazdādh and his troop.
      What's next? Is all mankind
   his terrible tribe?

4) You met them,
   leaving their faces
      torn from their necks,
   their guts in shreds,

5) On a battlefield
   where wretched death
      stood over them
   and stripped their lives away.

6) Their frozen souls
   ran as you reached them,
      then you slaked their thirst
   with steel.

7) When they saw you,
   they saw you father
      Muhammad in mail,
   and your uncle Muʿādh.

8) With a quick blow to the necks,
   you silenced their tongues
      from shouting:
   "There is no knight save him!"

9) You crashed down
   upon the fool

with a stormy brow
raining and pouring pain,

10) So you caught him
and soaked his cloak in blood,
while he pissed
down his thighs.

11) Your keen Yemeni sword
barred his way;
he had no retreat
to Aleppo or Baghdad.

12) He sought high rank at the front,
but he was from nowhere,
from Karkhayā
or Kalwādh.

13) Did he expect
spears to be sweet
like dates
from Barnī or Azādh?

14) He had never faced,
before you,
a lancer who savored
jousting thrusts,

15) A man
whose life is sour
until he executes
his decree,

16) A seasoned warrior:
coats of mail, his comfort,
his silk against the cold,
his cotton in blazing heat.

17) A wonder you seized him,
more wondrous still
had you not plundered
the likes of him!

Al-Mutanabbī opens his panegyric with a raging Musāwir returning from battling the Yazdādh tribe and ready for more. Musāwir, like his father and uncle before him, is an experienced veteran whose sharp blade hacks through his terrified enemies, leaving their bloody corpses strewn on the battlefield (vv. 1–7). Verse 8 is exceptional as al-Mutanabbī underscores his patron's prowess with a powerful phrase:

aᶜjalta alsunahum bi-ḍarbi riqābihim
ᶜan qawlihim lā fārisun illā dhā

With a quick blow to the necks
you silenced their tongues
from shouting:
"There is no knight save him!"

Lā fārisun illā dhā ("There is no knight save him!") echoes the first half of the traditional saying: "*lā fatā illā ᶜAlī wa-lā sayfa illā Dhū al-Faqār*" ("There is no hero save ᶜAlī and no sword save Dhū al-Faqār"). ᶜAlī ibn Abī Ṭālib was the cousin and son-in-law of the Prophet Muḥammad, and within Islam, he has been extolled as the warrior *par excellence*, as he wielded the famous notched sword, Dhū al-Faqār.[17] To draw such a parallel between a patron and the noble ᶜAlī might be perceived as impious exaggeration, but then al-Mutanabbī teases his audience, for the warrior's blade is swifter than his foes' insolent tongues. Thus, it is left to the poet to sing this praise of his mighty hero, and he concludes this short panegyric by comparing the battle-hardened Musāwir to his unworthy, inexperienced foe (vv. 9–17).

Composing his *al-Dhālīyah* in the same meter and rhyme, Ibn al-Fāriḍ used seventeen of al-Mutanabbī's eighteen rhyme words. Such a conscious patterning of an earlier poem required by tradition that Ibn al-Fāriḍ expand and improve on the original, and so his *al-Dhālīyah* is more than three times longer than that by al-Mutanabbī. Ibn al-Fāriḍ occasionally reused the same rhyme word but with different meanings, adding yet another stylistic flourish to his poem, which likewise begins with a rhetorical question:[18]

ṣaddun ḥamā ẓama'ī limāka li-mādhā
wa-hawāka qalbī ṣāra minhu judhādhā

1) A barrier guarded your dark lips
from my burning thirst;

why, since love of you
has hacked my heart to bits?

2) If you are content to stay
as I go to my ruin
drowning in passion,
I will savor it.

3) You plundered my healthy heart,
so give it back
as my last request,
though it be torn to shreds.

4) O archer
shooting eye arrows
from the bow of your brow,
piercing the heart,

5) How could you leave me?
One who slanders me
is full of malice,
and crazy ravings,

6) And one who attacked me
to keep me from you,
he was confused,
a hypocrite and liar!

7) O blamer,
you will not find me forgetting
one who seized and holds
mankind's loveliness.

8) How handsome he is,
a fawn making fair
his trading my fair state
for a squalid life.

9) He appeared
with beneficence and beauty,
bestowing rare things,
plundering souls;

10) A sword his eyelids
draw against the heart;
I see their languor
its whetstone;

11) A sudden death
he springs upon us,
bringing to mind victims of Musāwir
among the Banī Yazdādh.

12) No wonder he made
his downy cheek a sword belt
since he is quick to strike,
leaving his victims to die.

13) There is magic in his eyes!
Had Hārūt beheld their power,
he would have found there
his mentor and master.

14) Blamer, you rave on
the full moon in the sky above;
such crazy talk!
That is not my friend.

15) Sun and gazelle
fell captive to his face
as he looked back at them;
both sought refuge in him.

16) He was finer than
the fragrant east wind;
his delicate nature scorned
even a shirt of finest silk.

17) His tender cheek complained
against its blushing rose,
but his hard heart
told of steel.

18) The mole burning on his cheek
consumed a friend

tied to him by a passion
rejecting salvation.

19) The dark red of his lips
is cool and sweet to kiss
in the early morning before the toothpick;
he reigned over musk, scenting it.

20) From his mouth and glance
is my drunken state;
I see a vintner
in his every limb!

21) The belts on his narrow waist
said it all
when the silent signet rings
hurt his little pinkies.[19]

22) The belts were delicate;
his waist was fine,
like the words of my love song
and their meanings refined!

23) Like the bough, his stature
bright as the morning,
like a long dark night, his hair
falling down his back.

24) My love for him taught me
austerity since he was like
Muᶜādh in chastity,
fearful of the world to come.

25) So I threw away all shame
to veil him
and protect him
from a kiss on the cheek.

26) In Minā's Khayf are Arabs dear to us
but before them stands
the death of desire,
foe to a lover seeking refuge there.

27) In the winding tract of that sacred vale
a stag stood
guarding with sharp eye-arrows
a pool

28) Formed
by lovers' tears
as they fell on the mountain slopes
and flowed in the valley.

29) How many canals came there
to this sandy ground,
not to the stream,
begging a drink!

30) Before the troop divided,
we were a mighty tribe,
but the long journey
broke us into clans.

31) I was soon alone after union,
far away in Syria,
while they pitched their tents
near Baghdad.

32) The distance gathered
fear within me
that had before been scattered
when I was close to them.

33) Like a brief shower on stone
are their promises made at Ṣafā
But why? I am pure
and will not break the bond!

34) Bearing their absence is bitter myrrh,
yet bearing with them
seems to me a pain
sweet as dates of Azādh

35) Solace was hard to find,
grave my rapture with them

who were shelter in the deep of night,
but then they cut the tie.

36) O white gazelle of the desert plains,
leave me alone,
for they colored my eyes with dark black kohl;
do not make me look away in sadness.

37) I swear by him
whose torturing me
I find sweet as I savor
his degrading me,

38) My eye never found
anyone lovely but him,
and though he took another, not me,
I remained true.

39) Those who slipped in to spy,
watching without being seen,
saw only a man
shattered by grief.

40) He was a lion taming
the lions of the jungle
until he fell victim
to a young gazelle.

41) So it happened
that passion's fire filled him;
he sees its burning
but no relief.

42) Bewildered he is now;
if you met him, you would say:
"I see him pulled
every which way!"

43) Thirsty; his ribs embrace a sorrow
beyond the doctors' power,
so he clinched his teeth
as pain bit deep,

44) At the point of death;
stung within and plundered of life,
his sleepless state proved him to be
a match for Mimshādh.

45) A plague seized him,
and he suffered
to see on his body
the oozing ganglion.

46) Patiently, he put on
black garments of grief
to mourn when youth died,
shattered in his silver temples.

47) So his enemies were pleased
to see his youthful prime
loose as a shirt,
his hair, turban white.

48) Cold beds: there is no end
to their spreading sorrow.
So fate commands
and executes its decree.

49) His eyes never hold back,
but always give,
raining and pouring tears
for the lovers' cruel ways.

50) He showered the mountains
with tear drops
when the clouds refused,
and filled their hollow pools.

51) When the women visiting the sick
saw him, they said:
"If anyone be slain by passion,
surely it is this one!"

Similar to al-Mutanabbī, Ibn al-Fāriḍ begins his poem praising a hero, but one of love, not of war. In the opening verses of his panegyric, al-Mutanabbī recounts Musāwir's battle with his foes, whereas Ibn al-Fāriḍ describes the beauty and prowess of the conquering beloved and the wounds he inflicts when plundering his lover's heart (vv. 1–13). Ibn al-Fāriḍ pays homage to al-Mutanabbī by comparing his fearsome beloved to Musāwir, scourge of the Banī Yazdādh. Yet, the beloved is not a hardened warrior, but a young man, slender like a gazelle, with a soft cheek, and eyes so enchanting that they would captivate Hārūt, a fallen angel who taught magic to human beings.[20] Ibn al-Fāriḍ shifts further away from the knightly motifs of the panegyric to present this image of his more refined beloved. Al-Mutanabbī praises his patron's marshal skills and power as he rips the faces from his foes (v. 4), while Ibn al-Fāriḍ refers to the beloved's radiant face (v. 15):

ᶜanati-l-ghazālatu wa-l-ghazālu li-wajhihi
mutalaffitan wa-bihi ᶜiyādhan lādhā

Sun and gazelle
fell captive to his face
as he looked back at them;
both sought refuge in him.

Some of the more mystical passages of the Qur'ān mention God's face or countenance (wajh), which is present throughout creation (2:115). Save "God's face," all things will perish (28:88), but on the judgment day, He will look with mercy upon those of His creatures whose "faces submit" (*ᶜanati-l-wujūhu*) humbly to Him (20:111). Similarly, the Qur'ān repeatedly urges believers to "seek refuge in God" (e.g., 16:98), before whom even the sun and moon bow down (22:18).[21] But this holy image of the beloved becomes more earthly in the verses that follow, which depict him as a delicate, pampered youth, with cool lips, a sweet kiss, and a fragrant scent. Like a fine wine, he intoxicates the lover (vv. 16–23), although a restrained spiritual relationship may be implied by Ibn al-Fāriḍ's use of several terms with established Sufi meanings (v. 18: *wajd*: "passion," "rapture;" v. 20: *sukr*: "intoxication;" v. 24: *tanassuk*: "austerity," "asceticism"). Whereas Musāwir, in the heat of battle, resembles his manly uncle, Muᶜādh, the beloved of Ibn al-Fāriḍ's poem resembles the handsome ascetic Muᶜādh ibn Jabal, a pious and dear companion of the Prophet Muhammad (v. 24).[22] This led Arberry to assert:[23]

> The choice of the name is thus particularly apposite, apart from its rhetorical elegance. The reference suggests that

> the poet now has in mind a mortal beloved, no doubt a handsome disciple, in whom he is seeing after Sufi fashion the embodiment of the Divine Beloved.

Ibn al-Fāriḍ's description of the beloved in the *al-Dhālīyah* is one of the more detailed and embodied examples to be found in any of his poems. This beloved also is noteworthy in that he is male, not female as often is the case in Ibn al-Fāriḍ's verse, and this may have prompted Arberry's provocative remark. Nevertheless, the poet's close imitation of al-Mutanabbī's panegyric poem required a male beloved, as well as the use of the rhyme word Muᶜādh. Moreover, the Qur'ānic references in verse 15 might suggest the beloved is God, although not as convincingly as in his *al-Lāmīyah.* There, Ibn al-Fāriḍ's allusions to the pre-eternal covenant, annihilation and union in love, the heart and *dhikr,* all imply a divine beloved. In the *al-Dhālīyah,* the beloved's male gender together with mention of the toothpick (v. 19: *siwāk*) might allude to the Prophet Muhammad, who according to tradition, used the toothpick first thing in the morning.[24] But such prophetic or religious allusions were standard in many earlier *ghazals,* as poets praised their ideal loves, and similarly, in the *al-Dhālīyah,* Ibn al-Fāriḍ presents the Muslim ideal of a handsome, delicate youth. Significantly, this young, healthy and handsome beloved stands in marked contrast to the aged lover's fallen state that later becomes the poem's focus.[25]

In verses 21–22, Ibn al-Fāriḍ boasts that the beloved's thin belts and slender waist are comparable to the delicate and refined quality of his *nasīb* (vv. 21–22). Frequently, in Ibn al-Fāriḍ's verse, such conscious self-praise signals a transition, and here the poet introduces the standard *ghazal* theme of the lover's perseverance before the cruelties of his beloved. Although the beloved resembles Muᶜādh ibn Jabal in piety and beauty, the lover must learn from Muᶜādh's martyrdom and purge his self-regard and willful desires if he is to protect the beloved from others and from himself (vv. 24–25). The poet then recalls the beloved far away in Arabia. There a stag once guarded a pool of lovers' tears in a sacred precinct (*ḥimā*), and this powerful mythic image suggests both the sexuality of the stag, and the water's curative powers (vv. 26–29). The reverie of the *nasīb* persists as the lover sadly recalls the departure of the tribe, which has dispersed, but not in search of new pastures as in the pre-Islamic *nasīb.* Ibn al-Fāriḍ's references to al-Khayf, Minā, "the gathering," and al-Ṣafā in Mecca (vv. 26–27, 30–33) allude to the Hajj, the Muslim pilgrimage, suggesting that the sacred pool is the well of Zamzam. According to Arab poetic tradition, the Hajj is a time of rendezvous for lovers, whereas for lovers of God, the pilgrimage is a hallowed occasion for contemplation and prayer. Ibn al-Fāriḍ often combines both elements in his poems of meditation on life and love, which feature many of the rituals and places of the Muslim pilgrimage.[26]

The tribe of the *al-Dhālīyah*, then, is the community of Muslim pilgrims who, upon completion of the Hajj, depart by various routes. The lover longs to know why the pacts he made with them in Mecca were so quickly broken. Yet, if this is the beloved's wish, then he will deem it good, though separation is unbearable after the joys of union (vv. 33–35). The lover swears to his continued fidelity to the covenant and concludes with the description of his pitiful state; once a great man, a lion like al-Mutanabbī's Musāwir, the lover now resembles Mimshādh al-Dīnawarī, a Muslim ascetic worn out by sleepless devotion to God.[27] The raging fire of love has left the lover confused, thirsting, and near death (vv. 36–44). Infected with the plague of love, his body has lost its youth; fate has left him old, decrepit, and alone. Wasted by the pains of separation and haunted by memories of lost love, the lover, like a madman, wanders distraught, a victim of undying passion (vv. 45–51).

With this ending, Ibn al-Fāriḍ has, in effect, reversed the object of praise found in al-Mutanabbī's poem. Whereas Ibn al-Fāriḍ lauds the conquering beloved in the poem's opening section, beginning with verse 24, his hero becomes the victim broken by love. This role change underlies the contrasting allusions made by both poets with the name Muᶜādh. But the poets' differing goals are more vividly revealed by comparing two points of climax. In verse 8 of al-Mutanabbī's poem, Musāwir's victims realize at the moment of death that "There is no knight save him!" But Ibn al-Fāriḍ's final verse praises the slain and not the slayer:

qāla-l-ᶜawā'idu ᶜinda-mā abṣarnahu
in kāna man qatala-l-gharāmu fa-hādhā

When the women visiting the sick
saw him, they said:
"If anyone was slain by passion,
surely it is this one!"

This verse strikes the same theme as verse 34 of the *al-Lāmīyah*, but with a different tone. In his *al-Lāmīyah*, Ibn al-Fāriḍ's poetic persona is that of a wise and experienced teacher advising a young man on matters of love. Therefore, he recounts his own experience of self-sacrifice that led to his annihilation in love, so that now his beloved abides in his heart. But this joy is absent from the *al-Dhālīyah,* where the poetic persona is that of the imperfect lover. For in answer to the rhetorical question that began the poem regarding what prevents union, the lover still exists. So he must continue to suffer his slow, ignominious death in hopes of a union to come. Al-Mutanabbī's courtly panegyric is now a faint echo in Ibn al-Fāriḍ's lamentation on love.

Yet, Ibn al-Fārid's *al-Dhālīyah* represents a literary as well as spiritual endeavor. In his *al-Lāmīyah,* Ibn al-Fāriḍ was less rigorous in his adherence to a specific work by al-Mutanabbī while composing a beautiful and independent poem. However, in the *al-Dhālīyah,* Ibn al-Fāriḍ's careful use and play on al-Mutanabbī's motifs and rhyme words resulted in several difficult, if necessary, verses (e.g., vv. 5, 14, 21, 29, 34, 43–44). Furthermore, in verse 22, Ibn al-Fāriḍ boasts of his poetic skills and this, too, strongly suggests a literary motive in composing the *al-Dhālīyah.* For the imitation of a poem by al-Mutanabbī, a recognized master of Arabic poetry, should only be dared by another self-confident poet, and Ibn al-Fāriḍ's very original improvisations on al-Mutanabbī must have delighted his learned companions whether they were Sufi adepts, established poets or, like Ibn al-Fāriḍ, both.

Transformations

Many of Ibn al-Fāriḍ's contemporaries would have been awed by the many clever and creative rhetorical elements in the *al-Dhālīyah.* Al-Mutanabbī used word plays in his verse, but far less than Ibn al-Fāriḍ and other poets of the seventh/thirteenth century among whom the *badī*ᶜ style was quite the rage. Ibn al-Fāriḍ's *al-Dhālīyah* is replete with various types of *jinās* ("paronomasia"), *ṭibāq* ("antithesis"), and other types of word play, many of which may be found in a single verse such as verse 8:

yā mā umayliḥahu rashan fīhi ḥalā
tabdīluhu ḥālī-l-ḥaliya badhādhā

How handsome he is, a fawn,
making fair
his trading my fair state
for shabbiness.

Here we find the standard Arabic metaphor of the beloved as a deer, but this verse also features Ibn al-Fāriḍ's trademark, the use of the diminutive to express endearment. In this extraordinary instance, Ibn al-Fāriḍ stresses his admiration for the beloved by invoking a rare diminutive of a fourth-form verbal idiom of wonder *mā amlaḥahu*: "What a handsome one is he!" The lover's total submission before this young beauty is further suggested by the extended word play between *ḥalā* ("to be sweet, pleasant, or fair"), *ḥālī* ("my state"), and *al-ḥaliya* ("adorned," "fair," "sweet"), and underscored by the antithesis between *al-ḥaliya* ("adorned," "fair," "sweet") and *badhādhā* ("shabby," "worn out"). Thus, whatever pleases the pleasing beloved pleases the lover even if, in other ways, it must pain him.[28] But there is more. Ibn al-Fāriḍ's diminutive, *mā umayliḥahu*, is derived from the root *m*l*ḥ*, which may refer to saltiness, wittiness or, as in this verse, to beauty. So, one might translate the expression in idiomatic American English as "What a sweetie he is!" However, the appearance in the same hemistich of *ḥalā* ("to be sweet") may cause the reader to imagine momentarily that the poet intends to establish an antithesis between *ḥalā* ("to be sweet") and *umaylaḥ* meaning "salty," when in fact he intends the diminutive as a description of the beloved's beauty. Such a word play in Arabic is known as *tawrīyah* ("double entendre") or *īhām* ("making someone to imagine something else"). Other examples of *īhām* found in Ibn al-Fāriḍ's *al-Dhālīyah* occur in verse 10, *jufūn*, "eyelids," may also mean "scabbards," while in verse 15, *ghazālah*, "rising sun," also may mean "she-gazelle." Ibn al-Fāriḍ makes another elaborate play in verse 18:

ᶜamma-shtiᶜālan khālu wajnatihi akhā
shugulin bihi wajdan abā-stnqādhā

The mole burning on his cheek
consumed a friend
tied to him by a passion
rejecting salvation.

Here, the words *ᶜamma* ("to consume," "encompass"), *khāl* ("mole"), *akhā* ("man," "companion"), and *abā* ("to reject, scorn"), pun on their respective meanings of "paternal uncle," "maternal uncle," "brother," and "father" (*wajd*, "passion," in context of this *īhām* brings to mind *wa-jadd*, "and grandfather").[29] Ibn al-Fāriḍ offers yet another extended play on words in verse 29:

kam min faqīrin thamma lā min jaᶜfarin
wāfā-l-ajāriᶜa sā'ilan shaḥḥādhā

How many canals came there
to this sandy ground,
not to the stream,
begging a drink!

Here the words *faqīr* ("mouth of a canal," "canal," "beggar") and *sā'il* ("flowing," "asking," "begging") may also be synonyms of *shaḥḥādh* meaning "beggar," all forming a kind of antithesis with *jaᶜfar* ("stream") if this word is taken as the personal name of the generous Abbasid vizier, Jaᶜfar al-Barmakī (d. 187/803).[30] These five examples of *īhām* from the *al-Dhālīyah* have well-known forerunners in the verse of earlier poets, and it should be assumed that Ibn al-Fāriḍ placed them in this poem as yet another demonstration of his extensive knowledge of Arabic poetics.[31]

Ibn al-Fāriḍ's habitual use of such elaborate word plays and other rhetorical displays has frequently been noted but rarely studied, especially by modern scholars whose own literary tastes have been at odds with the mannerism of the Ayyubid period. Although these critics praise the content of his *Dīwān*, they usually ignore or apologize for its poetic style. As a result, many readers have failed to appreciate the contributions of the *badīᶜ* style to the meaning and mood of Ibn al-Fāriḍ's verse. An exception is Issa Boullata who, in a short but insightful study, analyzed a section from Ibn al-Fāriḍ's *al-Tāīyah al-Kubrā* to illustrate the harmony of content and form to be found in this work.[32] Several of Boullata's conclusions are echoed in a later study of Ibn al-Fāriḍ's poetic style by Ramaḍān Ṣādiq. Ṣādiq cites and briefly analyzes instances in which Ibn al-Fāriḍ draws attention to his message and poetic originality by means of *jinās*, parallelism, antithesis, and phonemic patterning, as in the following verse:[33]

fa-l-wajdu bāqin wa-l-wiṣālu mumāṭilī
wa-ṣ-ṣabru fānin wa-l-liqā'u wusawwifī

My rapture stays while union is deferred me;
patience is gone, and the encounter put off.

In this verse, Ibn al-Fāriḍ embeds several well-known antithetical Sufi technical terms within parallel grammatical and rhythmic structures to present the lover's desperate state in separation from his beloved, as requisite patience (*ṣabr*) is annihilated (*fānin*) by a passionate rapture (*wajd*), which abides (*bāqin*) within the lover who hopes for union. Similarly, in the following verse, Ibn al-Fāriḍ uses four pairs of contrasting verbs in a rhetorical *tour du force* regarding lover's fidelity to his beloved:[34]

wa-humu humu ṣaddū danaw waddū jafaw
ghadarū wafaw hajarū rathaw li-ḍanā'ī

They are the same
whether they turn away or draw near,
love or hate, are treacherous or true,
leave or take pity for my illness.

Again, in verse 30 of the *al-Lāmīyah*, Ibn al-Fārid invokes antithesis this time within an *īhām* to infuse his love with a mystical spirit:

ḥadīthī qadīmun fī hawāhā wa-mā lahu
kamā ᶜalimat baᶜdun wa-laysa lahu qablu

My tale of love for her is ancient, as well she knows,
without before, without an after.

The *īhām* is between *ḥadīthī* ("my tale," "my speech") and *qadīm* ("ancient"). *Hadīth* may also mean "new" or "temporal" as opposed to "eternal" or "pre-eternal" (*qidam*), and it is precisely this temporal element that is denied by the verse with its contrasting prepositional phrases that create a paradox of timelessness. Within a Sufi context, the lover's ancient tale may well be the word *balā* ("yes") that, according to the Qur'ān 7:172, was the answer given by the progeny of Adam in pre-eternity, before creation, to God's question, "*alastu bi-rabbikum*:" "Am I not your Lord?" This primordial covenant (*mīthāq*) between God and humanity has been a source of hope and inspiration for many Muslims and for Sufis, in particular, and, as we shall see, it is a major theme in Ibn al-Fārid's poetry.[35]

As noted in several verses just presented, antithesis (*ṭibāq*) is a major element in Ibn al-Fāriḍ's verse. In the opening verses to the *al-Lāmīyah* above, Ibn al-Fāriḍ employs antitheses to transform al-Mutanabbī's courtly love into a mystical one: mind, or intellect, (*ᶜalq*) contrasts with heart (*ḥashā*); ease (*rāḥah*) with hardship (*ᶜanā*), first (*awwal*) with last (*akhir*) and, naturally, life (*ḥayāh/yaᶜish*) with death (*mawt/yamūt*). Ibn al-Fāriḍ combines antithesis with word play and internal rhyme in verse 5, to proclaim forcefully love's law, and to once again suggest that the world is not as it at first appears:[36]

fa-in shi'ta an taḥyā saᶜīdan fa-mut bihi
shahīdan wa-illā fa-l-gharāmu lahu ahlu

But if you want to live well, then die love's martyr,
and if not, well, love has its worthy ones.

Ibn al-Fāriḍ also uses antithesis along with personification and internal rhyme in verse 18 of the *al-Lāmīyah* to underscore the lover's readiness to joyfully accept love's consequences:

wa-taᶜdhībukum ᶜadhbun ladayya wa-jawrukum
ᶜalayya bi-mā yaqḍī-l-hawā lakumu ᶜadlu

Your torturing me delights me, and your tyranny
over me, as passion decreed for you, is just.

As in this verse, Ibn al-Fāriḍ frequently combines antithesis with simile or metaphor to allude to hidden dimensions of reality and to probe deeper meanings, especially regarding the beloved with her transcendent, intoxicating nature:[37]

saqatnī ḥumayyā-l-ḥubbi rāḥatu muqlatī
wa-ka'sī muḥayyā man ᶜani-l-ḥusni jallati

The palm of my eye handed me
love's heady wine to drink,
and my glass was a face
of one revealing loveliness.

Although this deft *badīᶜ* style often adds depth to the meaning of his verse, Ibn al-Fāriḍ also heightened the emotional pitch of a poem via stylistic and rhetorical elements. On one occasion, he used a peculiar device known as *radd al-ᶜajz ᶜalā al-ṣadr* in which the last word of a verse is identical to the first word. This device appears in three successive verses at the conclusion of the *al-Yā'īyah*, where the repetition of the word *ayy* ("what," "alas," "oh," "which") reverberates with loss and lamentation (vv. 146–48):[38]

ayyu ᶜayshin marra lī fī ẓillihi
asafī idh ṣāra ḥazzī minhu ayy

ayy layālī-l-waṣli hal min ᶜawdatin
wa-mina-t-taᶜlīli qawlu-ṣ-ṣabbi ayy
wa-bi-ayyi-ṭ-ṭurqi arjū rajᶜahā
rubbamā aqḍī wa-mā adrī ayy

What life passed for me in the encampment's shade?
O, now my portion of it is what?
Alas, will the nights of union ever return?
And for distraction, the impassioned lover moans "Alas!"
By which road may I hope for their return?
Perhaps I'm dying and do not know which way.

As we see in these and other verses, Ibn al-Fāriḍ might call on rhyme, rhythm, and metrical form, simile, metaphor, and other rhetorical devices to unleash a dazzling display of his poetic skills. Yet even in such instances, he creatively employs various formal and rhetorical elements to add layers of meaning and feeling to his words. In this way, he urges others to listen carefully to his verse and to the larger world around them in order to witness the unity that lies hidden under the changing surfaces of things.[39]

Riddles and Rubāᶜīyāt

Although Ibn al-Fāriḍ often employed the *badīᶜ* style to create emotional tension, he also chose *badīᶜ* for witty and humorous verse, as is readily apparent in his riddles and *rubāᶜīyāt*. The posing of riddles (*lughz/ alghāz*) was a popular pastime among litterateurs and scholars of the Ayyubid period. Riddles were exchanged and given in answer to other riddles and, undoubtedly, this literary game provided entertaining demonstrations of abstruse knowledge and rhetorical ingenuity. Usually, riddles consisted of a few verses on virtually any topic, abstract or concrete, sacred or profane.[40] Among the solutions to Ibn al-Fāriḍ's twenty-one recorded riddles are the names of birds, plants, and foods, the name of a city (Aleppo), a personal name (Shaᶜbān), and several, more abstract notions such as "excellence" (*ḥusn*) and "well-being" (*salāmah*).[41] Although the answers to these riddles are simple enough, deducing them involves a complex process of metathesis (*qalb*) and substitution of radicals, either by other radicals (*taṣḥīf*) or by their numerical values, according to established rules, which were known by every gifted litterateur.[42] With such intricacies, many riddles convey a playful quality difficult to capture in translation:[43]

mā ismu shay'in mina-n-nabāti idhā mā
qalabūhu wajadtahu ḥayawānā
wa-idhā mā ṣaḥḥafta thulthayhi ḥāshā
bad'ahu kunta wāṣifan insānā

What plant becomes an animal
when you juggle its name?
Toss up two letters, but hold the first;
catch a human attribute!

The first verse tells the reader that Ibn al-Fāriḍ has in mind the name of a plant that, through metathesis becomes the name of an animal. The second verse limits the number of possibilities by hinting that the word has three radicals and that it becomes an adjective describing a human being when its final two radicals are changed following the rules of *taṣḥīf*. Sorting through the numerous three radical names for plants, one arrives at *līf* ("fibers of a palm tree"). If we switch the consonants by metathesis, this word becomes *fīl* ("elephant"), an animal. Keeping the first radical of *līf*, we then apply the substitution rules in *taṣḥīf*, so *bā'* is substituted for *yā'* and *qaf* for *fā'* resulting in *labaq* ("clever," "suave"), which describes anyone who is able to solve this riddle.[44]

In the following riddle, Ibn al-Fāriḍ plays on fractions and the numerical values of words and their radicals to hint at a solution:[45]

yā khabīran bi-l-lughzi bayyin la-nā mā
ḥayawānun taṣḥīfuhu baᶜḍu ᶜāmi
rubᶜuhu in aḍaftahu la-ka minhu
niṣfuhu in ḥasabtahu ᶜan tamāmi

Oh riddles' expert explain to us
which animal's *taṣḥīf* is part of the year?
One fourth, if you possess it,
is half the whole when you count it!

The first verse limits the answer to an animal whose name, following radical substitution, is equal to a portion of the year. Reviewing the names of the months, we find that the name of the second month, Ṣafar becomes *ṣaqr* ("falcon") after substituting for the second radical. This answer is confirmed by the riddle's second verse. To possess the falcon means to add the first-person pronominal suffix to the word producing *ṣaqrī* ("my falcon"). One-fourth of *ṣaqrī* equals one of its four radicals, and this letter must be equal to one-half of the word's value of four hundred, as computed by adding the values traditionally assigned to the four radicals. The *rā'* alone is equal to two hundred and, so, although being one-fourth of the word, the letter *rā'* is worth one-half of the whole word.[46]

These and other riddles by Ibn al-Fāriḍ demonstrate his knowledge of Arabic grammar and etymology, but more importantly they reveal a sense of humor and literary wit. This playfulness, however, has disturbed some modern scholars who find such "frivolities" as riddles incongruous with their image of Ibn al-Fāriḍ as a pious and solemn Sufi. Due to such convictions, the riddles have usually been ignored, and there has even been an attempt to dismiss them as forgeries by the poet's grandson, ᶜAlī.[47] Perhaps for similar reasons, Ibn al-Fāriḍ's occasional verse has been overlooked by more recent readers of his *Dīwān.* Nevertheless, many of the poet's educated contemporaries in Egypt probably enjoyed his humorous short poem in praise of Cairo. Ibn al-Fāriḍ's grandson ᶜAlī noted that his grandfather had once traveled to Damascus where he found the populace complaining of plague. When Ibn al-Fārid returned to Cairo, he composed this poem in the meter *ramal*:[48]

Damascus is the garden
  of the haughty and proud,
    and her hills I would desire
  if not for their disease.

I was asked to describe
  her Baradā as Kawthar:
    her Baradā is dear,
  with death!

Cairo is my homeland,
  she is my goal,
    and my eyes' desire
  her Mushtahā.

If my soul
  dwells elsewhere,
    then ask her, my friends,
  what consoles her?

Most of Ibn al-Fāriḍ's shorter poems take the form of *rubāᶜīyāt* ("quatrains"). A poetic genre of Persian origin, *rubāᶜīyāt* were very popular in Ayyubid Egypt, where they were known as *dū bayt*, a Persian phrase meaning a couplet, that is, four hemstitches (= *rubāʿī*). In a good quatrain, the first, second, and fourth hemstitches were required to rhyme, and the third might also. Some Ayyubid poets, such as Bahā' al-Dīn Zuhayr, composed *rubāʿīyāt* in the spirit of the fifth/eleventh-century Persian master ʿUmar Khayyām to make pointed observations on life and destiny:[49]

kam yadhhabu hadhā-l-ʿumru fī khusrāni
  mā aghfalanī ʿanhu wa-mā ansānī
in lam yakuni-l-yawma falāḥī fa-matā
  hal baʿdaka yā ʿumriya ʿumrun thānī

How long this life has passed in loss;
  how heedless I am, how forgetful.
If I don't profit today, then when?
  "Life, after you, is there another?"

In contrast to such lamentations, most of Ibn al-Fāriḍ's *rubāʿīyāt* address love themes similar to those found in his longer poems. The broken covenant, the pain of separation, and longing for union are frequent themes, while in the following quatrain, Ibn al-Fāriḍ combines the ancient motif of the nocturnal visit by the beloved's phantom with the motif of the blamer who unintentionally gladdens the lover by mentioning the beloved in his censure of the lover's conduct:[50]

al-ʿādhilu ka-l-ʿādhiri ʿindī yā qawm
  ahdā lī man ahwāhu fī ṭayfi-l-lawm
lā aʿtibuhu in lam yazur fī ḥulumī
  fa-s-samʿu yarā mā lā yarā ṭarfu-n-nawm

My people, the accuser is my excuser,
  he guides my love to me, a phantom in his blame.
So I don't blame my love when he visits not my dreams,
  for the ear sees what sleep's eye does not.

In another *rubāʿī*, Ibn al-Fāriḍ extols the sustenance of love:[51]

lam akhsha wa-anta sākinun aḥshā'ī
  in aṣbaḥa ʿannī kullu khillin nā'ī
fa-n-nāsu-thnāni wāḥidun aʿshaquhu
  wa-l-ākharu lam aḥsibhu fī-l-aḥyā'i

While you dwell in my heart, I will not dread,
  though my dearest friends move far away.
For people are of two kinds:
  those I dearly love, and those I count as dead.

By contrast, Ibn al-Fāriḍ is contrite in the next quatrain, as he laments having fallen short in love before his death:[52]

rūḥī li-liqāka yā munāhā-shtāqat
  wa-l-arḍu ᶜalayya ka-ḥtiyālī ḍāqat
wa-n-nafsu fa-qad dhābat gharāman wa-assā
  fī janbi riḍāka fī-l-hawā mā lāqat

My spirit longed to meet you, my desire,
  while the earth oppressed me like my deceit.
Though my selfish soul melted from passion and pain,
  next to your acceptance, it was unfit for love.

This *rubāᶜī* and most others by Ibn al-Fāriḍ have been interpreted mystically due to the Sufi technical terms and references that may be found in some of them. In this particular quatrain, Ibn al-Fāriḍ makes the standard Sufi contrast between the divine spirit (*rūḥ*) and human concupiscence or selfishness (*nafs*). In true love, selfishness must be restrained and tempered so that the spirit may return to its creator once the body is buried in the grave. Yet despite his sincere efforts, the lover must still pray for God's acceptance (*riḍā*) of him on the Day of Judgment (*yawm al-liqā'*).[53] In addition to their possible religious themes, however, a number of Ibn al-Fāriḍ's quatrains appear to be poetic exercises in which he has reworked themes and entire hemstitches found in other quatrains:

ahwā rasha'an kulla-l-asā lī baᶜathā
  mudh ᶜāyanahu taṣabburī mā labithā
nādaytu wa qad fakkartu fī khilqatihi
  subḥānaka mā khalaqta hadhā ᶜabathā

I desire a fawn who sends every grief to me.
  After my patience saw him, it would not stay.
I cried out when I admired his form:
  "Glory be to You! You did not form this one in jest!"[54]

ahwā rasha'an hawāhu li-r-rūḥi ghidhā
mā aḥsana fiᶜlahu wa-law kāna adhā
lam ansa wa-qad qultu lahu al-waṣlu mattā
mawlāya idhā muttu hawan qāla idhā[55]

I desire a fawn whose love nourished the spirit.
How lovely his deed, had it even caused harm.
I will never forget when I asked him: "Oh, my master,
"When is union? Must I die of desire?" He said: "Then!"

ahwā rasha'an rushayiqa-l-qaddi ḥulay
qad ḥakkamahu-l-gharāmu wa-l-wajdu ᶜalay
in qultu khudhi-r-rūḥa yaqul lī ᶜajaban
ar-rūḥu lanā fa-hāti min ᶜindika shay[56]

I desire a dear fawn, slender of shape,
for passion and rapture made him judge over me.
When I said: "Take my spirit!" He replied: "Amazing!
"The spirit is ours? Then give us a little now!"

Whatever the mystical content of some quatrains, the following *rubāᶜī* is rather risqué at first glance:[57]

mā aṭyaba mā bitnā maᶜan fī burdi
idh lāṣaqa khadduhu-ᶜtināqan khaddī
ḥattā rashaḥāt min ᶜaraqin wajnatuhu
lā zāla naṣībī minhu mā'a-l-wardi

How sweet to spend the night together in a cloak,
his cheek embracing mine,
until his cheek began to sweat.
My share of it? Rose water!

This *rubāᶜī* has been admired for its elegant comparison of the cheek's perspiration to rose water, an extension of the hackneyed motif of the beloved's cheek red like the rose. But these verses may also allude to the prophet Muhammad who once gave his cloak (*burdah*) to a poet as a reward. Furthermore, according to popular legend, the prophet's sweat was the original source for the rose.[58] Once these allusions are understood, much of the quatrain's scandal is dissipated. Given the literary customs of the period, Ibn al-Fāriḍ may have composed this quatrain to convey a message of thanks to a friend for a pleasant evening of conversation and poetry.[59]

Several other quatrains ascribed to Ibn al-Fāriḍ may serve as further illustrations of his intricate *badīʿ* style. The poet ends each hemistich of the following *rubāʿī* with the word *khaṭā* but with four different meanings: "turning grey"; "walk away"; "Khaṭā," the name of a city; and "mistake." With this extended word play, Ibn al-Fāriḍ draws a parallel between the foolish old man who visits the brothels, and the dishonor it brings him:[60]

lammā nazala-sh-shaybu bi-ra'sī wa-khaṭā
  wa-l-ʿumru maʿa-sh-shabābī wallā wa-khaṭā
aṣbaḥtu bi-sumri Samarqandin wa-Khaṭā
  lā afruqu mā bayna-ṣawābin wa-khaṭā

When hoariness fell upon my head turning it grey,
  and life with youth turned and walked away,
Then I awoke with the tawny beauties of Samarqand and Cathay.
  Now, I can not tell what is right from what leads astray.

The poet again uses homonyms and punning (*jinās*) to drive home his point in the following quatrain which, according to tradition, Ibn al-Fāriḍ recited near the end of his life:[61]

khalīlaya in zurtumā manzilī
  wa-lam tajidāhu fasīḥan fa-sīḥā
wa-in rumtumā manṭiqan min famī
  wa-lam tarayāhu faṣīḥan fa-ṣīḥā

My two dear friends, if you visit my house,
  but find it cramped, then out!
And if you crave a phrase from my mouth,
  but find it rough, then shout!

In addition to their literary value, these *rubāʿīyāt* and riddles, as this last example illustrates, are noteworthy for their portrayal of Ibn al-Fāriḍ as a witty, educated poet. Although the authenticity of the last two quatrains is open to some question, their style and tone echo that of Ibn al-Fāriḍ's other occasional verses, which exhibit his knowledge of Arabic and, too, a sense of humor. Moreover, as the examples illustrate, *badīʿ* is an essential component of Ibn al-Fāriḍ's sophisticated poetry. This *badīʿ* style, together with Ibn al-Fāriḍ's riddles, *rubāʿīyāt*, and improvisations on verse by his literary predecessors challenge persistent views of him as a divinely possessed poet spontaneously reciting from the depths of mystical trance. However, it would be equally wrong to regard the significance and function of his *badīᶜ* as merely the decorative product of the mannered poetry of his time. For Ibn al-Fāriḍ's selection and use of the *badīᶜ* style was particularly appropriate to his mystical themes whose expression required a highly symbolic language with deeply subliminal associations, as is clear in his *ghazals*, or love poems.

2

Love's Secrets

Tryst

From the start, love and poetry have been intimate companions with Islamic mysticism. The love between God and humanity is an essential element of the Sufi tradition, and this relationship, with its many permutations, is central to Arabic religious verse. This poetry, like love and mysticism, is more or less oblique, for it shares with them a fundamental problem regarding language, namely, how does one discuss the larger world of experience with language that has evolved to satisfy specific everyday needs. With striking images and metaphors, structural and phonemic patterning, and the beat of rhythm and rhyme, a poem can evoke moods and convey meaning by drawing attention to language via language itself. In this way, the poet urges others to listen more closely and so invest renewed attention in their immediate surroundings, which are psychological and spiritual, as well as physical and temporal.

Verse, then, marks a return, a recollection, and a remembrance that are of equal importance to love and mysticism, and so Muslim mystics naturally turned to love poetry to voice their feelings and beliefs. Early Sufi love poetry draws many of its themes and images directly from the Arabic *ghazal* tradition, whether embodied in the pre-Islamic *nasīb*, the chaste laments by Jamīl and other ᶜUdhrī poets, or in the playful love songs of such poets as ᶜUmar Ibn Abī Rabīᶜah. But Islamic mysticism, Arabic poetry, and love have reciprocal relationships, and by the fourth/tenth century, many professional poets found inspiration in Sufism. Al-Mutanabbī employed the mystical language of antithesis and paradox to amaze and praise his royal patrons, whereas the Andalusian poet Ibn Zaydūn (d. 463/1071) relied on mystical allusions to intimate the spiritual nature of his abiding love for a fickle lover. Such unions were encouraged and strengthened by medieval views of love, particularly those influenced by neo-Platonism, which saw all forms of love as emanating from one divine source.[1]

Nevertheless, permissible love relationships, as well as their forms of public expression, were matters of concern to religious scholars and litterateurs, alike. The theologian and mystic Muhammad al-Ghazālī (d. 505/1111) warned that public recitation of love poetry might arouse lust and unseemly behavior among the ignorant masses, and the Ḥanbalī scholar Ibn al-Jawzī (d. 597/1200) was scandalized when amorous verses by Ibn al-Rūmī were recited from the pulpit during a Friday sermon. By contrast, as we have seen, the literary critic al-Thaᶜālibī censured al-Mutanabbī for using the Sufis "tangled words and abstruse meanings" in his poetry, whereas others criticized Sufi poets for composing love poetry at all.[2] This seems to have also been the case when Ibn al-ᶜArabī compiled a collection of his poems entitled the *Turjumān al-Ashwāq* ("The Interpreter of Desires"). In the original preface to this work, Ibn al-ᶜArabī noted that when he arrived in Mecca in 598/1202, he began to study with an Iranian scholar who had a daughter named Niẓām. This woman's physical and spiritual beauty inspired Ibn al-ᶜArabī to compose poems using the style and expressions from *ghazal* poetry that, he said, fell far short of his true feelings:[3]

> Nevertheless, I have put into verse for her sake, some of the longing thoughts suggested by those precious memories, and I have uttered the sentiments of a yearning soul and have indicated the sincere attachment, which I feel, fixing my mind on the bygone days and those scenes, which her society endeared to me. Whenever I mention a name in this book, I always allude to her, and whenever I mourn over an abode, I mean her abode. In these poems, I always signify divine influences, spiritual revelations, and sublime analogies according to our most exemplary way (*ṭarīqah*)—for the next world is dearer to us than this one—and due to her understanding of what I was alluding to. May God preserve the reader from thinking of anything unbecoming to souls that scorn evil, and to lofty spirits that are attached to the things of heaven!

Despite Ibn al-ᶜArabī's assertion that he followed the Sufi path in his poems, a number of these love lyrics have no clear mystical referents, leaving them open to more worldly interpretations, and so an overly literal reader complained that Ibn al-ᶜArabī, as a scholar of religion, had no business composing erotic verse. As a result, Ibn al-ᶜArabī compiled a new edition of the *Turjumān al-Ashwāq*, claiming that his use of "the erotic style and form of expression" (*lisān al-ghazal wa-t-tashbīb*) was allegorical in intent; because people liked erotic poetry, it was a useful medium for his mystical message. However, to avoid further misunderstandings, Ibn al-ᶜArabī added an extensive commentary on the spiritual and mystical allusions to be found in each poem.[4]

The verse of Ibn al-ᶜArabī's Egyptian contemporary, Ibn al-Fāriḍ has faced similar criticism on occasion. A century after the poet's death, several critics took exception with Ibn al-Fāriḍ's monistic mystical doctrines, along with his depiction of God as a feminine beloved in his *Naẓm al-Sulūk* ("Poem of the Sufi Way"). For this reason, one critic, al-Ḥusayn Ibn al-Ahdal (d. 855/1451) forbade Muslims from reading or listening to the *Naẓm al-Sulūk*. As for Ibn al-Fāriḍ's love poems, Ibn al-Ahdal dismissed them as comparable to verse by the pre-Islamic Arabs; while a Muslim was permitted to listen to such infidel poetry, it was better left alone.[5] As was the case with the *al-Lāmīyah* and the *al-Dhālīyah*, close readings of Ibn al-Fāriḍ's other poems encourage their mystical interpretation, but Ibn al-Ahdal's comparison, nevertheless, points out the poet's continuity with earlier Arabic verse. This is particularly the case with Ibn al-Fāriḍ's love poetry.

Love Talk

Like other Arabic genres of unified theme, the *ghazal*, or love poem, echoes the moods and themes of the pre-Islamic ode (*qaṣīdah*) and, in this case, specifically those of its elegiac prelude, the *nasīb*. Following the *nasīb*'s opening recollections of the departed beloved, the poet might describe his mistress or his past encounters with her and her companions who often chided him for being immoderate and reckless.[6] The early *ghazals* of the Umayyad period developed these and other elements of the *nasīb*, especially the dialogue between the poet and his beloved, and so significantly enhanced the *nasīb*'s lyrical qualities. Whereas the pre-Islamic *nasīb* generally dwells on a failed love affair in the past, the *ghazal* usually addresses a current beloved, and *ghazals* are sentimental, not heroic like the early *qasīdahs*. This shift probably reflects, in part, increasingly individual and less tribal perceptions of life refined by life in the cities of the Ḥijāz and, later, Syria. The influence of singing girls and folk poetry also is apparent in the simple charm of this urban poetry, which is well illustrated by the Ḥijāzī *ghazals* of ᶜUmar Ibn Abī Rabīᶜah with their playful seductions of noble ladies:[7]

thumma qālat li-llatī maʿahā
lā tudīmī naḥwahu-n-naẓarā

Then she said to her friend,
"Don't keep staring at him!
Slyly, sister, coyly,"
and I listened in.
"Sister, he'll leave us
if he gets what he needs!"
I said, "You've got real class;
I see nothing to fear from me.
So take a lover, one ready to die.
Then let God shame whoever's unfaithful!"

This early sensual poetry of illicit love and sexual gratification may express individual and collective yearnings, particularly the desire to be free from the ambivalent and confining strictures of conscience and society, restraints tightened by Islam and the political centralization of the Umayyad caliphate.[8] Social and economic tensions may also underlie the ʿUdhrī *ghazal*, which retains the deep sentiments of the early *nasīb*. Poems by Jamīl ibn Maʿmar (d. ca. 82/701) of the ʿUdhrah tribe,[9] and similar verse by other poets of the first/seventh century, sadly relate tales of an undying love that is never consummated as fate and society scheme to prevent a happy union between the lover and his beloved. A sense of loss and despair pervades these poems of passive resistance against social and religious norms, and the martyrdom of love becomes a substitute for the heroic quest. Unable to attain the object of his desire, the ʿUdhrī poet wastes away or is driven insane, as was said to have been the case with the legendary Qays ibn al-Mulawwah, known as Majnūn, the "Possessed."[10] This chaste ʿUdhrī love became an Arab-Muslim ideal sanctified by the prophetic tradition: "One who loves, remains chaste, never reveals the secret, and dies, dies the death of a martyr." The spiritual nature of this ʿUdhrī love is also underscored by frequent references to God, the Qur'ān, and Islamic beliefs and rituals. Still, it is the beloved's will, or the law of love, that must be obeyed at all cost, even if this will lead to the violation of social and religious norms:[11]

yā ḥabbadhā ʿamalu-Sh-Shaytāni min ʿamalin
in kāna min ʿamali-Sh-Shaytāni ḥubbīhā

How lovely the work of Satan
if from his work is my love for her!

Unlike ᶜUmar ibn Abī Rabīᶜah's compliant lady, the beloved of ᶜUdhrī poetry is a sacred ideal aspired to but never won. Though the beloved is praised for her beauty, she is rarely described, and her lover must renounce his physical existence and self-will, and passively accept the cruelties of unrequited love. Remaining chaste, mortifying the flesh, the lover longs for a reunion between spirits destined for each other since pre-eternity:[12]

taᶜallaqa rūḥī rūḥahā qabla khalqinā
wa-min baᶜdimā kunnā niṭāfan wa-fī-l-mahdi

My spirit clung to hers before our creation
and after we were sperm drops, and then in the cradle.

Yet, due to social and religious barriers, this union may never be consummated before death and, so, the lover flames with the fire of passion and is consumed in an exaltation of emotion. The unattainable beloved remains his despair and, like the pre-Islamic Arab poet mourning in the abandoned campsite, the ᶜUdhrī poet laments his lost garden of Paradise:[13]

khalīlayya Laylā jannatī wa-biᶜāduhā
jahīmī wa-nuskī in aradtu ṣalātiyā

Oh my friends, Laylā is my garden,
her staying away, my hell,
and my ascetic devotion
when I want to pray.

Beginning in the late second/eighth century, during the Abbasid period, ᶜUdhrī love blended with ideas of aesthetic refinement (*adab*) producing a spirit of courtliness, which permeated many later *ghazals*. The ᶜUdhrī ideals were gradually altered, as courtly love and its themes were increasingly applied to panegyrics, as we see in the verse of such poets as Abū Tamām and, later, al-Mutanabbī. Human love continued to be a powerful force, and the bliss of union and the pains of separation remained central poetic concerns. But more realistic, sometimes erotic and humorous love poetry tempered the self-effacing and masochistic aspects of ᶜUdhrī love, as is clear in the *ghazal* poetry composed by Abū Nuwās (d.c. 198/813), whether his love interest was male or female, ideal or human:[14]

aḍramta nāra-l-ḥubbi fī qalbī
thumma tabarra'ta mina-dh-dhanbi

You set love's fire in my heart,
then washed your hands of the crime!
Even as I plunged into the sea of passion,
as the waves crashed upon my heart,
you divulged my secret and forgot about me.
Is that justice, my dear?
Suppose I can't defend myself from passion;
won't you at least fear the Lord?

Still, the ᶜUdhrī passion for an ideal beloved and union with her were preserved and transfigured in later Arabic verse, particularly, Sufi poetry.[15] Given the centrality of love within the Islamic mystical tradition, it is not surprising that Sufis appropriated and allegorized Arabic love poetry to speak of mystical concerns. In fact, their reinterpretation of this poetry was so thorough that the ᶜUdhrī poet Majnūn became the archetypal mystic obsessed with God to the point of apparent insanity.[16] Even ᶜUmar ibn Abī Rabīᶜah's risqué conversational style found a place in Sufi verse:[17]

wa-lammā-ddaᶜaytu-l-ḥubba qālat kadhabatnī
fa-mā lī arā-l-aᶜḍā'a minka kawāsiyā
fa-mā-l-ḥubbu ḥattā yalṣaqa-l-jildu bil-ḥashā
wa-tadhbula ḥattā lā tujība-l-munādiyā
wa-tanḥala ḥattā la yubaqqī laka-l-hawā
siwā muqlatin tabkī bihā aw tunājiyā

And when I claimed love, she countered: "You lied to me!
Why are your limbs still clothed in flesh?
There's no love till skin clings to bone,
and you, so parched, can't answer the caller,
and you dry up till passion leaves you nothing
save an eye to weep and confide!"

In these verses, the famous Baghdadi Sufi Sarī al-Saqaṭī (d. 253/867) transforms the traditional theme of the blaming woman who chides her presumptuous suitor, into a harangue on the importance of the *via negativa* for the mystical life. Read in terms of al-Saqaṭī's mystical ideas, this poem demands the eradication of the seeker's selfish desires and volition as a prerequisite for pure spiritual love. Yet this mystical reading is plausible only because these verses were cited in the clear mystical context of a Sufi manual.[18] For al-Saqaṭī's poem, like the majority of Arabic Sufi love poetry, is part of a larger poetic tradition that resonated with classical Greek and later Hellenistic love theories, which asserted love's power to transform the individual spiritually, and so overcome physical mortality. The influence of these theories is readily apparent in medieval Arab treatises on love, especially those by the Ikhwān al-Ṣafā' (fl. fourth/tenth CE), Ibn Dāwūd (d. 279/909), the celebrated philosopher Ibn Sīnā (Avicenna, d. 428/1039), and his contemporary in Spain, Ibn Ḥazm (d. 456/1064) of Cordova. For instance, grounding Ibn Ḥazm's famous treatise on love, the *Ṭawq al-Ḥamāmah* ("The Ring of the Dove"), is the familiar Platonic distinction between bestial sensuality and pure and ennobling spiritual love, and Ibn Ḥazm goes so far as to suggest that the human beloved may, in fact, embody and manifest celestial realities.[19] Similarly, when praising his mistress who had left him, Ibn Zaydūn likens Wallādah's incomparable beauty to God:[20]

lasnā nusammīki ijlālan wa-takrimatan
wa-qadruki-l-muᶜtalī ᶜan dhāki yughnīnā
idha-nfaradti wa-mā shūrikti fī ṣifatin
fa-ḥasbunā-l-waṣfu īḍāḥan wa-tabyīnā

We cannot name, exalt, or praise you.
Your high majesty frees us from that.
You are unique, without equal in quality.
So it's enough that we tried to describe.

Clearly, by the sixth/eleventh century, mystical love was an integral part of many *ghazals*, whether composed by court poets or Sufi masters. Still, some in their audience inevitably failed to recognize the spiritual dimensions of love, and so dismissed love as lust. Had Ibn al-Ahdal listened more closely to Ibn al-Fāriḍ's love poems, he might have heard something quite different than erotic verse by the pre-Islamic Arabs.

Hymns of Devotion

iḥfaẓ fu'ādaka in mararta bi-Ḥājiri
fa-ẓibā'uhu minhā-ẓ-ẓubā bi-maḥājiri[21]

Protect you heart if you pass by Ḥājir,
for sharp arrows fly from the eyes of its gazelles.
So the heart is slain by passing there;
if it is saved, sanity's at risk.
Upon a solitary dune is a tribe whose fawns
felled lions with their eyes.

I love a tawny one protected there by a shining sword
 whose sheath is lashed deep within my heart.

Six of the fifteen core poems in Ibn al-Fāriḍ's *Dīwān* are *ghazals*, each beginning with a highly emotional and lyrical introduction describing the lover's present predicament. The poet invokes love and the beloved, and attests to his inevitable destruction at their hands:[22]

qalbī yuḥaddithunī bi-annaka mutlifī
 rūḥī fidāka ᶜarafta am lam taᶜrifi
lam aqḍi ḥaqqa hawāka in kuntu-l-ladhī
 lam aqḍi fīhi asan wa-mithlī man yafī
mā lī siwā rūḥī wa-bādhilu-nafsihi
 fī ḥubbi man yahwāhu laysa bi-musrifi
fa-la'in raḍīta bi-hā fa-qad asᶜaftanī
 yā khaybata-l-masᶜā idhā lam tusᶜifi

My heart tells me
 you are my destruction;
  my spirit be your ransom
 whether you know it or not.

I have not paid passion's due for you
 if I do not die for it, afflicted,
  but one like me
 always pays in full!

I have only my spirit,
 but one who spends himself
  in love for one desired,
 he is no waster.

If you are satisfied with this,
 then you have helped me,
  but oh the wasted effort,
 if you do not help.

In these opening verses to Ibn al-Fāriḍ's *al-Fā'īyah*, the lover declares his willingness to pay the ultimate price for love. These verses, like those beginning the *al-Lāmīyah*, have Sufi reverberations. The heart (*qalb*), through which the mystic communes with God, informs the lover that he must die to prove his love (v. 1); base desires and self-will (*nafs*, v. 3) must be eliminated, and the spirit (*rūḥ*) returned to the beloved (v. 2). The lover longs to be totally obedient and so prove his fidelity, but his efforts are useless without the beloved's satisfaction (*raḍīta*) and assistance (v. 4). The final verse of this passage offers a ray of hope, for the Qur'ān declares that contented souls who are satisfying to God will be accepted on the Judgment Day when they will enter the garden of Paradise (Q. 89:27–30).[23] The lover appears to speak face to face with his love, but later in the poem we learn that the lover has been separated from his beloved sometime in the past. In fact, in all of Ibn al-Fāriḍ's poems, the beloved is not physically present, and the beloved's absence and sacred memories of their previous encounter elicit the lover's complaint:[24]

He is inaccessible; we have no union with him
  save the vain imagining of a visiting phantom.
I would return to his dark lips, thirsting like one dying for a drink,
  denied to the Euphrates, and I always came back quenched!

Ibn al-Fāriḍ's reveries and recollections of the beloved pose the crucial question of the lover's worthiness to be reunited with his beloved. This issue of separation and reunion is so central to his *ghazals* that the dialogues between lover and beloved must, of necessity, be framed in the past or represent a message from the lover to the beloved. Even in the following verses, the beloved is far away:[25]

tih dalālan fa-anta ahlun li-dhākā
  wa-taḥakkam fa-l-ḥusnu qad aᶜṭākā
wa-laka-l-amru fa-qḍi mā anta qāḍin
  fa-ᶜalayya-l-jamālu qad wallākā
wa-talāfī in kāna fīhi-'tilāfī
  bi-ka ᶜajjil bihi juᶜiltu fidāka

1) Be proud in coquetry, you are worthy of that,
  and pass judgment, for loveliness endowed you.
2) You possess the command, so decree what you will,
  for beauty made you ruler over me
3) And if in my destruction is intimacy with you,
  then hurry with it, may I be your ransom!

* * * * *

fa-ᶜasā fī-l-manāmi taᶜriḍu li-l-wah-
  mi fa-yūḥī sirran illayya surākā

16) And perhaps in sleep, you will appear in a dream
revealing in secret, your night-journey to me.

The openings of Ibn al-Fāriḍ's *ghazals* set the scene, tone, and mood of the poem as they enunciate a desperate desire to be fit for another encounter with the beloved. The subsequent sections of the *ghazal* present aspects of love and the lover's dilemma featuring a number of themes and motifs common to ᶜUdhrī verse; the pains of separation are detailed as are the lover's many maladies and sufferings.[26] Yet, Ibn al-Fāriḍ places these ᶜUdhrī allegories in mystical contexts with the addition of Sufi technical terms and rhetorical devices, especially antithesis. Read in this light, the separation from the beloved in the following passage from the *al-Lāmīyah* leads not only to an imprisonment in base matter and love sickness, but also to the dark night of the soul when the mystic's passions and desires are progressively purged and his self-will annihilated that he may abide in a new spiritual life:[27]

A token of what I encountered and suffered for her—
and I have kept my words short, not long—is this:
Wasting away, I disappeared; my visitor could not find me.
How can those visiting the sick see one without a shadow?
No eye ever stumbled across my track,
for those wide eyes left no trace of me in love.
Yet, when I remember her, a resolve rises within me,
and when she is mentioned (*dhikrāhā*), my cheap spirit
grows rich.

The lover strives to purify himself through suffering and remembrance of the beloved, and his physical wasting away is emblematic of his renunciation of his selfish will and the attainment of spiritual passivity.[28] Still, he must humbly beseech her mercy if he is to attain his aim, for she alone decides his fate. This is quite evident in the following verses, which further demonstrate Ibn al-Fāriḍ's use of antithesis and contrasting Sufi terms to enhance his poetry. The final verse, in particular, pairs wild rapture (*wajd*) with patience (*ṣabr*), and abiding (*bāqin*) with annihilation (*fānin*) as the lover's heart (*qalb*) is broken in seeking union (*wiṣāl, liqā'*) with the beloved:[29]

yā mānicī ṭība-l-manāmi wa-māniḥī
thawba-s-saqāmi bihi wa-wajdī-l-mutlifi

ʿaṭfan ʿalā ramaqī wa-mā abqayta lī
min jismiya-l-muḍnā wa-qalbī-l-mudnafi
fa-l-wajdu bāqin wa-l-wiṣālu mumāṭilī
wa-ṣ-ṣabru fānin wa-l-liqā'u wusawwifī

Oh you forbidding me sweet sleep,
bestowing upon me
the robe of disease
and my destructive rapture,

Have a care for my last gasp
and for what you have allowed to remain
of my wasted body
and broken heart.

My rapture abides
while union is deferred me;
patience is destroyed,
and the meeting put off.

Comparable to the physical maladies of love are love's psychological and spiritual effects often personified by the lover's antagonists: the blamer (*lā'im*/*lāhin*/*ʿādhil*), the spy (*raqīb*), and the slanderer (*wāshin*). These were standard characters in the repertoire of classical Arab love poetry. The blamer often upholds social norms and the opinions of others; the spy may represent the lover's intellect and conscience, whereas the slanderer embodies the sensual desires that oppose chaste love. Within a Sufi context, these characters may also represent the mystic's volitional, rational, and physical natures, which must be tamed for selfless obedience. As was the case in ʿUdhrī verse, in Ibn al-Fāriḍ's poems the lover's physical condition mirrors his psychological and spiritual states as well, and so the wasting of the lover's body is linked to his turning a deaf ear to his various critics:[30]

Say to the blamer:
"Long have you blamed me, relishing
that blame will stop me
from passion.

"Don't be rude to me!
Taste the food of passion,

and if you love passionately,
then after that, blame me."

* * * * *

My eye never found
anyone lovely but him,
and though he took another, not me,
I remained true.

Those who slipped in to spy,
watching without being seen,
saw only a man
shattered by grief.[31]

* * * * *

I find comfort from the slanderers between her and me,
for then she knows what afflicts me, but she is not naïve.
And I long for the blamers, loving mention of her,
as if they were messengers of passion between us.[32]

By rejecting the advice and blame heaped on him, the lover disregards his good reputation and welcomes shame and public disgrace. However, in Sufi terms, the lover destroys his selfishness as well as his self-righteousness, which takes pride in spiritual achievements and so smothers selfless love:[33]

wa-fī ḥubbihā biʿtu-s-saʿādata bi-s-shaqā
ḍalālan wa- ʿaqlī ʿan hudāya bihi ʿaqlu
wa-qultu li-rushdī wa-t-tanassuki wa-t-tuqā
takhallū wa-mā baynī wa-bayna-l-hawā khallū
wa-farraghtu qalbī min wujūdiya mukhliṣan
laʿalliya fī shughlī bihā maʿahā akhlū

For love of her I went astray, selling happiness for distress;
my reason was hobbled unable to follow right guidance,
And I said to my good faith, to asceticism and piety:
"Go, leave me alone with passion!"
And I emptied my heart, cleansed of my existence,
that, perhaps, busy with her, we could be alone together.

Throughout these physical and psychological trials, the lover is required to keep the secret of love. In early Arabic love poetry, the *sirr* or "secret" probably referred to the intimate sexual union between lovers, although over time, the secret was said to be the beloved's name and identity that must be concealed to protect her honor and reputation. But the ᶜUdhrī poets increasingly praised the principle of love more than any material beloved, and the hidden secret was transformed into a sacred life-giving mystery.[34] The secret was spiritualized further by the Sufis who often played on multiple meanings and homonyms of the this term *sirr* to allude to the inexpressible joy (*sirr*) of union with God experienced by the mystic within his innermost being, or "heart secret," also termed *sirr*.[35] The secret of mystical love, then, is not so much a concealed thing as it is an ineffable experience, and attempts to describe or define this powerful moment can only fall short of its reality. To conceptualize the experience of love, mystical or otherwise, is to lose it, and so rational consciousness can never fully know the secret, which is not a problem to be solved but a mystery to be lived:[36]

akhfaytu ḥubbakumu fa-akhfānī asan
ḥattā la-ᶜamrī kidtu ᶜannī akhtafī
wa-katamtuhu ᶜannī fa-law abdaytuhu
la-wajadtuhu akhfā mina-l-luṭfi-l-khafī

I hid my love for you,
so affliction hid me
until, by my life,
I was nearly hidden from myself.

And I concealed it from me
for had I revealed it,
I would have found it
more hidden than hidden grace.

Although the secret or essence of personal experience, by definition, may never be fully described to another person in everyday language, poets and mystics have often alluded to the nonrational character and profound effects of emotional and spiritual experiences. As we have seen, of special importance to Ibn al-Fāriḍ and many other poets and mystics was the analogy to be drawn between human love and mystical experience with their comparable pains, sorrows, and indescribable joys in union.[37] Moreover, similar to earlier Sufis,

Ibn al-Fāriḍ relied heavily on antithesis to construct a paradox to underscore the complex and confusing nature of his abiding love:[38]

O you taking my heart away in breach of faith,
  why did you not take the rest of me to follow behind?
Because of you, part of me is jealous of my other part,
  for my outer half envies my inner half where you are.
And when you are recalled in a gathering, my eye longs
  to become an ear heeding him who speaks to me at night,
Accustomed to him always fulfilling his threats,
  while putting off his rare promise to me.
Because he is far away, bright noon has turned dark to me,
  just as when he was near, my darkness was all bright.

Once again, Ibn al-Fārid recounts an experience of union to remember its loss. Such reveries are colored by a melancholy reminiscent of the pre-Islamic *nasīb*, accompanied by a sense of resignation and, on occasion, hope. Poignant and emotionally charged, these hallowed memories of an earlier covenant often return in Ibn al-Fāriḍ's climactic conclusions to his *ghazals*:[39]

By the sanctity of the pact (*ᶜahd*) between us from which
    I never withdrew,
  and by the bond of hands between us never to be loosed,
Whether in parting's anger or passion's acceptance,
  you are with me, my heart holding you every hour.
Do you think one day my eyes will see those I love,
  and my destiny please me with the gathering reunited?
Yet in essence, they never left; I see them with me.
  Though they be far in form, they stay in the mind.

These verses near the end of the *al-Lāmīyah* illustrate the pivotal theme of Ibn al-Fāriḍ's *ghazals*. The beloved has gone leaving the longing lover alone to remember their covenant. In the final two verses, Ibn al-Fārid employs contrasting verbs, participles, and prepositions eloquently to rest his case. Despite his shortcomings, the lover must remain true to his pact, enduring separation's trials in hopes of a reunion with his beloved:[40]

fa-hum nuṣba ᶜaynī ẓāhiran ḥaythumā saraw
  wa-hum fī fu'ādī bāṭinan aynamā ḥallū
la-hum abadan minnī ḥunūwun wa-in jafaw
  wa-lī abadan maylun ilayhim wa-in mallū

They are the eye's idol, manifest, whenever they journey
by night;
they are in my heart, hidden, wherever they alight.
Always, I have affection for them, though they were
cruel to me,
always, I am inclined toward them, though they are
weary of me.

Sun and Full Moon

In the *al-Lāmīyah*, Ibn al-Fāriḍ presents his lady love, naming her Nuᶜm, although like the ᶜUdhrī poets, he never describes her physical features. This female beloved is in contrast to the male beloveds found in the other five *ghazals*. In most of these poems, too, Ibn al-Fāriḍ does not describe physically his beloved beyond an occasional reference to his bright, moon-like face, his dark eyes, deep red lips, or the shining teeth and sweet saliva of his mouth.[41] As we have seen, the exception is Ibn al-Fāriḍ's extended description of the beloved as a handsome youth in the *al-Dhālīyah*.[42] In earlier Arabic love poetry, a female beloved might be referred to as a young man in yet another attempt to conceal the secret of the mistress' true identity. By the sixth/twelfth century, however, this masculine image of the beloved was standard in panegyrics, which had appropriated elements of the *ghazal* to praise rulers and patrons. Because Ibn al-Fāriḍ modeled his *al-Dhālīyah* on a panegyric by al-Mutanabbī, he may have felt that a longer, more traditional description of the beloved was called for than was the case for his ᶜUdhrī style *ghazals*. Moreover, in Sufi circles, a beardless young man was, at times, regarded as a mirror of divine beauty in accord with two traditions ascribed to the prophet Muhammad: "I saw my Lord in the most beautiful shape," and "I saw my Lord with his cap awry." Ibn al-Fārid alludes to these and similar traditions in his *Poem of the Sufi Way*, to support his view of the divine origin of all beauty.[43] The male beloved in Ibn al-Fāriḍ's *ghazals* has also led to speculation that this figure was none other than the prophet Muhammad and his prophetic spirit or light.[44]

Sufi doctrines of the prophetic Reality of Muhammad (*al-Ḥaqīqah al-Muḥammadīyah*) or the Light of Muhammad (*Nūr Muḥammad*) were developed early in Islam and became an important element in Islamic mystical theology. Muhammad's light has functioned as an instrument of creation through which the unseen absolute God articulates Himself in pre-eternity. There, this light gazes upon God, contemplating and worshipping Him. Furthermore, the lights of the other prophets, of the heavenly kingdom and the hereafter, and, finally, the light of this world emanate from Muhammad's light.[45] Significantly, some Sufis held that the progeny of Adam who made their covenant with God in pre-eternity emanated from the *Nūr Muḥammad,* which also transmits prophecy to all of the prophets beginning with Adam and ending in the historical, physical Muhammad. So as the essential instrument for the primordial events of creation and their unfolding, and as the source of prophecy, the Light of Muhammad serves as a vital link between humanity and God. If the mystic can never hope to be reunited with God prior to the Day of Resurrection, he may still aspire to enlighten his divine spirit with this prophetic light. Thus, Sufi poets have longed for and venerated this shining Light of Muhammad, this moon illuminating all others.[46]

Ibn al-Fāriḍ may have referred to the prophet Muhammad in several *ghazals,* including the *al-Dhālīyah* with its mention of the toothbrush (*siwāk*), the daily use of which is ascribed to Muhammad by Muslim tradition.[47] More explicitly, Ibn al-Fāriḍ makes several allusions to the prophet and his light in the *al-Kāfīyah*:[48]

abqi lī muqlatan laᶜalliya yawman
qabla mawtī arā bihā man ra'ākā

19) Leave me an eye that perhaps one day
before I die I may see one you saw.

* * * * *

fīka maᶜnan ḥallāka fī ᶜayni ᶜaqlī
wa-bihi nāẓirī muᶜannā ḥilākā
fuqta ahla-l-jamāli ḥusnan wa-ḥusnā
fa-bihim fāqatun ilā maᶜnākā
yuḥsharu-l-ᶜāshiqūna taḥta liwā'ī
wa-jamīᶜu-l-milāḥi taḥta liwākā

37) In you is a meaning; it adorned you to my intellect's eye,
and made my vision a captive to your adornments.
38) You surpassed beauty's worthy ones in loveliness
and handsomeness, so they need your meaning.
39) The lovers will gather under my banner
and all of the beauties under yours.

* * * * *

ahlu badrin rakbun sarayta bi-laylin
fīhi bal sāra fī nahāri ḍiyākā

49) Badr's men were riders, you rode with them by night,
while they rode in the day of your light.

The final verse is the most obvious allusion to Muhammad. According to Muslim tradition, the prophet's holy light, bright like the full moon (*badr*), shone on his loyal supporters prior to the legendary Battle of Badr and the defeat of the Meccan pagans. Verses 37–39 of the *al-Kāfīyah* likewise allude to the prophet when praising the beloved; according to a popular tradition, Muhammad will stand before the ranks of humanity on the Day of Resurrection holding the Banner of Praise.[49] Similarly, in verse 19, the "one you saw" could be Muhammad, though the commentator al-Nābalusī held that this verse alludes to the Light of Muhammad that contemplates God in pre-eternity.[50] The beloved in another of Ibn al-Fāriḍ's *ghazals*, the *al-Fā'īyah*, also appears to reflect the Light of Muhammad, particularly in verses 38–49:[51]

38) Had they let Jacob hear mention
of his handsome face,
he would have forgotten
Joseph's beauty,

39) Or in the past, had Job seen him
in the dreaminess of sleep,
visiting him in his sickness,
his affliction would have been cured.

40) All full moons long for him,
as does every slender body,
when he reveals himself
coming forth.

41) If I said: "I have every longing for you!"
He would reply: "I have handsomeness;
every loveliness
is in me!"

42) His good qualities were perfect!
Had he shown his brightness

to the full moon,
it would not have been eclipsed,

43) And despite the artistry
of those who describe his loveliness,
time will pass away
with much still to be described.

44) By the hand of his loveliness,
I have spent all of me for his love,
and so I praised
my lovely economy.

45) For the eye desires
the form of loveliness
in which the spirit longs
for a hidden meaning.

46) Gladden me, dear brother,
and sing to me his tale (*bi-ḥadīthihi*),
scatter on my ear its ornament
and adorn it,

47) That hearing's eye
may see a witness (*shāhid*)
to his loveliness in meaning;
grant me that and honor me.

48) Oh sister of Saᶜd
coming from my beloved (*ḥabībī*)
with a message (*bi-risālatin*),
presenting it with kindness,

49) *fa-samiᶜtu mā lam tasmaᶜī wa-naẓartu mā*
lam tanẓurī wa-ᶜaraftu mā lam taᶜrifī
I heard what you did not hear,
and saw what you did not see,
and knew
what you never knew.

These verses proclaim the beloved's shining countenance to be brighter than all others, more beautiful than Joseph, able to console

Jacob and heal the tortured Job (vv. 38–40). The poet then presents the lover burning for the beloved's all-consuming radiance, which, if fully revealed, could prevent the moon's eclipse (vv. 41–42), a possible reference to Muhammad's alleged miracle of splitting the moon.[52] Ibn al-Fāriḍ then ends his account by praising the beloved's transcendent perfection (v. 43). Following a declaration of fidelity (vv. 44–45), the lover returns to memories of the beloved by calling on a friend and a messenger, stock characters who comfort the grieving lover with news of his absent love. The lover asks his companion to recite a *ḥadīth*, a "tale" of the beloved but, of course, this term usually designates a tradition of the prophet Muhammad (vv. 46–47).[53] This tale will let the lover "witness" (*shāhid*) the beloved, perhaps alluding to the "witnessing" (*shahādah*) to God's oneness and Muhammad as God's *rasūl*, His messenger. This reading is encouraged by verse 48 and the "message" (*risālah*) that is brought to the poet. The "sister of Saᶜd," then, could refer to Ḥalīmah of the Saᶜd tribe, Muhammad's wet nurse, and, in this context, the word *ḥabīb*, "beloved," echoes the popular Muslim epithet for Muhammad, *ḥabīb Allāh*, "the beloved of God."[54] Ḥalīmah nourished the infant Muhammad and, saw his shining face, and so, in a sense, Ḥalīmah delivered him to the world. Yet what she experienced falls short of what the lover knows (*ᶜaraftu*) from gnosis and recognition (*maᶜrifah*) of the beloved's pre-eternal light (v. 49).

Based on these verses, it is tempting to interpret the beloved in all of Ibn al-Fāriḍ's *ghazals* as a symbol for Muhammad and/or his prophetic Light. Yet, in most instances, the beloved's identity remains ambiguous. Significantly, Ibn al-Fāriḍ never uses the name Muhammad in his *ghazals* and only rarely does he explicitly mention the prophet's lineage, his virtues and epithets, or the city of Medina where Muhammad died. These elements became requisite features in poems praising the prophet Muhammad composed in Egypt within a generation of Ibn al-Fāriḍ's death, and so it is not surprising that a later Sufi poet of the Mamluk Period, Ibn Abī Ḥajalah (d. 776/1375) stated that Ibn al-Fāriḍ had not composed panegyrics on Muhammad.[55] Moreover, two noted commentators on Ibn al-Fāriḍ's verse, al-Būrīnī and al-Nābulusī, often interpreted the beloved of Ibn al-Fāriḍ's *ghazals* as God and the lover as the longing human spirit.[56] Verses from most *ghazals* also could support such a divine beloved. For instance, in the opening verses of the *al-Kāfīyah*, quoted above, Ibn al-Fāriḍ presents the beloved as a judge possessing the "command" (*amr*), and so decreeing the lover's fate. According to Qur'ānic precedent and Islamic tradition, the supreme judge and possessor of the divine command (*amr*) is God.[57] A similar situation arises near the end of the poem:[58]

qāla lī ḥusnu kulli shay'in tajallā
bī tamallā fa-qultu qaṣdī warākā
lī ḥabībun arāka fīhi muᶜannan
ghurra ghayrī wa-fīhi maᶜnan arākā
in tawallā ᶜalā-n-nufūsi tawallā
aw tajallā yastaᶜbidu-n-nussākā
fīhi ᶜūwiḍtu ᶜan hudāya ḍalālan
wa-rashādī ghayyan wa-sitrī-nhitākā
waḥḥada-l-qalb ḥubbahu fa-ltifātī
laka shirkun wa-lā arā-l-ishrākā

53) The loveliness of every revealed thing said to me:
"Take pleasure in me." But I said: "My goal is beyond you.
54) "I have a beloved, in whom I see you captive.
Others, not I, were deceived; I see you as a meaning in him.
55) "If he turns away from souls, he subdues them;
if he reveals himself, he enslaves the ascetics.
56) "For his sake, I traded my guidance for error,
my straight path for a wrong way, and my wrap was rent.
57) "The heart declared his love as one, so my glancing back at you
is polytheism, and I do not believe in partnership!"

Although this passage follows verses containing plausible allusions to Muhammad, the beloved here takes on divine proportions. Ibn al-Fāriḍ may have believed the Light of Muhammad was the instrument of creation, yet God is its ultimate ground of beauty and love (vv. 53–54). Even if we allow the Light of Muhammad, God's beloved (*ḥabīb*, v. 54), to assume this spiritual function, the Light would never be permitted to "take worshippers" for itself, a related meaning of *yastaᶜbidu* ("to take captive" in v. 55).[59] But a furtherer argument for reading the beloved of this passage as possibly alluding to God is verses 56–57. There, the lover renounces all regard for the things of this world, including his good reputation and self-will, so that his heart (*qalb*) may proclaim that he loves only the beloved. This profession of absolute love in verse 57, *waḥḥada-l-qalbu ḥubbahu*, "The heart declared his love as one," is based on the creed *waḥḥada-Allāh*, "God is one," and this phrase, like *amr* in verse 2 of the same poem, implies a divine beloved.

The beloved of Ibn al-Fāriḍ's *ghazals*, then, may at times allude to a physical beloved, to love, Muhammad, his light, or God, and, occasionally, all together. Yet the result is usually the same for a key to understanding Ibn al-Fāriḍ's *ghazals* is his recollection of the covenant with the beloved. In pre-Islamic poetry, the covenant (*ᶜahd*) was between the poet and a woman, usually from a neighboring tribe. Often, the tribes were at odds, and the beloved broke the pact when she departed with her people, an event that presaged imminent tribal warfare.[60] Following the revelation of the Qur'ān, the pre-Islamic pact was altered, if not totally replaced, by God's covenant with all of humanity. An elegant blending of the two traditions is found in a poem by the ᶜUdhrī poet Jamīl. After lamenting his lost youth and desiring union with his beloved, he declares to her that despite the vicissitudes of time, their love must survive for their covenant (*mīthāq*) was given by God in pre-eternity:[61]

wa-qultu lahā baynī wa-baynaki fa-ᶜlamī
mina-llāhi mīthāqun lahu wa-ᶜuhūdu

I said to her:
"Know that between you and me,
given by God,
is a covenant with Him and pacts."

However, for the Sufis, the *mīthāq*, or covenant, is not primarily between two humans or even their divine spirits. Rather, based on the Qur'ān 7:172, this pact was taken from humanity by God prior to creation, binding all humans to their divine creator. Once in creation and separated from God, the devout Muslim must faithfully recollect his first union and the prospect of a final encounter on the Judgment Day. As the Sufi Abū al-Ḥasan al-Daylamī (d.c. 392/1001) noted in his book on mystical love:[62]

> When God spoke to men while they were still seed and received the Covenant from them with theses words: "And when your Lord took from the children of Adam, from their loins, their seed, and made them testify touching themselves, "Am I not your Lord?" they said "Yes . . ." (7:172), and so on to the end of the verse, men heard this speech and saw Him, and He caused them to experience the pleasure of that vision and the sweetness of that speech. The pleasure and sweetness they experienced in what they heard and saw, moreover, remained in them, and when God created them in the second existence and spoke to them of servanthood, that pleasure was stirred up from within their spirits and produced love in them. And they were bewildered with love as a result of it.

To savor this sweet love, the Sufi recollects God through the practice of *dhikr* in order to lift the veils between himself and his Lord so as to abide in unifying love. As an early Sufi master, Abū Muḥammad Ruwaym (d. 303/915) noted:[63]

> Indeed, the folk heard the first *dhikr* when He addressed them saying: "Am I not your Lord?" So it was hidden in their heart secrets (*asrār*), just as the fact of its happening was hidden in their intellects. Thus, when they hear the secret contents of their hearts, they are carried away, just as when the secret contents of their intellects appeared when He spoke, and they believed.

Still, such moments of spiritual joy generally pass quickly and fade. The mystic, then, strives to remain true to his covenant and the demands of selfless spiritual love in hopes that God will be satisfied and grace him with union once more on the Day of Resurrection. Separation, loss, and hope of a reunion are parts of the human condition, and they underlay Ibn al-Fāriḍ's *ghazals* and, especially, his *al-Jīmīyah*.

"You Have Been Remembered"

mā bayna muᶜtaraki-l-aḥdāqi wa-l-muhaji
anā-l-qatīlu bilā ithmin wa-lā ḥaraji[64]

1) On the battle ground
between hearts and glances,
I am slain
without sin or guilt.

2) Prior to passion,
I bade my spirit adieu
due to the loveliness my eyes beheld
in that lovely site.

3) By God, for your sake,
eyelids are sleepless, longing for you,
and a heart was choked
by burning desire.

4) And ribs were wasted
by heartbreak,
their curves nearly set straight
by my fevered heart,

5) And tears rained down without end;
I was barely saved
from oceans deep
by the breath of passion's fire.

6) How lovely the sickness
that for your sake
hid me from myself;
there stand my proofs before passion.

7) Morning and evening
I grieved for you,
but I never burst out:
"Let the crisis end!"

8) I fly to every heart
obsessed with desire,
and to every tongue
addicted to love,

9) To every ear
deaf to the blamer,
and to every eye
untouched by sleep.

10) There never was a rapture
with tear ducts dry,
nor a burning passion
with unkindled desires.

11) Torment me as you will—
but not by separation from you—
and you will find a faithful lover
rejoicing in what pleases you.

12) So take what you left
of life's last breath;
there is no good in love
if it lets the heart stay.

13) Who will help me spend my spirit
for love of a fawn,
his qualities sweet
and mingled with spirits?

14) Whoever dies desiring him
lives exalted
to the highest degree
among passion's worthy ones.

15) He is a veiled one;
but were he to pass in a darkness
black as his forelock,
his blazing face would suffice him light.

16) So if I stray for a night
in his black locks,
his brow's bright morn
gives guidance to my eyes,

17) When he breaths, musk confesses
to those who know its sweetness:
"My fragrance spreads
from his breath!"

18) Years of his acceptance
are as brief as a day,
but a day of his rejection
is long like the years.

19) So if he is traveling far away,
then my heart depart,
and if he is visiting near at hand,
then my eyes rejoice!

20) Say to him who blames
and abuses me for his sake:

"Lay off me and my affair;
take back your poor advice.

21) "Blame is base;
no one was ever praised for it;
did you ever see a lover
mocked for burning desire?"

22) You of tranquil heart,
do not look to one who comforts me;
profit from your own heart;
beware the dark eyes' spell!

23) I am upright and kind, my friend,
and I have offered all my counsel:
do not turn aside
at that quarter!

24) There, I stripped off my shame,
and threw away my piety
and what was pleasing and approved
of my pilgrimages.

25) Then my passion's face
grew bright from loving him,
while the face of blaming me for his sake
turned black with proofs.

26) Blessed be God!
How sweet are his qualities;
how many hearts have they slain for him
then brought them back to life!

27) To hear mention of his name
my ear desires to hear
one pressing me with blame,
but blame never sinks in.

28) I pity the lightning flashing at night,
when it is compared to his smile,
for it is shamed
by the space between his teeth.

29) Though he is absent from me,
every grasping sense sees him
in every subtle sense
lovely and pure.

30) In the melody of the lyre
and gentle flute
when they embrace
in trilling notes of song.

31) In the meadows
of the forest gazelle,
in twilight's cool,
and daybreak's glow,

32) Where the mist
falls from clouds
on a blossoming carpet
woven from flowers,

33) Where the zephyr
sweeps its skirts,
guiding to me at dawn
the sweetest scent,

34) And in my kissing
the cup's lip
sipping wine drops
in secluded pleasure.

35) I never knew exile from homelands
while he was with me,
and wherever we were,
my mind was at rest.

36) So my tent is the one
where my love has settled;
whenever he appears, I turn aside
at the shifting dunes.

37) Farwell to the riders,
traveling by night with a light

dawning from you as you go
with them on their trek.

38) Let the riders
do as they will;
they are Badr's men
and shall not fear sin.

39) By the right to break from one
blaming me because of you,
and by the fire blazing in my ribs
bound to rapture,

40) Look to a heart
melted by burning love of you,
and to an eye drowned deep
in bloody tears.

41) Pity my stumbling hopes
and my falling back
on delusion in hopes
of the promised release.

42) Turn toward
my broken desire
with a "Maybe" or "Perhaps,"
and ease my breast of anguish.

43) How welcome the words
I was unworthy to receive
from the bearer of glad tidings,
proclaiming relief after despair:

44) "Good news for you,
so strip off what is on you,
for you have been remembered
despite your crooked ways!"

In the opening verse of the *al-Jīmīyah,* the lover is mortally wounded by the beloved's glances, which pierce his heart like sharp arrows:

mā bayna muᶜtaraki-l-aḥdāqi wa-l-muhaji
anā-l-qatīlu bilā ithmin wa-lā ḥaraji

1) On the battle ground
between hearts and glances,
I am slain
without sin or guilt.

As Angelika Neuwirth has pointed out, this verse brings to mind the first verse of Ta'abbata Sharran's famous pre-Islamic elegy for his slain uncle:[65]

inna bi-sh-shiᶜbi-l-ladhī dūna Salᶜin
la-qatīlan damuhu mā yuṭallū

On the mountain pass below Salᶜ is one slain;
his blood shall not flow unavenged!

Although in his poem Ta'abbata Sharran will pursue and eventually slay his uncle's killers, no such vengeance will be taken for Ibn al-Fāriḍ's dying lover. According to the commentator al-Nābulusī, the beloved of this *ghazal* is God, who then "is free to do what He wants with His property, fair in His judgment, and so not to be questioned about what He does."[66] Yet even if the beloved is not divine, the lover is still not entitled to compensation for, although he may be an innocent victim, he has not been killed by a person, but by love, a natural or, perhaps, supernatural cause of death. As noted by al-Daylamī in his manual on love: "The bonds of the prisoner of eros are tightly tied. Seldom is the one felled by it revived and no blood money is paid for the one it kills."[67] Such a death may be extraordinary, but it does not violate the norms of religion or society, being the natural consequence of selfless love.

Indeed, the lover knew beforehand that death would be his fate in love. Proceeding from the beloved's penetrating eyes to his own sleepless ones, the lover swears by God to his true love; his heart has been choked with desire, his body wasted, and his eyes filled with tears (vv. 2–5). As in his *al-Dhālīyah*, Ibn al-Fāriḍ once again praises the martyr of love, and he rhetorically draws attention to the lover's dire state, beginning verses 4 to 5 with nouns in the same plural form (*aḍluᶜ*, "ribs"; *admuᶜ*, "tears") and by contrasting the lover's flaming heart, which nearly straightens his crooked ribs, to the flood of tears overwhelming him.[68] The lover's fidelity to the beloved is strong, and for his sake, he gladly endures love's sickness, which emaciates his body, thus proving his unfailing, selfless devotion (v. 6). Verses 6 and 7 repeat the expression *fīka* ("for your sake," "for you"), and so reiterate the lover's claim to have borne patiently the pain and grief of separation. His condition compels him to seek out others like himself who are absorbed in their love (vv. 8–9). Ibn al-Fāriḍ underscores the totality of this state by repeating the word *kull* ("every") followed by nouns representing the spirit, reason, and the senses (e.g., "every heart," "every tongue," "every ear," "every eyelid").[69] Then, in verse 10, he uses parallelism to stress the inevitable suffering of those in rapture:

lā kāna wajdun bihi-l-āmāqu jāmidatun
wa-lā gharāmun bihi-l-āshwāqu lam tahiji

10) There was never a rapture
with tear ducts dry,
or a burning passion
with unkindled desires.

The impassioned lover asks the beloved to test him in anyway he pleases, save with separation, in order to prove his sincere devotion. Nevertheless, the lover's selflessness will be complete only when the beloved finally extinguishes the lover's last breath (vv. 11–12). Ibn al-Fāriḍ obliquely refers to the mystical nature of this desired annihilation (*fanā'*) with a word play (*jinās*) involving *baqīyah*, *abqayta*, and *abqā*, all related to *baqā'* ("abiding"), the Sufi antonym to *fanā'* and a technical term for union:

wa-khudh baqīyata mā abqayta min ramaqin
lā khayra fī-l-ḥubbi in abqā ʿalā-l-muhaji

12) So take what you left
of life's last breath;
there is no good in love
if it lets the heart stay.

Because the beloved is far away in this *ghazal*, as in all others by Ibn al-Fāriḍ, the lover futilely seeks his own destruction from others. Could they annihilate him, he would taste the love of his fawn-like beloved whose "sweet qualities" (*shamā'il*) are "mingled with spirits" (*bi-l-arwāḥi mumtaziji*) and so resemble an invigorating wine (v. 13). Then, as a transition to his portrayal of the beloved, Ibn al-Fāriḍ again employs antithesis to declare the law of love: the lover must die to all selfishness if he is to live among the worthy lovers of lore (v. 14):[70]

man māta fīhi gharāman ᶜāsha murtaqīyan
mā bayna ahli-l-hawā fī arfaᶜi-d-daraji

14) Whoever dies desiring him
lives exalted
to the highest degree
among passion's worthy ones.

Verses 15 to 19 portray a beloved who may not be described fully, for he is veiled (*muḥajjab*). Al-Nābalusī and Arberry have interpreted this to mean that God is veiled in or by His creation that, nevertheless, glows with His eternal light.[71] Yet, in this *ghazal, muḥajjab* strongly suggests the inability of reason to comprehend emotional and spiritual matters, particularly, love. This interpretation is supported by the image of the beloved's dark tresses that border the blinding brilliance of his face:[72]

muḥajjabin law sarā fī mithli ṭurratihi
aghnathu ghurratuhu-l-gharā ᶜani-s-suruji
wa-in ḍalaltu bi-laylin min dhawā'ibihi
ahdā li-aynī-l-hudā ṣubḥun mina-l-balaji

15) He is a veiled one;
but were he to pass in a darkness
black as his forelock,
his blazing face would suffice him light.

16) So if I stray for a night
in his black locks,
his brow's bright morn
will give guidance to my eyes.

By using a series of antitheses (dark/bright; night/day; astray/right guidance; acceptance/ rejection; brief day/long year), Ibn al-Fāriḍ asserts the extraordinary nature of encountering this ethereal beloved (vv. 15–18). Then in verse 19, Ibn al-Fāriḍ combines internal rhymes with antithesis to chart the lover's course:

fa-in na'ā sā'iran yā muhjatī-rtaḥilī
wa-in dānā zā'iran yā muqlatī-btahijī

19) So if he is traveling far away,
then my heart depart,
and if he is visiting near at hand,
then my eyes rejoice!

Following this charge, the lover dismisses his blamer with a play on the poetic genres of panegyric (*madīh*) and invective (*hijā'*) verse (vv. 20–21):

fa-l-lawmu lu'mun wa-lam yumdaḥ bihi aḥadun
wa-hal ra'ayta muḥibban bi-l-gharāmi hujī

21) "Blame is base;
no one was ever praised for it;
did you ever see a lover
mocked for burning desire?"

The lover then advises his companion to stay clear of the beloved's quarter if what he seeks is self-contentment, not selfless love (vv. 22–25). For, he warns him, true love demands absolute submission from the lover who must forget everything, including all thought of religious merit or saintly reputation (v. 24). Though a lover must bear worldly disgrace, his true honor is purified by love, while the blamer's reputation is blackened by the proofs of the lover's sincerity (v. 25). Ibn al-Fāriḍ highlights this contrast again with antithesis and internal rhyme:

fa-byaḍḍa wajhu gharāmī fī maḥabbatihi
wa-swadda wajhu malāmī fīhi bi-l-ḥujaji

25) Then my passion's face
grew bright from loving him,
while the face of blaming me for his sake
turned black with proofs.

Moreover, this verse resonates with Qur'ān 3:106–107 regarding the Judgment Day, when those destined for heaven will beam with delight, whereas those bound for hell will despair: "On a day when some faces will be bright and others black." Ibn al-Fāriḍ again implies that only selfless love can transform the lover.[73]

To this point, Ibn al-Fāriḍ has only hinted at the holy status of the beloved, who "guides" (*ahdā*) those astray (v. 16); his breath is the source of fragrant musk (v. 17); and his quarter (*ḥayy*) appears to be the site of the lover's pilgrimages (v. 24). But the true nature of the beloved emerges more clearly beginning with verses 26 and 27:

tabāraka-llāhu mā aḥlā shamā'ilahu
fa-kam amātat wa-aḥyat fīhi min muhaji
yahwā li-dhikri-smihi man lajja fī ᶜadhalī
samᶜī ᶜalā anna ᶜadlī fīhi lam yaliji

26) Blessed be God!
How sweet are his/His qualities;
how many hearts have they slain for him/Him
then brought them back to life!

27) To hear mention of his/His name
my ear desires to hear
one pressing me with blame,
though blaming me for him/Him never sinks in.

The phrase *tabāraka-llāhu* ("Blessed be God!") is a frequent exclamation of wonder in Arabic and, in verse 26, it obviously lauds the fawn-like beloved's marvelous qualities. However, because *Allāh* is the only masculine noun in this verse, it is grammatically correct to read the Arabic pronominal suffix *hu/hi* ("his" and "him") as referring directly to *Allāh*. In this case, God is the subject of both the verse and the praise; hence, He is the beloved. Such a reading is supported by the beloved's ability to restore to life those who have died for love of him. In numerous passages, the Qur'ān declares that God will cause the dead to live again (e.g., 2:73; 22:6; 30:40; 42:9; 45:26) and that He will reward His martyrs with eternal life in Paradise (e.g., 2:154; 3:169-171; 22:58–59).[74] Furthermore, in verse 27, to hear word of the beloved arouses the lover's affection even for his blamer because the latter, while censuring the lover, mentions the beloved's name (*dhikri-smihi*). This last phrase also may allude to the practice of *dhikr* in which Sufis remember God by recollecting passages from the Qur'ān, specific religious formula, or one of His many divine names. Not surprisingly, a favorite name is Allāh, which is sometimes reduced during the *dhikr* to its last letter, *hā'*. Significantly, *hā'* also is the consonant of the masculine pronominal suffix *hu/hi* ("him"; "his") occurring throughout this poem and four times in verses 26 and 27. Furthermore, the Qur'ān often mentions recalling God's name in worship, and the word *ism* is most often found in the *Basmallāh*—"In the name of God, the compassionate, the merciful"—which begins each chapter of the Qur'ān and, in fact, nearly every book or letter written by a pious Muslim.[75]

Through remembrance, the lover spiritually perceives the beloved within his body and in all things around him, although the beloved is far away. Thus, lightning recalls to the lover the beloved's flashing teeth. Although lightning pales next to the beloved's smile, this comparison suggests that nature is a reflection of the beloved's heavenly splendor (v. 28). Verses 29 to 36 elegantly elaborate such a vision in an extraordinary example of descriptive poetry adapted to allude to deeper meanings:

tarāhu in ghāba ʿannī kullu jāriḥatin
fī kulli maʿnan laṭīfin rā'iqin bahiji
fī naghmati-l-ʿūdi wa-n-nāyi-r-rakhīmi idhā
ta'allafā bayna alḥānin mina-l-hazaji
wa-fī masāriḥi ghizlāni-l-khamā'ili fī
bardi-l-aṣā'ili wa-l-iṣbāḥi fī-l-buluji
wa-fī masāqiṭi andā'i-l-ghamāmi ʿalā
bisāṭi nawrin mina-l-azhāri muntasiji
wa-fī masāḥibi adhyāli-n-nasīmi idhā
ahdā ilayya suḥayran aṭyaba-l-araji
wa-fī-ltithāmiya thaghra-l-ka'si murtashifan
rīqa-l-mudāmati fī mustanzahin fariji
lam adri mā ghurbata-l-awṭāni wa-hwa maʿī
wa-khāṭirī ayna kunnā ghayru munzaʿiji
fa-d-dāru dārī wa-ḥibbī ḥāḍirun wa-matā
badā fa-munaʿraju-l-jarʿā'i munaʿrajī

29) Though he is absent from me,
every grasping sense sees him
in every subtle sense
lovely and pure.

30) In the melody of the lyre
and gentle flute
when they embrace
in trilling notes of song.

31) In the meadows
of the forest gazelle,
in twilight's cool,
and daybreak's glow,

32) Where the mist
falls from clouds

on a blossoming carpet
woven from flowers,

33) Where the zephyr
sweeps its skirts,
guiding to me at dawn
the sweetest scent,

34) And in my kissing
the cup's lip
sipping wine drops
in secluded pleasure.

35) I never knew exile from homelands
while he was with me,
and wherever we were,
my mind was at rest.

36) So my tent is the one
where my love has settled;
whenever he appears, I turn aside
at the shifting dunes.

This highly lyrical passage conjures Arcadian images of peace and serenity and evokes a metaphysical spirit as a reflection of the lover's inner state. Each of the five verses involves one of the five senses (v. 30: hearing; v. 31: sight; v. 32: touch; v. 33: smell; v. 34: taste), all united in perceiving the beloved in various guises.[76] These verses are further united by their common first word *fī* ("in") and, in verses 31 to 33, by the noun form *mafāʿil,* which immediately follows this preposition. Verse 34 is of particular importance for its image of the cup whose wine is as sweet as the beloved's saliva. Both liquids were considered intoxicating and so frequently functioned as Sufi symbols of love and gnosis.[77] Thus, when in union with the beloved, the lover was oblivious to exile (*gurbah*), while dwelling in the beloved's presence (*ḥāḍir*). The appearance in verses 35 and 36 of this contrasting pair of Sufi technical terms comparable to *fanā'* and *baqā'*, again strongly suggests the mystical nature of this meeting.[78] Furthermore, in context of verses 37 and 38 that follow, the "shifting dunes" in verse 36 might allude to the desert camp near Badr where Muhammad stayed with his followers in preparation of their celebrated battle:[79]

li-yuhna rakbun saraw laylan wa-anta bihim
bi-sayarihim fī ṣabāḥin minka munbaliji
wa-l-yaṣnaᶜi-l-qawmu mā shā'ū li-anfusihim
hum ahlu Badrin fa-lā yakhshaw mina-l-ḥaraji

37) Farwell to the riders,
traveling by night with a light
dawning from you as you go
with them on their trek.

38) Let the riders
do as they will;
they are Badr's men
and shall not fear sin.

"The riders" refer to the Muslims who fought at the Battle of Badr as verse 38 clearly indicates with its direct reference to a *ḥadīth* regarding their favor with God. These warriors had long been incorporated into the Islamic mystical tradition as among the earliest spiritual adepts and, in context of Ibn al-Fāriḍ's poems, they probably represent the elite selfless lovers graced by God.[80] As a result, Arberry interpreted the beloved in these verses, as symbolizing the Spirit of Muhammad.[81] The commentator al-Būrīnī also noted that verse 37 is a variation on a theme found in a verse of another *ghazal* by the Ibn al-Fāriḍ, which appears to praise the prophet:[82]

ahlu Badrin rakbun sarayta bi-laylin
fīhi bal sāra fī nahāri ḍiyākā

Badr's men were riders;
you rode with them by night,
while they rode
in the day of your light.

Moreover, al-Būrīnī pointed out that both verses appear to refer to Qur'ān 17:1:

subḥāna-l-ladhī asrā bi-ᶜabdihi laylan . . . . . . "Praise be to Him who traveled by night with His servant (i.e., Muhammad) . . ."

This Qur'ānic verse relates to one of the prophet Muhammad's powerful visionary experiences traditionally referred to as Muhammad's Night Journey and Heavenly Ascension to God. Yet, because the subject of the Qur'ānic verse was God, al-Būrīnī surmised that He was also the beloved in verse 37 of the *al-Jīmīyah*. Al-Nābulusī concurred, and while he, too, mentioned Qur'ān 17:1 and Muhammad's Night Journey in his gloss of the verb *sarā* ("to travel at night"), he did not elaborate. Instead, he applied the light images in these verses to God's illumination and grace for His elect mystics.[83]

Yet, "Badr's men" is the most obvious clue to the beloved's identity in this passage, as they rode into battle with the prophet Muḥammad. Further, "traveling by night" is a probable reference to Muhammad's Night Journey and Heavenly Ascension, so central to Islamic mysticism and mythology. Earlier, in verse 15, Ibn al-Fāriḍ said:

muḥajjabin law sarā fī mithli ṭurratihi
aghnathu ghurratuhu-l-gharā ᶜani-s-suruji

(15) He is a veiled one,
but were he to pass in a darkness
black as his forelock,
his blazing face would suffice him light.

As we have seen, Arberry followed al-Nābulusī in his interpretation of the "veiled one," by stating, "the Divine Presence is shrouded in the darkness of the phenomenal world, yet the radiance of His Beauty shines forth and manifests Him to all who have eyes to see."[84] However, by reading verse 15 together with verses 37 and 38, we find that Ibn al-Fāriḍ has rendered in verse the iconic image found in the many paintings of the prophet Muhammad depicting his Night Journey and Heavenly Ascension: The prophet is mounted on his mythical steed, his face veiled, head wreathed in a blazing fire as he ascends to heaven to meet his Lord.[85]

Verse 39 begins the lover's final petition to be numbered among the martyrs of love:

bi-ḥaqqi ᶜiṣyāniya-l-lāḥī ᶜalayka wa-mā
bi-aḍluᶜī ṭāᶜatan lil-wajdi min wahaji
unẓur ilā kabidin dhābat ᶜalayka jawan
wa-muqlatin min najīᶜi-d-damᶜi fī lujaji
wa-rḥam taᶜaththura āmālī wa-murtajaᶜī
ilā khidāᶜi tamannī-l-waᶜdi bi-l-faraji

wa-ᶜṭif ᶜalā dhulli aṭmāᶜī bi-hal wa-ᶜasā
wa-mnun ᶜalayya bi-sharḥi-s-ṣadri min ḥaraji
ahlan bi-mā lam akun ahlan li-mawqiᶜihi
qawli-l-mubashshiri baᶜda-l-ya'si bi-l-faraji
laka-l-bishāratu fa-khlaᶜ mā ᶜalayka fa-qad
dhukirta thamma ᶜalā mā fīka min ᶜiwaji

39) By the right to break from one
blaming me because of you,
and by the fire blazing in my ribs
bound to rapture,

40) Look to a heart
melted by burning love of you,
and to an eye drowned deep
in bloody tears.

41) Pity my stumbling hopes
and my falling back
on delusion in hope
of the promised release.

42) Turn toward
my broken desire
with a "Maybe" or "Perhaps,"
and ease my breast of anguish.

43) How welcome the words
I was unworthy to receive
from the bearer of glad tidings,
proclaiming relief after despair:

44) "Good news for you,
so strip off what is on you,
for you have been remembered
despite your crooked ways!"

The lover swears by his undying loyalty, recalling again rapture's burning fire within his ribs, his flowing tears, and his humbled condition that began the poem (vv. 39–42). Verses 40 to 42, in particular, constitute the lover's prayer to the beloved as each verse begins with a verb in the imperative form: *unẓur . . .wa-rḥam . . . wa-ʿṭif . . . wa-mnun* ("Look . . . and have mercy . . . and show sympathy . . . and grant . . ."). Emaciated and humiliated, the lover no longer dares to seek union, but only desires to relieve his distress with the words *hal* ("Maybe," "Is there") and *ʿasā* ("Perhaps"). However, the precise meaning of both terms in this context has long puzzled commentators. Al-Būrīnī and al-Nābulusī understood the words as a dialogue between the lover and his beloved:[86]

> Lover: "Ask after me, if only with a single: 'How are you?' "
> Beloved: "Perhaps, I will turn to look at you. Perhaps, I will grant you union with me."

But the meaning that Ibn al-Fārid intended for *hal* is suggested by verse 77 of his ode *al-Tā'īyah al-Ṣughrā*:[87]

> *fa-lil-ʿayni wa-l-aḥshā'i awwala hal atā*
> *talā ʿā'idī-l-āsī wa-thālitha tabbati*

> To the eye and heart
> my sorrowing visitor recited
> the first part of "Has it come?" (*hal atā*)
> and the third part of "Accursed be!" (*tabbati*).

Hal atā is the beginning of chapter 76 of the Qur'ān (*Sūrat al-Insān*): *hal atā ʿalā-l-insāni ḥīna mina-d-dahri lam yakun shay'an madhkūran;* "Has there come upon the human a time when he was not a thing remembered (by God)?" Similarly, "the third part of 'Accursed be!' " refers to the Qur'ān, chapter 111, and the blazing hell to be experienced by Abū Lahab and his wife for vigorously opposing Muhammad.[88] Based on verse 77 of the *al-Tā'īyah al-Ṣughrā*, *hal* in verse 42 of the *al-Jīmīyah* also may designate the first verse of *Sūrat al-Insān*, which assures humanity of God's concern for them. In this light, *asā*, too, may refer to a Qur'ānic passage in *Sūrat al-Isrā'* (17), whose first verse was referred to earlier by Ibn al-Fāriḍ in verse 37 of the *al-Jīmīyah*. *Sūrat al-Isrā'* verses 8 and 9 read:

> Perhaps (*asā*) your Lord will have mercy (*yarḥama*) on you, but if you return again (to error), We will repeat (the punishment) and make Hell a prison for the infidels. Indeed, this Qur'ān guides to that which is the straightest, and gives glad tidings (*yubashshiru*) to the believers who do good works; to them is certainly a great reward!

In addition to the words *hal* and *asā*, other elements of both Qur'ānic passages are found in the final verses of the *al-Jīmīyah*: *arḥam* ("Have mercy") in verse 41; *al-mubashshir* ("the bearer of glad tidings") and *al-bishārah* ("glad tidings," "good news") in verse 43, and *dhukirta* ("You have been remembered") in verse 44. Furthermore, verses 41 and 42 contain additional Qur'ānic references, in this case to 94:1–6, which states *a-lam nashraḥ laka ṣadraka*: "Did We not ease your breast . . ." and promising *inna maᶜa-l-ᶜusri yusran*: "Surely with hardship comes ease!"

In this powerful climax to the *al-Jīmīyah*, the lover prays that the beloved will console him by remembering his humble servant and so have mercy and forgive and accept him. Here Ibn al-Fāriḍ reuses a number of phrases and rhyme words with their earlier meanings in the poem, a rare exception in his verse. However, this repetition highlights key words, particularly *ᶜiwaj* ("crookedness"), *ḥaraj* ("guilt"), and *faraj* ("joyous relief"), and so reinforces this *ghazal's* underlying themes of human selfishness and ingratitude, and the transformative power of love.[89] For the final two verses of the *ghazal* reveal that the beloved has indeed answered the lover's prayer, though by grace and despite the lover's waywardness. In this light, the *al-Jīmīyah*, like Ibn al-Fāriḍ's other *ghazals*, may be read as a devotional hymn to God and His prophet Muhammad for whose sake the lover struggles to lead a worthy life in love. Although separate from God since pre-eternity, the lover perseveres in recalling his beloved and their original covenant. Though confronted by the world's trials and his own selfish desires and defects, the longing lover, like all believing Muslims, seeks to stay on the path of right guidance, hoping for God's grace and mercy and, on the Day of Resurrection, His lasting satisfaction.[90]

Although five of Ibn al-Fāriḍ's six *ghazals* end with the lover's oath of fealty and hopes of reunion, the lover's prayer is answered in the *al-Jīmīyah*. Thus, in the final verse, the lover ceases to speak as his voice gives way to the messenger's words. In verse 12, the lover said:

wa-khudh baqīyata mā abqayta min ramaqin
lā khayra fī-l-ḥubbi in abqā ᶜalā-l-muhaji

So take what you left
of life's last breath;
there is no good in love
if it lets the heart stay.

When we recall the ancient pairings of self, voice, breath, and life, alluded to in this verse, the lover's silence at the end of the poem may presage his final annihilation in love as declared in the opening verse. As a result, the structure of the *al-Jīmīyah* resembles what critic Stanley Fish has termed "a self-consuming artifact." When analyzing religious poems by the George Herbert, Fish notes:[91]

> These poems, as they ask their readers to acknowledge their complete dependence, act out that acknowledgment by calling attention to what they are not doing, and indeed could not do. In their final radical modesty, they perform what they require of us, for as they undermine our reliance on discursive forms of thought, and urge us to rest in the immediate apprehension of God's all-effective omnipresence, they become the vehicles of their own abandonment. "God only is" . . .

Significantly, at the end of the *al-Jīmīyah*, the ʿUdhrī poem gives way to the sacred language of the Qur'ān from which Ibn al-Fāriḍ drew the beloved's message. If *hal* and *asā* represent Qur'ānic verses, then they are the words of God, who becomes the beloved at the end of this *ghazal*. By extension, "the bearer of glad tidings" is the prophet Muḥammad (cf. Qur'ān 17:105; 25:56; 33:45; 48: 8;), praised earlier in the *ghazal*, while the "good news" represents the revelations sent by God as guidance and a sure sign of His continuing remembrance and love for humanity (cf. Qur'ān 16:89, 102; 2:97; 3:126; 7:10).[92] Invoking God's word and His messenger, the poem replaces the poet with the prophet and so ends, consumed in the beloved's presence and the sacred message, *dhukirta*: "You have been remembered."

3

Joined at the Crossroads

The Arabic *ghazal* shares many characteristics with the *nasīb*, the opening section of the *qaṣīdah*, or ode. The nostalgic mood, descriptions of the lover's sickness and emaciation, the poet's friends and foes, his steadfast keeping of his secret, all play their parts in both. The *qaṣīdah* also recollects events of the past, and in its classical form, the ode contains additional sections and themes, most notably the hero's journey (*raḥīl*), scenes of wine drinking and/or battle, and a final section of invective or hopeful praise. With the coming of Islam, the *qaṣīdah* became the primary genre for panegyrics composed for caliphs, sultans, and other officials, but Sufi poets occasionally used the genre, as well. Ibn al-Fāriḍ applied the ode to his mystical concerns, and although his *qaṣīdah* retained vital links to the past, his mystical innovations caught the attention of his contemporaries and set new standards for later Sufi verse.

The Changing Ode

The earliest *qaṣīdahs* date from the pre-Islamic period. Often in these odes, the poet shakes himself free of his memories of the beloved and sets out on his she-camel to cross the hostile wastelands. The aim of this heroic quest, however, is not a reunion with the beloved, but often a return to his own tribe or patron:[1]

li-mani-d-diyāru ᶜafwana bi-l-Ḥubsi
  āyātuhā ka-mahāriqu-l-fursi

Whose encampments are these at Ḥubs,
  faded traces like the Persians' scrolls?
There is nothing there save doe herds,
  white oryx, black-cheeked, shining like the sun,

And the hoof prints left by noble steeds
etched in the hard ridge, sign of the beaten track.
I halted the riders there, second guessing past affairs,
as always, a dreamer.
Until the gazelles wrapped themselves
in lengths of shade and napped in their shelters,
And I lost hope due to the pain she left behind for me,
and nothing consoles like despair.
Then I rose up on a she-camel strong as a stallion,
hammering stones with her hardened pads,
Her hide worn, scarred and ragged
like pieces of fur flying on a rocky plain.
Will you not turn her toward a king,
wise in guidance, with a glorious soul,
To Ibn Mārīyah, the generous?
Is there another like Abū Ḥassān among men?[2]
He bestows on you coats of mail reaching below the waist,
and black stallions, tall and sturdy as palm trees,
And ingots of yellow gold, he gives in pairs,
and slave girls, white and red-lipped.
He expects nothing for his wealth as he goes through it;
all the same to him is the lucky star and one of ill-omen.
For fortune is with him there, never against him,
when the folk go hungry in misery.

This short ode by al-Ḥārith ibn Ḥillizah al-Yashkurī (fl. sixth CE) is among the earliest extant Arabic poems. Although most of this poetry was probably composed no earlier than the sixth century CE, its highly standardized form and content are indicative of substantial previous development. This pre-Islamic Arabic poetry addressed erotic, elegiac, descriptive, and heroic themes, either separately in pieces of a few verses (*qitʿah* or *al-qaṣīdah al-qaṣīrah*) or, as in al-Ḥārith's poem, in combinations, which could exceed one hundred verses. This latter form, the *qaṣīdah*, with its thematic and genre differentiation, became a foundation for the Arabic poetic tradition. Early Western studies of the *qaṣīdah* emphasized its detailed descriptions of flora and fauna and so classified it as a type of primitive realism, although later works have sought its cathartic function for the ancient Arabs who faced life and death issues in a harsh environment.[3]

Significantly, scholars have turned their attention to the moods and meanings underlying the formal and thematic structures of the poem with its deeply symbolic and archetypal nature.[4] As we see in al-Ḥārith's short ode, the pre-Islamic *qaṣīdah* begins with the *nasīb*, a slow, elegiac opening in which the poet halts at an abandoned campsite to grieve for his lost beloved. Amid the ruins, the poet may wistfully recall the blissful days of union with his beautiful lover and sadly recount the departure of her caravan. The reverie ends when the poet suppresses the past and sets out on his she-camel to cross forbidding and dangerous terrain in quest of fame and fortune (*raḥīl*). Correspondingly, the poem's tempo increases during accounts of the journey or of conflict and battle, rising to a crescendo when the poet ends his poem with an invective toward his enemies (*hijā'*), or in self-praise (*fakhr*) or praise of his tribe or patron (*madīḥ*).

The evocative power of the pre-Islamic *qaṣīdah* stems from its rigorous formal continuity and its stylized conventions, which crystallize complex metaphorical relationships among myth, ritual, archetype, and image.[5] In this light, the pre-Islamic *qaṣīdah* may be construed as a rite of passage and its sections read in terms of separation, liminality, and aggregation as defined by cultural anthropologists. The *nasīb* with its encampments and memories of the beloved may represent, on one level, the naïve and idyllic state of childhood, which is suddenly disrupted at puberty when the sexually maturing male must leave the society of women and enter a new world of men. At this juncture, the anxious adolescent must overcome and tame his natural instincts. The *raḥīl* section thus presents a liminal period of trial and testing through which the hero attempts to assert his individuality and become a responsible member of society. If the youth successfully passes this period of trial and proves his manhood, he is welcomed back to the victorious tribe as a mature adult member with commensurate rights and responsibilities (*fakhr*).[6] Concomitantly, a number of the pre-Islamic and early Umayyad *qaṣīdahs*, also may be read in terms of pollution and purification, sacrifice and ritual exchange, meant to strengthen the tribe and/or redeem the poet, as we see in an ode by Bishr ibn Abī Khāzim (fl. sixth CE) with its scenes of violent warfare:[7]

Ask Tamīm and ᶜĀmir of their wars with us;
  is a man who knows nothing equal
to one seasoned by experience?
  Tamīm were angry the ᶜĀmir were slaughtered
at the Battle of Nisār,
  so they followed them into disaster and death.
When they clamored loud for war,
  we brought them to their senses

with a charge that shocked them hard;
We battered helmets with swords,
shouting the names of our fathers,
while the horses' necks were streaked in blood.

In Bishr's ode and many similar ones by other Arab poets, the tripartite *qaṣidah* embodies a rite of renewal: The feelings of loss expressed in the *nasīb* may express mortification, the *raḥil* a process of purgation, and the final section with its boast, praise, or invective, the subsequent invigoration and jubilation at a successful outcome, whether that be in war, the hunt, or in seeking a superior's pardon in exchange for praising him.[8] Such readings of the early Arabic *qaṣīdah* underscore the ritual significance of this poetry, which had become the synthesis and precipitate of Arab culture's view of itself and its human and historical experience. Whether in new compositions or continued recitations, the *qaṣīdah* served as a ritual paradigm invoked repeatedly in attempts to give stability and meaning to life and society.[9]

Yet, as was the case with the Arabic *ghazal*, the *qaṣīdah* underwent change during the Umayyad period, particularly in the *raḥīl*. Although this section retained some mythical and psychological meaning, it slowly lost its efficacy within an increasingly urban milieu. Not only was the harsh desert environment of the Bedouin foreign to most later poets, but the heroic tribal ethos of the *qaṣīdah* had been challenged by the Qur'ānic ideal of the individual believer living a life of moderation in obedience to God.[10] As a result, much of the ritual significance of the early *qaṣīdah* waned as Arab culture realigned itself under Islamic influence. The poet was no longer the tribe's shaman or seer but, rather, he served to praise the defenders of the faith. Thus, the *qaṣīdah* became a vehicle for courtly ceremony and legitimation, with public declarations of allegiance in exchange for royal patronage.[11] By the Abbasid period, the *raḥīl* section of many odes served largely to assert rhetorically the panegyrist's worthiness to receive reward.[12] This was clearly the view of the noted Arab critic Ibn Qutaybah (d. 276/889):[13]

> Now, when the poet had assured himself of an attentive hearing, he followed up his advantage and set forth his claim: thus he went on to complain of fatigue and want of sleep and travelling by night and of the noonday heat, and how his camel had been reduced to leanness. And when, after representing all the discomfort and danger of his journey, he knew that he had fully justified his hope and expectation of receiving his due meed from the person

to whom the poem was addressed, he entered upon the panegyric.

Devoid of the deeper meanings of the quest, such *raḥīls* became largely irrelevant to most *qaṣīdahs,* although some Abbasid poets employed the *raḥīl* as a kind of travelogue, recounting actual trips that they had made. Abū Nuwās composed such a *raḥīl,* as did al-Mutanabbī[14] but another example from the latter's verse vividly illustrates the *raḥīl's* generally abbreviated form. In one poem al-Mutanabbī concludes his *nasīb* and begins his section of self-praise (*fakhr*) with only a passing allusion to the *raḥīl*:[15]

My bed is the back of a stead,
  while my shirt is a mail of iron!

The forbidding, chaotic and womb-like desert of the pre-Islamic *raḥīl* has almost disappeared and, significantly, the poet's mount is not the sturdy she-camel but the knightly horse. If any quest remains to the poet it is not for catharsis and social integration, but for personal glory in defending the faith or, perhaps more realistically, in self-aggrandizement. The symbolic importance of the *qaṣīdah* and its *raḥīl,* however, was occasionally maintained in Arabic philosophical and mystical verse, including the "Ode to the Soul" ascribed to the celebrated Muslim philosopher, Ibn Sīnā, which begins:[16]

habaṭat ilayka min-l-maḥalli-l-arfaᶜi
  warqā'u dhātu taᶜazzuzin wa-tamannuᶜi

1) She flew down to you from her high perch,
   a dove, proud and free,
2) Invisible to the gnostic's eyes
   though she was bright, unveiled.
3) She joined you reluctantly;
   now she suffers, reluctant to leave you.[16]

This allegorical poem is more philosophical than mystical, yet it demonstrates that the *qaṣīdah* remained a viable pattern for speaking about spiritual enlightenment. Using the ancient symbol of the bird to represent the immortal spirit, Ibn Sīnā recounts the spirit's descent from heaven, her imprisonment in matter, and her growing attachment to the body (vv. 1–6). Forgetful of her noble past, the spirit becomes ensnared by her attachments and grieved by her imprisonment:

7) Burdened and bound, she awoke
amid the traces and ruins (*ṭulūl*) of the campsite.
8) She cries, bathing in tears, when she recalls
the abodes at the sacred precinct (*ḥimā*).

Elements of the *nasīb* appear when Ibn Sīnā describes the pain and sorrow of the dove/spirit caused by her separation from her heavenly home (*ḥimā*). Like the poet standing in the abandoned and ruined encampment (*ṭulūl*), the spirit cries within the body with a mournful lament for a lost paradise (vv. 7–10). Then, setting out from the confines of this encampment, the spirit soars on a quest (*raḥīl*) for knowledge:

11) Until the time for departure to the precinct drew near
and the trek (*raḥīl*) to the plain was at hand.
12) The veil removed, she began to coo
and saw what sleepy eyes can never grasp.

Once this self-knowledge is attained, the enlightened spirit returns to its primordial land freed from time and space as determined by God's inscrutable plan (vv. 16–20):[17]

15) For what purpose was she sent down
from an apogee to a perigee far below?
16) Indeed, God sent her for a wise reason (*ḥikmah*)
hidden from the wisest sage.
17) So she had to fall, her affliction required,
that she might hear the unheard,
18) So she returns, her feathers unruffled,
knowing every secret in the two worlds.
19) For time had blocked her path (*ṭarīqah*),
til she was lost with no way to rise.
20) She was like lightning flashing in the precinct
then gone as if never was.

Sacred Fire

As was the case in Ibn Sīnā's ode, elements from the *qaṣīdah* are also found in some shorter Sufi poems prior to those of Ibn al-Fāriḍ, including verse by Ibn al-Shahrazūrī:[18]

wa-mā raḥalū illā wa-qalbī amāmahum
wa-mā nazalū illā wa-kāna lahum arḍan
yamīlu ilayhim ḥaythu mālū fa-innahu
yarā ṭāʿata-l-maḥbūbi fī-ḥubbihi farḍan

They never set out, but my heart goes before them,
and they never alight, save my heart is their land.
It turns to them wherever they turn, for it sees submission
in love to the beloved as a sacred duty.

In these verses, Ibn al-Shahrazūrī employs the traditional motif of the beloved's departing caravan to stress the theme of the selflessness nature of true love. When the beloved's tribe departed, the lover's heart went obediently with them as love required. Similar to the ʿUdhrī poets, Ibn al- Shahrazūrī implies that love is his religion, for he regards obedience as a *farḍ*, a religious obligation comparable to the required daily prayers, or the Hajj pilgrimage. However, these verses have a mystical flavor; from the many Arabic words for heart, Ibn al-Shahrazūrī chooses *qalb*, a favorite Sufi term for the site of spiritual illumination and vision. Hence, the heart "sees" obedience to the beloved as its duty. Other surviving verse by Ibn al-Shahrazūrī suggests that he may have preferred the *ghazal* to the ode, yet he composed one of the earliest known Sufi *qaṣīdahs*, the *al-Mawṣilīyah*, named after the city of Mosul, where he preached:[19]

lamaʿat nāruhum wa-qad ʿasʿasa-al-lay-
lu wa-malla-l-ḥādī wa-ḥāra-d-dalīlu

1) Their fire shivered as the night grew dark.
The camel-driver was weary; the guide confused.
2) I hoped to see it, but it was so far from me.
My concentration was broken, my sight weak.
3) And my heart is that captive heart,
my affliction that inner passion.
4) Then I looked to the fire and to my companions said:
"This is Laylā's fire; turn there!"

In the opening to this *qaṣīdah*, Ibn al-Shahrazūrī blends traditional *raḥīl* elements into the *nasīb*. As night enfolds the caravan, the camel driver grows tired, and the guide loses the trail. In the dark distance, the lover catches the faintest flicker of a campfire. This fire was a featured element of many classical desert crossings, and its promise of light, warmth, and companionship contrasts starkly to the dark, cold, and lonely night through which the riders must pass on their quest. Within the *nasīb*, the campfire is usually that of the departed beloved pursued by her former lover (v. 1). Ibn al-Shahrazūrī then suggests that his ode is to be understood as a mystical allegory: The lover strains to see (*ta'ammaltu*; v. 2) the fire, and this verb in a Sufi context may mean both "to contemplate," and "to meditate."[20] The poet then explicitly tells his audience that he is the lover whose heart is afflicted by inner desire for none other than Laylā, the name of one of the great ᶜUdhrī beloveds (vv. 3–4).

The lover's companions cannot see the fire despite their strong eyesight. Rather than believe the lover who has a firmer resolve, they turn to berate him, claiming that he saw lightning or a phantom form of his beloved. As is the case in the *ghazal*, this blaming is a part of the *nasīb*, and it recounts the companions' attempts to dissuade the lover from seeking his lost love. Ibn al-Shahrazūrī has the lover leave his blamers, riding off with his personified desire mounted on his passion and stalked by love. Once again, Ibn al-Shahrazūrī makes clear his allegorical intent:

fa-tajannabtuhum wa-miltu ilayhā
wa-l-hawā markabī wa-shawqī-l-zamīlu
wa-maᶜī ṣāḥibun atā yaqtafī-l-ā-
thāri wa-l-ḥubbu sharṭuhu-l-taṭfīlu

7) So I shunned them and turned toward the light;
passion my mount, and desire my fellow rider.
8) And a companion trailed behind me;
it was love who intrudes uninvited!

Clearly, this love has been fated, and so the lover presses on until he stumbles upon the encampment. There, he is blocked from reaching the fire by "barren ruins" (*ṭulūl muḥūl*), which lie littered across the landscape of the classical *nasīb*. These are generally the remains of the former dwellings of the beloved's tribe, and they evoke a sense of sadness and nostalgia in those who return to them. Ibn Shahrazūrī underscores the sense of loss as sighs and moans arise from the ruins (vv. 9–10). As is custom in the classical *qaṣīdah*, the lover questions the ruins:

11) I said: "Who is in the encampments?"
They answered: "A shackled captive, a wounded man, another slain.
12) "What did you come for?" I said: "A guest has come seeking hospitality. Where do I alight?"
13) The ruins motioned: "Alight where you are, and hamstring your camel for the guest never leaves.
14) "He who comes to us throws down his travel staff."
I asked: "Who will take me to the fire? Where is the path?"

In most odes, the ruins are dumb, but here they speak to tell the lover that the sighs and moans arise from love's victims. They pointedly ask the lover what he has come for, and when he claims his right to hospitality, they tell him to hamstring his camel. In other words, though the host is obliged to feed his guest, the ruins ominously inform the lover that his she-camel is to be the feast, and that their guests never leave (vv. 11–14). The lover then alights where once a tribe was "felled by wine before it was tasted" (v. 15). As we shall see, this is a Sufi reference to the wine of love or gnosis, and this mystical allusion is underscored in verse 16 and elsewhere in the poem where *wajd*, or, "rapture," overwhelms the seekers:

16) Rapture (*wajd*) effaced every trace of them,
so it was a trace in which the tribe settled.
17) Among them was one so effaced
no place remained for tears or complaint.

Using several other Sufi technical terms, the lover mentions the conditions of other lovers to whom little remains (*lam yabqa*; v. 19). Whereas Sufis often use the verb *fanā* ("to annihilate") to speak of the effect of mystical rapture, Ibn al-Shahrazūrī chose *ʿafā* ("to efface"; v. 17), a verb better suited to the *nasīb*, where the winds efface the remains of the campsite, in which only passion and rapture remain. Ibn al-Shahrazūrī appears to distinguish between mystics who have attained near total union and so have been obliterated by love, and those whose ecstasy has permitted a little something to remain. Only this last group is able to allude to their experiences and point out the way to others. The poet assigns each lover a permanent mystical station (*maqām*), but he excuses himself from further elaboration (v. 20). Keeping within the *nasīb* tradition, the lover greets the folk dwelling at the camp, and he pleads his case hoping for acceptance. The lover claims fidelity for his burning desire, which has never faltered no matter what adversity befell him. Moreover, he will not offer an excuse for his love and obsessive behavior, for to do so would prove that he is still concerned with his own welfare and reputation and, so, not a truly selfless lover. The lover hopes to be admitted into the company of the beloved's tribe, and so he begs to approach the fire:

> 25) "I came to warm myself this early morning.
> Do I have a path to your fire?"

But the ancient stones warn the traveler not to be overly excited by the Eden like meadows beyond, which are difficult to attain. Many others have tried to reach them and the beloveds there only to falter when union was nearly within reach, their false pretenses to love being exposed by "the people of realities" (*ahlu-l-ḥaqā'iq*; vv. 21–30):

> 30) "And the banner of fulfillment unfurled in the hand of rapture,
> and the people of realities shouted: 'Race on!
> 31) "'Where are those who make false claim to us?
> This day, the dye of claims runs red!'"

Ibn al-Shahrazūrī has now moved from the *nasīb*, and *raḥīl*, to a scene of battle as the selfless spiritual warriors charge the pretenders. Those falsely claiming love offered too little for union, and so they are overwhelmed and dashed upon the ruins (vv. 31–35). Ibn al-Shahrazūrī then brings his ode to a close by returning to the fire and its true identity:

> 36) "This, our fire, shines for him who travels by night
> but you will never reach it.
> 37) "The most it offers is a glance,
> but those who grasp that are few."

Ibn al-Shahrazūrī now reveals the fire's deeper meaning beginning with several important allusions to the Qur'ān. The fire "shines for him who travels by night" (*tuḍī'u li-man yasrī bi-laylin*). This resonates with the beginning of Qur'ān 17:1: *subḥāna-l-ladhī asrā bi-ʿabdihi laylan*: "Blessed be He who traveled with His servant by night," which is the basis for the Night Journey and Heavenly Ascension of the prophet Muhammad, noted earlier. In this case, the fire and its light may belong to Muhammad and/or God as they both "traveled at night." Given the fire's holy character, the mortal lover can never reach it. Even the glimpses of it that occasionally occur, are rarely understood (vv. 36–37). Then in verses 38 and 39, Ibn al-Shahrazūrī provides the key to the entire ode:

jā'ahā man ᶜarafta yabghī-qtibāsan
wa-lahu-l-basṭu wa-l-munā wa-s-sūlu
fa-taᶜālat ᶜani-l-munāli wa-ᶜazzat
ᶜan dunūwin ilayhi wa-hwa rasūlu

38) "One you know came to the fire seeking a torch,
begging with desire, arms outstretched.
39) "But it was out of reach, too exalted
to be near him, and he was a messenger!"

In the ode and *ghazal*, the messenger brings the lover news of the beloved, and here, the messenger is none other than the prophet Moses who brought humanity a revelation from God. Specifically, these verses refer to an earlier encounter with the fire, namely that of Moses and the Burning Bush as found in the Qur'ān 27:7–10:

7. Then Moses said to his people: "I perceive a fire. I will bring news from it or I will bring you a torch (*shihāb qabas*) that perhaps you can warm yourselves (*taṣṭalūna*)."

8. So when he came (*jā'ahā*) to it, there called out: "Blessed be He who is in the fire and He who is around it, and praise be to God, Lord of the Worlds!

9. "Oh Moses, He is Me, God, the exalted, the all-knowing!

10. "Throw down your staff (*alqi ᶜaṣāka*) . . .

Ibn al-Shahrazūrī's messenger seeks a torch (*iqtibās*, v. 38), and the diction of the Qur'ānic account influenced Ibn al-Shahrazūrī's verb choice in verse 39, *jā'ahā* ("He came to it"), his use in verse 25 of the verb *iṣṭalā* ("to warm oneself'), as well as the expression in verse 14 *'alqī ᶜaṣā-s-sayr* ("throw down the staff of travel"). These parallels to the Qur'ānic account point to the identity of the fire; it is a holy manifestation of God. This being the case, no creature can take from this fire and so share in the divine nature, not even a prophet. Nevertheless, Muhammad, Moses, and the spiritually elect ("the people of realities," *ahl al-ḥaqā'iq*, v. 30) may approach close enough to see its light and feel its warmth. Near the fire, the mystics are consumed by rapture (vv. 16–20) while the prophets return with God's revelations to humanity (vv. 38–39). As for the rest of humanity, they can only stand afar, staring in bewilderment, searching for the fire in the dark of night:

41) "We ward off time with hope; so settle for a heart (*qalb*)
 whose sustenance is two drinks:
42) "Whenever it tastes the cup of bitter sorrow,
 another cup comes sweetened with hope,
43) "And when selfishness (*nafs*) entices it to some affair,
 the heart is turned and told: 'Dignified patience!'
44) "This is our state and what knowledge has attained,
 but all states change."

As in many classical *qaṣīdahs*, this one, too, ends with a flicker of hope that perhaps one day the lover may draw closer to the fire's light and warmth. For bitter disappointment may be followed by the sweet sense of hope. Ibn al-Shahrazūrī contrasts the heart (*qalb*; v. 41), the site of love and divine inspiration, to selfish concupiscence (*nafs*; v. 43), which leads astray:

fa-idhā sawwalat lahu-n-nafsu amran
 ḥīda ᶜanhu wa-qīla ṣabrun jamīlu

43) "And when selfishness entices it to some affair,
 the heart is turned and told: 'Dignified patience!'"

Here, again, Ibn al-Shahrazūrī invokes the Qur'ān. In this instance, these are words of prophet Jacob in response to his sons who brought news that his son Joseph had been devoured by a wolf, when in fact, they had thrown him into a well (12:18):

> *bal sawwalat lakum anfusukum amran fa-ṣabrun jamīlun wa-llahu-l-mustaᶜānu ᶜalā mā taṣifūna*: "No! Your selfish souls have enticed you to an affair! But dignified patience! May God help concerning what you have described!"

In the end, Jacob was reunited with his beloved Joseph, and perhaps Ibn al-Shahrazūrī implies that sincere and patient seekers will return to the lost garden of Paradise after death (vv. 43–44).

Ibn al-Shahrazūrī's *qaṣīdah* hangs together well, gradually unfolding the theme of the holy fire, which he introduces in the opening verse. Similar to other poets of the Abbasid period, he did not strictly follow the classical *qaṣīdah* form of *nasīb*, *raḥīl*, and *madīḥ/fakhr/hijā'*. Rather, he selected those elements from each section that would lend themselves to his mystical allegory with its dramatic tone. Ibn al-Shahrazūrī was famous for his preaching, and one could image him reciting this poem during a sermon on Moses or on God's manifestations to humanity.[21] This also could account for the absence of provocative love imagery in the poem. Moreover, Ibn al-Shahrazūrī presents clearly defined metaphors regarding the heart and its desire, the mystics in rapture, and the fire, in particular. In this way, he leads his audience to imagine the abandoned campsite and its ruins as creation, and he has the ruins speak to reveal their true meaning. The homiletic character of this ode also is suggested by the development and resolution of the central quest theme. Clearly, the lover of the poem does not number himself among the spiritually elect; rather, he is a seeker who has glimpsed the fire. He is not a prophet or an enraptured mystic, although he aspires to gnosis, so he must tame his selfish nature and be patient under God's decrees, hoping for divine mercy.

Ibn al-Shahrazūrī's *al-Mawṣilīyah* is important within Arabic poetry as an example of a mystical ode with a sustained poetic discourse on the quest for spiritual illumination. The historian Ibn Khallikān cited the ode in full, he said, because it was hard to find although much appreciated as a *qaṣdah* "on the Sufi path."[22] Other Sufis poets also would draw from the *qaṣīdah*, and from *nasīb* section in particular, to speak on matters of love and longing. However, their poems were generally short and rarely touched on the *raḥīl* as a quest theme. In the following poem, the Egyptian ascetic and Sufi Ibn al-Kīzānī echoes the *nasīb* and the departure of the beloved and ends with a depiction of the beloved as the lover's judge:[23]

ayya ṣabrun taraktumu
liya lammā raḥaltum

What patience did you leave me
when you set out?
I have a heart enslaved by love
traveling along where ever you go.
In any event, I am your servant
if that would please you.
I remain under your judgment
whether you oppress or give justice.

But if you are merciful, you will rule
in favor of violent passion!

Ibn al-Kīzānī generally employed traditional themes and forms in his few odes, and this also is true of the odes by Ibn al-ᶜArabī, Ibn al-Fāriḍ's contemporary:[24]

qif bi-l-manāzili wa-ndubi-l-aṭlālā
wa-sali-r-rubūᶜa-d-dārisāti su'ālā

1) Stop at the alighting place and weep over the ruins,
then question the bare spring camping grounds:
2) "Where are the beloveds? Where have the roan ones gone?"
There they are cutting through the hazy wastelands!
3) You see them like gardens in a mirage;
their shapes magnified in haze.
4) They set out seeking to drink at ᶜUdhayb
water cool like life.
5) So I tracked them asking the east wind:
"Have they pitched camp or sought the *ḍāl* tree's shade?"
6) It replied: "I left their tents at sandy Zarūd,
their camels complaining, tired from their journey.
7) "They had lowered curtains over the tents,
shielding beauty from mid-day's heat.
8) "So mount up and track them
race your roan camel on toward them!
9) "Then, when you stop at the markers of Ḥājir
and cross through its highlands and lowlands,
10) "Their places will be near, and their fire will appear,
a fire causing passion to blaze up!
11) "Kneel your camel there, and fear not their lions,
for desire will make them seem to you as cubs."

Although Ibn al-ᶜArabī uses few Sufi terms in this poem, the recurring image of the haze and mirage and reference to the water of life suggest a mystical element to this ode as the lover tracks after his beloved (vv. 1–4). In his commentary to this ode, Ibn al-ᶜArabī states explicitly that this poem alludes to those seeking spiritual mysteries. The east wind is the lover's companion who helps him to visualize the hidden beauties, and it urges the lover on to action, envisioning the quest to find them (vv. 5–8). The final three verses of this ode recall themes in Ibn al-Shahrazūrī's *al-Mawṣulīyah,* as the Eden-like gardens (v. 3) may be reached only after the obstacles surrounding them are surmounted (v. 9). The fire of enlightenment beckons invitingly, causing the seeker's passion to rage to such a degree that the ferocious guardians of divine secrets will appear to him as playful cubs (vv. 10–11).[25] Ibn al-ᶜArabī mentions several places by name in this poem, ᶜUdhayb (v. 4), Zarūd (v. 6), and Ḥājir (v. 9), the latter identified as Madāin Ṣāliḥ, whose people, the Qur'ān states, where destroyed by God for their disobedience.[26] In his commentary, Ibn al-ᶜArabī notes that Zarūd is a sandy track whose shifting sands represent the unstable spiritual state of the novice seekers. As for Ḥājir, Ibn al-ᶜArabī plays on its etymological root referring to restriction, noting that it represents the barrier between aspiring mystics and the union that they desire.[27] Significantly, both ᶜUdhayb and Zarūd are on the pilgrimage route from Kufa to Mecca, although in his commentary, Ibn al-ᶜArabī does not mention this.[28] Other place names associated with the pilgrimage and holy cites of Arabia occasionally appear in other odes by Ibn al-ᶜArabī.[29] However, an explicit and more sustained series of references to the pilgrimage in Sufi poetry may be found in an earlier short poem by the noted North African Sufi theologian Ibn al-ᶜArīf (d. 536/1141):[30]

shaddū-l-maṭīya wa-qad nālū-l-munā bi-Minan
wa-kulluhum bi-alīmi-sh-shawqi qad bāḥā

1) They saddled their mounts
having attained their desires at Minā,
and each of them had revealed
the anguish of desire.

2) Their camels set out,
their fragrance spreading sweetly,
their fine shapes
pleasing to the band of travelers.

3) They were refreshed by a breeze
from the tomb of the chosen Prophet,
when, from memory of him,
they drink a wine.

4) Oh you who have arrived
at the chosen of Muḍar's line,

you visit in the body
while we visit in spirit!

5) We remained behind,
excused by necessity,
and those who stay, excused,
are like those who travel.

Ibn al-ᶜArīf's verses revolve around the pilgrimage to Mecca, which concludes with the *ᶜĪd al-Adḥā*, or "Festival of the Sacrifice," and other celebrations at Minā near Mecca. Subsequently, many pilgrims travel several hundred miles north to Medina to visit Muhammad's tomb there. Ibn al-ᶜArīf envisions this blessed group of pilgrims, and praises the spiritual benefits to those who recollect the Prophet and visit his grave:

nasīmu qabri-n-nabī-l-muṣṭafā la-humu
rawḥun idhā sharibū min dhikrihi rāḥā

3) They were refreshed by a breeze
from the tomb of the chosen Prophet,
when, from memory of him,
they drink a wine.

The final two verses contrast those who have the opportunity to complete the Hajj and visit the Prophet's shrine in person, to those who cannot go due to illness or some other valid reason. Yet those left behind may still recall the blessed prophet and vicariously participate in the sacred rights and blessings through the imagination (vv. 4–5). In this short poem, Ibn al-ᶜArīf reinterpreted the ancient *raḥīl* in light of the Muslim pilgrimage, and this would become an increasing trend in Sufi verse in the sixth–seventh/eleventh–twelfth centuries. Perhaps more than any earlier poet, Ibn al-Fāriḍ would consciously develop this aspect of the ode to speak of the spiritual quest.

Turn Aside at Ṭai

Six of the core poems in Ibn al-Fāriḍ's *Dīwān* may be classified as *qaṣīdahs*, ranging in length from 18 to 151 verses. Each poem opens with images drawn from the classical *nasīb* tradition as the poet recalls his beloved and their separation in the past:[31]

a-wamīḍu barqin bi-l-Ubayriqi lāḥā
am fī rubā Najdin arā miṣbāḥā

Did lightning flash
at dear Abraq,
or do I see a lantern
in the hills of Najd?

Or did Laylā al-ʿĀmirīyah
unveil her face that night
and so turned evening
to dawn?

* * * * *

hal nāru Laylā badat laylan bi-Dhī Salami
am bāriqun lāḥā bi-Z-Zawrā' fa-l-ʿAlami

Did Laylā's fire shine at Dhū Salam,
or did lightning flash at al-Zawrā' and al-ʿAlam?[32]

In two odes, the lover's memories are stirred not by a distant light, but by the early morning breeze that blows to him from his beloved's camp far away:[33]

naʿam bi-ṣ-ṣabā qalbī ṣabā li-aḥibbatī
fa-yā ḥabbadhā dhāka-sh-shadhā ḥīna habbati

1) Yes, because of the east wind
my heart yearned for my beloveds;
how lovely that scent
when it arose!

2) It traveled through the night
and near dawn divulged to the heart
tales (*aḥādīth*) of the neighbors at ʿUdhayb,
bringing joy.

3) Quietly rustling in the meadows,
soft its cloak, a languid breeze,
in whose very nature
is the recovery for my disease,

4) Setting in motion
the sweet grasses of al-Ghuwayr.
I was drunk from that,
not from my companions' wine.

5) *tudhakkirunī-l-ᶜahda-l-qadīma li-annahā*
ḥadīthatu ᶜahdin min uhayli mawaddatī

The breeze reminded me
of the ancient pact,
for it had recently met
the dear ones of my love.

Here in the opening of the *al-Tā'īyah al-Ṣughrā* ("Ode Rhyming in T—Minor"), Ibn al-Fāriḍ likens the gentle east wind to the beloved's night messenger who brings the lover glad tidings of a possible union (vv. 1–3). The memories evoked by the breeze induce a state of intoxication that leads the poet to recollect (*tudhakkirunī*) the "ancient pact" (*al-ᶜahd al-qadīm*; vv. 4–5). This probable allusion to the *mīthāq*, or primordial covenant, is conveyed and reinforced by word play and antithesis (*al-ᶜahd al-qadīm*, "ancient pact;" *ḥadīthatu ᶜahd*, "recent meeting") suggesting the paradox of a timeless permanence amid temporal transience. Ibn al-Fāriḍ's use in verse 2 of *aḥādīth* ("traditions," "tales") appears to allude to the Prophet Muhammad, which is certainly the case in the following ode:[34]

araju-n-nasīmi sarā mina-Z-Zawrā'i
saḥaran fa-aḥyā mayyita-l-aḥyā'i

1) The breeze's sweet scent traveled by night
arriving at dawn from al-Zawrā',
bringing back to life
one dead among the living.

2) Its fragrance guided
the winds of Najd to us,
so the air everywhere
smelled of ambergris,

3) And it told tales
of the beloveds,
traced back to a fragrant rush
and thorn bush at Athākhir.

4) I was drunk with that fragrant scent
  from the hems of its cloak,
    and the flush of recovery
      spread through my disease.

In this opening from the *al-Hamzīyah*, the winds (v. 2: *arwāḥ*, also meaning "spirits") from Arabia once again arrive at dawn to revive the lover who is dead to all save his beloved. The heady fragrance carried by the breezes from Najd, the ᶜUdhrī Arcadia, is termed *ᶜarf* (v. 2), suggesting a related Sufi word, *ᶜirfān*, gnosis. Moreover, the fragrance guides (*ahdā*) the winds bearing news of the beloved just as the Qur'ān brings God's guidance to humanity. Ibn al-Fāriḍ hints further at the religious character of the feelings aroused by this fragrance with a sustained word play (*īhām*) involving the science of *ḥadīth* (v. 3):

wa-rawā aḥādītha-l-aḥibbati musnidan
  ᶜan idhkhirin bi-Adhākirin wa-salḥā'i

And it told tales
  of the beloveds
    traced back to a fragrant rush
      and thorn bush at Adhākhir.

Aḥādīth clearly refers to the prophetic traditions of Muhammad, which are related (*rawā*) based on a chain of authority (*musnad*). Similar to the opening scene from the *al-Tā'īyah al-Ṣughrā*, the fragrant wind is likened to a medicinal wine, which relieves the poet's love sickness (v. 4).[35] As in several *ghazals*, mention of *ḥadīth* suggests that the beloved of both odes may refer to the prophet Muhammad and/or his Light, and this impression is strengthened by Ibn al-Fāriḍ's mention of al-Zawrā', a place in Medina near the Prophet's mosque, and Adhākhir, the place of Muhammad's encampment prior to his conquest of Mecca.[36] Finally, the word for cloak in verse 4 of the *al-Hamzīyah*, *burd*, has a common variant, *burdah*, a term traditionally used to refer to Muhammad's cloak or mantle, which is a Muslim symbol for forgiveness.[37]

In all six of his *qaṣīdahs*, Ibn al-Fāriḍ recounts the departure of a caravan, which in the classical *qaṣīdah*, referred to the beloved's departure, and two odes begin with this scene of separation:[38]

sā'iqa-l-aẓᶜāni yaṭwī-l-bīda ṭai
  munᶜiman ᶜarrij ᶜalā kuthbāni Ṭai

1) Driver of the howdahs rolling up the perilous deserts,
kindly turn aside at the dunes of Ṭai,
2) And at Dhāt al-Shīh, if you pass a tribe of dear Arabs
of the winding valley, greet them for me,
3) And show kindness to them and quickly mention me;
perhaps they will look to me with affection.

* * * * *

khaffifi-s-sayra wa-tta'id yā ḥādī
innamā anta sā'iqun bi-fu'ādī[39]

1) Ease the pace and slow, O leader of the caravan,
for you are driving on with my heart.

Similar passages immediately follow the opening verses of the other four *qaṣīdahs*, and Ibn al-Fāriḍ's use of key words, phrases, and images sets the desert scene:[40]

yā rākiba-l-wajnā'i bullighta-l-munā
ᶜuj bi-l-ḥimā in juzta bi-l-jarᶜā'i

O rider of the strong she-camel,
may you be granted your desire,
turn aside at the sacred precinct
if you pass by the sandy ground.

In this last instance, the greeting and blessing of the caravan leader signals the beginning of a journey as the poet imagines the route taken by the camels and their stops along the way until the caravan alights at the beloved's campground. Once at the site, the driver is asked to present to the beloved an account of the lover's emaciated and distraught condition. As in Ibn al-Fāriḍ's *ghazals*, the lover then dismisses his blamers and, occasionally, he recalls the beloved's beauty and cruelty. Following the ᶜUdhrī tradition, the female beloved of Ibn al-Fāriḍ's odes usually is the ideal perfect woman. She may be compared with Majnūn's Laylā or Qays' Lubnā, but even these legendary beauties fall short of the beloved's magnificence:[41]

bi-farṭi gharāmī dhikra Qaysin bi-wajdihi
wa-bahjatihā Lubnā amattu wa-ammati

With my excessive passion,
I slew the memory of Qays in his rapture,
just as she preceded Lubnā
in splendor.

As with the beloved in his *ghazals*, Ibn al-Fāriḍ rarely details her physical features in his *qaṣīdahs* as she is veiled.[42] The one exception in the odes appears in the *al-Yā'īyah*:[43]

51) My desire is for her bright face
while my heart thirsts for those full, red lips.
52) Both those lips and her glances made me drunk;
how sweet my two intoxications!
53) I believe wine was drunk from the breath of her lips,
while honey, confused, is humbled before them.
54) Always her glances are Dhū al-Faqār,
while my insides are Huyai and ᶜAmr!
55) Her waist wasted my body to her slender shape,
so wasting away is my finest robe.
56) If she sways, she is a bough on a dune bearing the full moon
at night, dark tresses of a tawny beauty.
57) If she turns away, my heart turns too,
but if she unveils (*tajallat*) all reason is her booty

Ibn al-Fāriḍ's portrayal of the beloved leaves little doubt as to her ideal status; she has a face bright like the moon, long hair black as night, a slender waist, red, honeyed lips, an intoxicating breath, and deadly eyes whose glances pierce the lover like the famed sword Dhū al-Faqār, which ᶜAlī ibn Abī Ṭālib used to run through his infidel enemies including ᶜAmr ibn ᶜAbd Wudd and Ḥuyai ibn Akhṭab.[44] The commentator al-Nābulusī noted that Ibn al-Fāriḍ used the word *wajh* (v. 51) for the beloved's face as an allusion to Qur'ān 2:115: "To God belongs the east and west, so wherever you turn, there is the face (*wajh*) of God, the omnipresent, the omniscient!"[45] Later, in the *al-Yā'īyah*, Ibn al-Fāriḍ suggests the divine nature of the beloved when she proclaims her omnipotence in matters of love:[46]

lastu ansā bi-th-thanāyā qawlahā
kullu man fī-l-ḥayyi asrā fī yadai
salhumu mustakhbiran anfasahum
hal najat anfusuhum min qabḍatai

fa-l-qaḍā mā bayna sukhṭī wa-r-raḍā
man lahu uqṣi qaḍā aw udni ḥai
khātiba-l-khatbi daʿi-d-daʿwā fa-mā
bi-r-ruqā tarqā ilā waṣli Ruqai.
ruḥ muʿāfan wa-ghtanim nuṣḥī wa-in
shi'ta an tahwā fa-lil-balwā tahai
wa-bi-suqmin himtu bi-l-ajfāni an
zānahā waṣfan tazayyan wa-tazai
kam qatīlin min qabīlin mā lahu
qawadun fī ḥubbinā min kulli ḥai
bābu waṣlī-s-sāmu min subli-d-ḍanā
minhu lī mā dumta ḥayyan lam tabai
fa-ini-staghnayta ʿan ʿizzi-l-baqā
fa-ilā waṣlī bi-badhli-n-nafsi ḥai
qultu rūḥī in tarā basṭaki fī
qabḍihā ʿishtu fa-ra'yī an tarai

81) I have not forgotten her words at the narrow passes:
"Everyone of the tribe is a prisoner in my two hands.
82) "Ask them, if you seek to know what is most precious to them,
if their souls escaped from my two fists.
83) "For judgment is between my displeasure and satisfaction:
one I put afar, dies; one I bring near, lives.
84) "O you engaging in an important affair, give up false claims;
not with amulets will you ascend to union with Ruqai.
85) "Leave in good health and profit from my advice,
but if you wish to love, be ready for affliction.
86) "For I desperately love eyes embellished by disease,
so adorn and dress them up!
87) "In loving us, how many have been slain
from every type and tribe without retaliation.
88) "The door to union with me is death by wasting away;
you will not come back to me as long as you live.
89) "So if you can be free of glorious mortality and give up your soul,
then welcome to my union!"
90) I said: "If you see your unbound joy in my spirit's oppression,
then I will live, seeing as you do."

This is one of only a few passages in Ibn al-Fāriḍ's verse in which the beloved speaks, and her words are replete with word plays, antithesis, and Sufi technical terms as the beloved asks her lover to suffer affliction (*balwā;* v. 85) and death, to give up his selfish soul (*nafs;* v. 89) and thoughts of permanence (*baqā';* v. 89) if he is to attain her satisfaction (*riḍā;* v. 83) and union with her (*waṣl;* v. 88). Ibn al-Fāriḍ also underscores the spiritual nature of this death by using several Sufi terms and their antithesis in the lover's eager reply to meet the beloved's demands; he is ready to permit her to oppress (*qabḍ*) his spirit (*rūḥ*) if that will bring her exhilaration (*basṭ*), as her wish becomes his command (v. 90). Furthermore, the beloved, like God in the Qur'ān, speaks with the "royal We" (v. 87), and has the power to grant life or death to whom she wills (v. 83). Jalāl al-Dīn al-Suyūṭī (d. 911/1405), perhaps the earliest scholar to compose a commentary on this poem, finds an allusion in verse 83 to a prophetic tradition, which declares that at the time of Adam's creation, God drew two handfuls from Adam's loins. The fistful from the right side contained those of Adam's progeny destined for Paradise, while the fistful from the left side had those destined for Hell.[47] Similarly, the beloved of this poem judges her lovers as she sees fit, and only those who willingly submit themselves to her will become the unavenged martyrs of love blessed with union.[48]

Following the classical *qaṣīdah* tradition in his odes, Ibn al-Fāriḍ portrays life as a test, and the lover plagued by fear of failure. Returning to the somber and sorrowful mood of the *nasīb*, Ibn al-Fāriḍ generally concludes his *qaṣīdahs* with the lover's cherished memories of union with the beloved during the pilgrimage at Mecca:[49]

wāhan ʿalā dhāka-z-zamāni wa-ṭībihi
ayyāma kuntu mina-l-lughūbi murāḥā
qasaman bi-Zamzama wa-l-Maqāmi wa-man atā-l-
Bayta-l-Ḥarāma mulabbiyan sayyāḥā
mā rannahat rīḥu-ṣ-ṣabā shīḥa-r-rubā
illā wa-ahdat minkumu arwāḥā

24) Ah, for that time
and its sweetness,
days when I had rest
from toil.

25) I swear by the well of Zamzam
and Abraham's Station,
and by the pilgrim passing the Sacred House
crying; "I'm here to serve, O Lord!"

26) Never did the breeze of the east wind
rustle the wormwoods of the hills
save it brought
reviving spirits from you!

* * * * *

āhan li-ayyāminā bi-l-Khayfi law baqiyat
ᶜashran wa-wāhan ᶜalayhā kayfa lam tadumi[50]

14) Ah, for our days at al-Khayf,
had they been ten, but how could they last?
15) If only my grief could cure me,
and my remorse recover what has passed.
16) Fawns of the winding valleys, leave me alone, please,
I have bound my eye to face only them.
17) Obeying a judge who decreed a wondrous thing:
the shedding of my blood in unhallowed and sacred grounds.
18) Deaf, he did not hear the plea; dumb, he did not answer,
blind to the case of one burning with desire.

In several poems, and in these verses from the ode beginning "Did Laylā's fire shine at Dhū Salam," Ibn al-Fāriḍ alludes to the ᶜUdhrī love cycle of Majnūn-Laylā. According to the oldest accounts of their sad tale, Qays ibn al-Mulawwah was unable to wed his kinswomen Laylā, and so he went insane, hence his nickname Majnūn, the "mad man." He often would face toward the Najd longing to feel the east wind and some trace of his beloved, but to no avail. Hoping to cure him, his father took him on pilgrimage to Mecca, but there at Minā, Majnūn heard the name Laylā and fell unconscious thinking only of her, not of God. Later, Majnūn roamed distraught with wild animals, including gazelles, and when a man tried to intercede with Laylā's family on Majnūn's behalf, he was told that the caliph had given them permission to shed the blood of Majnūn with impunity were they to encounter him.[51] Ibn al-Fāriḍ's ode invoking Laylā's name ends with the gazelles, which could be a metaphor for human beloveds. Yet, this reference to gazelles, together with the Muslim holy land, and the judge's decree to allow shedding the lover's blood, all resonate with Majnūn's tragic tale of unrequited love and eventual death.[52] Furthermore, at the end of several other odes, Ibn al-Fāriḍ has the lover voice a desperate hope that he be accepted once more and granted a reprieve from his desolate exile. He calls on the spring rains to water the encampments of the beloved so that, perhaps, her love in days long past will likewise be renewed:[53]

145) Give life, O spring rains, to the tribe's spring campground;
 may my father be ransom for our neighbors there.
146) What life passed for me in the encampment's shade?
 O, now, my portion of it is what?
147) Alas, will the nights of union ever return?
 And for distraction, the impassioned lover moans "Alas!"
148) By which road may I hope for their return?
 Perhaps I am dying and do not know which way.
149) O my neighbors, my bewilderment is between
 fate standing behind me and passion before.
150) Life has gone to waste, come to an end in vain,
 if I win nothing from you,
151) Were it not for the trust to me of my bond of fidelity
 to him truly sent from Quṣai.

The first verse of this conclusion to the *al-Yā'īyah* begins with an elaborate series of word plays:

ḥayyī rabᶜīya-l-ḥayā rabᶜa-l-ḥayā
bi-abī jīratunā fīhi wa-bai

Give life, O spring rains, to the tribe's spring campground;
may my father be ransom for our neighbors there.

The listener hears the recurrent sounds *ḥaiya* and *rabaᶜa,* which conjure images of life (*ḥaiya,* "to live") and fertility (*rabiᶜ*, "spring"). It is the loss of both that the lover mourns, and he repeats *ai* ('what," "alas," "O," "which") at the beginning and end of three successive verses to underscore his confusion and despair (vv. 146–148). Then in his climax, Ibn al-Fāriḍ calls on word play (*ḥayratī/jīratī*) and antithesis ("behind me"/"before me") to etch indelibly the human condition (v. 149):[54]

ḥayratī bayna qaḍā'in jīratī
min warā'ī wa-hawan bayna yadai

O my neighbors, my bewilderment is between
fate standing behind me and passion before.

Fated to be tested in a life without apparent meaning, the lover longs for a reunion that may never be. Ibn al-Fāriḍ leaves aside rhetorical display in the final two verses, lending them a quality of frankness, as the lover grieves over the past, for his lost youth, and a life perhaps squandered for nothing. In the final verse, Ibn al-Fāriḍ alludes to Muhammad by way of the prophet's ancestor Quṣai,[55] as the lover still hopes that his devotion to the prophet Muhammad may ultimately lead him to union once more.

Holy Pilgrimage

As in the last passage, Ibn al-Fāriḍ often cites Arabian proper nouns in his odes, particularly when he recounts the route taken by the caravan. Such direct naming had long been a part of the *qaṣīdah* tradition, though some commentators have felt that Ibn al-Fāriḍ's references to Arabia were the natural result of his own stay in the Ḥijāz.[56] Moreover, several scholars have considered these references to be an integral part of the poet's expressions of devotion and veneration for the Prophet and his homeland.[57] In several odes, the caravan does indeed arrive at or pass by Medina, the holy site of Muhammad's mosque and tomb, as we find in the *al-Tā'īyah al-Ṣughrā*:[58]

Bless you, driver,
  if you see Tūḍiḥ at forenoon
    and cross the desert lowlands
      of the white antelopes of Wajrah,

And put aside ᶜUrayḍ's dunes,
  avoiding Ḥuzwā's
    rugged hard ground,
      driving on to Suwayqah,

Leaving behind the willows
  on the way from Ṭuwayliᶜ to Salᶜ,
    ask after an encampment
      set up there,

And halt among the party,
  may you be safe,
    and greet the dear Arabs
      on my behalf.

For among those dear tents
I have one who
is stingy to me with union
but generous with parting.

Ibn al-Fāriḍ's caravan in this passage does not appear to follow a clear route. Ṭūdiḥ is located in central Arabia while Wajrah is on the pilgrimage road between Basra and Mecca; al-ᶜUrayḍ is a valley at Medina, and Ḥuzwā and Suwayqah may be there too. Ṭuwayliᶜ is the name of a number of places, the best known being a hill near Mecca, but the caravan's stopping at Salᶜ is a certain reference to Medina. Of course, Ibn al-Fāriḍ may not have selected these place names for their exact geographic location, but for their poetic possibilities with their subliminal or rhetorical associations since most of the names figure prominently in the alliterations, assonances, and word plays in the verses.[59] Nevertheless, the caravan driver is asked to halt at Salᶜ, a site in Medina, to greet the beloved and appeal to her on the lover's behalf. Yet, although Medina often may be an alighting place for the caravan, it is not the final destination, and later in the ode, the lover recalls his meeting the beloved near the Kaᶜbah in Mecca, where the caravan makes its way in the other odes, as well:[60]

yā rākiba-l-wajnā'i wuqqīta-r-raḍā
in juzta ḥaznan aw ṭawayta biṭāḥā

Oh rider of the strong she-camel,
may you be guarded from destruction,
if you cross the rugged hard ground,
or roll up the wide-spread torrent beds,

And travel by Naᶜmān al-Arāk,
turn aside
to a wide valley there,
one which I have known,

And to the right of ᶜAlamān,
to the east,
stop and seek out
its sweet fragrant *arīn* plants.

And when you reach the folds of the sandy tract,
call out for a heart

that wandered away to destruction
in that dear torrent bed,

And recite a greeting on my behalf
to its dear folk and say:
"I left him starved
for your courtyard!"

The rider's destination in this ode is the sacred precincts of Mecca as the caravan travels from Naᶜmān al-Arāk ("Naᶜmān of the Arāk trees"), a valley two leagues from Mt. ᶜArafāt, to al-ᶜAlamān ("the Two Markers"), which lies on the pilgrims' path between ᶜArafāt and Minā where the pilgrims camp. As for the courtyard (*janāb*), this is a standard reference to the area immediately adjacent to the Kaᶜbah.[61] In fact, the poet's imagined final destination in all of his odes is not Medina but Mecca. Although Ibn al-Fāriḍ certainly pays his respects to Muhammad and Medina in several of his odes, his *qaṣīdahs* are not panegyrics to the Prophet as his *ghazals* appear to be, but rather devoted recollections of the Hajj, the Muslim pilgrimage. For the pilgrimage at Mecca was the time and place of the lover's close encounter with the beloved:[62]

wa-humu bi-qalbī in tanā'at dāruhum
ᶜannī wa-sukhtī fī-l-hawā wa-riḍā'ī
wa-ᶜalā mahallī bayna zahrānayhimi
bi-l-Akhshabayni atūfu hawla ḥimā'ī
wa-ᶜalā-ᶜtināqī li-r-rifāqi musalliman
ᶜinda-stilāmi-r-Rukni bi-l-īmā'ī
wa-ᶜalā muqāmī bi-l-Maqāmi aqāma fī
jismī-s-saqāmu wa-lāta hina shifā'i
wa-tadhakkurī ajyāda wirdī fī-ḍ-ḍuḥā
wa-tahajjudī fī-laylati-l-laylā'i

27) And they are in my heart though their abode be far from me;
in passion, they are my grief and satisfaction.
28) I remember my place among them at Akhshabān
my circumambulating my sacred place,
29) Embracing my companions, greeting them with a nod,
when kissing the Stone of the Corner,
30) Standing at Abraham's Station as disease stood in my body
too late for a cure.
31) My recollecting Ajyād is my litany at noon
and my vigil in the dark of night.

Ibn al-Fāriḍ recalls the lover's days among his beloveds at al-Akhshabān, two hills located in the vicinity of Mecca (v. 27). Using antithesis, word play, internal rhyme, and beginning three consecutive verses with the phrase *wa-ᶜalā*, the poet quickly sketches the lover's moments within the holy mosque of Mecca; he circumambulated the Kaᶜbah, kissed its black stone, and embraced his companions. Then near the Kaᶜbah, he stood at Abraham's Station, consumed by love (vv. 28–30). The lover proclaims that his constant recollection (*tadhakkurī*) of his stay at Ajyād, another mountain near Mecca, has become his mystical prayer (*wird*, v. 31). Clearly, there is a strong mystical current running through Ibn al-Fāriḍ's accounts of meeting his beloved in the Muslim holy land:[63]

wa-lammā tawāfaynā ᶜishā'an wa-ḍammanā
sawā'u sabīlay Dhī Ṭuwā wa-th-Thanīyati

42) In the twilight when we gathered
joined at the crossroads
from Dhū Ṭuwā
and Thanīyah,

43) She did not grudge giving me
a moment's pause
equal to my standing
at ᶜArafāt.

44) Then I reproved her, but she did not care,
as if no meeting, nothing,
had happened save that
I pointed, and she nodded.

45) O Kaᶜbah of loveliness,
the hearts of the wise
make pilgrimage to your beauty
and cry: "At you service!"

46) The lightning's precious gleam
in the narrow pass
flashed us your shining teeth,
the best of gifts,

47) And revealed to my eye that my heart
was a neighbor to your precinct,

so my eye desired and yearned
  for your beauty.

The meeting is in the evening, but the very special one at Mt. ᶜArafāt where the pilgrims stand and pray at sunset on the second day of the pilgrimage. The lover and his beloved have come from their respective campsites, Dhū Ṭawā and al-Thanīyah, both located in Mecca. She pauses with him for a brief moment at ᶜArafāt where he reproves her (vv. 42–43). Poetically this reproof is for the beloved's neglect of the lover. But the beloved does not grant him more than a glance, which passes so quickly that the he wonders if it even happened. Yet this is enough to arouse the lover's yearning desire to see her again (vv. 44–47).[64] These verses from the *al-Tā'īyah al-Ṣughrā* have a strong mystical flavor. The encounter at ᶜArafāt may well allude to an experience of gnosis (*maᶜrifah*), and Ibn al-Fāriḍ's references to the beloved in terms of the pilgrimage rites leave little doubt as to her exalted nature; she is the Kaᶜbah toward which the hearts of those with insight (v. 45: *qulūb al-uwilā*) turn in prayer. In this light, the beloved's fleeting glance may be an immediate experience of the holy presence, which is the essence of the pilgrimage. Standing at ᶜArafāt or before the Kaᶜbah, the lovers of God see within their hearts the flash of gnosis, God's grace to His worshippers who are blessed with the knowledge that their Lord is always near (v. 47).[65] For a timeless moment they are again in the divine realm of pre-eternity:[66]

saqā bi-S-Safā-r-ribᶜīyu rabᶜan bihi-ṣafā
  wa-jāda bi-Ajyādin tharan minhu tharwatī
mukhayyamu ladhdhātī wa-sūqu ma'āribī
  wa-qiblatu āmālī wa-mawtinu ṣabwatī
manāzilu unsin kāna lam ansa dhikrahā
  bi-man buᶜduhā wa-l-qurbu nārī wa-jannatī

81) May the spring rains at Ṣafā
  quench a pure spring encampment
    and fall abundantly at Ajyād
      whose moist soil is my treasure.

82) There is the camp of my delights,
  my market of aims,
    my *qiblah* of desires,
      my abode of youthful passion.

83) They were stations of intimacy
whose recollection I have not forgotten:
because of her, her distance is my Hell,
her proximity my Paradise.

This reunion experienced during the pilgrimage is the crucial event in Ibn al-Fāriḍ's odes, as we see in this passage from the *al-Tā'īyah al-Ṣughrā*. Ibn al-Fāriḍ again recalls the places and events of the pilgrimage in Sufi terms, especially in verse 83, in which he uses *uns*, ("intimacy"), *dhikr* ("recollection"), and *qurb* ("proximity").[67] Ibn al-Fāriḍ was certainly not the first Muslim to explore the mystical dimensions of the Hajj. Earlier, the Sufi writer al-Sarrāj (d. 378/988) had stressed the importance of the pilgrim's intentions and attitude during these rites whose outward forms clothed inner truths, and al-Hujwirī (d. 469/1077) related a story of third/tenth-century Sufi master al-Junayd, which is a fine example of a Sufi interpretation of the Hajj:[68]

> A certain man came to Junayd. Junayd asked him whence he came. He replied: "I have been on the pilgrimage." Junayd said: "From the time when you first journeyed from your home have you also journeyed away from your sins?" He said: "No." "Then," said Junayd, "you have made no journey. At every stage where you halted for the night did you traverse a station on the way to God?" He said: "No." "Then," said Junayd, "you have not trodden the road stage by stage. When you put on the pilgrim's garb at the proper place did you discard the attributes of humanity as you cast off your ordinary clothes?" "No." "Then you have not put on the pilgrim's garb. When you stood at ᶜArafāt did you stand one instant in contemplation of God?" "No." "Then you have not stood on ᶜArafāt. When you went to Muzdalifa and achieved your desire did you renounce all sensual desires?" "No." "Then you have not gone to Muzdalifa. When you circumambulated the Temple [the Kaᶜbah] did you behold the immaterial beauty of God in the abode of purification?" "No." "Then you have not circumambulated the Temple. When you ran between Safā and Marwā did you attain to the rank of purity (*ṣafā*) and virtue (*muruwat*)?" "No." "Then you have not run. When you came to Minā did all your wishes (*munyathā*) cease?" "No." "Then you have not yet visited Minā. When you reached the slaughter-place and offered the sacrifice did

> you sacrifice the objects of sensual desire?" "No." "Then you have not sacrificed. When you threw stones did you throw away whatever sensual thoughts were accompanying you?" "No." "Then you have not thrown stones, and you have not performed the pilgrimage. Return and perform the pilgrimage in the manner which I have described in order that you may arrive at the Station of Abraham."

Many of Ibn al-Fāriḍ's poetic allusions to the Hajj strikingly parallel al-Junayd's interpretations of the pilgrimage rites. As we have seen, Ibn al-Fāriḍ places particular stress on the pilgrim's journey and stopping places, the lover's discarding of selfish thoughts, and the momentary encounter at ᶜArafāt; his beloved, too, is the "Kaᶜbah of beauty," and the lover's mystical ascent is from "Abraham's Station." Furthermore, Ibn al-Fāriḍ makes nearly identical etymological word plays involving such sites as al-Ṣafā, al-Marwā, and Minā.[69] As important, for both al-Junayd and Ibn al-Fāriḍ, the Hajj is not merely a symbol for the mystical quest and experience, but the actual site and occasion for it. For the pilgrimage and the standing at ᶜArafāt, in particular, are the most pronounced example of Muslim solidarity and communion in humility before God. An older contemporary of Ibn al-Fāriḍ, Ibn Jubayr (d. 613/1217) left an account of his pilgrimage and some of the profound feelings he experienced at ᶜArafāt:[70]

> Upon that Friday morning there was on ᶜArafāt a multitude that could have no like save that which will be on the Day of Resurrection; but, within the will of God Most High, it was a gathering that will win reward, giving promise as it does of God's mercy and forgiveness when men assemble for the Day of Reckoning. . . . When on Friday, the midday and afternoon prayers were said together, the people stood contrite and in tears, humbly beseeching the mercy of Great and Glorious God. The cries of "God is Great!" rose high, and loud were the voices of men in prayer. Never has there been seen a day of such weeping, such penitence of heart, and such bending of the neck in reverential submission and humility before God. In this fashion the pilgrims continued, with the sun burning their faces, until its orb had sunk and the time of the sunset prayers was at hand. . . . What a standing it had been, how awesome to regard and what hopes of happy reward it

> had brought to the soul. God grant that we may be among those on whom He there conferred His approbation and covered with His bounty. For He is bounteous, generous, compassionate, and beneficent.

Ibn Jubayr compared the Standing at ʿArafāt to the gathering on the Day of Resurrection, and Ibn al-Fāriḍ, too, in his odes likens the encounter there to a foretaste of the permanent joy to be savored in Paradise. Like many other Muslims, Ibn al-Fāriḍ apparently viewed the Standing at ʿArafāt to be a second point of direct contact between humanity and God following their first meeting on the Day of the Primordial Covenant (*yawm al-mīthāq*). At ʿArafāt the eternal and temporal meet for a moment, and believing Muslims may briefly raise the veil of selfishness to glimpse their reward to come if God forgives and accepts them on the Day of Resurrection (*yawm al-qīyāmah*), their third and final meeting.

Ibn al-Fāriḍ followed well-established Sufi tradition in regarding ʿArafāt as the nexus of gnosis (*maʿrifah*),[71] but he may have been the first poet to consciously reinterpret the *qaṣīdah* in terms of the Hajj and the deeply religious feelings aroused at Mecca. In this context, his *nasībs* are recollections of the illumination to be experienced there, or memories brought by the breeze from those holy sites. The caravan whose driver he beseeches is the annual pilgrimage caravan that leaves Cairo and journeys to Mecca perhaps stopping en route at Medina in order to pay homage to the prophet Muhammad and seek his blessings. The departure of the caravan causes the lover to remember his own inner journey and final destination, which was not some earthly lord or ruler, as had been in the pre-Islamic and later panegyric odes but, rather, God, Lord of the Worlds. Thus, the caravan sections of Ibn al-Fāriḍ's odes combine the motif of the departing beloved, traditionally recounted in the past tense, with elements of the heroic *raḥīl*, often related in the present.[72] But in stark contrast to the classical *raḥīl* and its cathartic psychological rite of passage, the journey in Ibn al-Fāriḍ's odes is both the physical trek to Mecca and an interior quest to recover the primordial union lost in creation. The lover of Ibn al-Fāriḍ's odes longs for this encounter experienced during the rites of renewal performed in the sacred precincts of Mecca. As one of Ibn al-Fāriḍ's commentators, Sibṭ al-Marṣafī (fl. 960/1562) astutely observed, the ruins and spring encampments of other poets have become in Ibn al-Fāriḍ's odes, Medina, Mecca, and their places of pilgrimage.[73] Thus, Ibn al-Fāriḍ channels the ancient and evocative power of the classical *qaṣīdah* into the sites and rites of the Muslim pilgrimage to communicate a mystical vision of life and love. This very original contribution to Islamic mysticism and Arabic poetry is beautifully illustrated by Ibn al-Fāriḍ's *al-Dālīyah*.[74]

"Greetings from Suᶜād"

khaffifi-s-sayra wa-tta'id yā ḥādī
innamā anta sā'iqun bi-fu'ādī

1) Ease the pace and slow, O leader of the caravan,
for you are driving on with my heart.
2) Do you not see the reddish white camels being driven and longing,
starved and thirsty for the spring encampments' springtime?
3) The wastelands have not left them any body
other than skin stretched over protruding bones.
4) Their pads have dried up, burning like coals,
but they walk on from their grief.
5) Fatigue has whittled them away and loosened their nose rings;
let them quench themselves on the depressions' panic grass.
6) Running will wear them away if you do not water them,
so give them a drink on the run amid the lowland's large pools,
7) And race with them, but spare them,
for they are your means to win the best of valleys.
8) May God lengthen your life! If you pass by Yanbuᶜ oasis,
then Dahnā, then Badr, setting out early,
9) And journey to Naqā, then to the wetlands of Waddān,
and to Rābigh with well-watered pools,
10) And you cross the stony tacks aiming for the tents of Qudayd,
the dwellings of the glorious ones,
11) And draw near to Khulayṣ, then ᶜUsfān,
and Marr al-Ẓahrān, the bedouins' meeting place,
12) And arrive to drink at Jumūm, then Qaṣr and Daknā',
one and all watering holes for those coming for drink,
13) And you come to Tanᶜīm, then to Zāhir,
radiant with blossoms to its mountain tops,
14) And cross over to Ḥajūn and pass through,
choosing to visit the shrines of the saints,
15) And reach the tents, then give my greetings carefully
to the dear Arabs of that assembly.

16) Be kind, and recall to them
a part of my passion, never to be exhausted.
17) O my friends, will the time of drawing near you
in the sacred precinct return with my sleep?
18) O neighbors of the quarter, how bitter is separation,
how sweet the meeting together after loneliness.
19) How can a captive savor life
while in his heart are striking sparks?
20) His life and endurance wane,
while burning passion and rapture grow:
21) In Egypt's villages, his body; near Syria,
his dear companions; in Ajyād, his heart.
22) If we could stand again on those dear rocks at dusk,
I would be happy after being afar.
23) May God preserve our day at Muṣallā
where we were called to wisdom's path,
24) While the riders' domed howdahs swiftly set out early
between ᶜAlamān toward Ma'zimān.
25) May He shower our union at Jamᶜ with gentle rains
and our dear nights at Khayf with a cloud of spring showers.
26) Some crave wealth and a fine place to dwell,
but my desire is Minā, my highest hope.
27) O dear ones of the Ḥijāz, if time decrees separation,
executing a willed command,
28) Then my ancient affection for you will be my affliction,
for my love, as you know well, remains my desire.
29) Long ago you took up residence in the core of my heart
and in the dark black center of my eye.
30) O my night companion, refresh my spirit,
singing of Mecca if you wish to cheer me,
31) For her courtyard has my herds, her soil is my grassland,
and her torrent channel is my place of water and provision.
32) In her was my intimacy and the ascent of my sanctity;
my station was Abraham's and the enlightenment clear.
33) But the fortunes carried me away from her;
cut off from water, my drinking could not last.
34) O, if only time would permit a return;
perhaps then my festive days would return to me.
35) I swear by Ḥaṭīm and the Corner, by the Coverings,
and the two Marwahs where the worshippers run,
36) By the Courtyard's shadows, by Ḥijr and the Spout,
and the Place of Answering for those who seek it,

37) I have never smelled balsam save
it brought to my heart greetings from Suʿād!

Ibn al-Fāriḍ begins this ode *in medias res*, as the lover begs the leader of the caravan to go easy on his camels, which the poet identifies with the lover's aching heart. As is common in the pre-Islamic *qaṣīdah*, the she-camel is the poet's alter ego, and her physical trials and afflictions suffered while crossing the forbidding desert reflect the lover's psychological condition.[75] In this instance both are driven hard by their passion, becoming famished and parched, longing to reach the fertile and verdant encampments (vv. 1–2). The joy to be encountered there is in contrast to the stark wastelands, which may symbolize the lover's ascetic devotions and/or his desolate emotional and spiritual state. He is emaciated, skin and bones without volition, living on in excruciating pain (vv. 3–4). He cries out to the harsh and unrelenting driver, perhaps a symbol for his passion, to grant him a taste of the water of life before he is consumed by the fire of love and desire (vv. 5–6).

Ibn al-Fāriḍ then moves to an account of the caravan's route, foretelling its destination by advising the driver to spare his mounts so that they may fly to the "best of valleys" which, in an Islamic context, often refers to Mecca (v. 7).[76] Following his usual formulaic blessing of the driver, the lover recollects a journey he once made. Ibn al-Fāriḍ begins verses 8 to 14 with verbs of motion and travel, and mentions numerous places along the way. Commentators have identified many of the sites as lying between Medina and Mecca, and al-Nābulusī in his customary zeal to find hidden spiritual meanings in every word linked each name to a stage on the mystic's path to God.[77] Another more recent scholar also has claimed that Ibn al-Fāriḍ's lengthy itinerary is intended to convey the monotony of the pilgrimage caravan, the pilgrim's hardships, and their joy upon reaching Mecca.[78] Yet, Ibn al-Fāriḍ's descriptions of several places (Rābigh, v. 9; Qudayd, v. 10; al-Zāhir, v. 13) suggest a fondness for these alighting places. Moreover, what has apparently gone unnoticed is that the identified place names are cited by Ibn al-Fāriḍ in their correct geographical order along the pilgrimage route from Cairo to Mecca.[79] This poetic map of the way, then, may recount Ibn al-Fāriḍ's own historical pilgrimage to Mecca and so exhibits the travelogue quality of some Abbasid *raḥīls*.[80] Nevertheless, this journey retains an archetypal character because he recounts it in a reverie, envisioning the pilgrimage route followed or aspired to by many Muslims in Egypt and North Africa.

The caravan passes al-Ḥajūn where an important Meccan cemetery was located, hence Ibn al-Fāriḍ's reference to visiting the "shrines of the saints" (*mashāhid awtād;* v. 14). Loosely translated as "saints," *awtād* literally means "tent-pegs," and this term was traditionally used by Sufis to designate the saints who occupied a very high spiritual rank.[81] Ibn al-Fāriḍ then plays on the literal meaning of this term as he mentions the tents of the beloved (v. 15). He concludes this journey by obliging the caravan driver to greet the beloved and relate to her the desperate state of her devoted servant (vv. 15–16).

By recollecting the pilgrimage, the lover has re-enacted this liminal phase in hopes of reliving his moment of union with the beloved, but he wakes from his reverie. Maintaining the lyrical tone of the *nasīb,* the lover wonders if the phantom of his beloved will come to him in a dream and so relieve his distress caused by their separation. He longs for death and the Day of Resurrection (v. 18: *yawm al-tilāqī*) for his present life is misery due to the pains of separation. Physically he remains bound to Egypt, while his pilgrimage companions have returned to their homes in Syria, yet, spiritually, his heart remains attached to Mecca (v. 21: Ajyād). The thought of Mecca stirs the lover's hallowed memories of the Standing (*waqfah*) at ᶜArafāt, and were he to experience this precious moment again all would be well (v. 22). His reverie returns with his recollection of other pilgrimage rites: praying at al-Muṣallā after the ᶜĪd al-Adhā, or the Festival of Sacrifice following the day of Standing; the running from ᶜArafāt through al-ᶜAlamān and al-Ma'zimān to the gathering (*jamᶜ*—a word full of allusion to mystical union) at Muzdalifah where more prayers are said; then spending the night at al-Khayf before proceeding on to Minā for the final days of the Hajj (vv. 23–26).[82] Ibn al-Fārid ends this daydream with an elaborate series of word plays, which distinguishes those who love God from those who love mammon (v. 26):

man tamannā mālan wa-ḥusna ma'ālin
fa-munā'ī Minan wa-aqṣā murādī

Some crave wealth and a fine place to dwell,
but my desire is Minā, my highest hope.

The lover claims to have given up all concern for this world and his own security, choosing instead to bear the burden of love in total obedience to the beloved. He swears to his ancient (*qadīm*) passion for his beloved and his fidelity to their covenant (*ᶜahidtum,* "you know well," and ᶜ*ahd*, "pact, covenant"), although the beloved has decreed the lover's exile, perhaps to test him (vv. 27–28). The lover has little choice but to suffer patiently, for the beloved is in his heart, at the center of his very being (v. 29). Here, Ibn al-Fāriḍ refers to a famous Sufi tradition in which God says: "My earth and My heaven do not contain me but the heart of My believing servant does."[83] The lover is obsessed with Mecca, and its recollection alone provides him with solace; the courtyard of the Kaᶜbah has become his protective enclosure, its soil his sweet pasturage (*ṭībah*), and the well of Zamzam (*Ṭībah*) his source for life-giving water (vv. 30–31). There, the lover tasted a moment of intimate union (*uns*) and spiritual enlightenment (*fatḥ*). Like Muhammad whose body, according to tradition, was purified with the water of Zamzam thus enabling him to travel to Jerusalem (al-Quds) and rise from the Farthest Mosque (al-Masjid al-Aqṣā) to heaven in his spiritual ascent (*miᶜrāj*), so does the lover express the occasion for enlightenment as a *miᶜrāju qudsī*, "ascent to my sanctification," or "my Jerusalem ascension," which is pre-figured by Ibn al-Fāriḍ's use of the word *aqṣā* ("farthest," "highest") in verse 26.[84] As so often is the case, Ibn al-Fārid focuses the listener's attention on this key, climactic verse with word play and internal rhyme:

kāna fīhā unsī wa-miᶜrāju qudsī
wa-muqāmī-l-maqāmu wa-l-fatḥu bādi

32) In her was my intimacy and the ascent of my sanctity,
my station was Abraham's and the enlightenment clear.

The doors to mystical insight suddenly open (*fatḥ*), and with God's help (*fatḥ*), the lover achieved a clear spiritual victory (*fatḥ*). For a moment the lover becomes God's intimate, and so he stands in the Station of Abraham, which symbolizes true friendship (*khullah*) (v. 32).[85] But this union is a transient one, and time deprives the lover of his draughts (*awrād*) of gnosis (*wird*, v. 33).[86] Ibn al-Fāriḍ poignantly expresses the desire to perform again the rites of pilgrimage and experience spiritual renewal by returning full circle to the elegiac mood of the *nasīb*:

mā shamamtu-l-bashāma illā wa-ahdā
li-fu'ādī taḥīyatan min Suᶜādi

37) I have never smelled balsam save
it brought to my heart greetings from Suᶜād!

The lover swears by all that is holy in Mecca's sacred precincts, that the breeze blowing from Mecca always brings to his heart greetings (*taḥīyah*), which keep alive (*taḥīyah*) his hope of one day attaining an auspicious (*saᶜd*) reunion with his beloved Suᶜād (vv. 35–37).[87] Suᶜād is also the beloved's name in Kaᶜb ibn Zuhayr's (d. after 10/632) famous panegyric on the Prophet in which Muhammad granted forgiveness to his former opponent by casting his mantle upon Kaᶜb. This led Arberry to assert that the beloved of Ibn al-Fāriḍ's ode must be Muhammad.[88] Ibn al-Fāriḍ is undoubtedly alluding to this celebrated poem in this final verse, yet his many references to the Mecca and the Hajj point toward God as the major focus of his devotion in the poem.

In Ibn al-Fāriḍ's *qaṣīdahs*, as in his *ghazals*, the joys of youth, of acceptance and union in pre-eternity, must invariably lead to separation and old age, to the lamentation for fleeting life and the longing for meaning or, at least, peace of mind. Life with its apparent capriciousness is God's test of humanity, and His worshippers must struggle to be true to their covenant. This pre-eternal pact and the certain final judgment delimit both Ibn al-Fāriḍ's love poems and his odes.[89] Yet, the *qaṣīdahs* with their pilgrimage go beyond accounts of mystical love and longing to underscore the mystic's obsessive endeavor to grasp in this life a moment of eternal heavenly joy. But once found, the experience is quickly lost for separation, not union, is humanity's lot. Thus, Ibn al-Fāriḍ's *qaṣīdahs* remain above all else elegies on the irremediable human condition, which for some may be rectified in the world to come.

4

The Beloved's Wine

Mystical themes resonate throughout Ibn al-Fāriḍ's verse, but especially in his wine odes. From its inception Arabic verse on wine carried spiritual and sacramental associations, which were developed and refined over the centuries. Ibn al-Fāriḍ knew this tradition well, and his celebrated wine ode the *al-Khamrīyah* is the mature product of a distinguished line of rarified spirits leading to union and ecstasy.

Blood-Red Wine

References to wine and intoxication are found in many of the oldest pre-Islamic *qaṣīdahs* and serve to reinforce the mood and meaning of the ode's various sections:[1]

fa-ẓaliltu fī dimani-d-dayāri ka-annī
nashwānu bākarahu ṣabūḥu mudāmi

Amid the ruined abodes
I stayed like a reeling drunk,
visited early
by a morning drink

Of an untouched vintage, aged,
the color of gazelle's blood,
from ᶜĀnah's wine
or Shabām's vines.

It was as if the drinker's tongue
had been hit by a pox,
mixing disease
in his body.

In these verses from a *nasīb* ascribed to Imru' al-Qays (fl. sixth century CE), the strong intoxicating wine suggests the powerful feelings of grief and bewilderment that overwhelm the poet as he stands among the traces of the campsite abandoned by his lover.[2] Emotionally confused, he wanders aimlessly unable to express his feelings, like a staggering drunk who slurs his words. Similarly, wine figures prominently in the opening of ᶜAmr ibn Kulthūm's (fl. sixth century CE), *Muᶜallaqah*. The poet calls for his morning drink, but his mistress does not respond, preparing instead to depart the camp with her tribe. On this fateful morning the poet will not feel the enlivening effects of wine or taste his beloved's lips:[3]

a-lā hubbī bi-ṣaḥniki fa-aṣbaḥīnā
wa-lā tubqī khumūra-l-Andarīnā

Arise, quench us with your cup;
don't hold back the wine of Andarūn
Beaming bright like golden saffron;
when it is mixed with water, we are munificent!
It leads one with affairs astray from his passion;
he tastes it, then softens.
When it is passed round to the stingy miser,
you will see him despise all his wealth for wine.
You withheld the cup from us, Umm ᶜAmr,
when it should have been circling to the right.

Wine and love are also joined in verse by al-Aᶜshā (sixth to seventh centuries CE) who frequently celebrates wine and its pleasures. In one of his finest odes, the poet bemoans his sorry, infirm state. He has grown old, and his beloved has left him for a younger man. Seeking consolation in memories of his past, the poet recalls his younger days:[4]

wa-qad aqūdu-ṣ-ṣibā yawman fa-yatbaᶜunī
wa-qad yuṣāḥibunī dhū-sh-shirrati-l-ghazilu

36) Sometimes I hold the reins of youth for a day, so it follows me,
and sometimes my companion is a hot-blooded stud.

37) And I have left early for the taverns,
following me a blade sharp, quick, erect, ready,

38) In the company of braves, like Indian swords,
who knew that no cunning could cut off death.

39) Reclining, I tossed them sweet-basil branches
and a fine, deep red wine its jar dripping.

40) They never came up for air while wine remained
except to shout for more, a second round, a third!

41) A cup-bearer ran with it decked in pearls,
busy bearing glasses, shirt-tails tucked,

42) And songs you would have thought heard from a Persian harp
were sung by the girl in the slip gown.

43) A day like that I relished, tempted
by amorous words and long pleasure,

44) And by the women sweeping their silk gowns,
trailing their trains, wine skins on hip.

The tone of this passage is heroic as reckless braves roam the taverns to satisfy their lusts. Aware of life's brevity and the inevitability of death, they seize the moment and drain their cups until the wine is exhausted. Coupled with the wine imagery are allusions to sexual potency and fertility: The youths are like phallic swords; the cup-bearer's pearls (*nuṭaf*, v. 41) resemble drops of semen (*nuṭaf*); the young women pouring the wine-skins (*ᶜijal*, v. 44) entice the braves like heifers (*ᶜijal*) receptive to rutting bulls. By imagining past days of vigorous youth, the poet may hope to relieve the pain and humiliation of rejection, to assert his manliness, and reinvigorate failing self-esteem.

Elsewhere in pre-Islamic poetry, the drinkers may be rebuked for squandering their wealth on wine and getting drunk, yet such behavior as recalled by al-Aᶜshā was normally considered proof of a man's generosity and fearlessness. Quite often, therefore, the *qaṣīdah's* drinking scenes are immediately followed by the perilous desert crossing or by bloody battles with the enemy as in ᶜAntarah's (fl. sixth century CE), *Muᶜallaqah*:[5]

fa-idhā sharibtu fa-innanī musthalikun
mālī wa-ᶜirḍī wāfirun lam yuklami

When I drink, I spend away my wealth,
  while my honor abounds untouched.
But when I sober up, I do not cut off spending;
  you know well my character and generosity.
And many is the beautiful woman whose spouse
  I left bent, his side whistling like the harelip's mouth.

Although wine in pre-Islamic poetry may offer solace and pleasure, in ᶜAntarah's ode wine's associations with women and love give way jarringly to violence and death. Wine has become the symbol for blood, for life itself, and this, in turn, accounts for the libations of wine poured by Arabs on the graves of their dead:[6]

khalīlayya hubbā ṭāla mā qad raqadtumā
  ajiddakumā lā taqdiyāni karākumā

My two friends, arise! How long you have slept;
  your slumber never ends.
Do you not know that in all of Rāwand and Khuzāq
  I have no friends but you?
I will stay by your graves not leaving the long nights
  until your owls answer.
I will pour wine on your graves;
  if you cannot taste it, I will moisten your earth,
And I will mourn you until death!
  But who will mourn for me?

The probable purpose of the wine libation in this elegy is to ease the burning thirst of two unavenged warriors. A tradition among pre-Islamic Arabs held that if a man were killed and not avenged, he would return to his grave as a fearsome owl crying out to be quenched with the blood of his killer.[7] Similarly, many other pre-Islamic references to wine are tied to the theme of blood vengeance. Avenging the death of one's relatives and protected clients was requisite if a young warrior was to prove his manhood and attain rank in his tribe, which he was sworn to protect. As in the *raḥīl*, the trials faced by the youth in his quest for vengeance nourish and strengthen him, as they do the entire tribe when the deed is done and their enemy slain. Therefore, the final climactic sections of many *qaṣīdahs* gruesomely depict the carnage wrought by the poet and his clan among the enemy whose corpses are dismembered and devoured by predators with the frenzy of the bacchantes. Gathering together after the battle, the victorious braves of the clan also share a meal and, in the company of beautiful maidens, they drink wine at the banquet symbolic of their revitalization at the expense of their victims:[8]

matā ta'tanī aṣbaḥka ka'san rawīyatan
wa-in kunta ʿanhā dhā ghinan fa-ghna wa-zdadi

When you come to me, I will give you
a quenching morning cup,
but if you have no need of it,
then do with out and prosper.

For when the tribe gathers
you will find me
at the peak
of the high sacred house.

My drinking mates are like blazing stars,
while a singing girl
rises to us in the evening
in a stripped saffron gown.

Her neckline is inviting;
to the companions' touch,
she is submissive,
smooth, disrobing.

When we call her to sing
she raises her voice to us
in her way, never harsh,
gently strumming.

A Liberated Spirit

In early Arabic poetry, then, wine often symbolizes blood and by extension, the poet's life and virility, and the tribe's continued vitality and well-being. These associations remained, although often transformed in later Arabic wine poetry, which expanded the images and themes of its pre-Islamic predecessors. In particular, wine became emblematic of a refined courtly life. The Byzantine and Sassanid empires heavily influenced their Arab client kingdoms, and a description of

Arab Ghassānid court, reportedly from the sixth century CE, suggests the creative blending of Greek, Persian, and Arab cultures:[9]

> I saw ten singing girls there; five were Greeks who sang Greek songs accompanied by lutes, and five sang the songs of the people of al-Ḥīrah. Arabs would come from Mecca and elsewhere and sing to (the king). When he held a drinking session, he would recline on a couch surrounded by myrtle, jasmine, and other aromatic herbs; ambergris and pure musk were presented to him in gold and silver vessels.

Among the Ghassānids and Lakhmids many Arabs embraced Christianity, which colored the verse composed at both courts. Not surprisingly, Christian influences enhanced the sacramental character of wine, and this trend continued after the advent of Islam among such noted poets as al-Akhṭal (d. pre 92/710), a Christian courtier of the Umayyads:[10]

sharibnā fa-mitnā mītatan jāhilīyatan
maḍā ahluhā lam yaʿrifū mā Muḥammadu

1) We drank and died the death of the Jāhilīyah—
whose people passed not knowing Muḥammad—
2) For three days; then when life's last breaths
stirred and arose and returned to us,
3) We lived again a life, but not by resurrection
or the next life promised yet to come,
4) But the hypocrites' life who sober up to suffer
the blamers' scorn and cold rebuke.
5) So we said to our cup-bearer: "Come, take us back
to yesterday's state, most-praised its return!"
6) So he brought it, as if the planet Mars
were in its vessel, pristine and pure,
7) Its sweet scent rose fragrant in water
as the cup passed from hand to hand.
8) It kills then revives: delicious its death,
but sweeter still is its praiseworthy life!

In this short poem, al-Akhṭal draws attention to the passing of the pagan era with the coming of Muhammad. For the pre-Islamic Arabs getting senselessly drunk might have been a metaphoric death, but now it could literally bring damnation since the Qur'ān forbade

Muslims from drinking wine. However, al-Akhṭal was a Christian and so could indulge. Other references to Christianity and Islam are also obvious as the poet revives after three days though not to the eternal life of the resurrection, but to the censure of others. Yet instead of changing his ways, the poet calls for more wine, which the cup-bearer brings. The wine is red like Mars, perhaps an allusion wine's pre-Islamic associations with war, blood, and death. But it is no longer an enemy who is conquered but the poet's senses as he seeks to free himself from the strictures of society and religion.[11]

Al-Akhṭal's poem points to the fact that wine verse was developing into a separate genre, later termed *khamrīyah* (*khamr* = wine). As had been the case with love poetry, the themes and subjects of wine verse were largely defined and refined within the urban centers of the Umayyad Empire. Along with al-Akhṭal, other poets of period, most of them Muslim, frequently described the wine that they drank and the effects of intoxication in spiritual terms. The Muslim poet al-Uqayshir (fl. late first\seventh century) wrote:[12]

wa-muqᶜadi qawmin qad mashā min sharābinā
  wa-aᶜmā saqīnāhu thulāthan fa-abṣarā

From our drink
  the tribe's cripple walked;
    three times we quenched a blind man—
      he saw!

Poems on wine and drinking sessions often were favorites of the royal court, and al-Walīd ibn Yazīd (d. 126/744), an Umayyad prince and later caliph, composed some of the most elegant verse on these subjects. Of course, that a caliph, the supposed defender of Islam, enjoyed wine scandalized devout Muslims who believed in the strict enforcement of the Qu'rānic prohibition of wine, but other Muslims tolerated wine's presence in the community. In fact, there appears to have been a small yet significant number of Muslims throughout the ages who have continued to drink wine in open opposition to Islamic law. Many Arabs, Persians, and Turks who accepted Islam refused to alter aspects of their lives with which they strongly identified, and so wine-drinking persisted becoming, at times, a symbol of social and religious protest.[13] This important dimension of Arabic wine poetry is present early on, but it is best illustrated by the verse of Abū Nuwās, the most renowned wine poet of the Abbasid period and of all Islamic literature. Many of his poems retain the pre-Islamic associations of wine and war, but his battlefield is the tavern and his conquest, the beloved, whether male or female. Like the iconoclastic court jester, Abū Nuwās continually rebuked and satirized established religious and literary traditions:[14]

lā tabki Laylā wa-lā taṭrab ilā Hindi
wa-shrab ᶜalā-l-wardi min ḥamrā'a ka-l-wardi

Don't cry for Laylā; don't grieve for Hind,
but drink on horse-back from one red like the rose.

* * * * *

yā Sulaymānu ghanninī
wa-mina-r-rāḥī fa-sqinī[15]

O Sulaymān, sing to me
and quench me with wine.
So if the glass comes round,
seize it and give it to me.
Don't you see morning has appeared
in a straw colored shawl?
Give me a cup of distraction
from the muezzin's call,
Give me wine to drink in public,
then cover and fuck me!

Time is a crucial element in many wine odes by Abū Nuwās and his Abbasid contemporaries. In al-Aᶜshā's verses cited above, recollections of wine and the tavern strengthen the poet's resolve to undertake the quest and attain glory before he falls prey to the ravages of time. By the Abbasid period, however, wine no longer gives the poet courage to stand against time, rather wine serves as a means to suspend or escape it:[16]

wa-fityatin ka-maṣābīḥi-d-dujā ghurarin
shummi-l-unūfi mina-ṣ-ṣīdi-l-maṣālīti

And many the braves burning bright
like lamps in blackest night,
proud ones
among princely, penetrating men,

They overpowered time
with the pleasure they embraced,
so their rope
is never sundered.

Time came round
with lucky stars for them,
and it turned aside and bowed
a lovely neck before them.

Clearly, a persistent theme in much of this verse is the brevity of life, which is lived but never understood. Thus the poet's calling for wine, drunkenness, and other forbidden pleasures is not only a form of protest against religious precepts; it is also an expression of an Epicurean attitude toward life, which is to be savored and enjoyed. Such philosophical elements of Arabic wine poetry often have been noted particularly in passages from Abū Nuwās that echo mystical or gnostic doctrines:[17]

isqinī yā Ibna Adhamā
wa-ttakhidhnī laka ibnamā

Quench me Ibn Adham
and take me to you like some boy.
Quench me with a choice wine (*sulāfatan*)
that preceded Adam's creation.
For it was and there was not
save heaven and earth.
It watched time (*dahr*) grow and mature,
and grow decrepit,
For it was a liberated spirit (*rūḥun mukhallaṣun*)
freed from flesh and blood.
Quench me with it
and sing in your sweet Persian voice,
But not of the campsite
with its crow of ill-omen and shit.

The poet's desire to transcend time and mortality is clear as the sought after wine is one fermented prior to Adam's creation. The priority of this primordial wine is stressed in the third verse by antithetical verbs:

fa-hya kānat idh-lam yakun
mā khalā-l-arḍa wa-s-samā

For it was when there was not
save heaven and earth.

This, in turn, produces a momentary paradox so characteristic of Sufi writings, and one stressing humanity's absence. Furthermore, this amazing wine also precedes time (*dahr*). *Sulāfah* ("choice wine") is related to *sālif* ("preceding"), which is found in the idiomatic expression *fī sālif al-dahr* ("in former times," "in priority of time"), and in the fourth verse, this wine is observing time itself passing through the stages of human life that ultimately end in death. In verse five, the wine is described as *rūḥ mukhallaṣ* ("a liberated spirit") freed from flesh and blood, suggesting two possible meanings. First, as earthly wine, it has been extracted and liberated from the grape and so is able to liberate (*mukhalliṣ*) its drinkers from the cares of this world. But given the preceding verses and the term *rūḥ*, this spirit may also represent the human spirit manifest in pre-eternity and ultimately liberated at death from the prison of its body.[18]

Allusions to wine's spiritual properties abound in the wine verse of the later Abbasid, Andalusian, and Ayyubid poets, many of whom imitated the wine odes of Abū Nuwās. Newer, popular poetic forms including the strophic *zajal* and *muwashshaḥ* were used for wine songs, yet the forcefulness of some of this verse was often replaced by a self-satisfied, even complacent view of existence. Wine odes composed by many of the court poets of this era were seldom revolutionary statements or existential musings. Rather, they were celebrations of the good life among like-minded, cultured friends and the ruling elite.[19] Nevertheless, wine remained an evocative spiritual metaphor as is clear from Abū Aᶜlā al-Maᶜarrī's (d. 449/1058) *Risālat al-Ghufrān* in which the pleasures of Paradise are often portrayed by pre-Islamic verses including those on wine. In such a context, the wine of pre-Islamic Arabia serves as a symbol for the immortality to be tasted in Heaven's eternal gardens.[20]

Two Intoxications

Of course, Sufis did their part to allegorize wine because they used sobriety (*ṣaḥw*) and intoxication (*sukr*) as metaphors for states of mystical experience. The individual heedless of God's living presence is described as sober, whereas the mystic overpowered by a spiritual state is said to be intoxicated due to his loss of self-consciousness and reason. Once the mystic has recovered from this bewildering yet blissful state, he again becomes sober. But many Sufis have regarded this second sobriety to be far superior to the first and to intoxication as well. Now the mystic is said to be aware of both God and the world and so less prone to error through unconscious exuberance.[21] It was only natural, then, that wine became a symbol of the powerful and intoxicating mystical love passing between God and His worshipper, and Sufi manuals often cite wine verse to illustrate this loving relationship:[22]

fa-ḥālāka lī ḥālāni ṣaḥwun wa-sakratun
fa-lā ziltu fī ḥālayya aṣḥū wa-askaru

Your two states are mine:
sobriety and drunkenness;
so I stay in both,
getting drunk while sober

* * * * *

lī sakratānī wa-li-n-nudmāni wāḥdatun
shay'un khuṣiṣtu bi-hi min baynahumu waḥdī

To me two intoxications,
to my companions one;
by this I am marked
among them alone![23]

Many such verses are cited anonymously in Sufi works, and the last example appears to have been taken from a poem by Abū Nuwās, clearly demonstrating the mystical reinterpretation of earlier wine poetry.[24] Sufis, however, also composed their own wine verses. Al-Ḥallāj, for instance, is credited with a number of short wine poems that refer to union with God in markedly Christian terms:[25]

muzijat rūḥuka fī rūḥī kamā
tumzaju-l-khamratu bi-l-mā'i-l-zalāli
fa-idhā massaka shai'un massanī
fa-idhā anta anā fī kulli ḥāli

Your spirit is mixed in mine
just as wine is mixed in purest water.
So if something touches you, it touches me,
since you are me in every state.

As we have seen, Muslim mystics, including al-Ḥallāj, often favored the *ghazal* tradition to speak of their love of God and union with Him, but mystical wine has always held a prominent place in their poetic canon. Like most early Sufi verse, that on wine rarely exceeds a verse or two, but longer wine poems were composed by Sufis including Ibn al-Shāhrazūrī, who is exuberant in the following poem on the transformative effects of spiritual intoxication among the Sufis (*qawm*, "folk"):[26]

yā nadīmī qarribi-l-qadaḥā
inna sukra-l-qawmi qad ṭafaḥā

O my drinking mate, bring the cup near
for the folk's intoxication has overflowed!
Quench me from its treasure troves—
ignore blamers and advisors—
With a deep red wine sparkling,
dancing joyously in its cup.
It was not defiled by mixing;
if filtered at night, bright noon would arise,
And one tempted to greed by selfishness
would become magnanimous.
He was veiled, but when its cup
came to his hand, he was revealed!

A similar tone is present in a poem by the North African Sufi master Abū Madyan who speaks of the wine of love whose intoxicating rapture (*wajd*) leads to a reeling dance and gnosis:[27]

qul li-lladhī yanhā ᶜana-l-wajdi 'ahlahu
idhā lam tadhuq maᶜanā sharāba-l-hawā daᶜnā

8) Say to one who forbids the folk from rapture (*wajd*):
"If you've not tasted the wine of passion with us, leave off!

9) "When spirits tremble longing for reunion,
then, yes, the bodies will dance, though you don't get it!

10) "Consider the caged bird, young man,
when it recalls its homelands, it is moved to sing,

11) "And what is in its heart breaks forth in song,
and without and within, it flaps its wings,

12) "And it dances in its cage longing for reunion,
as the bodies of sensitive souls are moved by its song.

13) "Such are the lovers' spirits, young man;
desires drive them on to the world sublime!"

Abū Madyan's analogy of the caged bird echoes Ibn Sīnā's "Ode to the Soul" (vv. 10–13). However, Abū Madyan's use of many Sufi technical terms throughout his poem leaves no doubt that it is the mystical rite of audition and recollection that intoxicated the lovers and left them with gnosis. The poet berates his blamer who is young and inexperienced and so requires instruction as to why the ecstatic lovers appear to loose control and shout and dance (vv. 1–18). Yet, they are not guilty of any sin, because it is love, not wine, that has intoxicated and so moved them (vv. 19–22).[28] Other Sufis, too, following well-established literary conventions, combined traditional love and wine imagery in longer poems to intimate mystical beliefs and experiences, as in the following verses by Yaḥyā al-Suhrawardī, who opens his wine ode with the image of lovers in the throes of separation pining for their beloved and an intoxicating union (vv. 1–2):[29]

abadan taḥinnu ilaykumu-l-arwāḥu
wa-wiṣālukum rayḥānuhā wa-r-rāḥu

1) Always the spirits long for you;
union with you is their sweet basil and wine.
2) The hearts (*qulūb*) of your worthy lovers yearn for you;
the delicious taste of your encounter will please them.

But the lovers face a dilemma: If they publicly profess their love, they will disgrace the beloved and reveal their own selfish weakness. Yet if the lovers try to conceal their feelings from others in order to protect the beloved from gossip and slander, their tears of anguish will give them away while the symptoms of love-sickness will leave no doubt as to the real source of their malady (vv. 3–6). It is for the beloved, then, to resolve the problem by excusing the lovers' unseemly behavior resulting from effusive passion. Were the beloved to show mercy to those who truly love him, it would not be a crime since, after all, the lovers' sole concern is for meeting (*liqā'*) and satisfying (*riḍā*) their lord. The poet beseeches the beloved to pierce the dark night of separation with union's illuminating rays (vv. 7–9), and the beloved grants his wish:

> 10) He loved them truly, and to him they were devoted,
> for in the light of their hearts were the niche and the lamp *(al-mishkātu wa-l-miṣbāḥu)*
> 11) They savored the moment (*waqt*) delicious with their nearness (*qurb*);
> the cups were delicate, the wine a delight.

Here, al-Suhrawardī alludes to the Qur'ān in his account of those who have attained union. The lovers have become totally absorbed in the beloved such that their hearts (*qulūb*) have been illuminated with the divine light. Al-Suhrawardī refers directly to one of the most mystical passages of the Qur'ān, the celebrated "Light Verse" (24:35):[30]

> God is the light of the heavens and the earth. A parable for His light is like a niche in which is a lamp, the lamp within a glass (*ka-mishkātin wa-fīhā miṣbāḥun*). The glass is like a shining star lit from a blessed olive tree of neither east nor west; its oil almost shines though fire has not touched it. Light upon light, God guides to His light whom He wills, and God strikes parables for humanity, and God is omniscient.

Al-Suhrawardī's wine ode resonates with that of Abū Madyan, as both use a number of Sufi technical terms, adding further mystical associations to this wine, as in verse 11 of al-Suhrawardī's poem where the moment (*waqt*) in proximity (*qurb*) to the beloved grants the enlightened lovers a taste of rarified wine. These accomplished lovers can reveal their secret (*sirr)* without guilt because they are totally absorbed in the beloved. By giving themselves totally to him, they receive a new life. Obediently, they wait upon their lord, desiring nothing else, and they savor the mention (*dhikr*) of the beloved, which transforms every moment of their existence (vv. 12–17). By means of their *dhikr*, their recollection, they come into the beloved's presence where they lose all sense of self and fall into ecstasy before the beatific vision (vv. 18–20).[31] Then, in the final verses of the poem, al-Suhrawardī exhorts his audience to imitate these great heroes, and once again he calls for a spiritual wine that will be found in religion, but not in the grape:

> 21) Try to copy them if you can't be like them,
> for imitation of nobility brings prosperity.
> 22) Rise, drinking mates, to the wine,
> for the cups have gone round in its tavern: Bring me
> 23) A vintage from generosity's vine in the flask of religion,
> not a wine crushed by a peasant!

Al-Suhrawardī composed this poem within the framework of the *khamrīyah* genre, and it is the lord and his drinking companions who are the poet's major concern. This poem clearly echoes earlier Arabic accounts of drinking sessions at the royal court, but al-Suhrawardī's Qur'ānic and Sufi references leave little doubt that the lord of his ode is God, while the court is His divine presence in Paradise. Within this extended analogy, wine symbolizes mystical union, which intoxicates and drowns the mystics; it deadens their physical senses and washes away all traces of their selfish wills in order to revive them in spiritual immortality. Though wine is occasionally mentioned in the poem, al-Suhrawardī did not substantially develop this topic and its related themes. About a century later, however, Ibn al-Fāriḍ would detail the amazing spiritual qualities of wine and its effects in several poems, one of which has come to be regarded as the finest mystical wine ode in Islam.

Drunk by a Glance

Ibn al-Fāriḍ's most famous poem on wine is called simply the *al-Khamrīyah*, the "Wine Ode." Yet, two of his other poems bear traces of the genre. First, perhaps his greatest poem, the *Naẓm al-Sulūk* ("Poem of the Sufi Way"), also called the *al-Tā'īyah al-Kubrā* ("Ode in T—Major"), begins and ends with explicit references to wine. However, due to the poem's great length and its diverse themes and references, the *Naẓm al-Sulūk* is far more than a poem on wine, and I will examine this poem in detail in the next chapter. A second poem also resonates with Arabic poetry on wine, though it may be read as a love poem as well:[32]

adir dhikra man ahwā wa-law bi-malāmī
fa-inna aḥādītha-l-ḥabībi mudāmī

1) Pass round remembrance of the one I desire,
though that be to blame me,
for tales of the beloved
are my wine.

2) Let my heart witness the one I love,
though she be far away,
in blame's fantasy,
not the phantom dream of sleep.

3) For her memory is sweet to me
in what ever form,
even if those rebuking me
mix it with bitter grief,

4) As if my blamer
brought good news of union,
though I had not hoped
for even "Peace!" in reply.

5) My spirit be her ransom,
in loving her I have lost it;
my fate was at hand
before my day of death.

6) Yet, because of her, my disgrace is sweet,
and savory still is being thrown
and broken down
from my high station.

7) For her sake, my open shame is right,
so too my wanton ways
and ride for sin,
not my righteous ways of old.

Similar to al-Suhrawardī and Abū Madyan, Ibn al-Fāriḍ likens remembrance (*dhikr*) of his lost love to wine, which, whether pure or mixed, is passed around to console the lover in the beloved's absence (vv. 1–3). Again, the lover claims to have traded his selfish life for one of true love, and so he is unscathed by those who blame him for immoderate passion. Because he does not sleep, vigilantly awaiting the beloved's return, the lover cannot find consolation in dreams of his love. Therefore, he hopes to refresh his memories with the blamers' reproach, which contains mention of the beloved. But here too, the success of his efforts is in doubt, for it is "as if" the blamer brought glad tidings of a future union (v. 4). Nevertheless, the lover savors the pains of separation and his public disgrace that still taste sweet because he suffers for love (vv. 5–7).

As is frequently the case in Arabic wine poetry, wine becomes mixed with the love and beloved of the *ghazal*.[33] Indeed, the mention of *aḥādīth*, the plural of *ḥadīth*, together with *ḥabīb*, in verse1 would seem to indicate that the beloved is Muhammad or his light, as was the case in several of Ibn al-Fāriḍ's *ghazals*.[34] But then we read verses 8 and 9:[35]

uṣallī fa-ashdū ḥīna atlū bi-dhikrihā
wa-aṭrabu fī-l-miḥrābi wa-hya imāmī
wa-bi-l-ḥajji in aḥramtu labbaytu bi-smihā
wa-ᶜanhā arā-l-imsāka fiṭra ṣiyāmī

8) I pray and so chant when I recite
in memory of her,
and I delight in the prayer-niche,
while she is my *imām*,

9) And on pilgrimage, in a pure state,
I cry "*labbayka*" in her name,
and I see restraint
to be the breaking of my fast.

The Muslim rites named in these verses: Prayer, recitation of the Qur'ān, pilgrimage, and fasting, are properly performed in submission to and worship of God and to no one else, not even the prophet Muhammad. Furthermore, the religious intent of these verses becomes more pronounced when they are compared to two verses ascribed to the ᶜUdhrī poet Majnūn:[36]

arānī idhā ṣallaytu yammamtu naḥwahā
bi-wajhī wa-in kāna-l-muṣallā warā'iyā
wa-mābiyya ishrākun wa-lakinna ḥubbahā
wa-ᶜuẓmu-l-jawā aᶜayā-ṭ-ṭība-l-madāwiyā

I see myself when I pray
turning my face toward her
though the place of prayer
is behind me.

I am no polytheist,
but love for her
and awesome passion
baffle the doctor's cure!

Although the ʿUdhrī poet turns his back to the prayer niche and, by extension, to God in order to follow his passion, the lover of Ibn al-Fāriḍ's poem claims to behold his beloved leading him in prayer (*imāmī*) or, as the commentator al-Būrīnī has suggested, before him (*amāmī*) in the prayer niche.[37] This alternative reading agrees nicely with the lover's recitation of the Qur'ān in recollection (*dhikr*) of the beloved, his calling out in her name *labbayka*, "Here I am Lord, at Your service!" which is an essential rite of the pilgrimage, and with the lover's "fasting" from all things save the beloved.[38] However, the beloved's presence is fleeting, and the lover again describes his deteriorating physical and psychological state. This long section of the poem would be at home in any of Ibn al-Fāriḍ's *ghazals*:[39]

10) Yet my tears are clear proof of my affair
running fast over what has passed,
while my sobbing speaks true
of my love thirst.

11) On the edge of night,
my heart (*qalb*) is parched for love;
in the morning,
my anguished eyes shed tears.

12) My heart and eye:
one caught by her beauty's subtle sense (*maʿnā jamālihā*);
the other lured
by her soft, subtle stature.

13) So my sleep is lost,
while to morning I bid: "Stay!" (*baqā*)
for I have found sleeplessness
as my desire grows.

14) My bond (*ʿaqdī*) and pact (*ʿahdī*)
are neither loosed or withdrawn,
rapture (*wajd*) my joy,
burning passion my affliction.

15) As sickness wears my body out,
secrets show through,
my wasting bones becoming
an essence (*maʿnā*) among them,

16) Thrown down by love's passion,
ribs pierced,
eyelids lashed
by endless bloody tears,

17) Passion so pure, light as air
I flew with dawn's breeze,
the zephyr's breaths
my companions,

18) Sound yet sick, so seek me
from the east wind
where wasting willed
my station (*maqāmī*).

19) I was hidden, consumed,
concealed even from consumption
and from my disease's cure
and the cooling of my burning thirst.

20) I knew no one save passion
who knew my place,
my keeping the secrets,
and guarding my honor.

21) All that love left me
was sorrow,
grief and affliction,
endless disorders.

22) As for my burning desire,
my patience and consolation,

nothing remains (*lam yubqa*) with me
but their names.

23) Let one free of my passion
safely save his own soul.
As for you my soul:
"Leave in peace!"

24) "Forget her!" said my accuser,
burning to blame me
on her account.
"Forget blaming me!" I countered.

25) Could I seek solace instead?
Who would guide me,
since every guide in love
follows me?

26) In my every limb is every love
flowing toward her,
desire tugging
on my reins.

Once again, Ibn al-Fāriḍ's account of the lover's sufferings is replete with Sufi technical terms suggesting a spiritual purgation of selfishness in hopes of a union with the beloved.[40] In the final three verses of this passage the blamer returns to scold the poet, who promptly rebuffs him in the name of his abiding love. In many of Ibn al-Fāriḍ's *ghazals* and some of his *qaṣīdahs*, too, this is followed by the lover's oath of fidelity to the beloved, and his prayer for acceptance. Yet in this poem, the lover is reunited with his beloved:[41]

27) She swayed as she walked, so we thought
her quivering sides
to be branches on a dune;
beneath a full moon,

28) So in my every limb
was every heart
hit by every arrow
whenever she gazed with pleasure.

29) Had she unrolled my body,
she would have seen in every essence
every heart holding
every burning passion.

30) In union (*waṣl*) with her,
a year is but a moment to me,
while exile's hour
is like a year to bear.

31) When we met in the evening
joined by two straight paths,
one from her tent
the other from mine,

32) We swerved a little
from the tribe
to a place without a spy
or slanderer with lies.

33) And I rubbed my cheek in the dust
for her to step on,
so she said: "Good news for you!
Kiss my veil!"

34) But my soul (*nafsī*)
would not have it,
guarding me jealously
to keep my longing pure.

35) So we passed the night together
as my command willed over desires;
I saw kingship my kingdom
and time my slave!

For this scene of union, Ibn al-Fāriḍ drew on a number of motifs and themes common to early Arabic poetry. Perhaps these culturally laden images required little embellishment to be fully evocative, for Ibn al-Fāriḍ's rhetorical display is confined largely to antithesis and a few word plays. The lover and his companions marvel at the swaying beloved whose supple body accentuates her full buttocks and moonlike face (v. 27).[42] So enamored is the poet that he becomes the archetypal lover, encompassing within himself all passion and every heart wounded by love. This totality is rhetorically reinforced by the six-fold repetition within two verses of the word *kull* ("each," "every," "all"):

wa-lī kullu ᶜuḍwin fīhi kullu ḥashan bihā
idhā mā ranat waqᶜun li-kulli sihāmi
wa-law basaṭat jismī ra'at kulla jawharin
bihi kullu qalbin fīhi kullu gharāmi

28) So in my every limb
was every heart
hit by every arrow
whenever she gazed with pleasure.

29) Had she unrolled my body,
she would have seen in every essence
every heart holding
every burning passion.

The period of union (*waṣl*, v. 30) with the beloved is fleeting, while a moment of separation is an eternity. The rendezvous takes place in the evening, a time of transition neither day nor night in which physical surroundings gradually dissolve into darkness. The lover becomes oblivious not only to the material world but also to society ("tribe"), to his intellect ("spy"), and base desires ("slanderer"). True to the ᶜUdhrī ideal, no physical union takes place, yet the lover abides with his beloved. The lover restrains himself and his concupiscent desires (*nafsī*, v. 35) thus proving his pure, unselfish love:

wa-bitnā kamā shā'a-qtirāḥī ᶜalā-l-munā
arā-l-mulka milkī wa-l-zamāna ghulāmī

36) So we passed the night together
as my command willed over desires;
I saw kingship my kingdom
and time my slave!

In this final verse, Ibn al-Fāriḍ underscores the profundity of the meeting with references to time and the young slave (*ghulām*), which frequent Arabic wine poems. But in this special union, the lover does not lose his love to the tyrant time, rather time is at the lovers' bidding and so, in union, the lover conquers time and space.[43] Such a conclusion differs markedly from Ibn al-Fāriḍ's *ghazals* and *qaṣīdahs*, yet this is the rule for his wine odes where love eradicates selfish desire in a moment of intoxicating union, and this is most evident in Ibn al-Fāriḍ's *al-Khamrīyah*.

Immortal Wine

sharibnā ʿalā dhikri-l-ḥabībi mudāmata
sakirnā bihā min qabli an yukhlaqa-l-karmu[44]

1) In memory of the beloved
we drank a wine;
we were drunk with it
before creation of the vine.

2) The full moon its glass, the wine
a sun circled by a crescent;
when it is mixed,
how many stars appear!

3) If not for its bouquet,
I would not have found its tavern;
if not for its flashing gleam,
how could imagination picture it?

4) Time preserved nothing of it
save one last breath,
concealed like a secret
in the breasts of the wise.

5) But if it is recalled among the tribe
the worthy ones
are drunk by morn,
without shame or sin.

6) From the depths of the jars
it arose, though truly,
nothing remained
save a name.

7) Yet if one day
it crosses a man's mind,
then joy will dwell in him,
and anxiety depart.

8) Could the tavern mates see
the seal of its jar,
without the wine that seal alone
would make them drunk,

9) And could they sprinkle it
on a dead man's earth,
the spirit would return to him,
his body revived.

10) Could they fling
into the shadow of its trellised vine
a sick man on the point of death,
disease would flee him,

11) Could they bring a cripple
near its tavern, he would walk,
and from mention of its flavor,
the dumb would talk.

12) Could the breaths of its bouquet
spread out in the east,
one stuffed-up in the west
would smell again,

13) And were a touching palm
tinged by its cup,
one would not stray at night,
a star in hand.

14) Could it be unveiled in secret
to the blind, he would see,
and from the strainer's sound,
the deaf would hear,

15) Were the riders
to seek its soil

with one scorpion-stung among them,
the poison would not harm him.

16) Could the wizard write
the letters of its name
on the brow of one struck by the jinn,
the tracings would cure and cleanse him,

17) And were its name inscribed
upon the army's standard,
all beneath that banner
would fall drunk from the sign.

18) It refines the morals
of the tavern mates
and guides the irresolute
to resolution's path,

19) He whose hand never knew munificence
is generous,
while one lacking in forbearance
bears the rage of anger.

20) And could the stupid one among the folk
win a kiss from its strainer,
he would sense the hidden sense
of its fine qualities.

21) They say to me: "Do describe it,
for you know its character well!"
Indeed, I have word
of its attributes:

22) Purity not water,
subtlety not air,
light but not fire,
spirit without body.

23) Lovely features guiding
those describing it to praise;
how fine their prose and poetry
on wine.[45]

24) One who never knew it
is moved by its mention,
just as one longing for Nuʿm
is stirred when she is recalled.

25) But they said: "You have drunk sin!"
No, indeed, I drank only
that whose abstention
is sin to me.

26) So cheers to the monastery's folk!
How often they were drunk with it
though they never drank it,
but only longed to,

27) While it made me drunk
before my birth,
abiding always with me
though my bones be worn away.

28) So take it straight,
though if you must, then mix it,
but your turning away
from the beloved's mouth is wrong.

29) Watch for it in the tavern,
try to uncover it there
amid melodious tunes
where it becomes the prize.

30) It never dwells with anxiety
at any time or place,
just as sorrow
never lives with song.

31) Be drunk from it,
if only for the life of an hour,
and you will see time a willing slave
under your command.

32) For there is no life in this world
for one who lives here sober;

who does not die drunk on it,
prudence has passed him by.

33) So let him weep for himself,
one who wasted his time
never having won a share
or measure of this wine.

Ibn al-Fāriḍ's wine is something much more rarified than a vintage of the grape. Taking up a theme noted earlier in verse by Abū Nuwās, the poet says that his wine existed prior to creation,[46] intoxicating him and his companions as they drank to the memory of their beloved. Ibn al-Fāriḍ underscores the heavenly nature of this drink by combining several traditional astral images of the cup and its contents. He compares the round cup brimming with a shining white wine to a full moon reflecting the sun. This sun is circled by a crescent moon, perhaps a reference to the lip of the cup reflected in the wine, or to the cup-bearer, who circles among the drinkers bending to serve them. Star-like bubbles arise in the cup as the wine is mixed with water (vv. 1–2). This exceptional wine, however, is not easy to find, and to drink it may be impossible. If not for the wine's musky fragrance and brilliant flash, the poet would have never known of its existence or found the tavern where it was served. Although this wine flowed in pre-eternity, now within time it has all but disappeared. Here, as in earlier wine odes and the larger *qaṣīdah* tradition, time (*dahr*, v. 4) has sundered the poet from his beloved, and his paradise was lost (vv. 3–4).

Still, traces of this potent wine remain though hidden in time like half-forgotten secrets guarded by the wise. A mere mention of this wine could serve the tribe as an intoxicating morning draught, while a passing thought of it would fill a man with joy. Yet in either case, the poet tells us, no sin would be committed for although drinking wine is forbidden to all Muslims, there is no wine to drink (vv. 5–7). Indeed nothing is left of it save a name (*ism*, v. 6), but what miracles this wine could perform if only the wine were here. The sight of its sealed jar alone would make the drinking mates drunk; a libation sprinkled on a grave would bring the dead to life. In the shadow of its vine, the sick would be cured, and near its tavern, the crippled would walk. Mention of its taste would cause the dumb to speak; its scent would return smell to one with a stuffy nose, and its luminous hue would guide those lost in darkness. The blind would see if it was unveiled, and from the sound of its strainer, the deaf would hear. One stung by a scorpion would be cured by its soil, while the possessed man would be freed by a tracing of its letters, and could its name be written on an army's standard, the soldiers would become intoxicated, courageous warriors. This wine could make course companions refined, the faint of heart determined, the miser generous, one quick to anger forbearing, and the ignorant insightful (vv. 8–20).

But this will not happen as Ibn al-Fārid repeatedly stresses the phrase *wa-law* ("and if only . . ."). *Law* is the Arabic particle denoting the impossibility of the conditional sentence ("Were it that . . . but it is not to be"). The particle begins verses 8 to16, occurs in the middle of verse17, and then returns to begin verse 20. These verses, however, not only speak of the past and deny the earthly presence of this wine, they also assert the wine's other-worldly character, and Ibn al-Fārid consistently employs antithesis and word play to draw attention to the transformative power of this amazing vintage. Moreover Ibn al-Fārid has traced the wine from the soil, vine, and trellis, to its production and storage in the wine jar, which is wrapped, and sealed. Then the wine is decanted with a strainer, and Ibn al-Fāriḍ mentions the sound of the wine, its bouquet, hue, and flavor. The wine affects all the senses of the drinking companions and their human behavior, while this wine also has medicinal uses to cure poison, madness, and other maladies; in fact a libation of the wine could revive the dead. Ibn al-Fāriḍ's extensive list of miracles and cures covers an astonishing range of traditional wine themes and images, and this poetic *tour de force* demonstrates his considerable literary knowledge and skill, while leaving no doubt as to the spiritual essence of his wine.[47]

Ibn al-Fāriḍ then shifts to the present as he concludes his description of his beloved wine and builds to the poem's climax. The poet is asked to describe this wine, for he is clearly a connoisseur and familiar with its ethereal qualities (vv. 21–22):

ṣafā'un wa-lā mā'un wa-luṭfun wa-lā hawan
wa-nūrun wa-lā nārun wa-rūḥun wa-lā jismu

22) Purity not water;
subtlety not air;
light but not fire;
spirit without body.

Others, too, have praised this glorious wine, and accounts of it continue to stir up a desire to taste the wine and rekindle some lost love, even in those who never knew of it (vv. 23–24). The poet then rebukes his blamers who previously charged him with sin, for clearly his wine is not the forbidden one of the grape. The poem's mood now shifts from one of a nostalgic reverie characteristic of the *nasīb* to assume a more boisterous and assertive tone, a traditional favorite ending of many wine odes and *qaṣīdahs*. The poet wishes good health to the monks of the monastery, the purveyors of wine in many Arabic poems. Although the monks have never tasted this long-sought vintage, they are intoxicated with it, as is the poet. Indeed, the poet claims that prior to his birth, he was drunk and will remain so long after his bones have turned to dust (vv. 26–27):

wa-ᶜindiya minhā nashwatun qabla nasha'tī
maᶜī abadan tabqā wa-in baliya-l-ᶜaẓmu

27) While it made me drunk
before my birth,
abiding always with me
though my bones be worn away.

The poet was predestined for this intoxication just as the ᶜUdhrī lover will forever long for his fated beloved, and Ibn al-Fārid's verse once again resonates with one ascribed to Majnūn:[48]

khalīlayya adwā'ī bi-Laylā qadīmatun
muḥaddadatun tabqā wa-tablā ᶜiẓāmiyā

My two friends, my maladies from Laylā
are ancient and predestined;
they abide
while my bones are worn away.

Rising to the climax of the poem, Ibn al-Fāriḍ commands one coveting this wine to take it straight, though if that be too strong, he may mix the wine. But the seeker must never turn away from the beloved's mouth for this is the source of Ibn al-Fāriḍ's wine (v. 28). Often in classical Arabic poetry, the beloved has a cool mouth with a bright flashing smile and a fragrant, musky breath, and the poet longs to be intoxicated by her kiss, drunk on the wine-like moisture of her lips.[49] Ibn al-Fāriḍ elegantly blends these *khamrīyah* and *ghazal* motifs throughout this poem to intimate love's conquering power, and he explicitly links the wine, beloved, and intoxication beginning with his opening verse. At the beginning and end of his ode, Ibn al-Fārid refers to the object of his affection with the feminine pronoun *hā*, which can refer to wine or a female beloved, such as Nuᶜm. Mention of the wine and its taste (v. 11: *dhikrā madhāqatihā*, v. 24: *dhikrihā*) form obvious parallels with the recollection and mention of the beloved (v.1: *dhikr al-ḥabīb*; v.24: *dhukirat Nuᶜm*). Furthermore, the wine's bouquet has the scent of musk (*sadhā*), like the beloved's breath, while the wine's flashing splendor (*sanā*) resembles her bright teeth (*asnān*) (v. 3). The wine is "unveiled" in secret (v. 14), its strainer (v. 20: *lathm*) kissed like a veil (*lathm*), and wine's fine, cooling qualities (v. 20: *shamā'il*) are comparable to the beloved's bright smile (v. 28: *ẓalm*) and her moist teeth, cool and white like the snow (*ẓalm*). The dew of her lips is the poet's wine (v. 28). The secret revealed, Ibn al-Fāriḍ ends his ode, perhaps echoing Ṭarafah and al-Aᶜshā, as he commands the seeker to go to the tavern, where music plays and joy prevails, in order to "uncover" (*istajil*) the wine, to unveil it like a new bride (*istajlā*). Once in this wine's embrace, the intoxicated will seem to master time, if only for an hour. But time drives on this world below, and so one who lives sober will only die having passed up his chance to pass away dead to the world but alive in love (vv. 29–33).

Wine of the Covenant

This more literary reading of Ibn al-Fāriḍ's *al-Khamrīyah* does not exclude possible deeper meanings, which have been sought out for centuries by Muslim mystics. More than a dozen commentaries have been written on this poem, and of them, one of the oldest and certainly most influential is the *Sharḥ al-Qaṣīdah al-Khamrīyah* composed by Dāwūd al-Qayṣarī (d. ca. 747/1346). Al-Qayṣarī was an adherent of Ibn al-ᶜArabī's mystical theosophy, and he lucidly summarized his own related beliefs and theories in his introduction to this work. Although his doctrinal positions undoubtedly appealed to many later commentators who borrowed extensively from his work, one need not share those beliefs to appreciate and, at times, be persuaded by al-Qayṣarī's interpretations of Ibn al-Fāriḍ's wine ode.[50]

In light of Ibn al-Fāriḍ's *ghazals*, al-Qayṣarī finds an allusion to the primordial covenant between God and humanity in verse 1 of the *Wine Ode*. Al-Qayṣarī equates the beloved (*ḥabīb*) with God, the true reality (*al-Ḥaqq*) and real beloved (*al-maḥbūb al-ḥaqīqī*); the poet and his companions stand for the pre-eternal spirits of human beings, whereas the vine represents the world of manifestation. Thus, the wine drunk before the vine's creation is the wine of Paradise, which cleanses its drinker of all traces of human volition, selfhood, and duality, and so restores him to his original state as an entity (*ᶜayn*) rapt within the unique and eternal divine essence (*al-dhāt al-ilāhīyah*). For al-Qayṣarī, the underlying themes of the poem are this original and originating love relationship between God and His worshipper, and the overpowering effects of its recollection (*dhikr*).[51]

Most commentators have also followed al-Qayṣarī's subsequent interpretation of verses 2 and 3 as portraying the emanation of God's love (= wine) throughout limited creation (= cup). After the covenant, God's absolute oneness (= the sun) is reflected into the dark world by the Light of Muhammad (= the full moon, *badr*) who in turn passes on a portion of his spiritual wisdom to his cousin and son-in-law, ᶜAlī (= the crescent moon) and then on to the Muslim saints and Sufi masters (= stars), who guide others to gnosis (*maᶜrifah*). Al-Qayṣarī supports his readings with *ḥadīth* and Qur'ānic quotations including (Q. 16:16) *wa-bi-n-najmi hum yahtadūna*: "And by the stars they are guided."[52] In verses 1 to 3, Ibn al-Fāriḍ most certainly alludes to Muhammad, the "beloved of God" (*ḥabīb Allāh*) or his light; Badr (v. 2: "full moon"), as we have seen earlier, was also the name of the site of Muhammad's first great victory. Significantly, Ibn al-Fāriḍ uses the verb *ihtadā* (v. 3: "to be guided") when speaking of the wine's bright flash that led the poet to the tavern, and *shadhā* (v. 3: "fragrance") may also refer to the legendary toothpick (*shadhā*) of the prophet Muhammad, the guide (*hādin*) for his people (e.g., Qur'ān 13:7).[53]

Al-Qayṣarī understands the wine's bouquet and luster to be the traces of absolute beauty remaining in creation, especially as embodied in beloveds of flesh and blood. These vestiges of the divine inspire the spiritually sensitive to search for God (= the tavern) in hopes of a taste of this mystical wine of love, which will ease life's hardships. Furthermore, it is the mystics graced with abiding union (*baqā'*) who, unbeknownst to others, preserve (v. 4: *yubqī*) this holy love, which has been all but lost (v. 6: *lam yabqa . . . illā*) in time since the Day of the Covenant. Continuing this line of interpretation in verses 5 and 6, the great mystics are the worthy ones (*ahl*) of humanity (*qawm*, "tribe") who become mystically intoxicated when God's love for them is mentioned or recalled (*dhukirat*) during the practice of *dhikr*. But the drunken Sufis are not to be blamed for their ecstatic behavior since they are the ones who keep alive love's presence (= last breath) deep within their hearts (= depths of the jars). These enlightened few comprehend the gnosis of divine love, which is known only by name among the rest of humanity mired in selfish existence.[54] Such a reading is encouraged by Ibn al-Fārid's word play *ḥushāshah* (v.

4: "last breath") and *ahshā* (v. 6: "depths"). This "last breath" of the pre-eternal wine also may symbolize the primordial spirit yet to be awakened within most human beings, who may still find joy if they recall their ancient covenant with God.

Al-Qayṣarī and other commentators go to great lengths to interpret symbolically the various characters and objects mentioned in Ibn al-Fāriḍ's extensive list of the wine's miraculous powers (vv. 8–20). The drinking companions are God's elect gnostics among the Sufis who would have been spiritually intoxicated had they seen the wine's seal. But this could never be since the wine was in pre-eternity while the seal (*khatm*), the historical Muhammad, the seal of the prophets (*khātm al-nabīīn* Q. 33:40), long ago left this earth below.[55] Al-Qayṣarī reads the remaining miracles in a similar vein. Generally speaking, the wine is divine love or gnosis (*al-maḥabbah; al-maᶜrifah al-ilāhīyah*), whereas the drinking companions, the wizard, the standard (of Muhammad = *liwā'*), and the strainer are symbols of the Sufi masters who dispense mystical wisdom. By contrast, those who are dead, dying, or in some way crippled in mind or body, including the five senses (*bukm*/dumb; *mazkūm*/stuffed-up; *akmah*/blind; *ṣumm*/deaf; *maslūᶜ*/scorpion-stung), represent the spiritually ignorant, incapacitated by their lusts and desires.[56] Although many of the detailed commentaries on particular characters appear highly speculative and overly analytical, Ibn al-Fāriḍ is certainly contrasting those who are spiritually alive in love to those dead to everything save their own selfish lives.

As for aspiring mystics, the commentators have usually identified them with those who ask the poet to describe the wine (v. 21). The poet, however, contrasts the wine's attributes (*awṣāf*) to what they are not, perhaps indicating the ineffability of love and gnosis, which may be alluded to with words and symbols, but truly experienced and known only within the heart. Whatever the case, Ibn al-Fāriḍ affirms the quintessential nature of this wine, which is a pure, luminous, and subtle spirit (*rūḥ*) untouched by any element of materiality. Although such accounts are only approximate, they arouse primal memories of humanity's former state and a desire to return there, just as the *dhikr* during a *samāᶜ* session stirs up a longing for God (vv. 22–24).[57]

Still, the inexperienced and impertinent aspirants mistake the poet's mystical wine for that of the grape. But this is not the case for the monks, who al-Qayṣarī equates with the realized mystics living in love (= the monastery) untainted by the material world.[58] Though they never drank the wine, they are often intoxicated perhaps because, like the poet, they recollect (*dhikr*) the beloved and their original meeting on the Day of the Covenant, prior to creation. This enables them to abide (*baqā'*) mystically with God despite the pain (*balā'*) and tribulation (*ibtilā'*) of mortal existence with the inevitability of physical death (vv. 24–27).[59] Thus the seeker should personally experience divine love, if only in diluted form since union's annihilation might well destroy the uninitiated.[60] But even a limited religious experience is better than nothing and a life without love. One should search for the beloved wine in the tavern, which in this instance al-Qayṣarī interprets as whatever leads to ecstasy whether that be a reading of the Qur'ān, the performance of *dhikr*, or the audition (*samā*ᶜ) of melodious voices in mystical assemblies (vv. 28–30).[61]

The final verses then forcefully convey to al-Qayṣarī and others the liberating and life-giving qualities of this mystical love. Although direct experience of it may be transient, lasting only an hour, for that moment, the mystic is annihilated and so abides, one with the unique divine essence (*al-dhāt al-aḥadīyah*), beyond the constraints of time and space (v. 31). Summing up this central message, al-Qayṣarī reveals the meaning of the poem's final, classic paradox. One who does not die, who does not destroy his selfish will, can never find true, everlasting happiness; he wastes his life seduced and blinded by useless vanities, never tasting a moment of the eternal life to come (vv. 32–33).[62] Although the *al-Khamrīyah's* more allusive and evocative language hardly supports the detailed mystical theologies of al-Qayṣarī and other commentators, they are right in detecting a distinctly mystical flavor in the poem. This is especially the case when the *al-Khamrīyah* is read in context of Ibn al-Fāriḍ's longest "wine-ode," the *al-Tā'īyah al-Kubrā*.

5

Poem of the Sufi Way in "T"–Major

The Great Ode

Ibn al-Fāriḍ's *Naẓm al-Sulūk* is a landmark in Arabic mystical poetry. For centuries, Sufis had drawn inspiration from the larger Arabic poetic tradition, yet no one before Ibn al-Fāriḍ had ever made such a grand poetic presentation of mystical thought in Arabic verse. This poem is composed of 760 verses in the meter *ṭawīl*, forming one of the longer poems composed in Arabic and the most famous one rhyming in "T," hence the poems other name the *al-Tā'īyah al-Kubrā* ("Ode in T–Major"). However, in contrast to other lengthy Arabic poems, such as those on Islamic law or Arabic grammar, the *al-Tā'īyah al-Kubrā* is not a didactic presentation of its subject as Ibn al-Fāriḍ frequently speaks of mystical love and life in the lyrical language of the ode and *ghazal*.[1] Because of its explicit Sufi themes, the *al-Tā'īyah al-Kubrā* soon became the focus of scholarly attention, and four major commentaries were composed on it in the century following the poet's death by Saᶜīd al-Dīn al-Farghānī (d. 699/1300), ᶜAfīf al-Dīn al-Tilimsānī (d. 690/1291), ᶜIzz al-Dīn al-Kāshānī (d. 735/1334), and Dāwūd al-Qayṣarī. These commentaries are quite useful, particularly regarding Ibn al-Fāriḍ's references and possible allusions to the Qur'ān, *ḥadīth*, and religious beliefs and rituals, and, occasionally, a commentator may link specific themes and images in Ibn al-Fāriḍ's other poems to the poet's more explicit statements and interpretations in the *al-Tā'īyah al-Kubrā*.[2]

As the *al-Tā'īyah al-Kubrā* became popular, several stories arose highlighting its spiritual character. One tale recounts that in a dream, Ibn al-Fāriḍ saw the prophet Muhammad who ordered him to entitle his long poem the *Naẓm al-Sulūk*. Through double entendre this two-word title can mean, "Stringing the String of Poetry's Pearls,"

"Poem of the Sufi Way," or "Order of the Spiritual Life," and all three meanings point to the poem's theme of the pilgrim's progress, while attesting to the Ibn al-Fāriḍ's posthumous reputation as a celebrated poet, Sufi, and spiritual master. Similarly, a second story relates how the poet would fall into deathlike trances for days, then recover and spontaneously recite verses directly inspired by God; these verses were then collected to form the *Naẓm al-Sulūk*.[3] Both legends were relayed in the commentary tradition that asserted the inspired, perhaps, even sacred character of the *al-Tā'īyah al-Kubrā*, and, not surprisingly, this poem and its commentaries became the lenses through which later generations have read Ibn al-Fāriḍ's *Dīwān*. Moreover, due to its length and explicit religious character, the *al-Tā'īyah al-Kubrā* often has been detached from Ibn al-Fāriḍ's poetic corpus to be read and analyzed as a mystical treatise in support of later theosophical systems.[4]

Certainly, close study of this poem discloses some of Ibn al-Fāriḍ's ideals and beliefs, and suggests possible avenues of interpretation for his other poems. But a reading of the *al-Tā'īyah al-Kubrā* in context of the poet's *Dīwān* will also reveal critical religious and poetic dimensions of this poem that have remained largely obscure. For instance, Ibn al-Fāriḍ undoubtedly composed the lengthy *al-Tā'īyah al-Kubrā* in segments. One tradition regarding the poem notes that when an ecstatic Ibn al-Fāriḍ emerged from his spiritual trance, he would recite between thirty and fifty verses rhyming in "T," then stop and wait for further inspiration. Although it would be quixotic to divide the poem on the basis of this tale, in the following analysis, I attempt to identify integral coherent sections of the poem, some of which could represent recitations made by the poet on a single occasion.[5]

Together Alone

saqatnī ḥumayyā-l-ḥubbi rāḥatu muqlatī
wa-ka'sī muḥayyā man ᶜani-l-ḥusni jallati[6]

1) The palm of my eye handed me
love's heady wine to drink,
and my glass was a face
of one revealing loveliness.

2) Drunk by my glance I caused
my companions to suppose
that drinking their wine
had brought my heart joy.

3) But by the dark pupils of the eyes
I did without my drinking bowl;
from the fine qualities of eyes, not cold wine,
came my intoxication.

4) So in the tavern of my drunkenness
was the time of my thanks to brave young men;
for despite my infamy,
I completely hid my love with them.

5) Then, when sobriety ceased,
I sought union with her;
shame's grip did not seize me
as I stretched out for her.

6) There was no one present with me there—
no persistent spy of fortune—
in the seclusion of the bridal chamber
where I revealed my all to her.

7) With my state as witness to rushing love—
my finding her effacing me,
losing her transfixing me—
I said:

8) "Before love annihilates
what remains of me to see you,
allow me
one backward glance,

9) "Or, if you forbid my seeing you,
bless my ear with:
'You will never see me!'
words sweet to one before me."

As in his *Wine Ode*, Ibn al-Fāriḍ blends images of wine, women, and love in the opening verses of the *al-Tā'īyah al-Kubrā*. The lover once saw his beloved, and so he likens his eye to a *sāqī*, or cup-bearer, who gave him the strong wine of love (*ḥumayyā-l-ḥubbi*) from a glass, which was the beloved's beautiful and life-giving countenance (*muḥayyā*; v. 1). Though the lover led his companions to believe that he drank what they did, he had in fact been intoxicated by a single glance at his beloved's face, which filled his heart with joy. Another possible reading of this second verse is that the poet fooled his companions "by means of a glance."[7] Yet, in Arabic love theory and *ghazal* poetry, it is the morally questionable "glance" (*naẓar/naẓrah*) at the beloved that sparks and fuels the lover's infatuation, which may ultimately consume him in madness or death.[8]

Ibn al-Fāriḍ continues to stress the special character of this wine by using word play to underscore and extend his wine/countenance metaphor to contrast the fine qualities (*shamā'il*) of the beloved's intoxicating eyes with wine cooled by the north wind (*shamūl*, v. 3). As was the case in the *al-Khamrīyah*, the lover's wine is not that of the grape, but neither is it the dew of the beloved's lips as in the *Wine Ode*; here, intoxication arises from seeing the beloved's eyes. This true source and secret of his intoxication, however, remained totally concealed by the drunken revelry of the tavern mates, and Ibn al-Fāriḍ employs paronomasia to allude to intoxication's mixing of time and space as the tavern of the lover's drunkenness (*ḥāni sukrī*) became the time for his thanksgiving (*ḥāna shukrī*; v. 4). The drunken lover was without shame or inhibition, and in high spirits he sought union with his mistress. This apparently reprehensible intoxication and shameless gaze on the beloved, however, were rendered lawful in the bridal chamber (*jalwah*; v. 6). There in total privacy without the continual presence of spies or restrictions, the lover confessed his deepest feelings to the beloved (vv. 5–6).

Returning to verse 1, the beloved "revealing loveliness" also is beyond or surpassing beauty (*ᶜani-l-ḥusni jallati*; v. 1), and so a single glance (*naẓrah*) may reveal the ineffable secret (*sirr*) of the divine presence within the mystic's inner most being (*sirr*; v. 2). It is quite possible that Ibn al-Fāriḍ is referring here to the very controversial Sufi practice of gazing at fair faces in search of living proof of divine beauty.[9] But whether exterior, interior, or both, this glance or gaze suggests spiritual contemplation, which may result in moments of illumination.[10] This, in turn, blesses the lover with an intoxication denied to his companions, who lack his profound insight (vv. 3–4):

wa-lammā-nqaḍā ṣaḥwī taqāḍaytu waṣlahā
wa-lam yaghshanī fī basṭihā qabḍu khashyati
wa-abthathtuhā mā bī wa-lam yaku hāḍirī
raqību baqā ḥaẓẓin bi-khalwati jalwati

5) Then, when sobriety ceased,
I sought union with her;
shame's grip did not seize me
as I stretched out for her.

6) There was no one present with me there—
no persistent spy of fortune—
in the seclusion of the bridal chamber
where I revealed my all to her.

This drunkenness (*sukr*) brought an end to the lover's restraint (= *ṣahw*, "sobriety"), and a feeling of exhilaration (*basṭ*) replaced his spiritual desolation (*qabḍ*) as he craved union (*waṣl*) with his love (v. 5). Alone in his private meditation (*khalwah*), the lover eluded those who had sought to prevent his meeting with the beloved, and so he could finally divulge what is within him (v. 6).

In these and subsequent verses, Ibn al-Fāriḍ continues to use Sufi terminology to describe the lover's state (*ḥāl*) as bearing witness (*shāhid*) to his fluctuation between self-effacing (*māḥī*) rapture (*wajd*) when he finds (*wajd*) his beloved, and the painful loneliness when she is lost (v. 7). Love had all but annihilated the lover (*yufnī*), and so he beseeched his beloved to permit him one last look before love ruined him completely. If this were not possible, a simple "never" (*lan*) would suffice to ease his pain as it had for another before him (vv. 7–9). This ancestor in love is none other than the prophet Moses. According to the Qur'ān (7:143) when Moses went to Sinai he said: "My Lord, appear to me that I may gaze upon you" (*rabbī arinī anẓur ilayka*). To which God replied: "You will never see Me!" (*lan tarānī*). God then revealed His splendor to the mountain, which crumbled sending Moses into a swoon. Ibn al-Fāriḍ's Qur'ānic allusion implies that the lover can never see his beloved, who if she be God, may be seen only in Paradise. Still, the lover hoped for some word of consolation from his beloved, to ease his pain, just as God answered the prayers of His suffering prophets (vv. 9–16).[11]

The lover goes on to claim that his own intoxicating passion could have destroyed the mountain prior to God's appearance. Continuing to complain of his plight in Qur'ānic and prophetic terms, the lover says that passion blazes in him like firebrands taken from the Burning Bush; his tears are like Noah's flood, while the fire of his love burns like the flames surrounding Abraham. Jacob's sorrow for his lost Joseph can hardly compare with the lover's grief for his departed beloved, whereas Job's affliction is but a portion of his own tribulation (vv. 10–16). These many references to divine encounters and to tests and miracles sent by God to His chosen prophets, strongly suggest that the beloved of this poem is something more than flesh and blood. As we saw earlier, Qur'ānic allusion and quotation are among the devices employed by Ibn al-Fāriḍ to reinterpret mystically key images and motifs of Arabic poetry: the reverie and the beloved, wine and intoxication, love's secret and its concealment. Furthermore, Ibn al-Fāriḍ's consistent use in this poem of multiple terms and antitheses prominent in Sufi lexicons leaves little doubt that the *al-Tā'īyah al-Kubrā* is presenting, at one level, a mystical allegory.

Ibn al-Fāriḍ next compares the lover to the emaciated camel driven relentlessly by the riders. He is so wasted away that his true being as a lover has been exposed (vv. 17–29). Ibn al-Fāriḍ invokes this and other *qaṣīdah* and *ghazal* motifs to detail the lover's wretched condition and his necessary total destruction at the hands of love. The lover then excuses himself for revealing his love because total passivity is required with respect to the beloved (vv. 30–43). He ceases to complain and begins, instead, to praise the trials and afflictions that he has faced, because his physical and psychological distress has rendered him a worthy adherent of love's creed (vv. 44–61):

58) He who tangles with beauty,
I think will see
his soul thrown down
from precious life to ruin.

59) But a soul that thinks
it will not see trouble in love
is turned away
when it turns to passion.

60) For no stable spirit
ever won its wish;
no soul loving the quiet life
ever wished for love.

61) Where is tranquility?
Far from the lover's life;
enclosing Eden's garden
are hateful, horrible things (*al-makārih*)![12]

The lover claims to have remained loyal to love and the memory of his beloved despite her absence and scorn for him (vv. 62–63). He declares love to be his law and rite (*madhhab; millah*; v. 64) such that for him to think of anything beside the beloved would be apostasy. Ending his testimony before his beloved who will judge his case (vv. 65–66), the poet swears to his steadfast love:

67) By love's strong bond between us
never weakened
by thought of being broken—
the best of oaths;

68) By your taking the covenant of love
where I did not appear
in the soul's manifest disguise
in the passing shadow of my clay;

69) By the priority of a pact
unbroken since I pledged it,
and a subsequent bond beyond
being loosed by intervening time;

70) By the rays rising
in your glowing face—
from their splendor all full moons
will soon disappear—

71) And by the attribute of your perfection,
from which creation's fairest form
and most straight in stature
sought support;

72) By the quality of your majesty—
near it, my suffering is savory;
my slaughter sweet,
before it—

73) And by the secret of your beauty
with which every luminous face
arose in all the worlds
and waxed full;

74) By a loveliness captivating reason,
leading me to a passion
making my weakness lovely
before your strength,

75) And by a subtle sense in you
beneath that loveliness—

by it I saw it, as it was too fine
for the grasp of even an insightful eye—

76) Truly you are my heart's desire,
my farthest wish,
my final aim,
my choice and chosen.

These verses compose the longest pledge of fidelity to be found in the *Dīwān* as Ibn al-Fāriḍ raises the emotional pitch of the *al-Tā'īyah al-Kubrā* with a highly rhetorical succession of oaths. Like his ᶜUdhrī ancestors, the lover swears by his unbroken bond of eternal love with his beloved, whose refulgent beauty eclipses all others. Indeed, all loveliness in creation is derived from her perfection and beauty, which are beyond comprehension. Only by being slain in passion can the lover bear witness to his true love of her who is his sole desire. Once again, as in his other oaths and the opening verses of the *al-Khamrīyah*, Ibn al-Fāriḍ invokes the primordial covenant (*mīthāq*, v. 68), which God has never abrogated; the lover likewise claims to have kept his vow of obedience and servitude to his beloved. Ibn al-Fāriḍ underscores the timelessness of this pact with antithesis and paronomasia as the prior covenant (*ṣābiqi ᶜahdin*) is followed by the subsequent bond (*lāḥiqi ᶜaqdin*; v. 69). Although the covenant is that of pre-eternity, the bond may represent the lover's mystical bond on earth, and, by extension, the ties between various communities and their prophets.[13] In light of Ibn al-Fāriḍ's *ghazals*, this subsequent bond may refer to the Day of Resurrection when humanity will again come face to face with their creator following their intervening time of trial (*fatrah*; v. 69) on earth.[14]

Proceeding from the covenant to the beloved herself, Ibn al-Fāriḍ again draws upon astral images perhaps alluding to the widely held Sufi doctrine of the divine light as emanating throughout creation (vv. 70, 73). He likens the radiant sunlike beloved of this passage to God because the attributes (*waṣf*) of perfection (*kamāl*), majesty (*jalāl*), and beauty (*jamāl*) are often ascribed together to Him. God is necessarily perfect, and His majesty and beauty have been seen by Muslims as contrasting states within this perfection; *jalāl*, majesty, is associated with God's wrath (*mysterium tremendum*) while *jamāl*, beauty, expresses His satisfaction (*riḍā*) and kindness (*mysterium fascinans*).[15] From among these attributes, Ibn al-Fāriḍ designates perfection as the ultimate support for the finest and soundest created form (*aḥsanu ṣūratin wa-aqwāmuhā*), namely, the human being, the crown of creation

(v. 71).[16] As for majesty, the lover is slain in its presence, while the secret (*sirr*) of beauty is that it is the true source underlying every moon-faced beauty appearing in the transient material world. Ibn al-Fāriḍ draws attention to these three attributes and their effects in creation by means of parallelism, beginning each verse with similar noun forms and constructs, followed by contrasting prepositions (vv. 71–73):

wa-waṣfi kamālin fīki . . .
wa-naᶜti jalālin minki . . .
wa-sirri jamālin ᶜanki . . .

Although such beauty bewilders the intellect, it may be sensed by love. For behind loveliness is a subtle spiritual sense (*maᶜnā*; v. 75), an inner meaning never held by reason (*nuhā*; v. 74) but that may be touched by the heart (*qalb*; v. 76). Thus, the lover swears by his covenants with God and His prophets, by His essential attributes, and by the experience of beauty and love that his true and deepest desire has always been for the beloved alone.[17] Thus, the oath ends with verse 76, concluding the first tenth of the *al-Tā'īyah al-Kubrā*, which could stand alone as a separate wine ode in Ibn al-Fāriḍ's *Dīwān*. This section begins with the lover's reverie regarding the tavern and his recollection of spiritual intoxication at the sight of the beloved. The lover then recounts his meeting with the beloved and his complaint to her, which contains a description of his dire state, the creed of love, the declaration of continued fidelity, and, finally, his invocation of the primordial covenant with the hope that he may yet be granted union with her. In contrast to this unified section, the next two verses abruptly begin a new topic:[18]

78) "Stripping off restraint
    is my duty to you,
      and depravity is my custom
        though my folk despise to come near me."

Verse 78 picks up the use of legal technical terminology found earlier in verses 64 to 66, as the lover's obligation and custom (*farḍ; sunnah*) necessitate his total abasement before his beloved, a standard theme in Ibn al-Fāriḍ's *ghazals*. Like Majnūn, the lover shocks his tribe by casting off his self-regard to the point of violating both custom and religion (vv. 77–83). Having once again proclaimed his faithfulness, the lover recalls the beloved's candid response to his claims:[19]

84) But she said:
"You aimed for another's love
and fell short, blind
to the straight pilgrim's path to me.

85) "You were seduced
by a fickle soul's disguise
until you said what you said
and dressed in an ugly lie.

86) "For you coveted
the most precious thing
with an aggressive soul,
transgressing beyond its bounds.

87) "How can you win my love.
that most beautiful friendship,
with lying pretense,
that ugliest fraud?"

In this passage, Ibn al-Fāriḍ continues to allude to the beloved's divine-like status through references to the pilgrimage, and to the "straight path" (*sawā' al-sabīl*; v. 84), which brings to mind the *surāt al-mustaqīm*, the straight path of obedience to God mentioned in the often repeated opening chapter of the Qur'ān (1:5). It is precisely this total obedience that the lover has failed to achieve according to the beloved who accuses him of loving another; misled by concupiscence and selfishness (*nafs*), the lover has overstepped his proper place and made false claims of love (vv. 85–86).[20] His oath of fidelity, then, is a shameless lie as are his earlier complaints of trials and sufferings (vv. 87–88). In fact, the lover's assertions that his love-afflicted condition was more severe than those of various prophets (vv. 11–16) would certainly support the beloved's charge against him of pretense and duplicity. Although occasional reference to prophets and their plights was an established tradition within Arabic poetry, Ibn al-Fāriḍ's elaborate comparison may have been an intentional parody of the distraught Arab lover, meant to convey the conceit and impudence that stand in the way of selfless love. Indeed, the beloved declares the lover's selfishness to be his transgression (vv. 88–96):

97) "Now I will expose your passion
and who it is whose worn you out;

I will sweep away
your pretense to my love.

98) "You are love's ally, all right,
but for its sake, not mine;
as my proof: you have saved
an attribute of yours."

The true source of the lover's affliction, then, is not the beloved at all but his own selfish desires (*nafs*; v. 98), and this infidelity has led him to ostentatious behavior regarding his tribulation. As a result, the lover's physical and psychological trials have not served as a means of purification but, due to his loud lamentations, as a way of procuring a reputation and sympathy among human society; he has languished in pain for narcissistic pleasures thereby strengthening his selfish will (vv. 97–98). But true love demands the annihilation (*fāniyan, tafna*) of the lover's will and attributes (*waṣf*), and the realization within him of the beloved's image (*ṣūrah*; v. 99):[21]

fa-lam tahwanī mā lam takun fīya fāniyan
wa-lam tafna mā lam tujtalā fīka ṣūratī

99) "For you never loved me
so long as you were not lost in me,
and you will never be lost
without my form revealed in you."

100) "So give up claim to love,
call you heart to something else,
and drive away your erring ways
with that.

101) "Shun the courtyard of union,
that was not to be—
here you are living;
die if you are true!

102) "Such is love: if you do not die
you will derive nothing from the lover;
so decide on death
or leave my love alone."

Chastened, the lover replies that he now stands ready to sacrifice everything for his love, even if that means that he can never attain his beloved; to have sincerely tried is enough (vv. 103–114). Although the beloved will slay him, the lover remains confident that his death will be followed by immortal life in love, just as God's chosen friends (*walī/awliyā'*; v. 115) will receive the promised Paradise after death:[22]

115) "Your threat is my promise,
its execution a gift to a friend
steady with whatever befalls him
in love.

116) "I have come to hope
for what is feared;
so make a dead man happy
whose spirit is ready to live."

After recalling this conversation with the beloved, the lover next recounts the effects of his surrender to her. He was disgraced and scorned among worldly folk who thought him insane or possessed (vv. 117–127). But it was precisely his consuming passion and loss of reason that enabled him to uncover the ineffable secret of love, a secret that must be protected from rationalist reduction and selfish desires (vv. 126–138). In marked contrast to the lover's giddy almost manic state that began the *al-Tā'īyah al-Kubrā* is his new condition of humility:

139) My eyes are shut
if I desire a glance;
my hand is stopped
if I stretch out to touch.

Love now envelops the lover and fills his senses, as his whole being is fixed on the beloved (vv. 140–147). Then, as in his *qaṣīdahs*, Ibn al-Fāriḍ recalls the lover's past union with the beloved during the pilgrimage rites:

148) In truth, I led my prayer leader in prayer
with humanity behind me;
wherever I turned
was my way,

149) And my eye saw her before me
in my prayer,

my heart witnessing me (*yashhadunī*)
leading all my leaders.

150) It is no wonder
that the prayer leader prayed toward me
since she had settled in my heart,
as niche of my prayer niche.

151) All six directions faced me
with all there was
of piety and pilgrimage
both great and small.

152) To her I prayed my prayers
at Abraham's station,
while I witnessed (*ashhadu*) in them
that she did pray to me:

153) Both of us one worshipper
bowing to his reality
in union
in every prostration,

154) For no one prayed to me but I
nor were my prayers performed
to other than me
in each genuflection.

155) How long must I be brother to the veil?
I have rent it,
and its clasps were loosened
in the bond of my pledge.

156) I was given her protection
on a day not a day
in my priority before she appeared
to take the pact.

157) So I gained love of her,
but not by sound or sight,
not by fated acquisition,
or tugging disposition,

158) And I burned with thirst for her
in the World of the Command
where nothing was manifest,
drunk before my creation.

159) So passion annihilated
the attributes here between us
that never abided there
so they passed away,

160) And I found
what I had cast away
emerging to me, returning from me
in abundance.

161) In my contemplation (*shuhūdī*),
I saw (*shāhadtu*) my soul with the attributes
that had veiled me from myself
in my concealment,

162) I was she whom I loved
no doubt,
so for her, my soul (*nafsī*)
passed me on to me.

163) For my soul had burned for her unaware,
but in my witnessing (*shuhūdī*)
it was not ignorant
of the soul of the affair.

This meeting between the lover and his beloved takes place during prayer at the sacred precinct of the Kaᶜbah, and Ibn al-Fāriḍ's many references to Islamic mystical beliefs and doctrine suggest, once again, that the beloved is God who may be found in the human heart (*qalb*; v. 149). Because the lover has witnessed the beloved's presence within himself, it seems that others pray toward him, while his own prayer niche is God as manifest in all things. Thus, during this powerful experience of union, wherever the lover faces becomes his direction (*wijhah*; v. 148) for prayer just as the Qur'ān declares in one of its most mystical passages (2:115): "Wherever you turn, there is the face (*wajh*) of God" (vv. 148–150).[23] Since the poet is near the Kaᶜbah, which is the *qiblah*, or direction for the five daily Muslim prayers, all prayers, pious acts, and pilgrimages face toward him (vv. 148–151). There, praying to God at Abraham's Station (*maqām*), the poet stands in the mystical station (*maqām*; v. 152) of union (*jamᶜ*), finding oneness to be His/his true reality (*ḥaqīqatihi*; v. 153). This, then, finally tears away the veil of duplicity and selfish existence as required by the bond of allegiance to God and His prophets (*ᶜaqdi bayᶜatī*; v. 155). Mention of the bond leads to the pact (*ᶜahd*), namely, the primordial covenant and ultimate origin for humanity's love of God. In fact, the lover states that he was bound to the beloved preceding even the covenant, perhaps alluding to an earlier existence as an idea in the mind of God (v. 156). The lover's passion, then, is innate and, contrary to folk or academic notions, this love is not obtained through the senses, the natural dispositions, or any sort of acquisition. Indeed, love is not something the lover can possess; love possesses its lover (v. 157).[24]

In the World of the Command (*ᶜālam al-amr*), prior to God's creative command "Be!" the lover was first intoxicated by love (v. 158). Again, Ibn al-Fāriḍ turns to the swearing of the pre-eternal covenant, that event outside of time and manifest existence, to speak of an experience that momentarily dissolves (*afnā*) the lover's created attributes (*ṣifāt*; v. 159) to restore him to a pre-existent state. Leaving the narrow perspective of the material world for a union without time or space, the rapt lover now experiences the world anew through the beloved's attributes as she becomes the eye through which the lover sees (vv. 160–163).[25] Ibn al-Fāriḍ's recurrent use of words based on the root *sh*h*d* involving "witnessing" (vv. 149, 152, 161, 163) suggests the experiential character of this union, which triggers a radical shift in perspective. The lover no longer regards himself as an independent volitional entity. Rather, the lover realizes through his experience of union that, previously, he had blindly loved only himself (*nafs*). But in union's embrace, he is lost in the beloved as he beholds his one true love within himself (vv. 159–163).[26]

Shifiting Guises

wa-qad āna lī tafṣīlu mā qultu mujmalan
wa-ijmālu mā faṣṣaltu basṭan li-basṭatī

164) Now it is time for me to expand
on what I have said in sum,
and summarize what I have said
expansively in my expansive state.

Suddenly, the wine ode is gone. This abrupt transition and literary flourish indicates that Ibn al-Fāriḍ has concluded another section (vv. 77–163), which together with verses 1 to 76, forms a poem comparable to several of his longer odes.[27] Furthermore, this section concludes with the recollection of union, which also ends his two shorter wine odes. In terms of the *al-Tā'īyah al-Kubrā* as a whole, verse 164 further suggests that the lover's previous account of union may have been the product of spiritual excitement (*basṭ*), not rational detachment, and that what follows will be a more detailed explanation of matters touched on in the opening sections. In fact, the lover claims to have received new insight into the nature of love and life as a direct result of his previous experience. This has taught him that characters such as the slanderer and blamer are a necessary part of the spiritual path, helping the traveler to give up self-regard. For if union is to be attained, all thoughts of reward and profit must be sacrificed as well as spiritual poverty, which is only a means to an end, the beloved herself (vv. 165–171):

172) Giving up
my poverty and fortune
secured the merit of my quest,
so I tossed all merit aside.

173) But as I cast away,
prosperity appeared,
but my reward was her alone,
she who rewards me.

174) So I began to guide
one astray from the path of guidance,
to her, by her—not by me—
for she was guiding.

The intent and tone of the *al-Tā'īyah al-Kubrā* become increasingly pedagogic as the lover turns to advise the aspirant to union, and the themes and terminology in the following sections underscore the spiritual nature of this quest. Ibn al-Fāriḍ portrays poetically this master–disciple relationship by an elaborate use of imperative verbs, which begin many of the next twenty-two verses (vv. 175–196), as the master commands his student to suppress selfish thoughts and desires in humble obedience to the beloved.[28] Sloth and procrastination, in particular, must be shed if the quest is even to begin. The guide repeats that spiritual poverty, not material riches or worldly reputation, will bring the lover to his goal. But, likewise, he exhorts his disciple to avoid putting stock in religious rewards and to guard diligently against spiritual pride and conceit. For true humility and sincere obedience are the only sure way (*ṭarīqah*) by which the mystic may be transformed from a selfish seeker into God's selfless servant in union (*jamᶜ*) with Him:[29]

fa-kun baṣaran wa-nẓur wa-samᶜan wa-ᶜī wa-kun
lisānan wa-qul fa-l-jamᶜu ahdā ṭarīqati

194) So be sight and see,
and an ear and hear,
be a tongue and speak,
for union is the truest way!

The guide next cites his own spiritual life as an example of the quest. Drawing on well-known Sufi psychological theories, the guide recounts how he labored to discipline his disobedient, reproachful concupiscence (*nafs lawwāmah*; v. 197) until it was calmed (*iṭma'annat*; v. 201). Then every mystical station (*maqām*; v. 203) became one of servitude and obedience (*ᶜubūdīyah*/*ᶜubūdah*; v. 203). Following this renunciation of self-will, the guide experienced union:

fa-ṣirtu ḥabīban bal muḥibban li-nafsihi
wa-laysa ka-qawlin marra nafsī ḥabībatī

205) So I became a beloved,
indeed, one loving himself,
but not like was said before:
"My beloved is myself."

The guide thus contrasts his former deluded state of self-love, for which he was rebuked by the beloved (v. 98), with this experience of mystical union in which he was no longer conscious of himself but only of beloved who had assumed his will and senses (vv. 205–208).[30] Rhetorically, Ibn al-Fāriḍ mirrors the mystic's reversal from selfish to selfless love by reversing the tense and word positions that he had used earlier at the beginning of the poem. Instead of the lover vociferously complaining to the beloved in the privacy of the bridal chamber (*bi-khalwati jalwati*; v. 6), he is now passive and made to witnesses (*ushhidtu*) her in the bridal chamber of his private meditation (*bi-jalwati khalwatī*; v. 209). Continuing to play on his opening passage,

Ibn al-Fāriḍ leaves little doubt regarding the mystical character of love in the poem:

wa-ushhidtu ghaybī idh badat fa-wajadtunī
hunālika īyāhā bi-jalwati khalwatī
wa-ṭāḥa wujūdī fī shuhūdī wa-bintu ᶜan
wujūdi shuhūdī māḥīyan ghayra muthbiti
wa-ᶜānaqtu mā shāhadtu fī maḥwi shāhidin
bi-mushhidihi li-ṣ-ṣaḥwi min baᶜdi sakratī
fa-fī-ṣ-ṣaḥwi baᶜda-l-maḥwi lam aku ghayrahā
wa-dhātī bi-dhātī idh tajallat taḥallati

209) And I was made to witness
my absence when she appeared,
so I found me, her there
in the bridal chamber of my seclusion,

210) In my witnessing, my existence
was cast off, and I was far
from the existence of my witnessing,
effacing, not transfixing,

211) And I embraced what I witnessed
by bearing witness to it
in the effacement of my witness,
now sober after my drunkenness.

212) So in sobriety after effacement,
I was none other than her;
my essence adorned my essence
when she removed her veil.

The lover's meeting and embrace of his beloved leads to union and the birth of gnosis in his heart, and this passage clearly expresses the popular Sufi doctrine of mystical ecstasy and union discussed earlier in context of Ibn al-Fāriḍ's wine imagery. The mystic's rationality (= sobriety) is suddenly obliterated when, face to face with his beloved, he is shown the divine presence within his heart. The mystic finds (*wajadtu*; v. 209) union there, and this witnessing (*shuhūdī*) effaces his individual existence (*wujūdī*; v. 210) such that he cannot be said to be actively or consciously witnessing anything. Ibn al-Fāriḍ uses the passive tense "my existence was cast off," to underscore the mystic's surrender of his will that results in a state of spiritual intoxication (*sukr*). Yet this is followed by a second sobriety (*ṣahw*), which allows the mystic to view his existence within a new perspective (v. 211). Having undergone a spiritual death, he finds that, although he is physically and psychologically limited and transient, his underlying essence (*dhāt*) is nothing less than a reflection of the beloved's self-revelation (*tajallat*; v. 212).[31] Ibn al-Fāriḍ conveys the paradoxical nature of this state by using well-known Sufi terms in various combinations, but he clearly understands that any statement on mystical experience and union is, at best, instructive allusion:

213) Now I will make clear
my beginning in uniting,
and bring to an end my end
in abasing my exaltation:

214) Unveiling herself revealed
existence to my eye,
so in everything seen
I perceived her with my sight.

215) So my attribute is hers
since we are not called two,
and her shape is mine
since we are one.

216) If she is called,
it is me who answers,
and when I am summoned, she replies:
"*Labbayka*!" to one who calls me.

217) And if she speaks,
it is me who whispers,
just as when I tell a tale
she is the one who tells it.

218) For the second person's sign
become the first between us,
and this rose my rank
above the sect of separation.

The beloved had demanded that her lover pass away to his own attributes and consciously choose to become her reflection (v. 99), and this has now come to pass. In union (*ittiḥād*; v. 213), the guide saw only his beloved revealed (*jallat/tajallī*) in all created existence (*wujūd*); his attribute (*waṣf*) is hers, her form (*hay'ah*) is his (vv. 214–215). Mystically, God has assumed the lover's place to the degree that they appear as one, and this unity is underscored in religious terms: the guide answers those who call or pray to God (*duʿiyat*) who, in turn, responds to those who cry out to the guide "Here I am Lord at thy service!" during the pilgrimage; if the beloved speaks, it is the lover who whispers an intimate prayer, just as when the lover relates a *ḥadīth*, it is really the beloved who tells it (vv. 216–217).[32] In this passage, Ibn al-Fāriḍ creatively maintains a unity between content and form through antithesis and word play and, in verses 216 to 217, with parallelism:

fa-in duʿiyat kuntu-l-mujība wa-in-akun
munādan ajābat man daʿānī wa-labbati
wa-in naṭaqat kuntu-l-munājī kadhālika in
qaṣaṣtu ḥadīthan innamā hiya qaṣṣati

Ibn al-Fāriḍ then grammatically reinforces his message while drawing attention to his rhetorical display (v. 218):

fa-qad rufiʿat tā'u-l-mukhāṭabi baynanā
wa-fī rafʿihā ʿan firqati-l-farqi rifʿatī

For the second person's sign
became the first between us,
and this rose my rank
above the sect of separation.

In Arabic, the second-person past tense often is made by attaching to a verb either the masculine suffix *ta* or the feminine *ti*, but changed to the first person, the suffix becomes *tu*, which may be either masculine or feminine. Thus between lovers in union, this pronunciation of *t* with *u* (called *rafʿ*) has elevated (*rufiʿat*) the lover's rank (*rifʿatī*) above duality and differentiation.[33]

The guide next offers his skeptical listener insightful indications (*ishārāt*; v. 220) of how what appears as two may be or act as one. He cites the example of a cataleptic woman whose strange and prophetic words are really those of the jinni who possess her. Although these mysterious oracles are formed and spoken by the woman's tongue and lips, the jinni truly speaks them (vv. 219-226). Just so God may speak or act through His devoted servants, and this is clear to one who has directly experienced the truth of union. But those who continue to embrace dualism, whether consciously or not, will never grasp this oneness. Their constant preoccupation with themselves (*nafs*) has led them astray from God's guidance into hidden polytheism; they worship themselves not their beloved Lord. Of course, these wayward seekers are precisely those whom the guide hopes to help, and he is sympathetic to their plight since he, too, had once been beguiled by selfishness. For a time he had experienced states of unconsciousness (*faqd*) and rapture (*wajd*) in contemplation (*shuhūd*; v. 231), and this led him to suppose that spiritual intoxication (*sukr*) and effacement (*maḥw*; v. 233) were his crowning achievements. But then he recovered to discover that his frenzied intoxication was impoverished compared to a second sobriety, which enriched him with a union of unity (*jamᶜī ka-waḥdatī*; v. 235) not one of duality:[34]

236) So fight on!
Witness in you, from you,
a silence beyond my description,
when peace is found.

237) For after I fought, I witnessed
that he who made me see,
my guide to me, was me—
me, my own example.

Rhetorically, Ibn al-Fāriḍ highlights the guide's identity in oneness by repeating eight times in verse 238, the Arabic first-person pronominal suffix *ī* accompanied by four contrasting prepositions, as the guide arrives back at the pilgrimage, with the Standing at Mt. ᶜArafāt and prayers near the Kaᶜbah, which were the occasion and site for his union described earlier in the poem (vv. 148–163):[35]

fa-bī mawqifī lā bal ilayya tawajjuhī
kadhāka ṣalātī lī wa-minniya Kaᶜbatī

238) So with me was my Standing;
indeed, I turned to me,
just as I prayed to me,
and from me was my Kaᶜbah.

Having stressed the fundamental character of union, the guide returns to the issue of apparent duality, and he cautions the seeker not to be led astray from God, the creator, by the transient tinseled forms of His creation (vv. 239–241). To make this point, Ibn al-Fāriḍ elegantly combines early Islamic descriptions of the fickle mistress as a ghoul who shifts her form, with later ᶜUdhrī notions of the beloved's incomparable and ideal beauty. Thus, it was the beloved's lovely but ever-changing forms that beguiled and misled great lovers in the past, such as Jamīl and Majnūn. They never knew that absolute beauty (*iṭlāqi-l-jamāl*; v. 241) often is hidden by a disguise (*labs*; v. 244), appearing in only limited manifestations (*maẓāhir*; v. 245), as when it first appeared in the Garden of Eden to Adam in the form of Eve (vv. 239–248):[36]

249) Thus began the outward forms
and the love for one another
without one against them
to oppose with hate,

250) And for a reason, she continued
to appear and disappear
in every age
according to the times,

251) Coming forth to lovers
in every form of disguise,
in shapes
rare and lovely.

252) So one time as Lubnā,
and another as Buthaynah,
then as ᶜAzzah,
that fawn-like dear.

253) They are not other than her,
no, they never were,
for in loveliness,
she has no peer (*sharīkati*).

Ibn al-Fāriḍ again underscores the divine nature of this archetypal beloved with a Qur'ānic allusion to God "who has no peer."[37] God and love of Him, then, are at the root of all love in whatever guise, and opposite the beloved's many manifestations, the enraptured mystic assumes the role of the ideal lover seeking union with her:[38]

254) By the force of uniting
with her loveliness
as she appeared
garbed as another,

255) I appeared to her
in every lover enslaved
to every male and female
of rare beauty.

256) They were not other than me
nor prior to me in passion,
because of my priority
in the pre-eternal nights,

257) And there are no folk
but me in passion,
though I came forth to them
disguised in every form:

258) So one time as Qays
and another as Kuthayyir,
then appearing
as Buthaynah's Jamīl.

259) Without, I revealed myself to them;
within them, I lay hidden and veiled—
how wondrous an unveiling
by means of a veil.

260) The beloveds and the lovers,
and this is not a feeble guess,
appear from us, to us, as we reveal
ourselves in love and splendor.

261) So every hero in love
am I, and she
the beloved of every hero,
all names of a disguise,

262) Names that named me truly
as I appeared
to myself by a self
that was hidden.

263) I was still her
and she still me,
no separation:
my being loved hers.

264) There was nothing with me
there in the world but me,
so "withness"
never crossed my mind.

Again the guide appeals to the pre-eternal covenant as the basis for his ancient love. Though the legendary lovers of early Islam preceded the guide in time, he had stood with them previously prior to time on the Day of the Covenant when all pledged their obedience to God. But the guide then claims priority over all other lovers based on "the pre-eternal nights," which apparently preceded the Day of the Covenant (v. 256). This priority of the guide's love resonates strongly with Sufi traditions regarding Muhammad's spiritual precedence to all other prophets as his prophetic light was the first of God's creations prior to the Day of the Covenant by one thousand years, and this luminous presence grows as the poem continues.[39] As for the spirits in pre-eternity, they are pristine but, once in creation, they are clothed (*labisa*) in the garment (*labs*) of the physical body, which confuses or disguises (*labasa*) their divine origin (vv. 257–258). Multiplicity, with its time and space, becomes an ephemeral veil yet, as it covers, it not only hides but also gives shape to the divine essence within all of existence. Although many people remain heedless of this higher nature, the mystic looks beneath appearances (*ẓāhir*) to glimpse the inner (*bāṭin*) reality of God's self-manifestation (v. 259). Once in union, separation (*farq*) ends, and consciousness of a separate existence gives way to God's consciousness of Himself through His worshippers whom He loves (vv. 260–264).[40]

A sense of immediacy and personal participation characterizes this section of the poem as Ibn al-Fāriḍ's lyrical persona shifts its guises from the ʿUdhrī lover to the enlightened guide, and finally to the Light of Muhammad enamored of God before and after creation. Ibn al-Fāriḍ suggests the mysterious perpetual exchange of love between lovers within the unity of God's self-revelations, by constructing parallels in poetic form and content (vv. 255–256, 258 and 261–263). True union has led the lover from his initial self-centered exaltation in exhilaration's release (*khalāᶜiti basṭī*) to a state of passive servitude in chastity's restraint (*li-nqibāḍin bi-ᶜiffati*; v. 269). The realization of unity, then, does not negate the need for righteous conduct, and Ibn al-Fāriḍ catalogs some of the many pious deeds undertaken by the prophetic guide following his recovery in the second sobriety (vv. 268–276). Still, this renewed adherence to the letter of the law is not in hopes of spiritual reward or from fear of others' opinions. Rather, the guide aims to protect the high status of his saintly friends (*awliyā'*; v. 267) from charges of heresy, particularly, the charge of *ḥulūl* or belief in a divine incarnation (vv. 277–279).

To distinguish his notion of union from that of incarnation, Ibn al-Fāriḍ cites the story of Gabriel, the Spirit of Revelation, who was said to have appeared to Muhammad once in the form of a handsome youth named Diḥyah al-Kalbī. On this occasion, Muhammad saw Gabriel, while the prophet's companions saw only Diḥyah. Gabriel, however, was not dwelling within a living person, rather he was clothed or disguised (*labs*; v. 285) by an attractive form, which could be penetrated only by the spiritual vision of the prophet (vv. 280–285). Ibn al-Fāriḍ, thus clearly differentiates his conception of union from doctrines of incarnation, which posit the existence of two separate entities, one dwelling within the other. Such a dualist form of union is unacceptable to Ibn al-Fāriḍ, who prefers to speak instead of *labisa*, the "clothing" or "disguising" of one existent beneath a variety of forms. Naturally this one existent is the beloved God who, if He so wished, could disguise an angel as a man to confuse the unbelievers (Qur'ān 6:9). Ibn al-Fāriḍ explicitly cites the Qur'ān and *ḥadīth* in support of his view of union, which he claims to be within the bounds of true religion (vv. 284–285). For Ibn al-Fāriḍ does not conceive of union as the merging of two entities, still less the dwelling of one within another. Rather, union is based on the realization that God is the essence and source of all being including the human being.[41] Although this fact may be know intellectually (*ᶜilm*), its reality may be grasped only by the selfless mystic who, having rent the veil of duality, perceives with mystical insight (*kashf*) the truth beneath the disguise of appearances (v. 286):

286) I have bestowed on you knowledge;
if you want it unveiled,
then enter my path (*sabīlī*)
and follow my way (*sharīᶜatī*)

Once more, Ibn al-Fāriḍ's prophetic persona expands to praise his own high station in gnosis, which is far beyond the reach of scholars, ascetics, and other mystics (vv. 287–333). Ibn al-Fāriḍ appears to be alluding again to Muhammad or his prophetic light, as was earlier the case (vv. 254–264). He uses the term *sharīᶜah* ("way," "law"), which almost always refers to the divine law established by Muhammad to be followed (*ittbāᶜ*; v. 286) by believers. Furthermore, Ibn al-Fāriḍ quotes the Qur'ānic injunction (6:152) "and do not come near the wealth of the orphan" as an indication of the enraptured guide's unique and unapproachable mystical station (v. 289). This seems an obvious allusion to Muhammad who was an orphan and, according to Islamic tradition, the final and greatest prophet.[42] Thus, the excited guide goes on to boast:

wa-mā nāla shay'an minhu ghayrī siwā fatan
ᶜalā qadamī fī-l-qabḍi wa-l-basṭi mā fatī

290) No one but me drew from this deep,
save a young warrior determined
to follow my steps
in good times and bad.

If the persona of this section represents Muhammad or the mystic in union with his prophetic light, then the brave would likely designate the prophet's cousin and son-in-law ᶜAlī ibn Abī Ṭālib, who supported the prophet no matter the risks, and who many Muslims believe received a unique esoteric teaching from Muhammad.[43] Muhammad's own spiritual ascent (*miᶜrāj*) is then mentioned as the guide tells of ascending beyond even love in his oneness (*ittiḥādī*; v. 295). He then commands his disciple to adhere to "the heritage of the highest gnostic" (*mīrātha arfaᶜi ᶜārifīn*), probably meaning the life and teachings of Muhammad (v. 299).[44]

Within this larger passage, the poetic persona appears to speak on behalf of the "highest gnostic," as he advises his disciple to become a lover rapt in union's oneness (vv. 300–306). But just as Moses was less than Muhammad (vv. 289, 307–309), so too is the intoxicated aspirant's state inferior to that of his guide who claims to possess alone the "sobriety of union" (*ṣaḥwa-l-jamᶜi*; v. 311). Describing this gnostic further, Ibn al-Fāriḍ alludes to the "Tradition of Willing Devotions" and God's assumption of the mystic's senses and to those traditions asserting Muhammad's light as the source of prophecy. The gnostic's ear is that of Moses who heard God speak through the Burning

Bush; his heart (*qalb*) is inspired by the most praiseworthy (*aḥmad*) vision from an eye of Muhammad who, according to tradition, saw God during his spiritual ascent (v. 312). The guide's spirit (*rūḥ*) is the spirit of all spirits, while every lovely thing in existence is from the emanation of his clay (v. 313).[45] Moving beyond description and predication, the guide declares himself free of any separate existence that could acknowledge his separation from the beloved. In fact, terms like master, disciple, lover, and close companion often hide what they are meant to reveal (vv. 314–325):

325) I have no attribute;
that is a stamp, as a name is a brand,
but if you must, speak of me
allusively or with metaphor.

326) I ascended from "I am she"
to where there is no "to,"
sweetening my existence
by my return

327) From "I am me,"
for an inner wisdom
and outer laws
to begin my call.

Ibn al-Fārid again invokes the Qur'ān to drive home his message, as the guide continues his ascent back to his pre-eternal state. Returning to oneness in God, whom all things praise (v. 331; Qur'ān 17:44), the guide has let go of the idolatry of self-worship, and, in total obedience, he holds tight with the firmest bond of revelation (v. 332: *bi-awthaqi ᶜurwā*; Qur'ān 2:256, 31:22).[46]

Love's Sweet Season

333) Metaphorically I greet her:
"Peace!" I say,
but in reality my greeting
is from myself to me.

With this verse, Ibn al-Fāriḍ makes an elegant transition from his discourse on union to another account of the suffering lover and his ideal beloved. In this section of *al-Tā'īyah al-Kubrā*, as in the *qaṣīdahs*, the lover's greeting to his beloved is followed by a detailed description of his love sickness and willingness to die for her sake. In this instance, rhetorical elements lead to melodrama as Ibn al-Fāriḍ richly embellishes his account with paronomasia and antithesis (vv. 334–339). He uses the vocative particle *yā* ("O") in nine consecutive verses to beseech the various parts of his body, his health, and his welfare to surrender in spiritual death to the beloved who is the true source of all love (vv. 340–54). Her beauty fills the world, especially the Muslim holy lands. As noted earlier, throughout his *Dīwān*, Ibn al-Fāriḍ often employs the abodes and way stations of the classical *qaṣīdah* as symbols for Medina, Mecca, and stages of the pilgrimage, and in an extended metaphor, Ibn al-Fāriḍ joins these places ever closer to the beloved and love of her:

355) Every day is my holy day
when I see,
with an eye refreshed,
the beauty of her face;

356) Every night is the Night of Power
when she draws near,
and every day we meet
is one of union, holy Friday.

357) My running to her
is a pilgrimage,
with every standing at her door,
the Standing,

358) And so wherever she alights
among God's many lands,
though it delight my eye,
I see it not, but Mecca,

359) Any place that holds her
is a precinct holy;
every house where she resides
is Medina's land.

360) Wherever she dwells
is Jerusalem, most sacred,

whose soothing sight
cools my burning heart,

361) And my Farthest Mosque
is where she trails her robe,
my musk, the moist earth
where she walked.

362) The dwellings of my joy,
the tower of my desire,
the limits of my longings,
and refuge from my fear

363) Were abodes where fate
never entered between us,
nor did shifty time
ensnare us with separation.

Continuing his rhetorical display, Ibn al-Fāriḍ begins five successive verses with negative verbs to assert the untainted nature of this union with the beloved, a union not sundered by fate, time's vicissitudes, or by the slanderer, blamer, or spy (vv. 364–368). Using progressively longer intervals of time, together with the conditional tense and its play between, past, present, and future, Ibn al-Fāriḍ suggests the transformative power of a timeless moment of the eternal now:

368) No time was favored
over another in pleasure;
with her, all my moments
are seasons sweet:

369) My whole day is vesper time
if its first hours
spread her fragrant reply
to my greetings,

370) And my whole night there
is an enchanting dawn
if a sweet scented breeze
arises from her to me.

371) For if she comes at night,
my whole month by her becomes
the Night of Power, radiant,
as she visits me,

372) And if she draws near my home,
my whole year becomes
a temperate spring
luxuriant amid meadows.

373) For if she is pleased with me,
my whole life will be
the pleasant time of childhood
and the age of youth.

The guide then exalts his own high mystical station in a union that he had never before imagined (vv. 374–380). To accentuate the totality of this union and build toward his climax, Ibn al-Fāriḍ continues to repeat the word *kull* ("each," "every," "all," "whole") in seventeen more verses, this time accompanied by multiple prepositions. The mystic's intellect, senses, and entire being are filled by the divine beloved, by God, who will double for the believer whatever he spends in the cause of Islam (Qur'ān 57:11):[47]

381) I spent all of me
for the hand of her beauty
so her beneficence
doubled my every union,

382) Every atom of me
witnessing her loveliness
with every glance
of every shining eye,

383) All my subtle words
adoring her
with every tongue
profuse in praise,

384) Smelling her sweet scent
with my every fiber,
with every nose inhaling
every rising air,

385) Every bit of me
hearing her word
with every ear
of all hoping to hear,

386) Every part of me
kissing her veil
with every mouth
in each touching kiss.

387) Had she unrolled my body
she would have seen
every essence with every heart
holding every love.

Taken as a whole, verses 334 to 387 form one of the most elaborate and dramatic accounts in Arabic of love's mystical union.[48] Ibn al-Fāriḍ repeats various particles, words, and verb forms to quicken his poem's pace and heighten its emotional pitch while composing a coherent rhetorical elaboration of the *al-Tā'īyah al-Kubrā*'s opening scene. Within this lyrical interlude, form and content merge to tell of the mystic's progress from his surrender of self-regard (vv. 340–348) to an unobstructed union (vv. 364–368), which is both timeless (vv. 370–375) and total (vv. 381–387), as God assumes the senses of His beloved worshipper.

Spirit and Matter

Ibn al-Fāriḍ slows the pace to elaborate on mystical love and union, while continuing to use symbols and allusions, which, he says, tell more than discursive speech. He begins with further observations on the roles of the slanderer and blamer who, in relation to the aspiring lover, are obnoxious traveling companions, pestering him along the way. But they, too, are one with the beloved in union (vv. 390–399), and the slander only slanders the lover because he jealously guards the beloved out of his love for her. In terms of Sufi psychology, Ibn al-Fāriḍ relates this protagonist to the spirit (*rūḥ*), which longs to return to God and so steers the mystic toward self-annihilation via spiritual contemplation (*shuhūd*). By contrast, the blamer urges the lover to forget his beloved, and, so, Ibn al-Fāriḍ employs this character as a symbol of the unruly carnal soul or concupiscence (*nafs*), which races headlong toward immediate sensual gratification:

wa-innī wa-īyāh la-dhātun wa-man washā
bi-hā wa-thanā ᶜanhā ṣifātun tabaddati
fa-dhā maẓharun li-r-rūḥi hādin li-ufqihā
shuhūdan ghadā fī ṣīghatin maᶜnawīyati
wa-dhā muẓhirun li-n-nafsi ḥādin li-rufqihā
wujūdan ᶜadā fī ṣibghatin ṣuwarīyati

399) She and I are in essence one;
he who slandered me against her
and one who turned away from her
appeared as attributes:

400) The slanderer is the spirit's guise
guiding on to its horizon
with a witnessing
beginning in an ideal form,

401) While the blamer is the soul's display
driving on to its cronies
with an existence
ending in a formal mold.

These verses are another fine example of Ibn al-Fāriḍ's use of parallelism, paronomasia, and antithesis to articulate and accentuate essential aspects of his mystical perspective. Here, he succinctly contrasts the two sides of every human psyche as embodied in medieval Islamic thought: the *rūḥ*, or primordial spirit, and the *nafs*, concupiscence or the carnal soul. The first points with mystical vision toward its pre-eternal spiritual home, whereas the later pulls the individual down to those mired in the created material world. The contrast between spirit and matter, and the resulting conflict between the two, underlie much of the *al-Tā'īyah al-Kubrā*, and verses 400 to 443, in particular. Ibn al-Fāriḍ views temporal existence as an emanation (*fayḍ*; v. 404) from a single divine essence (*dhāt*; v. 403), but it is an emanation characterized by this dual aspect with which every mystic must come to terms (vv. 402–406).[49] Like the ᶜUdhrī lover, Ibn al-Fāriḍ's guide appears obsessed with transcending the body's limitations, seeking to break the cage of materiality so that his spirit might escape and soar to its heavenly home.

To illustrate the spirit's need and ability to transcend the body's confines, at least for a moment, Ibn al-Fāriḍ cites the example of the mystic's unitive trance induced by the Sufi practice of *samāᶜ*. Fair forms and the mournful tones of the Qur'ān chanter cause the mystic to witness (*yushāhidu*) the beloved in his thought (*fikr*), memory (*dhikr*), imagination (*wahm*), and understanding (*fahm*). The sights and sounds cause him to fall into a state of spiritual intoxication (*sukr*) and aesthetic rapture (*ṭarb*); his heart (*qalb*) joyously dances to the accompaniment of his trembling limbs, as his spirit plays the part of the singing girl. The lover's burning desire for the beloved purifies his carnal soul, and so all things in existence (*kā'ināt*) help him to merge his senses and limbs with hers (vv. 407–419). The five senses, which had previously veiled the lover from creation's inner unity, now lead him to discover the beloved's handiwork manifest throughout time and space:[50]

420) The north wind guides
her memory to my spirit
whenever it comes from her by night
rising up at dawn,

421) And my ear is pleased
when her memory is roused at noon
by dusky doves on branches
warbling and gently cooing.

422) My eye is blessed
when a lightning flash
relays to it from her
thought of her in the evening,

423) And I taste and touch
her memory in vessels of wine
when, at night,
they come round to me,

424) Thus my heart reveals to me
her memory within
by what the sense messengers
delivered from without.

Ibn al-Fāriḍ summons classical pastoral images to suggest the tranquility pervading the lover's entire being. The lover's reverie deepens as his senses pause amid the traces left behind by the beloved in creation, traces which arouse the nostalgic recollection (*dhikr*) of an earlier union.[51] Ibn al-Fāriḍ's references to such classical Arabic poetic motifs as the night breeze, lightning, doves, and wine within this overtly religious context support their mystical interpretation elsewhere in his *Dīwān*. But as important, these verses suggest Ibn al-Fāriḍ's understanding of the "Tradition of Willing Devotions" and God's assumption of the mystic's senses. A fresh experience of reality is born of this union, but it does not lead the mystic to encounter a new world so much as to see the old world anew. He ceases to view creation superficially as a collection of independent objects, and so finds the Creator within His creation. Seen from this perspective, God assumes the mystic's senses in order to inspire him and to reveal, by means of the mystic's heart (*qalb*), the inner spiritual reality (*bāṭin*) hidden beneath external appearance (*ẓāhir*; v. 424).[52] This transformation of experience occurs to the mystic during a *samā*ᶜ session where the chanting of the beloved's name causes him to witness her within. His spirit soars while his body, like that of an entranced dervish, falls to the ground. Just so, the human spirit yearns to fly to heaven while the body struggles to hold it down (vv. 425–429). Ibn al-Fāriḍ sees this conflict between the spirit and the body as an inevitable part of the human condition. Given concupiscence's power, the mystic must work vigilantly on the spirit's behalf, and so Ibn al-Fāriḍ forcefully defends the practice of *samā*ᶜ against its critics with an elegant allegory unprecedented in classical Arabic poetry:

431) When the infant moans
from the tight swaddling wrap
and restlessly yearns
for relief from distress,

432) He is soothed by lullabies and lays aside
the burden that covered him;
he listens silently
to one who soothes him.

433) The sweet speech makes him
forget his bitter state
and remember a secret whisper
of ancient ages.

434) His state makes clear
the conditions of audition
and confirms the dance
to be free of error.

435) For when he burns with desire
from lullabies,
anxious to fly
to his first abodes,

436) He is calmed
by his rocking cradle
as the hands of his nurse
gently sway it.

437) I have found in gripping rapture
when she is recalled
in the chanter's tones
and the singer's tunes

438) What a suffering man feels
when he gives up his soul,
when the messengers of death
come to take him.

439) One finding pain
in being driven asunder
is like one pained in rapture
yearning for friends.

440) The soul pitied the body
where it first appeared,
and my spirit rose
to its high beginnings.

441) My spirit soared past the gate
opening to beyond my union
where there is no veil
of communion.

The tightly swaddled baby of this passage obviously represents the spirit bound to the body. In time, the baby will loose its innocence, just as all humans soon forget their spirit's pre-eternal origin (v. 430). As the baby struggles against his wrap, he is comforted by lullabies, while the spirit, distressed by its fleshy bonds, is momentarily calmed by the melodious voice of the Qur'ān chanter who leads the spiritually attuned to recollect their pre-eternal covenant with God. Ibn al-Fāriḍ undoubtedly refers here to the *mīthāq*, the pre-eternal covenant, with the phrase *najwā ᶜuhūdin qadīmati*, "a secret whisper of ancient ages," which also may be translated as "a secret whisper of ancient covenants" (v. 433). But the lullabies that ease the baby's misery create a longing to return to the womb and, similarly, the chanting at the *samāᶜ* session strengthens the mystic's desire to be reunited with his Lord. The baby is then calmed by the gentle rocking of his cradle, while the entranced dervish finds relief in the swaying movements of the Sufi dance. At last, the chanter's recollection (*dhikr*) of the beloved's name wrenches the spirit from the body, freeing it to ascend beyond any notion of duality, even that of a union between lover and beloved (vv. 437–443).[53]

Yesterday's Tomorrow

Again calling attention to his profound verse and the deep wisdom to be found there, Ibn al-Fāriḍ begins a new section:

> 444) In the mirror of my words, I will show you
> the gate if you are determined,
> so attend to what I bestow
> upon the ear of insight.

The lyric persona resumes the role of the spiritual guide as he tells his disciple how he purged himself of his self-regard (vv. 445–447). As expected, this led him to an experience of union in which he, like the beloved before (vv. 355–363), was transformed into the sites of the pilgrimage; his heart (*qalb*) is the Kaᶜbah circumambulated by adoring pilgrims who pray there and kiss its black stone:

> 448) My heart is a holy house
> in which I dwell;
> before it, rising out of it
> my attributes appear from my veiling.

> 449) My right hand is a corner there
> kissed within me, and by wise decree
> my kiss comes to my mouth
> from my niche for prayer.

> 450) Spiritually, my turning
> is really round me,

and I ran toward myself
from my Ṣafā to my Marwā.

451) In a sanctuary within me
my appearance is safe,
but around it my neighbors
risk being snatched away.

452) By my fasting my soul alone
was purified from all others,
and gave as alms
the grace flowing from me,

453) And my existence,
bent double in my witnessing,
became straight and single in my oneness
as I awoke from sleep.

454) So the night journey of my heart secret
from special truth to me
is like my course
among the common cares of law.

455) Divinity (*lāhūt*) did not distract me
from the rules of my appearance,
nor did human nature (*nāsūt*) lead me to forget
where my wisdom was manifest.

Reference to the *Isrā'*, Muhammad's night-journey mentioned in the Qur'ān (17:1), suggests that the poetic persona again speaks as the prophetic Light. Having awakened from union's trance, he regards special mystical truth (*khuṣūṣi ḥaqīqatin*) and universal religious law (*ᶜumūmi-sh-sharīᶜati*) as necessary companions on the spiritual quest. Furthermore, this enables him to distinguish between his divine essence (*lāhūt*) and his human nature (*nāsūt*), while recognizing their respective complementary roles. Concupiscence must be restrained and the senses held in check by covenants and laws that are, in fact, derived from him (vv. 456–458). Indeed, he is their pre-eternal source:[54]

459) From the age of my covenant
before the era of my elements,

before my mission
warning of resurrection time,

460) I was a messenger
sent to me, from me,
and by my signs,
my being was led to me.

Muhammad's prophetic Light proclaims its lordship over the universe, which is an emanation (*fayḍ*) from him. When compared to his shining countenance (*wajh*), the sun is but a flash; the sea becomes a drop next to his overflowing creative being and custom (*sunnah*; vv. 461–470). Ibn al-Fāriḍ uses Qur'ānic allusions, together with the repetition of *wa-lā* ("And no") followed by various nouns of time and place, to stress the limitless and absolute character of this union (*jam*ᶜ) underlying the apparent multiplicity of things. For in reality, there is no doubt or direction, no number or time, no rival or opposite to create real duality; they are but the Light's means to disguise himself (*labastuhu*, v. 475) that he may see himself worship himself.[55] This is particularly apparent in the case of Adam, Moses, the historical Muhammad, and the other prophets sent with God's message to worship Him alone (vv. 471–479). Yet, the worshipper must not be misled by God's attributes (*ṣifātu iltibāsin*, v. 486), which mask His unity. People entranced by the senses, by reason (*ṣaḥw/suḥāwah*), or trance's intoxication (*nashāwā*, v. 485) retain traces of their selfish nature and so persist in polytheism, lost among their own shifting identities (*talwīn*, v. 484). But after annihilation in union (*fanā'*), the mystic may come to abide (*baqā'*) in God, and so witness (*shuhūd*) oneness (*aḥadīyah*; vv. 490–494):

495) And yesterday's "Am I not?" is not
other than what one will be tomorrow,
as my pitch dark night became bright morn,
and my day, my night,

496) For the secret of "Indeed, yes!" to God
is the mirror of His unveiling,
and the meaning of union is confirmed
with the denial of "withness."

Timeless yet in time, this paradoxical experience of the unity beneath multiplicity enables the mystic to join the pre-eternal Day of the Covenant to the last Day of Judgment and so bear witness to God's everlasting oneness. God is the First and the Last, unbound by notions of time, as future events coalesce with those of pre-eternity. For God drew forth the spirits of humanity from Himself, as a revelation to Himself, asking them "Am I not Your Lord?" only to answer Himself on their behalf, "Yes, indeed, We/we so witness!" (7:172).[56]

Manifest Sites

Once again speaking as the Light, the poetic persona proclaims himself to be beyond time and space; he is the pre-eternal *quṭb*, the pole or pivot around which the planets turn though he encompasses them all. Further, as the *quṭb*, he is the greatest of the saints and head of their ranks (*al-awtād; badalīyah*; vv. 497–502).[57] Of course, this high status is due to union's state, and so the prophetic guide gives yet another account of union with the divine beloved as he passed from the well-known Sufi stages of religious knowledge (*ᶜilm al-yaqīn*) to hidden knowledge (*ᶜayn al-yaqīn*) and, finally, to certain gnosis (*ḥaqq al-yaqīn*; vv. 503–514).[58] At this point, Ibn al-Fāriḍ begins to push Arabic's rhetorical possibilities toward their limits repeating and recasting many words and phrases to sketch the mystic's path (vv. 513–520) and his subsequent successful completion of his quest in union (vv. 522–533). Ibn al-Fāriḍ constructs a series of contrasting and antithetical pairs—name/attribute, soul/spirit, manifest/hidden; body/essence—highlighted by parallelisms in morphology and syntax to reiterate his now familiar view that all creation serves as God's theatre of manifestation (*maẓāhir*; vv. 534–545):

545) Names and attributes
were my manifest sights where I appeared,
though I was not hidden from myself
before the site of my epiphany,

546) And so speech—
I am all tongue speaking of me—
and sight—
I am all eyes gazing upon me—

547) And hearing—
I am all ears hearing the call,
and all of me is a hand
firm in fending off destruction—

548) Are the qualities of attributes
that fixed what lay behind the guise,
all the names of an essence
spreading what the senses relayed.

These verses make further reference to the "Tradition of Willing Devotions" and God's assumption of the senses through which the mystic experiences life. In this instance, however, the mystic not only senses the divine hidden beneath the manifest, as was earlier the case (vv. 381–387), but he has been so annihilated that he has become the very senses that God has assumed. Furthermore, Ibn al-Fāriḍ maintains that just as a person's attributes, senses, and sense-organs confirm the presence of one experiencing and manifesting himself through them, so too is there a divine essence (*dhāt*; v. 548) acting in creation beneath the guises of its apparent names and attributes.[59] Staying with this last idea, Ibn al-Fāriḍ passes from the mystic's experiential union to the ontological union underlying the divine names and attributes, and their emanation throughout creation. Ibn al-Fārid's rhetorical display now reaches staggering proportions in a series of verses long recognized as forming the most rhetorically ornate and intellectually abstruse passage of the *al-Tā'īyah al-Kubrā* and of the entire *Dīwān*. Divisible into three distinct sections, the odd verses (549–555; 557–563; 565–573)—horizontally as well as vertically—follow harmonious patterns in terms of morphology, case, and syntax, which are reflected in the similarly unified, though different, patterns of the even verses (vv. 550–556; 558–564; 566–574). A transliteration of several verses may give some idea of Ibn al-Fāriḍ's rhetorical *tour de force*:[60]

549) *fa-taṣrīfuhā min ḥāfiẓi-l-ᶜahdi awwalan*
bi-nafsin ᶜalayhā bi-l-walā'i ḥafīzati

550) *shawādī mubāhātin hawādī tanabbuhin*
bawādī fukāhātin ghawādī rajīyati

551) *wa-tawqīfuhā min mawthiqi-l-ᶜahdi ākhirin*
bi-nafsin ᶜalā ᶜizzi-l-ibā'i abīyati

552) *jawāhiru anbā'in zawāhiru wuṣlatin*
ẓawāhiru inbā'in qawāhiru ṣawlati

[Qualities of attributes] that flow out from one
who first preserves the covenant,

with a soul watching over them
in loyal love,

As chanters of high praise,
guides to vigilance,
purveyors of sweet joys,
clouds pouring what is desired.

They are set down from one
who last confirms the covenant,
with a soul scorning
haughty pride,

As gems of prophecy,
luminaries of union,
manifest tidings,
chargers of a sudden assault.

Once again, Ibn al-Fāriḍ's elaborate rhetorical forms have a function intimately linked to content, as each of the three formal sections is divided into four parts reflecting metaphysical and mystical concepts revolving around the divine names and attributes. Through the persistent use of parallelism and patterning, Ibn al-Fāriḍ conveys the then popular conception of the universe as a multilayered existence progressively manifest through God's names and attributes.[61] God is the first mover, possessing the divine names and attributes by which He brings about creation and revelation, which ended with the human Muhammad, the last prophet (vv. 549–552). The outward (*ẓāhir*) manifestations of these names and attributes in existence (*wujūd*) are defined and explained by the dedicated religious scholar, whereas their inner (*bāṭin*) qualities are discovered and witnessed in mystical contemplation (*shuhūd*) by the sincere mystic who has returned, if only momentarily, to his pre-eternal origins (vv. 553–556).

Naturally, God's divine names and attributes appear in different forms within the different contexts. In terms of the human being, the names and attributes are the source from which the physical body (*labs*) governed by Islam's wise ordinances attains discipline and happiness. The senses informed by a deeper faith (*imān*) will receive profound and illuminating experiences from the names and attributes, whereas the carnal soul (*nafs*) is granted spiritual subtleties provided that it has been restrained by prophetic example, striving to realize God's living presence within itself (*iḥsān*). Finally, the entire human (*jamᶜ*) witnessing the divine is blessed with moments of union (*jamᶜ; ḥudūthu-t-tiṣālātin*) by the names and attributes (vv. 557–564).[62] Moving from the human microcosm to the universal macrocosm, the divine names and attributes emanate from God and cascade down progressively into levels of existence. In the sensate, visible world (*ᶜālami-sh-shahādati*), they appear—like Ibn al-Fārid's verse—as expressions and indications of the truth, which correspond in the unseen world (*ᶜālami-l-ghaybi*) to the inner secrets of the outward forms. In the next higher world of dominion (*ᶜālami-l-malakūti*), the names and attributes are the source of scripture and its spiritual interpretation (*ta'wīl*). Then Ibn al-Fāriḍ comes full circle back to God and the world of omnipotence (*ᶜālami-l-jabarūti*). Here, God's unity (*tawḥīd*) reigns supreme among His names and attributes, which appear as His angels and throne (vv. 565–572).[63]

Thus, on whatever level, in whatever world, the steadfast, enlightened mystic will always encounter an emanation (*fayḍ*) of the divine names and attributes to nourish and support him (vv. 572–574). With this transition, Ibn al-Fāriḍ returns from mystical cosmology to the mystical experience of union. For although the names and attributes are the means of manifestation, the apparent distinctions that they engender are obliterated in the most complete form of union. In this "sobriety of union" (*ṣaḥw al-jamᶜ*), the gnostic merges with his senses (vv. 575–578):

579) So the whole of me was
a tongue, an eye, an ear, a hand
to speak and see
and hear and grasp.

But this time, Ibn al-Fārid does not stop here, and in a paradoxical and dizzying account, he details the fusing of the mystic's senses into a sentient whole: his tongue saw, and his eye heard; his ear spoke, while his hand listened (vv. 580–588). Now privy to an unseen world, the gnostic can read all knowledge in a single word, hear all voices in a moment, smell all the scents on the wind, survey the earth in a flash, and cross the heavens in a step (vv. 589–594). Indeed, all miracles and prophecy are from him who has achieved union with Muhammad's Light (vv. 595–617). Turning to the Light, Ibn al-Fāriḍ states that while prophecy culminated in the mission of the historical Muhammad, his prophetic Light continued to shine among his community via the first four caliphs. Ibn al-Fāriḍ praises all four, attesting to his Sunni convictions, but he singles out the last of them, ᶜAlī, Muhammad's cousin and son-in-law, as the one who clarified obscure passages of the Qur'ān by means of mystical interpretation (*ta'wīl*; vv. 617–626). As for later generations, the Light is to be found among the religious scholars, the mystics, and especially the saints (*awliyā'*) who are like "guiding stars" for persons lost in the darkness. Although these saints have never actually seen Muhammad in the flesh, he is, nevertheless, with them in spirit (vv. 618, 627–628).[64]

The prophetic Light now returns with dramatic effect to declare his priority to Adam and all of humanity, for he was the means through which God took the primordial covenant and initiated creation (vv. 629–637). The speaker's identity is clear as Ibn al-Fāriḍ alludes to a popular divine saying in which God says to Muhammad: "If not for you, I would not have created the heavens:"[65]

638) If not for me
existence and witness would not exist,
and covenants of protection
would not have been pledged.

639) No one lives
unless his life is from mine;
obedient to my will
is every aspiring soul.

640) No one speaks
unless his speech is from mine;
no one sees
but by the gaze of my eye.

641) No one listens
unless listening by my ear;
no one grasps
save by my might and strength.

642) For no one
is speaking, seeing, hearing,
in all of creation
but me!

The sense's cycle is now complete as the poetic persona has moved from the aspiring lover using his senses, to the mystic's having them assumed by God, to the guide being the senses themselves, and finally to the Light being the senses of all others in creation.

The prophetic Light, then, is not only the creative first principle, but the sustaining force of creation as well. Furthermore, in this passage Ibn al-Fāriḍ appears to interpret the "Tradition of Willing Devotions" more theologically than he had previously; sensate beings are themselves senses or instruments through which the Light, and so God, experiences creation. In fact, the Light may be the totality of God's self-reflection. Once more, Ibn al-Fāriḍ uses parallels in syntax, case, and morphology to bring an exhilarating passage to its climax. He begins eight consecutive verses (vv. 643–650) with the phrase *wa-fī* ("And in") followed by nouns designating the realms of matter and spirit, and contrasting mystical states, including those of contraction and expansion (*basṭ/qabḍ*).[66] In this way Ibn al-Fāriḍ suggests the ever-present and all encompassing nature of the Light, which contemplates and manifests his Lord in His majesty, beauty, and perfection (*jalāl, jamāl, kamāl*):[67]

643) In the composite world,
I appeared deep within
every shape and form
adorning them with beauty.

644) While in every subtle sense
not revealed by visible guise,
I was conceived and formed
but without a body's shape.

645) Yet in what the spirit sees
clairvoyantly,
I was rarified, concealed,
from this subtle sense confined.

646) In the mercy of expansion
all of me is a wish
expanding wide
the hopes of humanity,

647) While in the dread of contraction
all of me is awe;
wherever I cast my eye
I am honored.

648) In joining both attributes
all of me is proximity;

come, draw near
my inner beauty,

649) For in the end-place of "in,"
I still found with me
my majesty of witness
arising from my perfect nature,

650) And where there is no "in,"
I still witnessed within me
the beauty of my existence
without an eye to see!

Shadow Play

Once again the pace slows as the lyric persona resumes the role of the enlightened master. He exhorts his disciple to strive for true union while avoiding false beliefs, particularly those that posit the spirit's re-incarnation or transmigration. Both notions are misleading since they conceive of the human as being a permanent entity (vv. 651–654), and to clarify his point, the guide turns to consider individual existence and action. As usual, Ibn al-Fāriḍ makes a poetic transition signaling a new section:

655) Now the parables I strike
time after time about my state
are a blessing
from me to you.

Indeed, parables dominate this portion of the poem concerning human nature whose spiritual qualities have been obscured and forgotten. This time, however, the culprit is not so much the body or the material world but, rather, the *nafs*, the carnal soul or concupiscence, which suppresses the spirit (*rūḥ*) for its own selfish ends. By means of the senses and sensation, the *nafs* seduces the unwary person into believing that he, alone, is the crown of creation, that his existence is totally unique, independent, and, especially, ever-lasting. Like the rogue of the *maqāmāt*, or picaresque stories popular in Ibn al-Fāriḍ's day, the *nafs* constantly changes its disguise (*talwīn; iltibās*) in order to deceive and swindle its naive companion (vv. 656–658).[68] The guide therefore urges the aspirant to look beneath appearances to see for himself the crafty play of the *nafs*. The seeker must stop thinking solely in terms of the body and its physical senses, and consider the origins of his actions and his presumed role as actor. He must look deeper, listen more intently to discover the divine spirit within. But although the spirit is the goal, the guide sternly warns against dismissing the phenomenal world as merely transient and illusory. For it is only through phenomena that individuals become manifest and act at all, and when seen aright, phenomena reveal reality's hidden truth. A creator only exists with his creation, just as a puppeteer must rely on his puppets to perform his play (vv. 659–678):

679) In illusion's drowsy dream
the phantom shadow
leads you to what shimmers
through the screens.

680) You see the shapes of things
in every display
disclosed before you
from behind the veil's disguise,

681) And opposites were joined in them
for the sake of wisdom,
so their figures appear
in every form:

682) Silent, they seem to speak;
still, they seem to move,
shedding light,
though dark,

683) While amazed you laugh
giddy and full of cheer,
then cry bereaved like a mother
who lost her child,

684) You wail when they mourn
their plundered fortune,
and rejoice
when they sing a sweet song.

685) In the branches
you see birds cooing

and warbling sad songs
that stir you,

686) And you are awed by the sounds
of their many voices,
for they clearly spoke
in foreign tongues.

687) On land,
camels cleave the desert night,
on sea.
ships race amid the heaving deep,

688) And you see two armies
on land, at times,
other times, at sea,
in great formations.

689) Courageous,
dressed in iron mail,
they stand their guard
with swords and spears.

690) The soldiers of land—
knights on horse
or mainly
manly infantry—

691) And the heroes at sea—
riding the decks
or climbing
the lance-like masts—

692) Are violently striking
with shining sword,
thrusting the brown shaft
of a strong quivering spear,

693) Drowning in the fire
of striking arrows,
burning in the deluge
of piercing hot blades.

694) You see one charging headlong
giving up himself,
while another turns
broken and defeated,

695) And you witness
the hoisting of the catapult;
then it fires to destroy
fortresses strong and forbidding.

696) You glimpse specters,
like disembodied souls,
lying in stealth within
their genie land;

697) Wild attire, savage nature
set them apart from
the humanity of humans,
for the jinn are not humane.

698) Into the river,
the hunter's hand
casts the net
and quickly draws out fish,

699) And cunningly,
he sets his traps,
and hungry birds
are snared for seed.

700) Ravenous serpents
shatter ships at sea;
while lions in the jungle
claw their prey,

701) And in the air
some birds snatch others,
while savage beasts
hunt in the badlands.

702) You will see other shapes
that I have not mentioned,

but I will trust
in these choice few.

703) Consider and learn
what appeared to you
in that single span
without a long delay:

704) All that you witnessed
was the act of one
alone within
the cloistering veils.

705) But when he removes the screen
you see none but him;
no doubt lingers
about the shapes and forms,

706) And you realize
when the truth is shown,
that by his light you were guided
to his actions in the shadows.

Ibn al-Fāriḍ was not the first Muslim to draw parallels between a puppet and the human being to portray matters of individual existence and volition, but his account of medieval puppet theatre is an elegant addition to classical Arabic poetry.[69] Interpreting his own analogy, Ibn al-Fāriḍ first equates the puppeteer with the *nafs*. The illuminated screen obscuring the puppeteer's presence is the body, while the puppets and their actions stand for the senses and sensations by which the *nafs* acts and becomes manifest. The *nafs* uses the body and its senses together to create the illusion of an existence with independent volition where, in fact, none exists. Just as the puppeteer removes the screen to end his play, so too should the mystic unveil his selfish *nafs* that he might slay it and annihilate duality (vv. 707–715). With duality destroyed, the shadow play gains new meaning as the prophetic Light re-emerges. For the ultimate puppet-master is not the *nafs*, but God, who has veiled His absolute oneness with his His attributes so that His unity will not consume the theaters of its manifestation.[70] Thus, by means of these veils and manifestations in humanity and all creation, God presents His handiwork.[71] The individual, then, is like a puppet, which appears to speak and move on the screen, although it is God who truly acts. This is union's (*ittiḥād*) truth, confirmed by the "Tradition of Willing Devotions" in which God assumes the senses of those absorbed with Him; this is the central lesson of the parable and of the *al-Tā'īyah al-Kubrā* (vv. 716–721).[72]

In the exuberance of union and gnosis, the poetic persona again speaks as the Light of Muhammad from whom all religions have drawn their inspiration and message. Indeed, all faiths are true in so far as their true aim is God and His glorification; Muslim, Christian, Jew, all have their place. Even those who worship idols, the sun, or fire glorify God in fact, although they have gone astray by mistaking diverse and limited manifestations to be the absolute one.[73] Still, monotheists may be wayward too, and they should temper their scorn of others, for many of them love worldly things more than their Creator (vv. 721–736). Yet human beings, as all things, must follow the courses set for them by God's names and attributes according to divine decree, just as the puppeteer moves the puppets. Like an illusory shadow play, creation hides the divine actor, but it also reveals His presence and actions and the fact that existence is not some idle sport. In a moment out of time, with patience, persistence, and, no doubt, a touch of grace, the aspirant may come to realize the truth of the poet's message (vv. 722–749).[74]

Ibn al-Fāriḍ now draws his poem to a close. Creative to the end, he invokes the lyrical Light one last time to praise God, Muhammad and, of course, his own poetry (vv. 750–761):

750) I am not to blame
if I spread my bounty
and bestow my gracious gift
on those who follow me,

751) For I have received the sign of kinship
from one bringing news of union
when he greeted me with:
"Or nearer!"

752) From his light,
the niche of my essence enlightened me;
by means of me,
my nights blazed morning bright.

753) I made me witness my being here
for I was him;

I witnessed him as me
the light, my shining splendor.

754) By me the valley was made holy
and I flung my robe of honor—
my "taking off of sandals"—
on those summoned there.

755) I embraced my lights
and so was their guide;
how wondrous a soul
illuminating lights!

756) I firmly based my Sinais
and there prayed to myself;
I attained my every goal
as my essence spoke with me.

757) My full moon never waned;
my sun, it never set,
and all the blazing stars
followed my lead,

758) By my leave, in my realm
my planets moved,
and my angels bowed
down to my dominion.

759) In the world of remembrance
the soul has her ancient lore;
my young disciples
seek it from me.

760) So hurry to my union old
where I have found
the elders of the tribe
as newborn babes,

761) For my friends drink
what I left behind,
while those before me,
their fine qualities fall short of mine!

Conjuring images of light and invoking numerous Qur'ānic passages, the enlightened guide claims his right to lead others based on his own pre-eminence. He has been singled out by the *mufīḍ al-jamᶜ*, the one who bestows tidings of union (v. 751). Earlier in verse 615 of the poem, Ibn al-Fāriḍ used this word *mufīḍ* together with the term *khaṭm* or "seal," making a clear reference to Muhammad, "the seal of the prophets:"

wa-jā'a bi-asrāri-l-jamīᶜi mufīḍuhā
ᶜalaynā lahum khatman ᶜalā ḥīni fatrati

615) And the secrets of all [the prophets]
were brought and bestowed on us
by him who was their seal
in prophecy's due time.

The *mufīḍ al-jamᶜ*, then, could be read as again referring to Muhammad or his Light.[75] However, if we understand the poetic persona as speaking not to but as the prophetic Light, then the *mufīḍ* in this second instance could be God or Gabriel, the Spirit of revelation who, the Qur'ān suggests, descended to Muhammad at a distance "of two bows' lengths or nearer" (53:9). In either case, union's messenger brought the prophetic guide news of his spiritual kinship (*nisbah*), thereby kindling love's fire in niche of his heart (*mishkāt*; vv. 752–753). By the light of this lamp, the mystic finds his oneness with the prophetic Light and its progressive manifestations among God's prophets. It first appeared as Adam, before whom the angels bowed (v. 758), later to Moses at Sinai and to other prophets (vv. 754, 756), and finally, to the saints and Sufis who guide others to recollect their pre-eternal state and ancient pact (vv. 755, 757). But whatever the place or time, the prophets of the past and the master mystics of the present are but reflections of Muhammad's refulgent Light, for it is he, in truth, who shines over all (vv. 760–761).[76]

Poet and Guide

Ibn al-Fāriḍ's great ode challenges readers on several levels as form and content weave together 760 verses. Thematically, the *al-Tā'īyah al-Kubrā* may be divided into a number of relatively discreet sections marked, at times, by their own pronounced stylistic features. Further, Ibn al-Fāriḍ usually makes his transition between sections with references to his poetry and the power of its expression. But most prominent among the poem's formal characteristics is its division into two distinct parts: an opening wine ode (vv. 1–163), and the subsequent discourse on the Sufi way (vv. 164–761).[77] The ode section as a whole poses few problems and closely parallels Ibn al-Fāriḍ's love poetry in terms of motifs, meaning, and mood. Ibn al-Fāriḍ, however, implies that he will mystically interpret his ode (v. 164), which he never does, at least not in the same manner as most of his major commentators. These commentators have generally read the poem in terms of their own particular beliefs often derived from Ibn al-ᶜArabī's mystical theology. Perhaps following Ibn al-ᶜArabī's methods of interpretation for his own poems, commentators of the *al-Tā'īyah al-Kubrā* normally treat each verse as a largely independent unit; key words and themes are paired with their symbolic and mystical equivalents, and then briefly related to the particular theosophy driving the commentary. Such commentaries are certainly valuable as they cite Ibn al-Fāriḍ's many references to the Qur'ān, *ḥadīth*, and key Sufi doctrines, many of which were undoubtedly shared in common by the poet and his readers.

More helpful, however, are Ibn al-Fāriḍ's poetic musings, which make up the larger portion of his ode. In section after section, Ibn al-Fārid circles back to allude to the spiritual sense and significance pervading his verse, particularly in such motifs as the lover's protagonists, love-sickness, the transformation of the senses, and, of course, love, the beloved, and union with her. Nevertheless, even in these cases, the relationship between poetry and mysticism remains for the most part implicit, as do the connections between the ode's two major sections. In fact, it is possible that Ibn al-Fāriḍ did not intend his extended Sufi discourse to be a commentary at all. Rather, setting out to compose a poem, he began with what he knew best, an ᶜUdhrī style poem on love and wine, to which he appended a number of more didactic recitals on Sufi topics interspersed with lyrical interludes, and concluding with self-praise.[78] The barest traces of the Arabic *qaṣīdah* begin to show through. But the *al-Tā'īyah al-Kubrā* is hardly a formal *qaṣīdah* in its classical sense, for the number and variety of subjects featured in the poem's second section go far beyond the restricted range and themes of the classical ode. Beginning in the sixth/twelfth century, some scholars composed long Arabic works in rhymed couplets in the *rajaz* meter on numerous subjects including grammar, jurisprudence, agriculture, hunting, and sex.[79] Yet, Ibn al-Fāriḍ had no precedent within Arabic poetry for his Sufi discourse, which followed classical poetic standards with a single rhyme and the meter *ṭawīl*. Instead, he may have turned to Arabic Sufi prose for a model: the ever-popular guide for the perplexed. The poetic persona thus becomes the Sufi master (*murād*) who imparts the secrets of gnosis to his audience, his eager disciple (*murīd*).[80]

This choice had important literary consequences. The guide form gave Ibn al-Fāriḍ the freedom to outline and discuss in verse the requirements of the Sufi path, ecstatic experiences, union, oneness, and a host of other mystical and theological beliefs. In addition, by not exclusively relying on traditional poetic genres, Ibn al-Fāriḍ was able to compose two very lyrical and original passages of high literary caliber, namely, the account of the distressed infant (vv. 430–436) and the shadow play of life (vv. 679–706). Neither section was a part of the classical Arabic poetic canon, yet, they are two of the most moving allegories in the poem. This is due in part to their juxtaposing charged poetic language with appealing everyday subjects, and in this respect, both allegories resemble portions of the popular Persian narrative poems, including those by ᶜAṭṭār, and especially the *Mathnavī* of Jalāl al-Dīn Rūmī (d. 672/1273), which would be composed fifty years later.

Still, although the subjects of the *al-Tā'īyah al-Kubrā* occasionally take on a popular hue, its language does not; Ibn al-Fāriḍ's rhetorical *badī*ᶜ style is ever present. Some instances of paronomasia and antithesis no doubt resulted from unconscious associations between the sense of words and their Arabic root forms. However, in the ode's many highly rhetorical sections, Ibn al-Fāriḍ consistently and consciously employed literary devices to elicit mystical allusions and meanings. Nevertheless, Ibn al-Fāriḍ's extensive use of *badī*ᶜ was as much literary as mystical, for he often used rhetorical devices in order to be succinct or terse, and for purposes of summary and stress:

huwa-l-ḥubbu in lam taqḍi lam taqḍi ma'raban
mina-l-ḥibbi fa-khtar dhāka aw khalli khulatī

102) "Such is love: if you do not die
you will derive nothing from the lover;
so decide on death
or leave my love alone!"

Yet these same devices could as readily obscure easily understood ideas, as in the case of Ibn al-Fāriḍ's account of God's names and attributes (vv. 537–574). The abstruseness of this passage is not due to intellectual density or subtle esotericism, but to Ibn al-Fāriḍ's incessant use of parallelism, antithesis, and paronomasia over thirty-seven verses.

In terms of Sufi doctrine, this poetic account is a vague summary of well-known cosmology, but in terms of Arabic poetry, these verses form an incredible rhetorical display.

Covering Reality

Ibn al-Fāriḍ's *al-Tā'īyah al-Kubrā* broke new ground in Arabic mystical poetry, though most of the mystical beliefs and ideas in the poem may be found in noted Sufi writings from earlier centuries. Generally, Ibn al-Fāriḍ appears to have followed the mystical tradition associated with Sahl al-Tusturī (d. 283/896) and, especially, al-Junayd of Baghdad (d. 298/910). As noted earlier, Ibn al-Fāriḍ and al-Junayd employed the Hajj, its sites and rituals in their discussions of the mystical quest,[81] and Ibn al-Fāriḍ also appears to have followed al-Junayd on several other matters. Al-Junayd is frequently credited with formulating a doctrine of the enlightened life commonly referred to as the second sobriety. Ibn al-Fāriḍ explicitly refers to this doctrine several times in his poem (e.g., vv. 212, 223, 311, 480–486), and his references to the pre-eternal covenant (*mīthāq*) were probably influenced by al-Junayd as well.[82] Al-Junayd asserted that the spirits (*arwāḥ*) of humanity were called up by God through His will (*mashī'ah*) prior to the primordial covenant whose purpose was to testify to God's unique oneness:[83]

> . . . He brought them into existence for Himself with Him in pre-eternity, as His mounts for oneness (*aḥadīyah*). When He called them, they answered quickly due to a grace and a favor from Him to them; by means of it, He answered on their behalf when He brought them into existence, so they were the call from Him. And He made Himself known to them when they were not save a will (*mashī'ah*), which He established before Himself. By His decree (*irādah*), He transported them, then He made them like atoms (*dharr*), drawing them out by His will (*mashī'ah*) as a creation (*khalq*) and depositing them in the loins of Adam. . . . So He the most glorious and exalted said: "And when your Lord took from the loins of the children of Adam their progeny and made them witness against themselves, 'Am I not your Lord?' " (7:172). Thus, He . . . informs with this that He addressed them while they were non-existent save by His existing on their behalf. Thus, they existed due to the Real

> (*al-ḥaqq*) since they were non-existent as themselves. So in that, the Real existed in the Real in a sense (*maʿnā*) that no one may know or find save Him!

From this passage it would appear that al-Junayd held that the pre-eternal covenant was taken by God from Himself when He answered Himself on behalf of the spirits whose contingent being was derived from His necessary one. The spirits and the covenant thus serve as a means for God's self-manifestation of His oneness.[84] Ibn al-Fāriḍ succinctly expressed a similar view in verses 495 to 496:[85]

wa-laysa alastu-l-amsi ghayran li-man ghadā
wa-junḥī ghadā ṣubḥī wa-yawmiya laylatī
wa-sirru balā li-llāhi mirātu-kashfihi
wa-ithbātu maʿnā-l-jamʿi nafyu-l-maʿīyati

495) Yesterday's "Am I not?" is not
other than what one will be tomorrow,
as my pitch dark became bright morn,
and my day, my night.

496) For the secret of "Indeed, yes!" to God
is the mirror of His unveiling,
and the meaning of union is confirmed
with the denial of "withness."

Ibn al-Fāriḍ's description of the human condition also appears indebted to al-Junayd. In one of his letters, al-Junayd states that following the primordial covenant, God made the spirits forget the bliss of pre-eternity. Once in creation, they began to take pleasure in their own individuality, growing self-centered and selfish amid material existence, which veiled them from their original state of perfection. Seen in this light, al-Junayd regards individual existence and human attributes as the spirits' self-deception (*talabbus*), or as disguises (*talbīsāt*) masking their true nature.[86] Naturally, it is concupiscence or the carnal soul (*nafs*) that tempts the human being and binds him to the material world, while the troubled spirit (*rūḥ*) yearns to return to its Creator. This tribulation (*balā'*) initiates the spiritual quest of those who strive diligently to discipline and weaken their selfishness. During their trials and tribulations, these seekers may find solace in nature's beauty, which serves as a temporal vision of Paradise. God, however, continues to try them until He annihilates their selfish wills.[87] Then,

He graces them with the highest mystical experience, which al-Junayd likens to their first moment in pre-eternity:

> (The gnostic) is a phantom (*shabaḥ*)[88] standing before Him without a third between them, while His decree flows over him in the channel of the judgments of His omnipotence, in the fathomless depths of the seas of His unity (*tawḥīd*), due to the annihilation (*fanā'*) from himself (*nafsihi*), from His call to him, and from His answering on his behalf (at the taking of the covenant), by means of the realities of the existence of His unicity, in the reality of H/his proximity (*qurb*), with the vanishing of his senses and movements, because the Real (*al-ḥaqq*) has undertaken for him what He has willed for him. And the point of this is that the worshipper's end returns to his beginning, and he is as he was before he was![89]

Major parallels between several of al-Junayd's mystical beliefs and those of Ibn al-Fāriḍ should now be clear: the conflict between the *nafs* and the *rūḥ*, the tribulation of the *via purgativa* and nature's ability to sooth the lover's anguish, and the experience of union as a return to the spirit's pre-eternal state. Significantly, both men use derivatives from the Arabic root *l*b*s* to refer to the spirit's being veiled in and by creation, and this is rare in Sufi discussions of this subject.[90] Further, words from the root *sh*h*d* involving witnessing also appear frequently in al-Junayd's epistles and in Ibn al-Fāriḍ's *al-Tā'īyah al-Kubrā* where they generally refer to mystical vision. Moreover, it is clear from al-Junayd, that underlying this root's surface meaning of vision is an implied "witnessing" to God's oneness and lordship on the Day of the Covenant. Al-Junayd goes on to contrast this enlightened witnessing (*mushāhadah*) in union, to the ignorance of human existence (*wujūd*), and this may clarify further, Ibn al-Fāriḍ's frequent pairing of similar concepts and terms, as in verses 400 to 401:[91]

fa-dhā maẓharun li-r-rūḥi hādin li-ufqihā
  shuhūdan ghadā fī ṣīghatin maʿnawīyati
wa-dhā muẓhirun li-n-nafsi ḥādin li-rufqihā
  wujūdan ʿadā fī ṣibghatin ṣuwarīyati

400) (The slanderer) is the spirit's guise
    guiding to its high horizon

with a witnessing
beginning in an ideal form,

401) While (the blamer) is the soul's display
driving down to its cronies
with an existence
ending in a formal mould.[92]

Finally, al-Juanyd explicitly states that a human being can never receive this mystical enlightenment without God's help, for the primordial is beyond the keen of those in the transient world. The seeker, therefore, must be annihilated in God who alone knows the secret of pre-eternity.[93] At the moment of union, God overwhelms His worshipper and assumes his will and actions, becoming the sole actor, in much the same way as Ibn al-Fāriḍ's puppeteer controls the show.[94] In support of this understanding of union, al-Junayd cites the "Tradition of Willing Devotions" concerning God's assumption of His believer's senses,[95] and, as we have seen, this tradition is central to Ibn al-Fāriḍ poetry, especially to the *al-Tā'īyah al-Kubrā* where he alludes to this tradition in numerous verses, especially in verses 719 to 721 at the end of his poetic account of the shadow play.

Yet in contrast to these noted similarities between ideas and expressions in the *al-Tā'īyah al-Kubrā* and al-Junayd's epistles, there remains an important difference in their terms for union. Al-Junayd consistently speaks of *tawḥīd* ("unity"), whereas Ibn al-Fāriḍ usually refers to union as *ittiḥād* ("unification"). Both terms stem from the Arabic root *w*ḥ*d* with its basic meaning of singularity. Al-Junayd's particular term has strong theological and ontological connotations because *tawḥīd Allāh* means monotheism, the declaration of God's unique and unrivaled oneness, and al-Junayd certainly had this in mind when discussing mystical union.[96] By contrast, *ittiḥād* gives the impression of a joining or coalescence between two things in an intimate connection. Furthermore, Ibn al-Fāriḍ's use of synonyms like *jam*ᶜ, *waṣl*, and *wiṣāl* with their *ghazal* overtones, also suggests that he viewed mystical experience more in terms of a lovers' union than as an ontological event. Nevertheless, Ibn al-Fāriḍ's *ittiḥād* is not the joining of two separate and distinct essences or natures, a doctrine that he forcefully denied (vv. 277–285). In fact, like al-Junayd, he invokes the term *tawḥīd* in one passage to underscore the oneness of *ittiḥād*:

*wa-alsinatu-l-akwāni in kunta wā*ᶜ*iyan*
shuhūdun bi-tawḥīdī bi-ḥālin faṣīḥatī

wa-jā'a ḥadīthun fī-ttiḥādiya thābitun
riwāyatuhu fī-n-naqli ghayru ḍaʿīfati
yushīru bi-ḥubbi-l-ḥaqqi baʿda taqarrubin
ilayhi bi-naflin aw adā'i farīḍati
wa-mawḍiʿu tanbīhi-l-ishārati ẓāhirun
bi-kuntu lahu samʿan ka-nūri-ẓ-ẓahīrati

718) The tongues of all beings,
if you listen close,
witness with eloquence
to my unity (*tawḥīdī*)

719) While about my union (*ittiḥādī*)
a *ḥadīth* has come,
its transmission firm,
not weak,

720) Declaring the Real's love
for those who draw near Him
by willing acts devotions
or those decreed.

721) The point of its teaching
is clear
as noon-day light:
"I am his ear . . ."

The difference between the two related words, then, is one of aspect or perspective, as the mystic and theologian Muhammad al-Ghazālī (d. 505/1111) perceptively noted in his analysis of mystical union in his *Mishkāt al-Anwār* ("The Niche for Lights"), a commentary on the Qur'ānic "Light Verse" (24:35):[97]

> This state (of union), in attribution to the one immersed in it, is called, metaphorically speaking, a unification (*ittiḥād*) or, ontologically speaking, a realization of unity (*tawḥīd*).

Similar to al-Ghazālī, Ibn al-Fāriḍ appears to employ the term *ittiḥād* when referring to experiential or existential union, whereas *tawḥīd* serves to denote union's ontological dimension. Underlying this distinction are notions of existence and being, and al-Ghazālī's clear and concise discussion of both topics in the *Mishkāt* clarifies an implicit premise of Ibn al-Fāriḍ mystical beliefs as presented in the *al-Tā'īyah al-Kubrā*:[98]

> Existence (*wujūd*) is divided into that which a thing has from its essence (*dhāt*), and that which it has from something else. That which has existence from something else, its existence is borrowed and not self-sufficient. Indeed, when its essence is considered with respect to itself, it is pure nonexistence. Rather, the thing exists only with respect to its relationship to something else, and that is not a true existence. . . . Thus, the true existent is God most high, just as the true light is God . . .

Clearly indebted to the fifth/eleventh-century Muslim philosopher Ibn Sīnā, al-Ghazālī defines true existence as that which is necessarily so. This, in turn, he declares to be God who is, then, the source for all contingent being. The necessarily existent God is like the sun whose light represents contingent existence; just as a moving reflection is relative to and dependent on the sun, so too does the ever-changing contingent existence require a necessary being. Without the sun, the moon would be totally dark; without God, nothing would exist. All things can be viewed from this dual perspective: in relation to themselves, and in relation to God, and this al-Ghazālī calls the two faces of a thing:[99]

> Everything has two faces: a face (*wajhah*) toward itself, and a face toward its Lord. In respect to its own face, it is nonexistent, while in respect to God's face, it exists. Consequently, there is no existence save God (*lā wujūd illā Allāh*) most high, and His face. Thus: "Everything perishes save His face" [Q. 28:88] always and forever!

Al-Junayd, al-Tusturī, and other early Sufis probably held similar views of existence when they declared that the nonexistent spirits appeared in pre-eternity due to God's existing on their behalf. This was a truth revealed to the mystic in union, and al-Ghazālī, too, stated that the great mystics witness (*mushāhadah*) this reality during their spiritual ascension (*miʿrāj*). Illumined by the holy prophetic spirit (*al-rūḥ al-nabawī al-qudsī*), the spiritually realized saints, like the prophets before them, become enlightened guides following Muhammad who the Qur'ān calls "a shining lamp" (*sirāj munīr*; 33:46).[100] This light symbolism found in the *Mishkāt* is also reflected in Ibn al-Fāriḍ's ecstatic proclamations of spiritual illumination (vv. 750–761), and in his account of the prophetic light and its transmission from the prophets to the saints (vv. 615–631).

Moreover, for al-Ghazālī, creation and human existence are a series of reflections of God's light. Most people, however, fail to see this and so are veiled from the pure light by materiality, the senses, the imagination, or a weak intellect. As a result, the idolater worships stones while others prostrate before a beautiful person or the sun; Magians venerate fire, and still others praise all forms of physical light. Indeed, the divine light ultimately underlies all these faiths, but the worshippers are blinded to this by their own heedlessness.[101] This doctrine is very similar to that found near the end of the *al-Tā'īyah al-Kubrā* (vv. 738–746):

738) The eyes of every faith
have never strayed,
nor did the thoughts of any creed
ever swerve aside.

739) One dazed in the sun
is not deranged
for it shines from the light
of my blazing splendor, unveiled.

740) And when the Magi worship the fire
that, tradition tells,
has been burning bright
for a thousand years,

741) They aim only for me,
though they do not show
a firm resolve
as they seek another.

742) They saw the flash of my light, once,
and supposed it to be a fire,
so they went astray, misled,
by shinning rays.

743) If not for the veil of being
I would speak out,
yet respect for the laws of sense
keeps me silent.

744) This is no jest:
creatures were not created in vain,
though their actions
fall short of the mark.

745) Their affairs run the course
marked by the names,
while the attribute of essence
drives them on to the divine decree:

746) "No and no!"—dispatching with dispassion
two handfuls of humans,
one for a pleasant life,
one for misfortune.

Both al-Ghazālī and Ibn al-Fāriḍ posit the divine light as the original source of all religious faiths, which have, nevertheless, veiled the light to varying degrees. Neither man, however, is proclaiming the unity of diverse religious traditions, so much as the unity of God who is concealed within all of them. Al-Ghazālī categorically declares many worshippers to be in error, and Ibn al-Fāriḍ, while counseling religious tolerance, describes the Magians as being "led astray" (*ḍallū*) by fire from right guidance (v. 742).[102] Furthermore, Ibn al-Fāriḍ, similar to al-Ghazālī, takes an ᶜAsharite theological position regarding creation and predestination. In the final verse above, Ibn al-Fāriḍ refers to a divine saying on creation, which states that God gathered up the progeny of Adam in two handfuls and said: "These are for the garden, and I don't care, and these are for the fire, and I don't care."[103] Finally, there is a tantalizing similarity between al-Ghazālī's *Mishkāt al-Anwār* and Ibn al-Fāriḍ's ode when immediately following his verses on the divine light of religions, Ibn al-Fāriḍ concludes his *al-Tā'īyah al-Kubrā* in praise of mystical enlightenment (vv. 750–761). These final verses are replete with light symbolism and Qur'ānic references, including one to the Light Verse (24:35), as the prophetic guide declares in verses 751 to 752:

wa-lī ᶜan mufīḍi-l-jamᶜi ᶜinda salāmihi
ᶜalayya bi-aw adnā ishāratu nisbati
wa-min nūrihi mishkātu dhātī ashraqat
ᶜalayya fa-nārat bī ᶜishā'ī ka-ḍaḥwati

751) I have received the sign of kinship
from one bringing news of union

when he greeted me with
"Or nearer!"

752) From his light
the niche of my essence enlightened me;
by means of me,
my night blazed morning bright!

The contents of these verses and others in the *al-Tā'īyah al-Kubrā* seem to mirror al-Ghazālī's doctrines of illumination, though this does not establish a firm historical link between them. Al-Ghazālī was by no means the first to comment on the Light Verse, and, as noted earlier, Ibn al-Fāriḍ had read at least some of the Arabic writings of the illuminist Sufi Yaḥyā al-Suhrawardī. In fact, many of Ibn al-Fāriḍ's light images and symbols were, by this time, quite traditional.[104] Ibn al-Fāriḍ, then, may not have been directly influenced by the writings of al-Ghazālī, al-Tusturī, or al-Junayd, although it appears certain that many of the mystical views and beliefs expressed in the *al-Tā'īyah al-Kubrā* and other poems by Ibn al-Fāriḍ reflect a chain of Sufi tradition in which al-Tusturī, al-Junayd and al-Ghazālī were prominent links.[105]

Two Masters

Surprisingly, Ibn al-Fāriḍ has rarely been included among the spiritual heirs of these celebrated Sufis. Generally, he has been placed in the school of Ibn al-ᶜArabī, often as his respected colleague.[106] Perhaps best illustrating this latter view is a popular story, here related by the Andalusian historian al-Maqqarī (d. 1041/1632):

> . . . [T]he shaykh Muḥyī al-Dīn Ibn al-ᶜArabī sent to the master ᶜUmar [Ibn al-Fāriḍ], asking his permission to comment on the *al-Tā'īyah*. But (Ibn al-Fāriḍ) said, "Your book entitled *al-Futūḥāt al-Makkīyah* is a commentary on it."[107]

Although this particular story is probably apocryphal, it highlights the view in the later Sufi tradition of Ibn al-Fāriḍ and Ibn al-ᶜArabī as spiritual brothers. Essential to this relationship were a number of Ibn al-ᶜArabī's followers who read Ibn al-Fāriḍ's verse in light of their master's teachings. The first to do so may have been Ṣadr al-Dīn al-Qūnawī (d. 673/1274), Ibn al-ᶜArabī's stepson and, perhaps, his most influential student and disciple.[108] Al-Qūnawī visited Cairo during Ibn al-Fāriḍ's lifetime, though he did not meet the poet. Later, in 643/1246, about ten years after the poet's death, al-Qūnawī held teaching sessions in Cairo where he commented on Ibn al-Fāriḍ's *al-Tā'īyah al-Kubrā*. Among those attending was Shams al-Dīn al-Aykī (or al-Īkī; 627–697/1230–1298), who later became an accomplished Sufi master in his own right. Al-Aykī is known to have taught Ibn al-Fāriḍ's *al-Tā'īyah al-Kubrā*, which he had studied with al-Qūnawī. Ibn al-Fāriḍ's grandson, ᶜAlī (fl. eighth/fourteenth century), related the following story from al-Aykī, who said:[109]

> "I follow the school of our master the shaykh Ṣadr al-Dīn al-Qūnawī in loving the Shaykh Ibn al-Fāriḍ, believing in his creed, and devoting oneself to his ode *Poem of the Sufi Way*." Then the shaykh al-Aykī recited some of its verses including this one:
>
> If not for the veil of being
> I would speak out,
> yet my respect for the laws of sense
> keeps me silent.[110]
>
> Then the shaykh al-Aykī began to comment on the meanings of these verses, saying:
>
> "A group of scholars and students of religion would attend the teaching sessions of our shaykh Ṣadr al-Dīn al-Qūnawī, and he would discuss specific disciplines within the religious sciences. Then he would bring his discourse to a close by mentioning a verse from the ode *Poem of the Sufi Way*. He would discuss it in Persian, using rare and mystical terms, which were not understood save by those possessing mystical experience (*dhawq*) and desire. Then on the following day he would say, 'Another meaning has come to me regarding the commentary of the verse about which we spoke yesterday,' and he would say something even more amazing than the day before! Also, he used to say, 'The Sufi should memorize this ode, and one who understands the ode should comment on it.'"
>
> The shaykh al-Aykī, may God have mercy on him, added: "The shaykh Saᶜīd al-Dīn al-Farghānī devoted himself with determination to understanding what Ṣadr al-Dīn al-Qūnawī mentioned as commentary on this ode, and he wrote it down in his presence, first in Persian and then in Arabic. He made his famous commentary in two

volumes, and it is from the inspired sayings of our shaykh Ṣadr al-Dīn al-Qūnawī, may God have mercy upon him."[111]

Saᶜīd al-Dīn al-Farghānī, then, appears to mark the beginning of a long and extensive written commentary tradition on Ibn al-Fāriḍ's verse in light of Ibn al-ᶜArabī's teachings.[112] Nevertheless, there is no solid evidence that Ibn al-Fārid and Ibn al-ᶜArabī ever knew each other, although Ibn al-ᶜArabī had passed through Cairo on at least two occasions, and both men had gone on pilgrimage and spent a considerable time in Mecca.[113] Moreover, given that Ibn al-ᶜArabī's stepson and student al-Qūnawī is known to have possessed a copy of Ibn al-Fāriḍ's *Dīwān*, it seems likely that Ibn al-ᶜArabī was familiar with Ibn al-Fārid's verse.[114] Although several studies have drawn attention to differences in the technical terminology used by the two mystics,[115] both Ibn al-Fārid and Ibn al-ᶜArabī conceived of the universe as a unified divine reality in a constant state of self-disclosure. Intriguingly, both used the medieval shadow play as a simile to illustrate this point. In chapter 317 of his *al-Futūḥāt al-Makkīyah*, Ibn al-ᶜArabī takes up the issue of the relationship between the body and the spirit and, by extension, of the cosmos with God. Ibn al-ᶜArabī states:[116]

> God is the *rūḥ al-ᶜālam*, the spirit of the cosmos, and its ear, its eye, and its hand. By Him the cosmos hears, by Him it sees, by Him it speaks, by Him it grasps and by Him it runs, for there is no power or strength save in God, the most high, the tremendous! No one knows this save him who has drawn close to God through willing acts of devotion, as has been related in the sound prophetic traditions and the divine sayings.

Here, Ibn al-ᶜArabī refers directly to the "Tradition of Willing Devotions" mentioned earlier, in which God assumes the senses of His beloved worshipper. In fact, says Ibn al-ᶜArabī, God has already assumed our senses, but it is only by an act of His grace that one comes to realize and know this.[117] Then Ibn al-ᶜArabī concludes, saying:

> For one who wants to understand what I have alluded to here, let him observe the shadow play (*khayāl al-sitārah*) with its shapes, and one who speaks for them. Young children are kept a distance from the curtained screen, which separates them from the one who plays with those figures and speaks for them. Such is the actual situation (*amr*) for the shapes of the cosmos. Most people are those children, whom I

> have postulated, so think about where the performance is coming from. The children in that setting are having fun and enjoying [the play], but they are heedless, taking it in as sport and amusement. But those who know (*al-ᶜulamāʾ*) consider the matter and know that God has made this only to serve as a simile. Thus, a figure, called the narrator (*waṣṣāf*), comes out at first and gives a short sermon praising and glorifying God. Then he talks about each type of figure from among the shapes that will come out after him from behind this screen. Thus, the learned know that God has made this a likeness for His worshippers, so that they will take heed and know that the actual situation (*amr*) of the cosmos with God is like these figures with the one who moves them, and that this screen veils the mystery of the perfect measuring out of destiny (*sirr al-qadar al-muḥkam*) into all creatures. Still, with all of this, the heedless take it all in as sport and amusement, as He most high has said: "Those who take their religion as sport and amusement" [Q. 7:51]. Then the narrator vanishes, and he corresponds to the first to exist among us, namely Adam, upon whom be peace. When he vanished, his concealment (*ghaybah*) was from us as he is with his Lord behind the screen of the unseen, and God speaks only the truth and leads the way.[118]

As we have seen, Ibn al-Fārid offered a poetic account of the shadow play in his *al-Tāʾīyah al-Kubrā* as an allegory for the *nafs* and its control of the body and the senses to produce an illusion of selfish independence. Then Ibn al-Fāriḍ extended this metaphor to the divine Light suffused in the universe but veiled, so as not destroy creation in a blazing conflagration. This interpretation of the shadow play resonates with that by Ibn al-ᶜArabī, and both men invoke the "Tradition of Willing Devotions" to underscore God's control and presence within His creation. Furthermore, Ibn al-Fāriḍ and Ibn al-ᶜArabī frequently speak in their writings of God's self-manifestation (*tajallī*) as essential to creation.[119] Because there is no reliable evidence that either author borrowed from the other, these similarities suggest that the similes, metaphors, themes and ideas common to their works resulted from a shared Sufi heritage, which included the work of al-Tustarī, al-Junayd, al-Qushayrī, al-Ghazālī, Yaḥyā al-Suhrawardī, and many other well-known Sufi masters.[120] Nevertheless, for the later Islamic mystical tradition, Ibn al-Fāriḍ, "the sultan of the lovers," remained forever joined to Ibn al-ᶜArabī, "the greatest master."

Conclusion

The Poetry of Recollection

I But not "Me"

Within the commentary tradition on Ibn al-Fāriḍ's poetry, al-Farghānī, al-Tilimsānī (690/1291), al-Nābulusī (1143/1731), and others declare the poet's verse to be the product of divine inspiration. Many commentators cite the account by ᶜAlī, Ibn al-Fāriḍ's grandson, on how his grandfather would fall into a trance for days, then come to and recite verses for his *Poem of the Sufi Way*. In light of this story, al-Nābulusī, wrote:

> As for the poems of the gnostics of God, they are, in appearance, poetry in the manner of the words of poets, but at the same time they are a divine inspiration (*ilhām rabbānī*), a merciful utterance, a spiritual opening (*fatḥ rūḥānī*), and an emanation of grace![1]

Furthermore, most commentators have ascribed Ibn al-Fāriḍ's accounts of union in the *Poem of the Sufi Way* and other verse to the poet's manic, mystical states, which led him to speak "with the tongue of union" (*bi-lisāni-l-jamᶜ*) or "with the tongue of the unique reality" (*bi-lisāni-l-ḥaqīqati-l-aḥadīyah*).[2] For them, these passages confirmed Ibn al-Fāriḍ's high spiritual status and the truth of his message. Following in this tradition, Giuseppe Scattolin has read the *al-Tā'īyah al-Kubrā* as a spiritual autobiography, as Ibn al-Fāriḍ passed through the three stages of "division (*al-farq*)," "absolute unity or self-identity (*al-ittiḥād*)," and "universal union (*al-jamᶜ*)." Scattolin states:

> The three stages follow each other and are interwoven in each other throughout the poem in ten great units. These units are the basic structure of the poem, and they progress in a dynamic movement that represents the journey of the poet in the discovery of the dimensions and true identity of his own self (*anā*).[3]

As we have seen, the protagonist of the *al-Tā'īyah al-Kubrā* certainly undergoes a process of spiritual transformation from a self-centered youth to a penitent lover, to a mystic guide, and, ultimately, to the Light of Muhammad. However, Scattolin's assertion that this metamorphosis accurately reflects Ibn al-Fāriḍ's own personal mystical experience is an unwarranted assumption. Moreover, to commentators such as al-Tilimsānī and al-Nābulusī, who were also poets, terms like *bi-lisāni-l-jam*ᶜ or *bi-l-lisāni-l-Muḥammadī* might mean something other than that the poet was in the throes of union or possessed by Muhammad's spirit. For these phrases also can mean "in the language of union," and "in the voice of Muhammad," as his commentators were well aware.[4] Indeed, such a poetic or lyrical persona is essential to all of Ibn al-Fāriḍ's poems, whether they be *ghazals*, *qaṣīdahs*, or wine odes, as the poet assumes a number of guises to deliver his musings on love and life. To gloss over these multiple voices as speaking only about Ibn al-Fāriḍ's personal spiritual life is to lose literary depth and subtle nuance within these poems.[5] For instance, in several odes, Ibn al-Fāriḍ's hero is a well-known character of Arab legend:[6]

a-wamīḍu barqin bi-l-Ubayriqi lāḥā
am fī rubā Najdin arā miṣbāḥā
am tilka Laylā-l-ᶜĀmarīyatu asfarat
laylan fa-ṣayyarati-l-masā'a ṣabāḥā

Did lightning flash at dear Abraq,
or do I see a lantern in the hills of Najd?
Or did Laylā al-ᶜĀmirīyah unveil her face that night
and so turn evening to dawn?

Here Ibn al-Fāriḍ explicitly names the beloved Laylā al-ᶜĀmirīyah, the obsession of Majnūn who was driven to insanity and eventually death by the anguish of his love for her. Ostensibly, then, Majnūn, is the persona of this poem, implying that the lover is on the brink of madness and scorned by society, as Ibn al-Fāriḍ's audience might well have appreciated.[7] But this Udhrī lover is only one of Ibn al-Fāriḍ's personas, which also include the novice in love, the blamer, the longing pilgrim, the intoxicated lover, the enlightened guide, the Light of Muhammad, and, on several occasions, the beloved herself, and Ibn al-Fāriḍ calls on all of them to play their essential parts in his poems:[8]

And there are no lovers
but me in passion,

though I came forth to them
disguised in every form:

So one time as Qays
and another as Kuthayyir,
then appearing
as Buthaynah's Jamīl.

Boldly, I revealed myself among them;
within them, I lay hidden, veiled.
How wondrous an unveiling
by means of a veil!

The beloveds and the lovers,
and this is not some feeble guess,
appear from us, to us, as we reveal
ourselves in love and splendor.

Content *and* Form

Literary matters, such as the poetic persona, appear of little interest to most of Ibn al-Fāriḍ's classical commentators or more recent scholars of the poet, whose primary concern has been the poet's mystical message. Frequently influenced by ᶜAlī's hagiography of his grandfather, they have focused on Ibn al-Fāriḍ, the Sufi and saint, paying particular attention to the *al-Tā'īyah al-Kubrā* and the *al-Khamrīyah*. However, there have been a few exceptions; A.J. Arberry, Jean-Yves L'Hôpital, and Ramaḍān Ṣādiq have noted stylistic and rhetorical features prominent in Ibn al-Fāriḍ poems; Arberry and Yūsuf Sāmī al-Yūsuf looked for literary influence, while Issa Boullata and Stefan Sperl have examined briefly the interaction of content and form in the *al-Tā'īyah al-Kubrā*.[9]

Among earlier classical commentators, the Egyptian scholar Jamāl al-Dīn al-Suyūṭī (d. 911/1505) composed a commentary on Ibn al-Fāriḍ's long ode, the *al-Yā'īah*, in which he cataloged the various rhetorical elements that the poet employed in his verse.[10] About a century later, Ḥasan al-Būrīnī (d. 1024/1615), went substantially further than al-Suyūṭī's commentary to comment on most of Ibn al-Fāriḍ's *Dīwān*, with the noticeable omission of the *al-Tā'īyah al-Kubrā*, with its obvious Sufi content; al-Būrīnī felt that he lacked the requisite mystical state (*ḥāl*) required to bring out the inner spiritual meanings within that poem.[11] Not surprisingly, in his commentaries on Ibn al-Fāriḍ's other poems, al-Būrīnī said little about possible mystical allusions, although he carefully vocalized Ibn al-Fāriḍ's words and phrases, identified the various meters, and analyzed the antitheses, word plays, and other literary devices that he found in the poems.[12]

Like al-Būrīnī, Ibn al-Fāriḍ's contemporaries had earlier drawn attention, not to his teachings on Sufism, but to his creativity and deft poetic skill, as we saw with Ibn Khallikān. Several of Ibn al-Fāriḍ's students mentioned that they had studied poetry with him, and Arab Sufi poets of later generations, including al-Tilimsānī, ᶜĀ'ishah al-Bāᶜūnīyah (d. 922/1517), and al-Nābulusī, imitated Ibn al-Fāriḍ's lyrical poems, and composed mystical *tā'īyahs* of their own.[13] Ibn al-Fāriḍ became the master Arab Sufi poet, and even his detractors admired his beautiful and moving verse. His poetic influence is also found in later panegyrics on the prophet Muhammad (*al-madīḥ al-nabawī*), a genre of poetry that became especially popular soon after Ibn al-Fāriḍ's death. While Ibn al-Fāriḍ's beloved, at times, is implicitly the prophet, later poets were quite explicit in their hymns of praise, greatly popularized by Muhammad al-Būṣīrī (d.c. 695/1295), who modeled his famous *al-Burdah* poem ("The Prophet's Mantle") on a short ode by Ibn al-Fāriḍ.[14] Another Egyptian poet, Ibn Abī Ḥajalah (d. 776/1375) was an admiring critic of Ibn al-Fāriḍ's verse, and so he composed his own collection of poems praising Muhammad, basing each panegyric on a poem by Ibn al-Fāriḍ.[15]

Ibn al-Fāriḍ's own *Dīwān* has no such thematic unity, although nearly every one of his poems mentions love. Here again, form and content blend as Ibn al-Fāriḍ generally composed riddles for lighter verse, whereas his quatrains frequently appear as *munājāt*, intimate conversations with a lover and/or God. The poet's *ghazals* often contain hymns of devotion and praise for the prophet, just as Ibn al-Fāriḍ's lyrical odes re-enact the pilgrimage in hopes of returning to God's presence. So, too, the wine odes are songs of the union and ecstasy to be felt by one who follows the lessons in the *Poem of the Sufi Way*, which may serve as a guide for the spiritually perplexed.

Beginning to End

Ibn al-Fāriḍ employed various poetic forms and themes to elicit a range of tones and moods, while he carefully patterned his poems to modulate their aesthetic and emotional pitch. The importance of form also has been noted by Stefan Sperl, who draws attention to three parts of an ode: the opening verses that introduce the major themes and motifs; the middle section, often characterized by a catharsis or transformation; and the end with its return to themes and images found at the beginning of the poem, but often seen in the new light of transformation. He applies this general pattern to Ibn al-Fāriḍ's poem beginning:[16]

adir dhikra man ahwā wa-law bi-malāmī
fa-inna aḥādītha-l-ḥabībi mudāmī

1) Pass round remembrance of the one I desire,
though that be to blame me,
for tales of the beloved
are my wine.

Sperl notes that issues of love and blame open the poem, as the lover resists those who chastise him and submits to suffering, in hopes that his torment in separation will yield to the bliss of union (vv. 1–13). Sperl then highlights the poem's transition:

14) My bond and pact
are neither loosed or withdrawn,
rapture my joy,
burning passion my affliction.

This declaration of fealty leads to the lover's spiritual transformation as his physical emaciation suggests the dissipation of his selfish nature, to be replaced by love and the beloved (vv. 15–27):

28) So in my every limb
was every heart
hit by every arrow
whenever she gazed with pleasure.

29) Had she unrolled my body,
she would have seen in every essence
every heart holding
every burning passion.

In the final scene, the transformed lover meets the beloved at last (vv. 30–32) and experiences rapture in her presence:

33) And I rubbed my cheek in the dust
for her to step on,
so she said: "Good news for you!
Kiss my veil!"

34) But my soul
would not have it,
guarding me jealously
to keep my longing pure.

35) So we passed the night together
as my command willed over desires;
I saw kingship my kingdom
and time my slave!

Sperl concludes:[17]

> The final section of the poem, the metaphorical meeting with the beloved, follows thereafter and the triumphant note on which it ends is clearly the fruit of the mystical self-annihilation at the core of the poem, an experience which makes the poet strong enough to refrain from kissing the beloved's veil and yearn for a still higher goal.

Sperl also finds this "transformation of consciousness" during his brief analysis of the *al-Tā'īyah al-Kubrā*, and I would add that a similar note of triumph is found at the end of Ibn al-Fāriḍ's *al-Khamrīyah*, because all three poems are versions of the wine ode.[18] Yet in other poems by Ibn al-Fāriḍ, no such transformation or union occurs. Ibn al-Fāriḍ begins his *al-Dhālīyah* with the lover's lament:[19]

ṣaddun ḥamā ẓama'ī limāka li-mādhā
wa-hawāka qalbī ṣāra minhu judhādhā

1) A barrier blocked your dark lips
from my burning thirst;
why, since love of you
has hacked my heart to bits?

In this *ghazal* composed in imitation of a panegyric by al-Mutanabbī, Ibn al-Fāriḍ praises the beloved (vv. 8–23) whose health and handsomeness are in stark contrast to the dire condition of the suffering, yet still faithful lover (vv. 24–50). However, despite the lover's good intentions, there is no union at the poem's end:

> 51) When the women visiting the sick
> saw him, they said:
> "If anyone be slain by passion,
> surely it is this one!"

For despite the lover's claims to have died love's martyr, something of him still remains for the women to see; this is the "barrier" mentioned in the opening verse that must be broken down before union can occur.

In effect, then, the opening verses of Ibn al-Fāriḍ's poems set the stage and signal the audience as to the poems' major themes and eventual conclusions: Mention of wine turns to intoxication; a barrier or confusion is a presage to continued separation; the lover's death brings mystical annihilation; invocations to love and the beloved yield inner peace, whereas the appearance of the caravan and driver will eventually lead to the pilgrimage. Then, following the opening scene, Ibn al-Fāriḍ presents a series of well-known motifs and images appropriate to his theme within a changing tempo. This, in turn, may elicit a sympathetic emotive response from accustomed listeners, who become subsumed in the poem's lyrical persona and formal patterns, as they participate in an aesthetic ritual whose structures and meanings are sensed and internalized.[20]

Meditation and Recollection

Ibn al-Fāriḍ's verse, then, falls into the category of meditative poetry as defined by Louis Martz. Describing meditative poetry in seventeenth-century England, Martz wrote:[21]

> The nature of meditative poetry . . . may be defined by studying its close relation to the practice of religious meditation in that era. The relationship is shown by the poem's own internal action, as the mind engages in acts of interior dramatization. The speaker accuses himself; he talks to God within the self; he approaches the love of God through memory, understanding, and will; he sees, hears, smells, tastes, touches by the imagination the scenes of Christ's life as they are represented on a mental stage.

> Essentially, the meditative action consists of an interior drama, in which a man projects a self upon an inner stage, and there comes to know that self in the light of the divine presence.

Martz found that English poets of the time, including John Donne, George Herbert, Henry Vaughan, and Thomas Traherne had been influenced to varying degrees by Christian forms of meditation including those of Augustine and, especially, the *Spiritual Exercises* of Ignatius of Loyola, which they applied to the form and content of certain poems through a process of "preparation, composition, discourse, . . . and colloquy."[22] Moreover, because many of these poets had a Platonic or neo-Platonic perspective, their universe was "a vast net of correspondence which unites the whole multiplicity of being."[23]

Although Ibn al-Fāriḍ did not share the Christian faith of these English poets, the parallels between their meditative stance and his poems should be clear. The poet uses his mind, thought, inspiration, understanding, and, above all, his memory to recover the beloved's presence:[24]

412) My thought sees her
with my inspiration's eye,
while my memory hears her
with the ear of my mind,

413) And my imagination presents her (*yuḥḍiruhā*)
as an image to the soul,
so my understanding reckons her
my close confidant in sense.

As just noted, Ibn al-Fāriḍ's poems open with a scene and theme, which he developed in the ensuing verses. Again, we see the importance of the lyrical persona and the various actors in the poem as the lover is accused by his blamer, leading the lover to plead his case and swear to his covenant with his beloved, while recalling a union that once occurred during the pilgrimage, whose stopping places and rituals are lovingly described by the poet. Depending on the type of poem and its dominant theme, the lover may face the frustration of a continued separation, sense the beloved's living presence within his heart, or be spiritually intoxicated and transformed by love. But whatever the case, the poet and his audience will have learned something in their spiritual quest to return to the divine presence.

Although Martz was able to establish a strong connection between a number of seventeenth-century English poets and specific Christian meditative traditions, the case of Ibn al-Fāriḍ, living five centuries earlier, is not so clear. In the *Poem of the Sufi Way*, Ibn al-Fāriḍ explicitly refers to and describes the Sufi meditative practice of recollection (*dhikr*) and mystical audition (*samā*ᶜ), which he probably practiced in some form.[25] Additionally, *dhikr* elements are found throughout his poems, particularly the invocation of the beloved's name and attributes, which Sufis often used for meditation.[26] Still, we do not know to what extent Ibn al-Fāriḍ followed a particular form or practice of *dhikr* or whether he consciously composed his poems to be recited in *samā*ᶜ sessions. We do, know, however, that later Sufis in the Arabic-speaking world, including many today, have recited Ibn al-Fāriḍ's verse during their mystical recitals, which often have led participants into an ecstatic trance.[27]

Ibn al-Fāriḍ mentions *dhikr* in the opening verse to several poems, including the *Wine Ode*, where recollection is a major theme:

sharibnā ᶜalā dhikri-l-ḥabībi mudāmah,
sakirnā bihā min qabli an yukhlaqa-l-karmu[28]

1) In memory of the beloved
we drank a wine;
we were drunk with it
before creation of the vine.

Ibn al-Fāriḍ's recollection of the beloved follows a long-established tradition in Arabic poetry, but as his beloved takes on divine proportions and recollection leads to intoxication, Ibn al-Fāriḍ's *dhikr* resonates with the Qur'ān and Sufi practice. Moreover, Ibn al-Fāriḍ praises the mystical experience that results from recollection, which he clearly links to the Day of the Covenant, the "Tradition of Willing Devotions," and the Light of Muhammad, all central tenets of Sufi doctrine and the practice to remember God often.

Ibn al-Fāriḍ's poetry of recollection is most evident in his *al-Khamrīyah* and *al-Tā'īyah al-Kubrā*, yet his other poems reveal it is as well. His *ghazals* are meditations on love, loss, and longing for God and His prophet, while Ibn al-Fāriḍ's odes invoke recollections of the pilgrim's quest to the holy lands to stand before God once more. For in all of his poems, Ibn al-Fāriḍ reinterprets mystically the Arabic poetic tradition with its lyrical persona and ritual antecedents, to offer a moving portrayal of human existence, which may be shared by others. Together, the poet and his audience articulate and recapture their profound feelings of love by conjuring an image of their beloved or by imagining the pilgrimage with its ancient and revered rites. Through these poems, Ibn al-Fāriḍ and others might transcend their separate selfish existence, bound by history and the inevitability of death, and merge momentarily into a spiritually recreated community in the divine presence. By joining the symbolically rich Arabic poetic tradition to Islamic mysticism and the Muslim Hajj, Ibn al-Fāriḍ created a pattern to be traced again and again in order to find spiritual consolation and, at times, mystical transformation.

Notes

Preface

1. *Dīwān Ibn al-Fāriḍ*, ed. Guiseppe Scattolin (Cairo: Institut français d'archéologie orientale, 2004). Regarding various editions of Ibn al-Fāriḍ's *Dīwān*, see G. Scattolin, "The Oldest Text of Ibn al-Fāriḍ's *Dīwān*: A Manuscript of Konya," *MIDEO* 24 (2000):83–114; his "Towards a Critical Edition of Ibn al-Fāriḍ's Dīwān," *Annales Islamologique* 35 (2001):503–47, and Th. Emil Homerin, "Ibn al-Fāriḍ's Personal *Dīwān*," in *The Development of Sufism in Mamluk Egypt*, ed. Richard McGregor and Adam Sabra (Cairo: Institut français d'archéologie orientale, 2006), 233–43.

2. See the works of Louis L. Martz, especially his *The Poetry of Meditation* (New Haven: Yale University Press, 1954); *The Paradise Within* (New Haven: Yale University Press, 1964), and *The Poem of the Mind* (New York: Oxford University Press, 1966). Also see the conclusion below.

3. Robert Bly, *The Eight Stages of Translation* (Boston: Rowan Tree Press, 1983), 13–49.

Introduction

1. Th. Emil Homerin, *From Arab Poet to Muslim Saint: Ibn al-Fāriḍ, His Verse and His Shrine*, rev. ed. (Cairo: American University in Cairo Press, 2001), 15–17, and Homerin, *ʿUmar Ibn al-Fāriḍ: Sufi Verse, Saintly Life* (New York: Paulist Press, 2001), 10–14.

2. Th. Emil Homerin, "Saving Muslim Souls: The *Khānqāh* and the Sufi Duty in Mamluk Lands," *Mamlūk Studies Review* 3 (1999):59–83, esp. 65–66.

3. Homerin, *From Arab Poet*, 16.

4. Ibid., 15–17.

5. ʿAlī Sibṭ Ibn al-Fāriḍ, *Dībājat Dīwān Ibn al-Fāriḍ*, in *Dīwān Ibn al-Fāriḍ*, ed. Scattolin, 1–34 (tr. Homerin in *ʿUmar Ibn al-Fāriḍ*, 301–35).

6. Ibid.

7. Ṣalāḥ al-Dīn Khalīl al-Ṣafadī, *al-Wāfī bi-al-Wafīyāt*, ed. Sven Dedering et al. (Wiesbaden: In Kommission bei Franz Steiner Verlag, 1959), 4:50–56, and Homerin, *From Arab Poet*, 22–24.

8. ʿAlī Sibṭ Ibn al-Fāriḍ, *Dībājah*, and Homerin, *From Arab Poet*, 20–22. Interestingly, al-Malik al-Kāmil is similarly depicted in the Christian tradition as venerating holy men, particularly St. Francis of Assisi (d. 1226), who was said to have gone to Egypt to put a stop to a bloody crusade. See Ewert Cousins, *Bonaventure: The Soul's Journey to God; The Tree of Life; The Life of St. Francis* (New York: Paulist Press, 1978), 262–71.

9. ʿAlī Sibṭ Ibn al-Fāriḍ, *Dībājah*, and Homerin, *From Arab Poet*, 50–54.

10. Homerin, *ʿUmar Ibn al-Fāriḍ*, 19–37.

11. There are a number of good studies on the history of Sufism including Annemarie Schimmel, *Mystical Dimensions of Islam* (Chapel Hill: University of North Carolina Press, 1975), and Carl Ernst, *The Shambala Guide to Sufism* (Boston: Shambala Publications, 1997).

12. Concerning the origins and early centuries of Sufism see Ahmet Karamustafa, *Sufism: The Formative Period* (Edinburgh: Edinburgh University Press, 2007).

13. These *ḥadīth* are found in many collections including the popular one by Yaḥya al-Nawawī (d. 677/1277), *al-Arbaʿīn al-Nawawīyah*, ed. Ibrāhīm ibn Muhammad (Tanta, Egypt: Maktabat al-Ṣaḥābah, 1986), 18, 47, 78, 95 (= #2, 13, 40); my translation. For a complete translation of al-Nawawī's collection see: *An-Nawawi's Forty Hadith*, tr. Ezzedin Ibrahim and Denys Johnson-Davies (n.p., n.d.).

14. Al-Nawawī, *Al-Arbaʿīn al-Nawawīyah*, 93–94, #38. Also see William A. Graham, *Divine Word and Prophetic Word in Islam* (The Hague: Mouton, 1977), esp. 173–74, and *Divine Sayings: The Mishkāt al-Anwār of Ibn ʿArabī*, ed. Stephen Hirtenstein and Martin Notcutt (Oxford: Anqa Publishing, 2004).

15. For more on *dhikr* see *Encyclopaedia of Islam*, 2nd ed. (*EI2*), 2:223–26 (L. Gardet); Fritz Meir, "The Dervish Dance," in *Essays on Islamic Piety and Mysticism*, tr. John O'Kane (Leiden: E.J. Brill, 1999), 23–48; Jean During, *Musique et extase* (Paris: Albin Michel, 1988), esp. 155–68, and Earle H. Waugh, *Memory, Music and Religion: Morocco's Mystical Chanters* (Columbia, SC: University of South Carolina Press, 2005), esp. 17–43.

16. For a more detailed discussion of this topic, see chapter 5.

17. Dhū al-Nūn quoted in Abū Naṣr al-Sarrāj, *Al-Lumaʿ*, ed. ʿAbd al-Ḥalīm Maḥmūd and Tāhā ʿAbd al-Bāqī Surūr (Cairo: Dār al-Kutub al-Ḥadīthah, 1960), 318. Also see ʿAlī Ṣāfī al-Ḥusayn, *al-Adab al-Ṣūfīyah fī Miṣr fī al-Qarn al-Sābiʿ al-Hijrī* (Cairo: Dār al-Maʿārif, 1964), esp. 193–99; Annemarie Schimmel, *As Through A Veil: Mystical Poetry in Islam* (New York: Columbia University Press, 1982), 24–25; "*zuhdiyya*" (P.F. Kennedy) in *Encyclopedia of Arabic Literature*, (*EAL*), ed. Julie Scott Meisami and Paul Starky (London: Routledge, 1998), 1:828–29, and Andras Hamori, "Ascetic Poetry (*zuhdiyyāt*)" in *Cambridge History of Arabic Literature ʿAbbasid Belles Lettres* (*CHALABL*), ed. Julia Ashtiany et al. (Cambridge: Cambridge University Press, 1990), 265–74.

18. Rābiʿah al-ʿĀdawīyah cited by Muḥammad al-Ghazālī, *Iḥyā' ʿUlūm al-Dīn* (Cairo: ʿĪsā al-Bābī al-Ḥalabī, n.d.), 4:302. Also see Schimmel, *Veil*, 17–18, and Geert Jan van Gelder, "Rābiʿa's Poem on the Two Kinds of Love: A Mystification?" in *Verse and the Fair Sex*, ed. Frederick De Jong (Utrecht: M.Th. Houtsma Stichting, 1993), 66–76.

19. Regarding early Sufi verse see A.S. al-Ḥusayn, *al-Adab al-Ṣūfīyah,* 191–96; Schimmel, *Veil,* 11–48; Martin Lings, "Mystical Poetry," *CHALABL,* 235–64; S.H. Nadeem, *A Critical Appreciation of Arabic Mystical Poetry* (Lahore: Islamic Book Service, 1979), and "Ṣūfī Literature, poetry" (R. Radtke), *EAL,* 2:738–39.

20. See chapters 2–4.

21. See Suzanne P. Stetkevych, *Abū Tammām & the Poetics of the ᶜAbbāsid Age* (Leiden: E.J. Brill, 1991), 3–37; Stefan Sperl, *Mannerism in Arabic Poetry* (Cambridge: Cambridge University Press, 1989), 9–27, and *EAL* 2:122–23 (W.P. Heinrichs).

22. Cited in Stetkevych, *Abū Tammām,* 24, from Ibn al-Muᶜtazz, *Kitāb al-Badīᶜ*, ed. I. Kratchkovsky (London: Luzac & Co., 1935), 23, my translation. Also see *EAL* 1:47–49 (J. Meisami).

23. Stetkevych, *Abū Tammām,* 24–25, and see Sperl, *Mannerism,* 9–27.

24. Stetkevych, *Abū Tammām,* 31–32, and S. Stetkevych, "The ᶜAbbasid Poet Interprets History: Three Qaṣīdahs by Abū Tammām," *Journal of Arabic Literature* 10 (1979):49–65.

25. Concerning al-Ḥallāj see *EAL,* 1: 266-67 (J. Cooper); *EI2* 2:99–106 (L. Massignon - L. Gardet), and Louis Massignon, *The Passion of Hallāj,* tr. Herbert Mason (Princeton: Princeton University Press, 1982).

26. Al-Ḥallāj, *Sharḥ Dīwān al-Ḥallāj,* ed. Kāmil Muṣṭafā al-Shaybī (Beirut: Maktabat al-Nahdah, 1974), 279–85.

27. Al-Ḥallāj quoted in Abū al-Ḥasan al-Daylamī, *ᶜAṭf al-Alif al-Ma'lūf,* ed. J.-C. Vadet (Cairo: Maktabat al-Maᶜhad al-ᶜIlmī al-Faransī lil-Āthār al-Sharqīyah, 1962), 44. Also see al-Ḥallāj, *Sharḥ Dīwān,* 142–45; Schimmel, *Veil,* 22–23, 30–34; Lings, "Mystical Poerty," 245–48, and Th. Emil Homerin, "Tangled Words: Toward a Stylistics of Arabic Mystical Verse," in *Reorientations/Arabic and Persian Poetry,* ed. S.P. Stetkevych (Bloomington: University of Indiana Press, 1994), 190–98, esp. 193–97.

28. See al-Daylamī, *ᶜAṭf al-Alif al-Ma'lūf,* 44–45, and also see, Abū 'l-Ḥasan Alī b. Muḥammad al-Daylamī, *A Treatise on Mystical Love,* tr. Joseph N. Bell and Hassan Mahmood Adbul Latif Al Shafie (Edinburgh: Edingburgh University Press, 2005), lvi–lvii, lxiv, 70–72.

29. Homerin, "Tangled Words," and A.S. Ḥusayn *al-Adab al-Ṣūfīyah,* 196–99.

30. Al-Thaᶜālibī, *Yatīmat al-Dahr fī Shuᶜarā' al-ᶜAṣr* (Cairo: Maktabat al-Ḥusayn al-Tījārīyah, 1947), 1:171, and Homerin, "Tangled Words," 194–96.

31. See *EAL,* 2:558–60 (J.S. Meissami), and chapter 1 for an example of his poetry.

32. Al-Thaᶜālibī, *Yatīmat,* 1:171, and al-Mutanabbī, *Dīwān,* ed. Muṣṭfā al-Shayqā et al. (Cairo: Dār al-Maᶜrifah, 1936), 1:201, verse 43.

33. E.g., see ᶜAlī al-Jurjānī, *Kitāb al-Taᶜrīfāt* (Beirut: Dār al-Kutub al-ᶜIlmīyah, 1983), 174.

34. Al-Thaᶜālibī, *Yatīmat,* 1:171, and al-Mutanabbī, *Dīwān,* 3:343, verse 2.

35. Homerin, "Tangled Words," 194–97.

36. See James T. Monroe, "Hispano-Arabic Poetry During the Caliphate of Cordova: Theory and Practice" in *Arabic Poetry: Theory and Development,* ed.

G.E. Von Grunebaum (Wiesbaden: O. Harrassowitz, 1973), 125–54; van Gelder, "Rābiᶜa's Poem," 73–75, and Th. Emil Homerin, "In the Gardens of al-Zahrā': Love Echoes in a Poem by Ibn Zaydūn," in *The Shaping of an American Islamic Discourse*, ed. E.H. Waugh and F. Denny (Atlanta: Scholars Press, 1998), 215–32.

37. See Alexander Knysh, *Islamic Mysticsm: A Short History* (Leiden: E.J. Brill, 2000), 169–218; Erik S. Ohlander, *Sufism in the Age of Transition* (Leiden: E.J. Brill, 2008), and Homerin, "Sufis and Their Detractors in Mamluk Egypt," in *Islamic Mysticism Contested*, ed. Frederick de Jong and Bernd Radtke (Leiden: E.J. Brill, 1999), 225–47.

38. J.T.P. De Bruijn, *Of Piety and Poetry* (Leiden: E.J. Brill, 1983), and Schimmel, *Veil*, 49–81.

39. Farīd al-Dīn ᶜAṭṭār, *The Conference of the Birds*, tr. Afkham Darbandi and Dick Davies (Penguin Books, 1984); Schimmel, *Veil*, 65–81; *EI2* 1:752–55 (H. Ritter), and H. Ritter, *Das Meer der Seele* (Leiden: E.J. Brill, 1955).

40. Al-Ḥallāj, *Sharḥ Dīwān* and Abū Nuᶜaym al-Isfahānī, *Ḥilyāt al-Awliyā' wa-Ṭabaqāt al-Aṣfiyā'* (Reprint of the Cairo 1932 ed., Beirut: Dār al-Kutub al-ᶜArabī, 1980), 10:331–84.

41. See *EI2*, 3:1241–44 (H.R. Roemer); Tahera Qutbuddin, *al-Mu'ayyad al-Shīrāzī and Fatimid Daᶜwa Poetry* (Leiden: E.J. Brill, 2005); Jawdat Rikabi, *La Poesie profane sous les Ayyubides et ses principaux representants* (Paris: G.-P. Masionneuve & Co., 1949); A.S. Ḥusayn, *al-Adab al-Ṣūfī*, esp., 183–207, and G. E. Von Grunebaum, "The Nature of the Arab Literary Effort," *Journal of Near Eastern Studies* 7 (1948):116–122.

42. *EAL*, 1:344–45 (W. al-Qāḍī), and *EI2* 3:832–33 (J.W. Fück).

43. *EAL*, 1:361 (G.J.H. Van Gelder).

44. *EAL*, 1:302–303 (L. Alvarez).

45. *EAL*, 1:30–32 (H. Kilpatrick).

46. *EAL*, 1:363 (G.J.H. Van Gelder).

47. *EAL*, 1:318 (L. Alvarez).

48. *EAL*, 1:392–93 (C. Hillenbrand).

49. EAL,1:188–89 (J.E. Montgomery).

50. *EAL*, 2:791–92 (R. Jacobi), and see chapter 2.

51. *EAL*, 1:41–43 (G. Schoeler) and see chapters 2 and 4.

52. *EAL*,1:161–62 (J.S. Meisami).

53. Ibn Khallikān, *Wafayāt al-Aᶜyān*, ed. Iḥsān ᶜAbbās (Beirut: Dār al-Thaqāfah, 1968), 2:542–43 and paraphrased by Mac Guckin de Slane, *Ibn Khallikan's Biographical Dictionary* (Paris: Oriental Translation Fund of Great Britain and Ireland, 1842–1871), 1:668–70.

54. Ibid.

55. *EAL*, 1:369 (L. Alvarez).

56. *EAL*, 1:381 (G.J.H. Van Gelder).

57. *EI2*, 3:875–76 (J. Rikabi).

58. *EAL*, 1:127 (P. Smoor).

59. Ibn Khallikān *Wafayāt*, 3:332–338; 5:14–19, 6:61–66; 6:258–66 (de Slane, *Ibn Khallikan*, 1:542–45; 3:176–181; 3:589–93; 4:144–150). Also see Rikabi, *La*

Poesie, and Maḥmūd Zaghlūl Salām, *al-Adab fī al-ʿAsr al-Ayyūbī* (Cairo: Dār al-Maʿārif, 1983).

60. Ibid., 5:76–77(de Slane paraphrase, *Ibn Khallikan*, 3:237); my translation.

61. Ibid., 6:266 (de Slane paraphrase, *Ibn Khallikan*, 4:150), my translation.

62. Ibid., 3:205–8; 6:165 (de Slane translation, *Ibn Khallikan*, 2:152–56; 4:51).

63. Ibid., 1:91–92 (de Slane translation, *Ibn Khallikan*, 1:74).

64. Ibid., 4:216–19 (de Slane translation, *Ibn Khallikan*, 2:621–24).

65. Ibid., 3:446–48 (de Slane translation, *Ibn Khallikan*, 2:382–84).

66. Ibid., 1:168–70 (deSlane translation, *Ibn Khallikān*, 1:150–51); also see chapter 3.

67. Ibid., 3:204–205 (de Slane translation, *Ibn Khallikan*, 2:150–51).

68. Ibid., 1:171–72 (deSlane translation, *Ibn Khallikān*, 1:152–53).

69. Ibid., 3:447 (de Slane paraphrase, *Ibn Khallikan*, 2:383), my translation.

70. Ibid., 3:51 (de Slane translation and paraphrase, *Ibn Khallikan*, 2:29–32), and my translation in Th. Emil Homerin, "Preaching Poetry: The Forgotten Verse of Ibn al-Shahrazūrī," *Arabica* 38 (1991): 87–101.

71. Ibn Khallikān *Wafayāt*, 3:52 (de Slane, paraphrase, *Ibn Khallikan*, 2:31), my translation.

72. See Homerin, "Preaching Poetry," and several other examples below in chapters 2–4.

73. See chapter 3.

74. See ʿAlī Ṣāfā Ḥusayn, *Ibn al-Kīzānī: al-Shāʿir al-Ṣūfī al-Miṣrī* (Cairo: Dār al-Maʿārif, 1966), esp. 65–77, and Muḥammad Kāmil Ḥusayn, *Dirāsāt fī al-Shiʿr fī ʿAṣr al-Ayyūbīyīn* (Cairo: Dār al-Fikr al-ʿArabī, 1957), 50–80.

75. Ibn Khallikān *Wafayāt*, 4:461–62 (de Slane, paraphrase, *Ibn Khallikan*, 3:158), my translation.

76. A.S. Ḥusayn, *Ibn al-Kīzānī*, 103–37, and M. K. Ḥusayn, *Dirāsāt*, 50–80. All translations of Ibn al-Kīzānī's verse are my own.

77. A.S. Ḥusayn, *Ibn al-Kīzānī*, 87–89, 104.

78. A.S. Ḥusayn, *Ibn al-Kīzānī*, 104, and 111, 114, 127.

79. For more on these and other characters, see the chapters below.

80. A.S. Ḥusayn, *Ibn al-Kīzānī*, 134.

81. A.S. Ḥusayn, *Ibn al-Kīzānī*, 136, and cf. 125.

82. See chapter 3.

83. See chapter 4.

84. *EAL* 2:742–43 (I. Netton and J.S. Meisami), and chapter 4.

85. Ibn Khallikān *Wafayāt*, 6:268–74 (de Slane, translation, *Ibn Khallikan*, 4:153–159).

86. Ibid, 6:270 (de Slane paraphrase, *Ibn Khallikan*, 4:155), my translation. Also see Yaḥyā al-Suhrawardī, *The Mystical & Visionary Treaties of Suhrawardi*, tr. W.M. Thackson, Jr. (London: Octagon Press, 1982).

87. ʿAbd al-Razzāq al-Kāshānī, *Iṣṭalāḥāt al-Ṣūfīyah*, ed. A. ʿAbd a-Khāliq (Minya, Egypt: Dār Ḥarā', 1980), 115–16.

88. Muḥammad ibn Maḥmūd al-Shahrazūrī, *Kitāb Nuzhat al-Arwāḥ wa-Rawḍat al-Afrāḥ*, microfilm of manuscript 908, Istanbul: Yeni Cami, p. 236.

Also see Otto Spies and S.K. Khattak, *Three Treatises on Mysticism* (Stutgart: W. Kohlhamer, 1935), 108 for their edited Arabic text of the poem.

89. The throne (*ᶜarsh*) and the footstool (*kursī*) were interpreted by many Sufis as meaning the heart (*qalb*) and breast (*ṣadr*), the locus of divine manifestation within the individual; see Gerhard Böwering, *The Mystical Vision of Existence in Classical Islam* (Berlin: Walter De Gruyter, 1980), 163–164. For more on al-Suhrawardī, see the work of Henry Corbin including *Sohrawardī d'Alep* (Paris: Libraire orientale et americane, 1939), and S.H. Nasr, *Three Muslim Sages* (Cambridge, MA: Harvard University Press, 1963), 52–82.

90. Abū Madyan, *Dīwān*, ed. al-ᶜArabī ibn Muṣṭafā al-Shawwār al-Tilimsānī, (Damascus: Maṭbaᶜat al-Taraqqī, 1938), 57, my translation. Also see *EAL*, 1:39 (R.P. Scheindlin), and esp. Vincent Cornell, *The Way of Abū Madyan* (Cambridge: Islamic Texts Society, 1996), 174–175, along with his thorough introduction to Abū Madyan's life, teachings, and writings (1–38).

91. Cornell, *The Way of Abū Madyan*, 162–65; Abū Madyan, *Dīwān*, esp. 58–59, 66–67, 70–79, and see chapter 4.

92. Vincent Cornell notes that there is no known "example of Abū Madyān's writings that was written down in manuscript form less than two hundred years after the death of the shaykh himself." Cornell, *Way of Abū Madyan*, 36.

93. *EAL* 1:311–12 (R.L. Nettler).

94. Ibn Khallikān *Wafayāt*, 6:11 (de Slane, translation, *Ibn Khallikan*, 4:343).

95. See Alexander D. Knysh, *Ibn al-ᶜArabī in the Later Islamic Tradition* (Albany: State University of New York Press, 1999).

96. See William Chittick, *The Sufi Path of Knowledge* (Albany: State University of New York Press, 1989), and below chapter 5.

97. Ibn al-ᶜArabī, *Fuṣūṣ al-Ḥikam*, ed. A.A. ᶜAffifī (Cairo: ᶜĪsā al-Bābī al-Ḥalabī, 1946), 83, my translation. Also see the translation by R.W.J Austin, *Ibn Al-'Arabi: The Bezels of Wisdom* (New York: Paulist Press, 1980), 95. For a commentary on these and other verses in the *Fuṣūṣ*, see ᶜAbd al-Razzāq al-Kāshānī, *Sharḥ ᶜalā Fuṣūṣ al-Ḥikam* (Cairo, 1891).

98. See Michael Sells, "Bewildered Tongue: The Semantics of Mystical Union in Islam," in *Mystical Union in Judaism, Christianity, and Islam*, ed. Moshe Idel and Bernard McGinn (New York: Continuum, 1996), 87–124, esp. 122–24.

99. Ibn al-ᶜArabī, *Dīwān* (Būlāq, 1855, reprint edition, n.p., 1963), 135–136, 164–179, 206–210, 218–232, 313. Also see *EAL* 1:311–12 (R.L. Nettler), Schimmel, *Veil*, 37–41, Lings, "Mystical Poetry," 250–53, and ᶜAbd al-Fattāḥ al-Sayyid Muḥammad al-Damāsī, *al-Ḥubb al-Ilāh fī Shiᶜr Muḥyī al-Dīn Ibn al-ᶜArabī* (Cairo: Dār al-Thaqāfah, 1983), esp. 44–54.

100. Ibn al-ᶜArabī, *Turjumān al-Ashwāq* (Beirut: Dār Ṣādir, 1966), 7–9. Also See R.A. Nicholson's translation, *The Tarjuman Al-Ashwaq* (London: Royal Asiatic Society, 1911), iv–vii, 1–4, 11–13, the partial translation by Michael Sells, *Stations of Desire* (Jerusalem: Ibis Editions, 2000), and chaps. 2 and 3 below.

101. Schimmel, *Veil*, 40–41; Homerin, *Arab Poet*, 27–28, and chapter 5 below.

102. Ibn Khallikān *Wafayāt*, 3: 454–56 (tr. Homerin, *Arab Poet*, 17–19).

103. This is his *al-Tā'īyah al-Kubrā*, also known as *Naẓm al-Sulūk* ("Poem of the Sufi Way"); see below chapter 5.

104. Verses 43–44 of his *al-Jīmīyah*; for a translation of the poem see chapter 2.

105. Verses 8–9 of his *al-Fā'īyah*.

106. Verses 43 of his *al-Fā'īyah*.

107. *EAL* 1:272–73 (R. Droy).

108. Issa J. Boullata has noted: "In many Arab countries, butchers still actually [inflate] a slaughtered animal by mouth from a hole made in the skin of the lower part of the leg in order to make the flaying easier by separating the skin from the flesh by the air blown in." Issa J. Boullata, "Toward a Biography of Ibn al-Fāriḍ," *Arabica* 38(1981):38–56, esp. 40, n. 5.

109. Ibn al-Fāriḍ, *Dīwān*, 216, with a slight variation in the second hemistich.

110. Ibn al-Fāriḍ, *Dīwān*, 217. ʿAlī, Ibn al-Fāriḍ's grandson, cites the verses on the butcher boy based on Ibn Khallikān.

111. Ibn al-Fāriḍ explicitly mentions al-Ḥarīrī and his *al-Maqāmāt* in the *al-Tā'īyah al-Kubrā*; see below chapter 5.

112. Homerin, *Arab Poet*, 22–24, and A.S. Ḥusayn, *al-Adab al-Ṣūfīyah*, 109–12, 227–30.

Chapter 1: Mystical Improvisations

1. ʿAlī Ṣibt ibn al-Fāriḍ, *Dībājah*, 13–14, (tr. Homerin, *ʿUmar Ibn al-Fāriḍ*, 313).

2. See Homerin, *From Arab Poet*, 24–32.

3. Homerin, *From Arab Poet*, 22–24. Also see: A.E. Khairallah, *Love, Madness, and Poetry* (Beirut: Franz Steiner, 1980), A. J. Arberry, *The Mystical Poems of Ibn al-Fāriḍ* (London: Emery Walker, 1952, 1956), 2:11, and Lings, "Mystical Poetry," 253–55.

4. Al-Būrīnī, *Sharḥ Dīwān Sulṭān al-ʿĀshiqīn Sayyidī ʿUmar Ibn al-Fāriḍ*, ed. Rushayyid ibn Ghālib al-Daḥdāḥ (Cairo: al-Maṭbaʿah al-ʿĀmmah, 1888), 1:135, 146. Other poets whose verse is often quoted by al-Būrīnī include ʿUmar ibn Abī Rabīʿah, Abū Tammām, Ibn Khayyāt (d. 517/1123), al-Arrajānī (d. 544/1149), Ibn Sanā' al-Mulk, and Ibn ʿUnayn.

5. Arberry, *Mystical Poems*, 2:26, 37, and Yūsuf Sāmī al-Yūsuf, "Baʿḍ yanābīʿ Ibn al-Fāriḍ," *al-Maʿrifah* 350 (1992): 86–112.

6. For Ibn al-Fāriḍ's use of Ibn al-Kīzānī's verse compare Ibn al-Fāriḍ, *Dīwān*, 168, verse 1 with Ḥusayn, *Ibn al-Kīzānī*, 129, verse 1, and Ibn al-Fāriḍ, *Dīwān*, 154, verse 1 with Ḥusayn, *Ibn al-Kīzānī*, 106, verse 1.

7. See al-Būrīnī, *Sulṭān*, 1:89; 2:89, and Arberry, *Mystical Poems*, 2: 49–50, 77–78.

8. Al-Mutanabbī, *Dīwān*, 3:180–191. In verse 1, I follow Arberry (*Mystical Poems*, 2:77) in reading *al-ḥadaqu* for *al-ḥadaqa* cited in the Cairo edition

of al-Mutanabbī's *Dīwān*. Also see, Andras Hamori, "Al-Mutanabbī," in *CHALAB*, 300–14.

9. Regarding the poetic *ʿayn* see Suzanne Pinckney Stetkevych, *The Mute Immortals Speak* (Ithaca, NY: Cornell University Press, 1993), 177–79, and Homerin, "az-Zahrā'," 225–26. For an insightful discussion of panegyric poetry, in general, and of al-Mutanabbī, in particular, see S. P. Stetkevych, "Abbasid Panegyric and the Poetics of Political Allegiance: Two Poems of al-Mutanabbī on Kāfūr," in *Qasida Poetry in Islamic Asia and Africa*, eds. S. Sperl and C. Shackle (Leiden: E.J. Brill, 1996), 1:35–63; 2:92–105, 421–22.

10. Ibn al-Fāriḍ, *Dīwān*, 181–186. For Arberry's translation, see *Mystical Poems*, 2:73–77; for a French translation see Jean-Yves L'Hôpital, *ʿUmar b. al-Fārid: Poèmes mystiques* (Damascus: Institut Français d'Études Arabes de Damas, 2001), 198–215.

11. Ibn al-Fāriḍ, *Dīwān*, 181. See al-Būrīnī, *Sulṭān*, 2:89, Arberry, *Mystical Poems*, 2:78, n. 6, and al-Mutanabbī, *Dīwān*, 3:288–289, verse 9 for the motif of the bees and the honey. For *kohl* motifs, see al-Būrīnī, *Sulṭān*, 2:89, and Arberry, *Mystical Poems*, 2:79.

12. Al-Mutanabbī, *Dīwān*, 3:87, verse 43.

13. See Arberry's chart, *Mystical Poems*, 2:78. The Cairo edition of al-Mutanabbī's *Dīwān* gives twenty-nine verses to this poem, not thirty-one, as does the Beirut edition used by Arberry. The missing verses are verse 5 of the Beirut edition, ending in *kaḥlu*, and verse 6 ending with *dakhlu*. If the Beirut edition is correct, then al-Mutanabbī used *kaḥlu* twice, once in verse 5 and again in verse 20; he did not repeat any other rhyme words, however. As for *dakhlu*, this word does not appear in Ibn al-Fāriḍ's *al-Lāmīyah*. Further, verse 56 of the Cairo edition of Ibn al-Fāriḍ's *Dīwān* is verse 58 in Arberry's published edition of the Chester Beatty manuscript; *Mystical Poems*, 1:38. Verse 28 of the Chester Beatty manuscript is not found in the Cairo edition, nor is verse 38, which is identical to verse 4 of al-Mutanabbī's poem. Arberry found this last verse in the margin of the Chester Beatty manuscript and so included it in the text; *Mystical Poems*, 1:37; 2:78.

14. See Homerin, *ʿUmar Ibn al-Fāriḍ*, 24–27; "az-Zahrā'," 217, 225–26, and chapter 2.

15. For more on the Sufi understanding of the heart and this tradition, see Chittick, *Sufi Path of Knowledge*, 106–109; Böwering, *Mystical Vision*, 201–207, 241–53, and the introduction. For Ibn al-Fāriḍ's view of *dhikr*, see Homerin, *ʿUmar Ibn al-Fārid*, 30–34, and chapter 5.

16. Al-Mutanabbī, *Dīwān* 2:82–85. This poem was composed around 330/941 in the meter *kāmil*. Concerning the occasion of its composition and Musāwir see R. Blachere, *Abou T-Tayyib al-Motanabbī* (Paris: Adrien-Maisonneuve, 1935), 109. It should be added that a poem ascribed to Ibn al-Fāriḍ beginning: *mā bayna ḍāli al-munḥanā wa-ẓilālih*, *Dīwān*, 223–24, also is a *lāmīyah* with similarities to a poem by al-Mutanabbī, *Dīwān*, 3:53–65. Both are in the meter *kāmil*, and eight of the thirteen rhyme words in *mā bayna ḍāli* (and esp. v. 10; al-Būrīnī, *Sulṭān*, 2:5, and al-Mutanabbī, *Dīwān*, 2:53, v. 2) correspond to words or phrases in al-Mutanabbī's poem. These similarities would seem

to strengthen the case of *mā bayna ḍāli* as an authentic poem by Ibn al-Fāriḍ; see Homerin, "Ibn al-Fāriḍ's Personal *Dīwān*," 242–43.

17. See *EI2*, 2:233 (E. Mittwoch), and *EI2*, 2:961 (Cl. Cahen).

18. Ibn al-Fāriḍ, *Dīwān*, 50–54. Also see Arberry's translation, *Mystical Poems*, 2:45–56; and the French translations by Emile Derminghem and Bachir Messilkh in *Ibn al-Faridh: 2 poemes mystique* (Montpelliar: La Licorne, 1952), 11–14, and L'Hôpital, *Poemes*, 74–95. Arberry's chart comparing the rhyme words of the two poems (*Mystical Poems*, 2:50) omits the rhyme word *afkhādhā*, which is found in the Cairo edition of al-Mutannabī's *Dīwān*, verse 10, with the meaning "thighs"; Ibn al-Fāriḍ also used the word, but with an alternative meaning of "clans" (v. 30). The Egyptian poet Ẓāfir al-Ḥaddād (d. 529/1134) also composed a *dhālīyah* using many of al-Mutanabbī's rhyme words; see Ibn Khallikān, *Wafāyāt*, 2:540–41 (De Slane paraphrase, *Ibn Khallikān*, 2:668).

19. Cf. the verse by Ẓāfir al-Ḥaddād cited by Ibn Khallikān, *Wafayāt*, 2:543, and quoted in the introduction.

20. See *EI2*, 3:236–37 (G. Vajda).

21. See ʿAbd al-Ghānī al-Nābulusī, *Kashf al-Sirr al-Ghāmiḍ fī Sharḥ Dīwān Ibn al-Fāriḍ*, microfilm of manuscript 4104 (3223), Princeton: Yahuda Section, Garrett Collection, Princeton University, fol. 70b, and Arberry, *Mystical Poems*, 2:51, n. 15.

22. Al-Būrīnī, *Sulṭān*, 2:98, and Arberry, *Mystical Poems*, 2:53, n. 24; Muʿādh was martyred in 17 or 18/638–39; see Ibn Ḥajar al-ʿAsqalānī, *Kitāb Tahdhīb al-Tahdhīb* (Beirut: Dār Ṣādir, 1968), 10:186–88, and Ibn al-ʿImād, *Shadharāt al-Dhahab fī Akhbār Man Dhahab* (Cairo: Maktabat al-Qudsī, 1931), 1:29–30.

23. Arberry, *Mystical Poems*, 2:53, n. 24.

24. See Annemarie Schimmel, *And Muhammad is His Messenger* (Chapel Hill: University of North Carolina Press, 1985), 43.

25. Concerning religious allusions in early Arabic *ghazals*, see chapter 2.

26. See Homerin, *From Arab Poet*, 8–9, *ʿUmar Ibn al-Fāriḍ*, 8–10, 304–308; Arberry, *Mystical Poems*, 2:53, n. 27, and chapter 3.

27. Mimshādh al-Dīnawarī (d. 299/912) was an ascetic famous for his sleepless nights spent in prayer. See al-Būrīnī, *Sulṭān*, 2:104–105; al-Iṣfahānī, *Ḥilyāt al-Awliyā'*, 10:353–354; al-Sulamī, *Ṭabaqāt al-Ṣūfīyah*, ed. Aḥmad al-Sharbasī (Cairo: al-Shaʿb, 1962), 76–77, and Arberry, *Mystical Poems*, 2:55, n. 44.

28. Al-Būrīnī, *Sulṭān*, 1:87–88.

29. Ibid., 1:91–94.

30. Ibid., 1:99, and Arberry, *Mystical Poems*, 2: 53, n. 29. For a study of *tawrīyah* and *īhām*, see S. A. Bonebakker, *Some Early Definitions of the Tawryia and Safadī's Fadd al-Xitām ʿan at-Tawrīya wa'l-Istixdām* (The Hague: Mouton & Co., 1966).

31. For the play on *malḥ* see al-Buḥturī (Bonebakker, 12, 29); for *jufūn*, see Yaḥyā ibn Manṣūr al-Ḥanafī (ibid., 11–12) for *ghazālah*, see Qāḍī ʿIyāḍ and Masʿūd ibn Saʿd ibn Salmān (ibid., 11, 13) for the terms for relatives, see Abū ʿAlā al-Maʿarrī (ibid., 33). The play on *jaʿfar* may be found in a citation by Ibn Khallikān (ibid., 18). Bonebakker demonstrates that most of

these examples were repeatedly cited as examples of *tawrīyah* in discussions of this subject and so were well known.

32. Issa J. Boullata, "Verbal Arabesque and Mystical Union: A Study of Ibn al-Fāriḍ's al-Ta'iyya al-kubra," *Arab Studies Quarterly*, 3: no. 2 (Spring, 1981):152–169. For an analysis of this passage from the *al-Tā'īyah al-Kubrā* see chapter 5. For an excellent study of *badī*ᶜ in later Mamluk poetry, see Thomas Bauer, "Ibn Ḥajar and the Arabic Ghazal of the Mamluk Age," in *Ghazal as World Literature I: Transformation of a Literary Genre*, eds. T. Bauer and A. Neuwirth (Beirut: Orient-Institut Beirut, 2005), 35–55.

33. Ramaḍān Ṣādiq, *Shi*ᶜ*r Ibn al-Fāriḍ: Dirāsah Uslūbīyah* (Cairo: al-Hay'at al-Miṣrīyah al- ᶜĀmmah lil-Kitāb, 1998), 38–39. This is verse 7 of the *al-Fā'īyah*; Ibn al-Fāriḍ, *Dīwān*, 177. Also see chapter 2.

34. Ibn al-Fāriḍ, verse 25 of the *al-Hamzīyah*, *Dīwān*, 146, and Ṣādiq, *Shi*ᶜ*r Ibn al-Fāriḍ: Dirāsah Uslūbīyah*, 40.

35. See Arberry, *Mystical Poems*, 2: 80, n. 30. Concerning the *mīthāq*, see Schimmel, *Dimensions*, 24; Böwering, *Mystical Vision*, 148–57; the introduction above, and chapters 2 and 5.

36. Mīshāl Ghurayyib has noted Ibn al-Fāriḍ's creative use of *ṭibāq*, but in general Ghurayyib views Ibn al-Fāriḍ's *badī*ᶜ as excessive hyperbole; Mīshāl Ghurayyib, ᶜ*Umar Ibn al-Fāriḍ min khilal Shi*ᶜ*rihi* (Beirut: Dār Maktabat al-Ḥayāh, 1965), 116—-30. Also see Ṣādiq, *Shi*ᶜ*r Ibn al-Fāriḍ: Dirāsah Uslūbīyah*, 67–81, 203–04.

37. Ibn al-Fāriḍ, *Dīwān*, 66, verse 1. For an analysis of this verse, see chapter 5 below. Also see Ṣādiq, *Shi*ᶜ*r Ibn al-Fāriḍ: Dirāsah Uslūbīyah*, 153–204, for his overview of similes and metaphors in Ibn al-Fāriḍ's *Dīwān*.

38. Ibn al-Fāriḍ, *Dīwān*, 49, and al-Būrīnī, *Sulṭān*, 1:81–82. For further examples of the types of *badī*ᶜ to be found in Ibn al-Fāriḍ's verse, see Ṣādiq, *Shi*ᶜ*r Ibn al-Fāriḍ: Dirāsah Uslūbīyah*, and, especially, al-Būrīnī's *Sulṭān*.

39. See Ṣādiq, *Shi*ᶜ*r Ibn al-Fāriḍ: Dirāsah Uslūbīyah*, 35–48, 54–66, 203–04, who nevertheless appears to be unaware of earlier insightful studies of the *badī*ᶜ style by Sperl (*Mannerism*) and S. P. Stetkevych (*Abū Tammām*).

40. Concerning riddles see *EAL*, 2:479 (G.J.H. Van Gelder); Diyā' al-Dīn Ibn al-Athīr, *al-Mathāl al-Sā'ir*, ed. Muhammad Muḥyī al-Dīn ᶜAbd al-Ḥamīd (Cairo: Muṣṭfā al-Bābī al-Ḥalabī, 1939), 2:223–35; al-Suyūṭī, *al-Muzhir fī* ᶜ*Ulūm al-Lughah wa-Anwā*ᶜ*ihā*, 3rd ed. (Cairo: ᶜĪsā al-Bābī al-Ḥalabī, 1945), 1:578–621, with numerous examples; Aḥmad Aḥmad Badawī, *al-Ḥayāh al-Adabīyah fi* ᶜ*Aṣr al-Ḥurūb al-Ṣalibīyah fī Miṣr wa-al-Shām* (Cairo: Maktabat Nahdat Miṣr, 1952), 106-108; ᶜAbd al-Karīm Yāfī, *Dirāsāt Fannīyah fī al-Abab al-*ᶜ*Arabī* (Damascus: Maṭbaᶜat Jāmiᶜat Dimashq, 1972), 256–66. Among Ibn al-Fāriḍ's contemporaries, Ibn ᶜUnayn appears to have been the most prolific composer of riddles; see Ibn ᶜUnayn, *Dīwān*, ed. Khalil Mardam (Beirut: Dār Ṣādir, 1974), 149–78.

41. Ibn al-Fāriḍ, *Dīwān*, 207–15.

42. *Taṣḥīf* usually consists of the addition or subtraction of dots to the letters to obtain new ones, but this is not always the case; see al-Ṣuyūṭī, *al-Muzhir*, 1: 537–55.

43. Ibn al-Fārid, *Dīwān*, 208.

44. Something I could not do without al-Būrīnī's very helpful commentary; *Sulṭān,* 2:159–60.

45. Ibn al-Fāriḍ, *Dīwān,* 211.

46. See al-Būrīnī, *Sulṭān,* 2:164–65.

47. E.g., ʿAbd al-Khāliq Maḥmūd, *Shiʿr Ibn al-Fāriḍ* (Cairo: Dār al-Maʿārif, 1984), 61–62. The riddles are also found in the Chester Beatty and Konya manuscripts, which were apparently transmitted independently of ʿAlī, thus Ibn al-Fāriḍ's grandson could not have forged them. A.J. Naṣr dismisses Ibn al-Fāriḍ's riddles as affected, lifeless, and trivial poetry with no redeeming value, which is to misunderstand them completely; *Shiʿr ʿUmar Ibn al-Fāriḍ* (Beirut: Dār al-Andalus, 1982), 111. Nasr's student Ramaḍān Ṣādiq, also omits the riddles and quatrains from his structural analysis of the poet's verse; Ṣādiq, *Shiʿr Fāriḍ: Dirāsah Uslūbīyah,* 21. On the other hand, Ghurayyib ascribes the poet's sense of humor in his riddles to his "Egyptian constitution"; Ghurayyib, *ʿUmar Ibn al-Fāriḍ,* 119. One of the great twentieth-century scholars of Ibn al-Fāriḍ, Muhammad Muṣṭafā Ḥilmī, conjectured that Ibn al-Fāriḍ could have posed riddles as a way of relaxing his students after a strenuous Sufi session; Maḥmūd, *Shiʿr,* 62, n. 32. For his part, al-Yāfī takes the riddles as evidence of the well educated and refined company that the poet must have kept; *Dirāsāt Fannīyah,* 261–262.

48. Ibn al-Fāriḍ, *Dīwān,* 195. The Baradā is the major river of Damascus (*EI2,* 1:1029–1030; N. Elisséeff), while Kawthar is a river in Paradise (*EI2,* 4:805–806; J. Horovitz-L. Gardet). Al-Mushtahā was a mosque on the island of Roda where Ibn al-Fāriḍ liked to view the Nile at sunset; Homerin, *ʿUmar Ibn al-Fāriḍ,* 327.

49. Bahā' al-Dīn Zuhayr, *The Poetical Works of Behā-Ed-Dīn Zoheir,* ed and tr. E.H. Palmer (Cambridge: Cambridge University Press, 1876–78), 1:279; also see Palmer's translation, 2:316, and further examples of quatrains in the introduction. Also see *EI,* 3:1167–68 (Henri Masse). For further details on Arabic *rubāʿīyāt,* see Mohammad Ben Cheneb, *Tuhfat al-Adab fī Mīzān Ashʿar al-ʿArab* (Paris: Libraire d'amerique et orient, 1954), 114–17; Muṣṭafā al-Shaybī, *Dīwān al-Dūbayt fī al-Shiʿr al-ʿArabī* (Tripoli: Manshūrāt al-Jāmiʿah al-Lībīyah, 1967), and "*dūbayt,*" in *EAL,* 2:197–98 (W. Stozer).

50. Ibn al-Fāriḍ, *Dīwān,* 196–206; this *rubāʿī* is on page 201. The exact number of quatrains varies within the manuscript tradition; ʿAlī's edition has thirty-three.

51. Ibid., 197. Cf. al-ʿAbbās Ibn al-Aḥnaf, "Only lovers count as people"; *Dīwān,* ed. ʿĀtikah al-Khazrajī (Cairo: Dār al-Kutub al-Miṣrīyah, 1954), 197, and quoted in A. Hamori, "Love Poetry (*ghazl*)," in *CHALAB,* 210.

52. Ibn al-Fāriḍ, *Dīwān,* 197.

53. See al-Būrīnī, *Sulṭān,* 2:174. For mystical interpretations of the *rubāʿīyāt,* and of the riddles, too, see al-Nābulusī, *Kashf al-Sirr,* fols. 431b–57b.

54. Ibn al-Fāriḍ, *Dīwān,* 197. In the last verse, Ibn al-Fāriḍ paraphrases a portion of Qur'ān 3:191: "Those who consider the form of the heaven and the earth (say): "Our Lord, You did not form this in vain, glory be to You!" See al-Būrīnī, *Sulṭān,* 2:174.

55. Ibn al-Fāriḍ, *Dīwān*, 198; al-Būrīnī, *Sulṭān*, 2:177.
56. Ibn al-Fāriḍ, *Dīwān*, 206; al-Būrīnī, *Sulṭān*, 2:184.
57. Ibn al-Fāriḍ, *Dīwān*, 198; al-Būrīnī, *Sulṭān*, 2:176.
58. See Schimmel, *Muhammad*, 35, 180.
59. Al-Būrīnī, *Sulṭān*, 2:176.
60. Ibn al-Fāriḍ, *Dīwān*, 217.
61. Ibid.

Chapter 2: Loves Secrets

1. Homerin, "az-Zahrā'," 215–32, and see also Khairallah, *Madness*, 4, 23–25, 98–103.

2. Homerin, "Preaching Poetry," 87–90, and Homerin, "Tangled Words," 194–97.

3. Ibn al-ᶜArabī, *Turjumān al-Ashwāq*, 9–10, tr. Nicholson, *Tarjumān*, 3–4

4. Ibid; Nicholson's Arabic text (12), reads *nasīb* for *tashbīb*. For a more recent translation of many of these poems, see Sells, *Stations of Desire*.

5. Al-Ḥusayn Ibn al-Ahdal, *Kashf al-Ghiṭā'* (Tunis: Aḥmad Bakīr, 1964), 199–201, and Homerin, *From Arab Poet*, 62. Ibn al-Ahdal compared Ibn al-Fāriḍ to the pre-Islamic Jewish poet Umayyah ibn Abī al-Ṣalt (d.c. 9/631); for this poet see *EAL*, 2:793 (T. Bauer).

6. Regarding the pre-Islamic and classical *nasīb*, see Jaroslav Stetkevych, *The Zephrys of Najd* (Chicago: University of Chicago Press, 1993) 1–49; Thomas Bauer, *Liebe und Liebesdichtung in der Welt des 9. und 10. Jahrhunderts* (Wiesbaden: Harrassowitz, 1998), 20–39, and chapter 3. For studies of the Arabic *ghazal* see, Renate Jacobi, "Die Anfänge der arabischen Ġazalpoesie," *Der Islam* 61 (1984):218–50, and her "Time and Reality in *Nasīb* and *Ghazal*," *Journal of Arabic Literature* 16 (1988):1–17. Concise discussions of Arabic *ghazal* literature may be found in *EAL*, 1:249–50 (J.S. Meisami), and *EI2*, 2:1028–33 (R. Blachere). Also see J-C. Vadet, *L'Esprit courtois en orient* (Paris: G.-P. Maisonneuve et Larose, 1968), 25–60.

7. ᶜUmar ibn Abī Rabīᶜah, *Dīwān*, 2nd ed. (Beirut: Dār al-Andalus, 1983), 162–63. Also see Vadet, *L'Esprit*, 61–158; Jacobi, "Time," 6–8; her "Theme and Variation in Umayyad Ghazal Poetry," *Journal of Arabic Literature* 23 (1993):109–19, and her entry "ᶜUmar ibn Abī Rabīᶜah," in *EAL*, 2:791–92; J.C. Bürgel, "Love, Lust, and Longing: Eroticism in Early Islam as Reflected in Literary Sources," in *Society and the Sexes in Medieval Islam*, ed. Afaf Lutfi Marsot (Malibu, CA: University of California Press, 1979), 96–101, and Salma K. Jayyusi, "Umayyad Poetry," in *The Cambridge History of Arabic Literature: Arabic Literature to the End of the Umayyad Period* (= *CHALUP*), ed. by A.F.L. Beeston, et al. (Cambridge: Cambridge University Press, 1983), 1:387–432.

8. Jayyusi, "Umayyad Poetry," 387–90.

9. See *EAL*, 1:410–11 (R. Jacobi).

10. See *EAL*, 2:636–37 (Stefan Leder); Vadet, *L'Esprit*, 362–78; Muhammad Ghunaymī Hilāl, *Laylā wa-al-Majnūn* (Beirut: Dār al-ᶜAwdah, 1980); Khairallah, *Madness*, and chapter 3.

11. This verse ascribed to Majnūn is cited by Ibn Qutaybah, *al-Shiʿr wa-al-Shuʿarā'*, ed. M.J. De Goeje (Leiden: E.J.Brill, 1904), 364. Insightful interpretations of the larger ʿUdhrī tradition, includung Majnūn, may be found in Tahar Labib Djedidi, *La Poesie amoureuse des Arabes: le cas des ʿUdhrites* (Algiers, 1974), esp. 90–157; Andras Hamori, *The Art of Medieval Arabic Literature* (Princeton: Princeton University Press, 1974), 38–47, who also quotes this verse, as does Khairallah, *Madness*, 75–96. Also see R. Jacobi, "Anfänge"; her excellent entry, "*ʿUdhrī* Poetry," in *EAL*, 2:789–90; J. Stetkevych, *Zephrys*, 114–17, 143–45, and Bauer, *Liebe*, 40–55.

12. Jamīl, *Dīwān* (Beirut: Dār Ṣādir, 1966), 42, verse 10; also quoted by Hamouri, *Art*, 43–44, and see Khairallah, *Madness*, 77–96, and Djedidi, *ʿUdhrites*, 90–92. Also see *EI2*, 2:1030–33 (Blachere); Jacobi, "*ʿUdhrī* Poetry," and her "Al-Walīd ibn Yazīd, the Last Ghazal Poet of the Umayyad Period," in T. Bauer and A. Neuwirth, eds., *Ghazal*, 131–47.

13. *Kays B. al-Mulavvaḥ ve-Dīwāni*, ed. by Sevkiye Inalcik (Ankara: Turk Tarih Kumuru Basimevi, 1967), 96; also quoted in Khairallah, *Madness*, 76-77. Also see *EI2*, 2:1031–33 (Blachere), and Vadet, *L'Esprit*, 249–263.

14. Abū Nuwās, *Dīwān*, ed. ʿAli Faʿūr (Beirut: Dār al-Kutub al-ʿIlmīyah, 1987), 58–59. Also see G. Scholer, "Bashshār B. Burd, Abū 'L-Atahiyah and Abū Nuwās," in *CHALABL*, 290–95; R. Jacobi, "Abbasidische Dichtung," in *Grundris der arabischen Philologie*, ed. H. Gatje, (Wiesbaden: Ludwig Reichert, 1987), 2:41–64; her "*ʿUdhrī* Poetry"; Bauer, *Liebe*, 53–162; Andras Hamori, "Love Poetry," in *CHALABL*, 202–18, and Jaako Hämeen-Anttila, "Abū Nuwās and Ghazal as a Genre," in *Ghazal*, ed. by T. Bauer and A. Neuwirth, 87–105.

15. See Annemarie Schimmel, "'I Take off the dress of the body': Eros in Sufi Literature and Life," in *Religion and the Body*, ed. Sarah Coakly (Cambridge: Cambridge University Press, 1997), 262–88, and Simon Kuntze, "Love and God: The Influence of Ghazal on Mystic Poetry," in *Ghazal*, ed. by T. Bauer and A. Neuwirth, 157–79.

16. Khairallah, *Madness*.

17. Al-Sarrāj, *al-Lumaʿ*, 321–22, and see Homerin, "Tangled Words," 191–92

18. Homerin, "Tangled Words," and "az-Zahrā'," 221–22. Also see van Gelder, "Rābiʿa's Poem," 73–75. For further examples of Sufi love poetry, see the introduction.

19. James T. Monroe, "Hispaon-Arabic Poetry," 125–54. Also see A.S. Ḥusayn *al-Adab al-Ṣūfīyah*, 221–27.

20. Monroe, "Hispano-Arabic Poetry," 151–52, and Ibn Zaydūn, *Dīwān Ibn Zaydūn wa-Risā'iluhu*, ed. by ʿAlī ʿAbd al-ʿAẓīm (Cairo: Dār Nahḍat Miṣr, 1957), 145–46; see another translation by Michael Sells in *The Cambridge History of Arabic Literature: the Literature of al-Andalus*, ed. by M.R. Menocal et al. (Cambridge: Cambridge University Press, 2000), 494.

21. Ibn al-Fāriḍ, *Dīwān*, 166, verses 1–4.

22. Ibn al-Fāriḍ, *Dīwān*, 177, verses 1–4.

23. Cf. the ninth-century Sahl al-Tusturī's reading of this Qur'ānic passage "as a divine address to the spiritual self"; see Böwering, *Mystical Vision*, 242.

24. Ibn al-Fāriḍ, *Dīwān*, 166, verses 5–6.

25. Ibid., 168, verses 1–3, 16, and cf. Ibn al-Kīzānī, *Dīwān*, 129:
tih kayfa shi'ta dalālan lā ṣabrun lī ᶜanka lā lā
Be proud as you please in coquetry;
I have no patience away from you, no, no!

26. See Arberry, *Mystical Poems*, 2:13–16, for a list of these themes as found in Ibn al-Fāriḍ's *Dīwān*; also see Yūsuf Sāmī al-Yūsuf, "Baᶜḍ Yanābīᶜ," 92–99. For Love sickness and its signs in classical Arabic medicine and love theory see Hans Hinrich Biesterfeidt and Dimitri Gutas, "The Malady of Love," *Journal of the American Oriental Society* 104:1 (1984):21–55, and in a mystical context, al-Daylamī, *Kitāb ᶜAtf al-Alif*, tr. by Bell and Al Shafie, *Treatise*, esp. 116–26.

27. Ibn al-Fāriḍ, *Dīwān*, 183–84, verses 34–37, and see al-Nābulusī, *Kashf al-Sirr*, 322a–23a.

28. Cf. Schimmel, "Body," 267.

29. Ibn al-Fāriḍ, *Dīwān*, 177, verses 5–7. Regarding the use and meaning of these terms in al-Tusturī's discussions of human–divine encounters, see Bowering, *Mystical Vision*, esp. 166–72.

30. Ibn al-Fāriḍ, *Dīwān*, 179, verses 25–26. Concerning the poet's protagonists see R.A. Nicholson, *Studies in Islamic Mysticism*, (Cambridge: Cambridge University Press, 1921. Reprint ed. 1967), 157–59, and al-Nābulusī who interprets the *raqīb* (spy) as the Qur'ānic *al-nafs al-ammārah bi-al-sū'* ("the lower soul commanding evil") and the *wāshin* (slanderer) as the helper of Satan who obstructs the seeker's path to God; *Kashf al-Sirr*, 317a. Also see chapter 5, for further comments on these protagonists by Ibn al-Fāriḍ.

31. Ibn al-Fāriḍ, *Dīwān*, 53, verses 38–39.

32. Ibid., 185, verses 48–49.

33. Ibid., 184, verses 44–45, and see and see al-Nābulusī, *Kashf al-Sirr*, 324b–26a.

34. See Vadet, *L'espirit*, 76–81, and Ruqayya Yasmine Khan, "On the Significance of Secrecy in the Medieval Arabic Romances," *Journal of Arabic Literature* 31 (2000):238–53.

35. Ibid, and see al-Kalabādhī, *al-Taᶜarruf li-Madhhab ahl al-Taṣawwuf* (Beirut: Dār al-Kutub al-ᶜIlmīyah, 1980), 87, tr. A.J. Arberry, *Doctrine of the Ṣūfīs* (Cambridge: Cambridge University Press, 1935. Reprint ed. 1977), 76; al-Hujwirī, *The Kashf al-Maḥjūb*, tr. R.A. Nicholson (London: Luzac & Co., 1911. Reprint ed. 1959), 333, 385, and esp. Böwering, *Mystical Vision*, 185–201. Also see Annemarie Schimmel, "Secrecy in Sufism," in *Secrecy in Religion*, ed. K.W. Bolle (Leiden: E.J. Brill, 1987), 81–102.

36. Ibn al-Fāriḍ, *Dīwān*, 178, verses 21–22, and see al-Būrīnī, *Sulṭān*, 1:155–156, and Ibn al-Fāriḍ, *Dīwān*, 185, verses 46,

37. For an inventory of some of Ibn al-Fāriḍ's love terminology see Jean-Yves L'Hopital, "Le vocabulaire amoureux dans les poèmes de ᶜUmar b. al-Fāriḍ," *Annales Islamologiques* 36 (2002):77–116. Also see and Kees W. Bolle, "Secrecy in Religon" in *Secrecy in Religion*, ed. Bolle, 1–24.

38. Ibn al-Fāriḍ, *Dīwān*, 167, verses 17–21, and see al-Nābulusī, *Kashf al-Sirr*, 371a.

39. Ibn al-Fāriḍ, *Dīwān*, 185-86, verses 57–60; also see 167, verses 17–21; 172, verses 58–60; 180, verses 46–51.

40. Ibn al-Fāriḍ, *Dīwān*, 186, verses 61–62.

41. E.g., Ibn al-Fāriḍ, *Dīwān*, 166, verse 6; 170, verse 35; 179, verse 27, verse 37.

42. Ibn al-Fāriḍ, *Dīwān*, 50–52; for a translation, see chapter 1.

43. Ibn al-Fāriḍ, *Dīwān*, 104–105, verses 277–85, and see Homerin, *ᶜUmar Ibn al-Fāriḍ*, 152–54, and chapter 5.

44. See Arberry's comments prefacing the notes to his translations in *Mystical Poems*, vol. 2.

45. U. Rubin, "Pre-existence and Light: Aspects of the Concept of *Nūr Muhammad*," *Israel Oriental Studies* 5 (1975):62–119; Böwering, *Mystical Vision*, 147–57; Schimmel, *Dimensions*, 214–16, and Paul Nwyia, *Exégèse coranique et language mystique* (Beirut: Dar al-Machriq, 1970), 93–94.

46. Ibid., and especially see Rubin, "Pre-existence," and Schimmel, *Muhammad*, 123–143.

47. Schimmel, *Muhammad*, 43, and see chapter 1.

48. Ibn al-Fāriḍ, *Dīwān*, 168–72.

49. Arberry, *Mystical Poems*, 2:72, n. 39, and al-Nābulusī, *Kashf al-Sirr*, 397b–98a. Also see Schimmel, *Muhammad*, 86, 124, and her *Veil*, 173–76.

50. Arberry, *Mystical Poems*, 2:71, n. 19, and al-Nābulusī, *Kashf al-Sirr*, 391a.

51. Ibn al-Fāriḍ, *Dīwān*, 177–80, and also see Arberry's translation, *Mystical Poems*, 2:62–63.

52. Concerning this miracle see Schimmel, *Muhammad*, 69–71.

53. Al-Nābulusī, *Kashf al-Sirr*, 384a–b, and Arberry, *Mystical Poems*, 2:65.

54. For *ḥabīb Allāh* see Schimmel, *Muhammad*, 57. For Ḥalīmah of the Banī Saᶜd, the tribe of Ibn al-Fāriḍ's ancestors, see "Ḥalīmah Bint Abī Dhu'ayb," *EI2*, 3:94 (W. Montgomery Watt); Schimmel, *Muhammad*, 9, 68; Arberry, *Mystical Poems*, 2:66; Rubin, "Pre-existence," 63, 103–104, and Homerin, *ᶜUmar Ibn al-Fāriḍ*, 309.

55. Aḥmad ibn Yaḥyā Ibn Abī Ḥajalah, *al-Ghawth al-ᶜĀriḍ fī Muᶜāraḍat Ibn al-Fāriḍ*, Cairo: Arab League Manuscript Institute microfilm 319 (Taṣawwuf) of manuscript 31 (Adab) Maktabat Sūhāj, Sūhāj, Egypt, 1, and see Homerin, *Arab Poet*, 58. For discussion of the genre of panegyrics of the prophet Muhammad see Schimmel, *Veil*, 171–211, and Zakī Mubārak, *al-Madā'iḥ al-Nabawīyah* (Cairo: Muṣṭafā al-Bābī al-Ḥalabī, 1943).

56. E.g., al-Būrīnī, *Sulṭān*, 1:148. Al-Nābulusī often referred to the beloved as *al-maḥbūb al-ḥaqīqī* or *al-maḥbūbah al-ḥaqīqīyqh* ("the true/real beloved"), that is to say, God; e.g., *Kashf al-Sirr*, 371a–b. Also see A.S. Ḥusayn, *al-Adab al-Ṣūfīyah*, 96–102.

57. See Al-Nābulusī, *Kashf al-Sirr*, 386a–b. Concerning the *amr*, or "command," of God see J. M. S. Baljon, "The 'Amr of God in the Koran," *Acta Orientalia* 23 (1958):7–18; Fazlur Rahman, *Major Themes of the Qur'ān* (Chicago: Bibilotheca Islamica, 1980), 97–99; Böwering, *Mystical Vision*, 145–46, 154–55,

176–80, and Schimmel, *Dimmensions*, 223, who notes the 7th/14th c. theosophist al-Jilī equated the *amr* with the *al-Ḥaqīqah al-Muḥammadīyah*.

58. Ibn al-Fāriḍ, *Dīwān*, 172, verses 53–57.

59. Of course, Sufis also applied the term *ḥabīb* to God as well as to Muhammad; see Ignaz Goldziher, "Die Gottsliebe in der Islamischen Theologie," *Der Islam* 9(1919):144–45.

60. Hassan El-Banna Ezz El-Din, " 'No Solace for the Heart:' The Motif of the Departing Women in the Pre-Islamic Battle Ode," in *Reorientations*, ed. S.P. Stetkevych, 165–79.

61. Jamīl, *Dīwān*, 39, verse 11; also see 43, verse 22, and 55, verse 9, also quoted by Hamori, *Art*, 43–44.

62. See al-Daylamī, *Kitāb ʿAtf al-Alif*, tr. Bell and Al Shafie, *Treatise*, 133–34, and Böwering, *Mystical Vision*, 145–49.

63. Al-Kalābādhī, *al-Taʿarruf*, 161. Also see Arberry, *Doctrine*, 166–67; During, *Musique*, 164–65, and Böwering, *Mystical Vision*, 201–09.

64. Ibn al-Fāriḍ, *Dīwān*, 162–65. For other English translations see Arberry, *Mystical Poems*, 2:27–34, and Wheeler M. Thackston, Jr., "The *Jīmīyah*," in *Introduction to Classical Arabic Literature*, ed. Ilse Lichtenstadler (New York: Shocken Books, 1976), 312–14; for a French translation see L'Hôpital, *Poemes*, 245–63.

65. Angelika Neuwirth, "Victims Victorious: Violent Death in Classical and Modern Arabic Ghazal," in *Ghazal*, ed. T. Bauer and A. Neuwirth, 259–80. Also see Abū Tammām, *Sharh Dīwān al-Hamāsah* by Aḥmad ibn Muhammad al-Marzūqī, ed. Aḥmad Amīn and ʿAbd al-Salām Hārūn (Cairo:Maṭbaʿat Lajnat al-Ta'līf wa-al-Tarjamah wa-al-Nashr, 1952), 2:827.

66. Al-Nābulusī, *Kashf al-Sirr*, 349a.

67. Al-Daylamī, *Kitāb ʿAtf al-alif*, tr. Bell and Al Shafie, *Treatise*, 120.

68. See Arberrry, *Mystical Poems*, 2:30–34, for a brief sketch of the poem and his notes, which are largely based on al-Būrīnī, *Sulṭān*, 2: 47–64, and al-Nābulusī, *Kashf al-Sirr*, 348b–56a.

69. Arberry, *Mystical Poems*, 2:31.

70. Cf. verse 5 of the *al-Lāmīyah* quoted in chapter 1.

71. Al-Nābulusī, *Kashf al-sirr*, 354a; Arberry, *Mystical Poems*, 2:32, n. 15.

72. Al-Nābulusī felt that the human's *nafs* ("selfishness," "concupiscence") veiled the individual from seeing true reality; *Kashf al-Sirr*, 353b–54a. Also see verse 43 of *al-Fā'īyah* cited earlier in this chapter. For a Christian parallel see the 14th c. English mystical classic, *The Cloud of the Unknowing*, ed. Clifton Wolters (Penguin Books, 1974), 59–70.

73. Cf. al-Tusturī, who read this Qur'ānic verse as referring to the grace of the "light of faith," which extinguishes the "darkness of unbelief"; see Böwering, *Mystical Vision*, 216–20.

74. Al-Nābulusī, *Kashf al-Sirr*, 358a; Arberry, *Mystical Poems*, 2:33, n. 26.

75. See William Chittick, "Dhikr," in *Encyclopaedia of Religion*, ed. Mircea Eliade (New York: Macmillan, 1987), 4:341–44, and During, *Musique*, 162–63.

76. See al-Būrīnī, *Sulṭān*, 2:58-60; al-Nābulusī, *Kashf al-Sirr*, 359a–60a; Arberry, *Mystical Poems*, 2:31, 33, n. 31–34, and A.J. Naṣr, *Shiʿr ʿUmar Ibn al–Fāriḍ*, 247–48.

77. Al-Nābulusī, *Kashf al-Sirr*, 360b; Arberry, *Mystical Poems*, 2:33, n. 33-34, and chapter 4.

78. Al-Nābulusī, *Kashf al-Sirr*, 360b–61b. For *ghaybah* and *ḥudūr* see al-Qushayrī, *Al-Risālah al-Qushayrīyah*, ed. ᶜAbd al-Ḥalīm Maḥmūd and Maḥmūd Ibn al-Sharīf (Cairo: Dār al-Kutub al-Ḥadīthah, 1972–74), 1:232–35, and tr. Sells in *Early Islamic Mysticism*, 122–24.

79. Arberry, *Mystical Poems*, 2:33, n. 36.

80. Al-Būrīnī, *Sulṭān*, 2:61, and al-Nābulusī, *Kashf al-Sirr*, 362a–63a; al-Hujwirī, *The Kashf*, 45; al-Kalābādhī, *al-Taᶜarruf*, 77 (tr. Arberry, *Doctrine*, 64), and Arberry, *Mystical Poems*, 2:33, n. 38.

81. Arberry, *Mystical Poems*, 2: 31–34, esp. 33 nos. 36–38.

82. Ibn al-Fāriḍ, *Dīwān*, 172, verse 49, and al-Būrīnī, *Sulṭān*, 2:61.

83. Ibid., and al-Nābulusī, *Kashf al-Sirr*, 361b–63a.

84. Arberry, *Mystical Poems*, 32, n. 15.

85. Regarding the myths and stories associated with the Night Journey and Heavenly Ascension, see Schimmel, *Muhammad*, 159–75. Also see Thomas W. Arnold, *Painting in Islam* (New York: Dover Press, 1965), 117–22. ill. LVIII, and Christine Jacqueline Gruber, "The Prophet Muhammad's Ascension (*Mi'raj*) in Islamic Painting and Literature: Evidence from Cairo Collections," *Bulletin of the American Research Center in Egypt*, no. 185 (Summer, 2004):24–31.

86. Al-Nābulusī, *Kashf al-Sirr*, 364a–b, and see al-Būrīnī, *Sulṭān*, 2:63. Arberry thought both terms should be ascribed to the lover "illustrating his abject eagerness to clutch at any straw"; *Mystical Poems*, 2:34, n. 42.

87. Ibn al-Fāriḍ, *Dīwān*, 62, and also see Arberry's translation, *Mystical Poems*, 2:121.

88. For verse 77 of the *al-Tā'īyah al-Ṣughrā* see al-Būrīnī, *Sulṭān*, 1:138, and Arberry, *Mystical Poems*, 2:128, n. 77.

89. See Arberry, *Mystical Poems*, 2:30–31, who speaks of "key-words."

90. Cf. Böwering's comment's on al-Tusturī's view of the day of the Covenant and the Judgment Day: "Seen against the background of primordial covenant (*mīthāq*) and post-existential theophany (*tajallī*), the spiritual knowledge achieved by mystic man reactualizes his primal past and anticipates his eschatological future"; *Mystical Vision*, 229.

91. Stanley E. Fish, *Self-Consuming Artifacts* (Berkeley: University of California Press, 1972), 158.

92. Concerning God's merciful guidance to humanity see Rahman, *Themes*, 9, and al-Tusturī's notion of "recollection of God by virtue of the Object of recollection (*al-dhikr bi-l-madhkūr*)"; Böwering, *Mystical Vision*, 205–206.

Chapter 3: Joined at the Crossroads

1. *Al-Mufaḍḍalīyāt*, ed. Aḥmad Muhammad Shākir and ᶜAbd al-Salām Muhammad Hārūn, 7th printing (Cairo: Dār al-Maᶜārif, 1983), 132–34. Also see Charles Lyall's translation and notes in *The Mufaddalīyāt: an Anthology of Ancient Arabian Odes* (Oxford: Clarendon Press, 1918), 2:90–92. For a finely

nuanced discussion of the classical Arabic ode see the works of Jaroslav Stetkevych, especially *Zephyrs*, and his "Toward an Arabic Elegiac Lexicon: the Seven Words of the *Nasīb*," in *Reorientations*, ed. S.P. Stetkevych, 58–129. Also see the articles in S. Sperl and C. Shackle, eds., *Qasida Poetry*, especially Renate Jacobi's "The Origins of the Qasida Form," 1:21–34, and her "*qasīda*," in *EAL*, 2:630–33. For translations of some early odes also see Michael A. Sells, *Desert Tracings: Six Classical Odes by ᶜAlqama, Shanfara, Labid, ᶜAntara, Al-Aᶜsha, and Dhu ar-Rumma* (Middletown: Wesleyan University Press, 1993).

2. The poet's patron may have been the Ghassānid ruler al-Ḥārith ibn Mārīyah al-ᶜAraj (d. 569); see Lyall, *Mufaddalīyāt*, 2:90.

3. E.g., Ch. Lyall, "The Pictorial Aspects of Ancient Arabian Poetry," *Journal of the Royal Asiatic Society* (1912):133–52; R.A. Nicholson, *A Literary History of the Arabs* (Cambridge: Cambridge University Press, 1907), 77–79; Alfred Bloch, "Qasida," *Asiatisch Studien* 2 (1948):106–32; H. A. R. Gibb, *Arabic Literature* (Oxford: The Clarendon Press, 1963), 21–22; Renate Jacobi, *Studien zur Poetik der altararabischen Qaside* (Wiesbaden: F. Steiner, 1971); Andras Hamori, *Art*, 3–30; Kemal Abu Deeb, "Towards a Structural Analysis of Pre-Islamic Poetry, Pt. I," *International Journal of Middle Eastern Studies* 6 (1975):148–84, and Pt. II, *Edebiyat* 1 (1976):3–69, and A. Haydar, "The Mu'allaqa of Imru' al-Qays: Its Structure and Meaning," Pt. I, *Edebiyat* 2 (1977):227–61, and Pt. II, *Edebiyat* 3 (1978):51–82.

4. E.g., J. Stetkevych, *Zephyrs;* his "Some Observations on Arabic Poetry," *Journal of Near Eastern Studies*, 26 (1967):2–3.; his "The Arabic Lyrical Phenomenon in Context," *Journal of Arabic Literature* 6 (1975):55–77, and especially his "The Arabic Qaṣīdah: From Form and Content to Mood and Meaning," *Harvard Ukrainian Studies* 3–4 (1979– 80):774–81.

5. J. Stetkevych, "Arabic Qaṣīdah," 778–81.

6. Suzanne P. Stetkevych, "Structuralist Interpretations of Pre-Islamic Poetry: Critique in New Directions," *Journal of Near Eastern Studies*, 42 (1983):85–107, and especially her *The Mute Immortals Speak*. Also see Khairallah, *Madness*, 21–23.

7. *Al-Mufaḍḍalīyāt*, 345–46, and also see Lyall's translation, *The Mufaḍḍalīyāt*, 2:268–69, 283–85.

8. See especially, Suzanne Stekevych, "Pre-Islamic Panegyric and the Poetics of Redemption," in *Reorientations*, ed. S.P. Stetkevych, 1–49, and Hamori, *Art*, 11–19, 26–27. Also see Victor Turner, *The Ritual Process: Structure and Anti-Structure* (Ithaca, NY: Cornell University Press, 1977), 94–95; Marcel Mauss, *The Gift: Forms and Functions of Exchange in Archaic Societies*, tr. Ian Cunnison (New York: Norton and Co., 1967), and Theodor H. Gaster, *Thespis: Ritual, Myth, and Drama in the Ancient Near East* (New York: Norton and Co., 1977).

9. J. Stetkevych, "Arabic Qaṣīdah," 781–82; his "A *Qaṣīdah* by Ibn Muqbil," *Journal of Arabic Literature* 37 (2006):303–54, and S. P. Stetkevych, "Structuralist Interpretations," 98–107.

10. See Renate Jacobi, "The Camel Section of the Panegyrical Ode," *Journal of Arabic Literature* 13 (1982):1–22; Hamori, *Art*, 31–38, and Th. Emil Homerin,

"A Bird Ascends the Night: Elegy and Immortality in Islam," *Journal of the American Academy of Religion* 58 (1991):541–73.

11. S.P. Stetkevych, "Abbasid Panegyric," 1:35–63, and her *The Poetics of Islamic Legitimacy: Myth, Gender, and Ceremony in the Classical Arabic Ode* (Bloomington, IN: University of Indiana Press, 2002). Also see Sperl, *Mannerism*, 9–27, and the introduction.

12. Jacobi, "Camel Section," and also see M. M. Badawi, "From Primary to Secondary Qaṣīdas," *Journal of Arabic Literature* 11 (1980):1–31; G. E. Von Grunebaum, "Aspects of Urban Literature Mostly in the Ninth and Tenth Centuries," in *Themes In Medieval Arabic Literature*, ed. Dunning S. Wilson (London: Variorum Reprints, 1981) IV:281–300 (esp. 288–95), and his "The Response to Nature in Arabic Poetry," in *Themes*, VII:137–51.

13. Ibn Qutaybah, *al-Shiʿr*, 15; tr. Nicholson, *History*, 77–78. Also see Jacobi, "Camel Section," 1–3, 16–21, and Sperl, *Mannerism*, 26.

14. See Abū Nuwās' journey from Baghdad to Egypt; *Dīwān Abī Nuwās*, ed. Ahmad ʿAbd al-Majīd al-Ghazzālī (Cairo: Maṭbaʿat Miṣr, 1953), 480–83, and al-Mutanabbī, *Dīwān*, 3:372, verses 31–33.

15. Al-Mutanabbī, *Dīwān*, 1:319, verse 19.

16. There are several versions of this ode. I have followed Ibn Abī Uṣaybicah, *ʿUyūn al-Anbā' fī Ṭabaqāt al-Aṭibbā'* (Cairo: al-Maṭbaʿah al-Waḥḥabīyah, 1882), 2:10. Also see Ibn Khallikān, *Wafayāt*, 2:160–61 (paraphrased by de Slane, *Ibn Khallikan*, 1:443); A.J. Arberry's translation in *Avicenna: Scientist and Philosopher*, ed. G.M. Wickens (London: Luzac & Co., 1952), 28, and Mohd. Badruddin Alavi, "Some Aspects of the Literary and Poetical Activities of Avicenna," in *Avicenna Commemoration Volume*, ed. V. Courtois (Calcutta: Iran Society, 1956), 65–72.

17. For more on Ibn Sīnā's doctrine of the soul see Henry Corbin, *Avicenna and the Visionary Recital*, tr. Willard R. Trask (New York: Pantheon Books, 1960).

18. Al-Kātib al-Iṣfahānī, *Kharīdat al-Qaṣr wa-Jarīdat al-ʿAṣr* (Damascus: al-Maṭbaʿah al-Hāshmīyah, 1955), 2:316, and see Homerin, "Preaching Poetry."

19. Ibn Khallikān, *Wafayāt*, 3:49–51; and also see de Slane's paraphrase and symbolist interpretation, *Ibn Khallikān*, 2:31–32.

20. See chapter 2. For *ta'ammaltu*, see the verse by ʿUmar al-Suhrawardī in the introduction.

21. Homerin, "Preaching Poetry," 90–91, 97, 100–101.

22. Ibn Khallikān, *Wafayāt*, 3:49–51.

23. Alī Ṣafā Ḥusayn, *Ibn al-Kīzānī*, 135, and also see his similar short odes, 116, 130–31, 134. Several *qasīdahs* are also ascribed to Abū Madyan; see his *Dīwān*, 81–82.

24. Ibn al-ʿArabī, *Turjumān al-Ashwāq*, 71–74, and also see Nicholson's translation, *The Tarjumán*, 82–83, and that of Sells, *Stations of Desire*, 119–121.

25. Ibn al-ʿArabī, *Turjumān al-Ashwāq*, 71–74, and see Nicholson's translation, *The Tarjumán*, 82–83.

26. Sells, *Stations*, 141.

27. Ibn al-ʿArabī, *Turjumān al-Ashwāq*, 71–74, and see Nicholson's translation, *The Tarjumán*, 82–83.

28. See Yāqūt, *Muʿjam al-Buldān* (Beirut: Dār Aḥyā' al-Turāth al-ʿArabī, 1979), 3:139; 4:92.

29. See Sells, *Stations*, 26–30, 139–49. Also see a poem ascribed to Abū Madyan in which the poet mentions the prophet Muhammad and various pilgrimage stops, including the well of Zamzam and the black stone, as he seeks God's forgiveness; Abū Madyan, *Dīwān*, 86–87.

30. Ibn Khallikān, *Wafayāt*, 1:168–70 (also see deSlane's paraphrase, *Ibn Khallikān*, 1:150–51). For Ibn al-ʿArīf see *EI2*, 3:712–13 (A. Faure).

31. Ibn al-Fāriḍ, *Dīwān*, 149, verses 1–2.

32. Ibid., 152, verse 1. For other examples of Ibn al-Fāriḍ's use of rhetorical questions see, Ṣādiq, *Shiʿr Ibn al-Fāriḍ: Dirāsah Uslūbīyah*, 102–105.

33. Ibn al-Fāriḍ, *Dīwān*, 55, verses 1–5.

34. Ibid., 144, verses 1–4.

35. See al-Būrīnī, *Sulṭān*, 2:13–15, and Arberry, *Mystical Poems*, 2:24, n. 1–4.

36. Ibid.

37. Concerning the *burdah*, see Schimmel, *Muhammad*, 180, and her *Dimensions*, 225, for the *burdah's* curative powers; also see "Burda," *EI2*, 1:1314–15 (R. Basset).

38. Ibn al-Fāriḍ, *Dīwān*, 36, verses 1–3.

39. Ibid., 154, verse 1. Cf. a verse by Ibn al-Kīzānī (Husayn, *Ibn al-Kīzānī*, 106, v. 1):

yā ḥādī-l-ʿīsi iṣṭabir sāʿatan fa-muhjatī sārat maʿa-r-rakbi
Oh driver of the roan camels, stay awhile
for my heart travels with the riders!

40. Ibid., 144, verse 5 ff., and also see Ibn al-Fāriḍ, *Dīwān*, 55, verse 7ff., 149, verse 3ff., and 157, verse 3ff.

41. Ibn al-Fāriḍ, *Dīwān*, 57, verse 20.

42. E.g., ibid., 56, verse 12, and 60, verse 56.

43. Ibid., 40–41, verses 51–57.

44. Al-Būrīnī, *Sulṭān*, 1:42, and Arberry, *Mystical Poems*, 2:111, n. 53–56.

45. Al-Nābulusī, *Kashf al-Sirr*, 56b–58a.

46. Ibn al-Fāriḍ, *Dīwān*, 43–44, verses 81–90.

47. Jalāl al-Dīn al-Suyūṭī, *al-Barq al-Wāmiḍ fī Sharḥ Yā'īyat Ibn al-Fāriḍ*, manuscript 881 (Shiʿr Taymūr), Cairo: Dār al-Kutub al-Miṣrīyah, 23. For this *ḥadīth* also see Graham, *Divine Word*, 161–62, and chapter 5 where Ibn al-Fāriḍ refers to this tradition more explicitly in his *al-Tā'īyah al-Kubrā*.

48. Regarding this passage, al-Suyūṭī suggests that though the poet may follow the mystic path toward total selflessness, experiencing moments of great profundity, he can never know the everlasting bliss of the beatific vision in this life, as the prophet Muhammad related in a tradition: "You will not see your Lord until you die"; see al-Suyūṭī, *al-Barq al-Wāmiḍ*, 23–24. Also al-Būrīnī, *Sulṭān*, 1:54–58; al-Nābulusī, *Kashf al-Sirr*, 56b–58a, and Arberry's translation and comments, *Mystical Poems*, 2:102–103, 112–13, n. 82–90.

49. Ibid., 151, verses 24–26, and cf. Ibn al-Fāriḍ, *Dīwān*, 157, verses 34–37.

50. Ibn al-Fāriḍ, *Dīwān*, 153, verses 14–18.

51. For the Majnūn saga, see Ibn Qutaybah, *al-Shiʿr*, 355–64. A translation of this account and analysis of the love cycle is found in Khairallah, *Madness*, esp. 135–43. For a complete translation of this ode by Ibn al-Fāriḍ, see Homerin, *Arab Poet*, 5–9.

52. Cf. Ibn al-Fāriḍ, *Dīwān*, 149–51.

53. Ibn al-Fāriḍ, *Dīwān*, 49, verses 145–51, and cf. Ibn al-Fāriḍ, *Dīwān*, 148, verses 45–50; 65, verses 101–103.

54. For more details regarding Ibn Fāriḍ's elaborate rhetorical devices (*badīʿ*) in these verses see al-Suyūṭī, *al-Barq al-Wāmiḍ*, 35–37; al-Būrīnī, *Sulṭān*, 1:81–84, and chapter 1.

55. This is Quaṣi ibn Kilāb; see al-Suyūṭī, *al-Barq al-Wāmiḍ*, 37; al-Būrīnī, *Sulṭān*, 1:81–84, and Arberry, *Mystical Poems*, 2:107, 116, n. 151.

56. See, for example, Muṣṭafā Maḥmūd Ḥilmī, *Ibn al-Fāriḍ wa-al-Ḥubb al-Ilāhī*, 2nd. ed. (Cairo: Maṭbʿat Miṣr, 1971), 48–51. On the importance and power of names in classical Arabic poetry see J. Stetkevych, *Zephyrs of Najd*, 103, 114.

57. See Arberry's notes to these names throughout his translations, and Schimmel, *Muhammad*, 189.

58. Ibn al-Fāriḍ, *Dīwān*, 55–56, verses 7–11.

59. Concerning these specific place-names, see al-Būrīnī, *Sulṭān*, 1:111–13, and Arberry, *Mystical Poems*, 2:125, n. 7–10, based on Yāqūt, *Muʿjam al-Buldān*. Also see J. Stetkevych, *Zephyrs*, 87–88.

60. Ibn al-Fāriḍ, *Dīwān*, 149, verses 3–7, and 59, verses 42–45.

61. Concerning these place names see Yāqūt, *Muʿjam al-Buldān*, and Arberry, *Mystical Poems*, 2:37, n. 4–6.

62. Ibn al-Fāriḍ, *Dīwān*, 146, verses 27–31, and J. Stetkevych, *Zephyrs*, 87–88.

63. Ibn al-Fāriḍ, *Dīwān*, 59, verses 42–47.

64. For more on the glance, see chapter 5.

65. See al-Būrīnī, *Sulṭān*, 1:125, and Arberry, *Mystical Poems*, 2:126–27, n. 42–43.

66. Ibn al-Fāriḍ, *Dīwān*, 62–63, verses 81–83, preferring *ṣabwatī* for *ghurbati* in verse 82; also cf. ibid., 147–48, verses 41–44.

67. Cf. the verse by Majnūn cited in chapter 2, n. 13.

68. See al-Sarrāj, *al-Lumaʿ*, 222–30, esp. 228–29; al-Hujwirī, *Kashf al-Maḥjūb*, ed. by Valentin Zhukovskii, (Leningrad: Maṭbacat Dār al-ʿUlūm, 1926), 425–26, and tr. Nicholson, *The Kashf*, 328. Note the use of *ishtiqāq*, or etymological derivation, as a means of commentary.

69. For further parallels between al-Junayd and Ibn al-Fāriḍ, see chapter 5. Also cf. Ibn al-Fāriḍ, *Dīwān*, 40, verses 45–48; 52, verse 26; 75; 147–48, verses 40–50.

70. Ibn Jubayr, *Riḥlat Ibn Jubayr* (Beirut: Dār al-Sādir, 1964), 152–53, tr. R. J. C. Broadhurst in *Classical Arabic Literature*, ed. L. Lichtenstadler, 389–90.

71. For example see Hujwirī, *Kashf*, 422, tr. Nicholson, *The Kashf*, 326–27. For more interpretations of the pilgrimage, see al-Ghazālī, *Iḥyā'*, 1:267–73, and G. E. Von Grunebaum, *Muhammadan Festivals* (New York: Olive Branch Press, 1988), 44–49.

72. J. Stekevych, *Zephyrs*, 88.

73. Sibṭ al-Marṣafī, *Fatḥ al-Makkī al-Fā'iḍ Sharḥ Yā'īyat Ibn al-Fāriḍ*, manuscript 1566 (Adab), Cairo: Dār al-Kutub al-Misrīyah, 44b–45a. Also see J. Stetkevych, *Zephyrs*, 100–101.

74. Ibn al-Fāriḍ, *Dīwān*, 154–57.

75. See Jaroslav Stetkevych, "Name and Epithet: The Philology and Semiotics of Animal Nomenclature in Early Arabic Poetry," *Journal of Near Eastern Studies* 45 (1986):89–124.

76. See al-Būrīnī, *Sulṭān*, 2:64–78, and al-Nābulusī, *Kashf al-Sirr*, 301b–11a. Al-Nābulusī felt that the camel driver symbolized both God and the Light of Muhammad, which was created from God's light; ibid., 301a–302b.

77. Al-Nābulusī, *Kashf al-Sirr*, 303a–306a, and also see al-Būrīnī, *Sulṭān*, 2:69–71; Arberry, *Mystical Poems*, 2:43, n. 7–14, and A. J. Naṣr, *Shi*ᶜ*r* ᶜ*Umar Ibn al-Fāriḍ*, 195–203.

78. Ghurayyib, ᶜ*Umar Ibn al-Fāriḍ*, 143–46.

79. Beginning at Yanbuᶜ (lat. 24° 05′ – long. 38° 03′), the caravan passes on to al-Dahnā', then to Badr (23° 44′ – 38° 46′), al-Naqā, Waddān, and Rābigh (22° 48′ – 39° 02′), Qudayd (22° 27′ – 39° 06′), Khulayṣ (22° 09′ – 39° 19′), ᶜUsfān (21° 55′ – 39° 22′), to Marr al-Ẓahrān, a valley near Mecca, then to al-Jumūm (21° 37′ – 39° 42′), al-Qaṣr (probably Qaṣr Ibn ᶜAmr near Mecca), al-Daknā' and then entering the environs of Mecca, al-Tanᶜīm (21° 29′ – 39° 48′) where many pilgrims enter the state of ritual purity; see the United States Board on Geographic Names, *Official Standard Names Gazetteer: Saudi Arabia* (Washington D. C., 1978); Yāqūt, *Mu*ᶜ*jam al-Buldān*, 2:225, 493; 3:11, 342; 4:63, 121, 355; 5:365, and Arberry, *Mystical Poems*, 2:43, n. 12. Probably the unidentified names, too, such as al-Naqā' ("the sand dune," "purity") and al-Daknā' ("the black place") refer to lesser known alighting places. For more on the Cairo-Mecca Hajj route see ᶜAbdullah ᶜAnkawi, "The Pilgrimage to Mecca in Mamluk Times," *Arabian Studies* 1 (1974):146–70.

80. Ibn al-Fāriḍ made the pilgrimage at least twice, once when a young man and, again in 628/1231 four years before his death; see Homerin, ᶜ*Umar Ibn al-Fāriḍ*, 305, 324.

81. For al-Ḥajūn and its cemetery see Yāqūt, *Mu*ᶜ*jam al-Buldān*, 2:225. Concerning the *awtād*, see al-Nābulusī, *Kashf al-Sirr*, 305b–306a; Schimmel, *Mystical Dimensions*, 200–203, and Böwering, *Mystical Vision*, 236–37.

82. Regarding these places, see Von Grunebaum, *Muhammadan Festicals*, 15–49, and Arberry, *Mystical Poems*, 2:44, n. 22–26. Concerning the Sufi implications of *jam*ᶜ ("union") see al-Qushayrī, *Risālah*, 1:222–25 (tr. Sells, *Early Islamic Mysticism*, 116–19).

83. For this divine saying see Schimmel, *Mystical Dimensions*, 190, and the introduction.

84. Al-Būrīnī, *Sulṭān*, 2:76; al-Nābulusī, *Kashf al-Sirr*, 309a–310a, and Arberry, *Mystical Poems*, 2:44–45, n. 33. For more on Muhammad's *mi*ᶜ*rāj*, see *EI2*, 7:97–103 (J.E. Bencheikh); *Encyclopaedia of the Qur'ān*, (*EQ*) 1:176–8 (M. Sells); Schimmel, *Muhammad*, 159–75, and chapter 2.

85. Abraham was known as the *khalīl* (friend) of God. See al-Hujwirī for a mystical interpretation of this Station in *Kashf*, 423–26 (tr. Nicholson, *The Kashf*, 326–28).

86. For *wārid* see Hujwirī, *The Kashf*, tr. Nicholson, 385, 404, 407, and Arberry, *Mystical Poems*, 2:45, n. 34.

87. Concerning the sites mentioned in verses 35–36 and other places in and around the Kaᶜbah see Ibn Jubayr's description in *Riḥlah Ibn Jubayr*, 59–81, partially translated by Broadhurst in Lichtenstadler, ed., *Introduction*, 378–92, and see Arberry's references; *Mystical Poems*, 2: 45, n. 35–36. Regarding Ibn al-Fāriḍ's language of hope that ends many, though not all of his odes, see J. Stetkevych, *Zephyrs*, 88–89.

88. Arberry, *Mystical Poems*, 2:45, n. 37. Concerning Kaᶜb ibn Zuhayr and his panegyric to Muhammad, see Michael Sells, "Bānat Suᶜād: translation and introduction," *JAL* 21 (1990):140–54.

89. Cf. al-Tusturī's doctrine of the two Days in Böwering, *Mystical Vision*, 229–30.

Chapter 4: The Beloved's Wine

1. Imrū' al-Qays, *Sharḥ Dīwān Imrū' al-Qays* (Beirut: Dār al-Ṣādir, n.d.), 163, verses 7–9, and see Muhammad Muhammad Ḥusayn, *Asālīb al-Ṣināᶜā fī Shiᶜr al-Khamr wa-al-Naqā bayn al-Aᶜshā wa-al-Jāhilīyīn* (Alexandria: Munsha'at al-Maᶜārif, 1960), 7–8; Īliyā Hāwī, *Fann al-Shiᶜr al-Khamrī* (Beirut: Dār al-Thaqāfah, 1960), 9-75; *EI2*, 4: 998–1002 (J.E. Bencheikh); Abdulla El Tayib, "Pre-Islamic Poetry," in *CHALUP*, 100–102, and F. Harb, "Wine Poetry (*Khamriyyāt*)," in *CHALABL*, 219–22.

2. Concerning Imru' al-Qays, see *EI2*, 3:1176 (S. Boustany), and *EAL*, 1:394–95 (R. Jacobi).

3. Al-Ḥusayn ibn Aḥmad al-Zawzanī, *Sharḥ al-Muᶜallaqāt al-Sabᶜ* (Damascus: n.p., 1963), 118–19, verses 1–5. Concerning ᶜAmr ibn Kulthūm, see *EI2*, 1:452 (R. Blachère), and *EAL*, 1:87–88 (J.E. Montgomery).

4. Al-Aᶜshā, *Dīwān*, ed. Muḥammad Muḥammad Ḥusayn (Beirut: Mu'assasat al-Risālah, 1963), 109, verses 36–44; see Michael Sells, *Desert Tracings*, 57–66, for another translation of these verses and the entire poem. For more on al-Aᶜshā see *EI2*, 1:689–90 (W. Caskel); *EAL*, 1: 107 (T. Bauer); Hāwī, *al-Shiᶜr al-Khamrī*, 27–59; Philip F. Kennedy, *The Wine Song in Classical Arabic Poetry* (Oxford: Clarendon Press, 1997), esp. 245–61, and John Dennis Hyde, "A Study of the Poetry of Maymun Ibn Qays al-Aᶜsha," Ph.D. diss., Princeton University, 1977.

5. Al-Zawzanī, *al-Sabᶜ*, 146, verses 39–41. For ᶜAntarah see *EI2*, 1:521–22 (R. Blachère); *EAL*, 1:94 (T. Bauer), and Sells, *Desert Tracings*, 45–56, for a translation of the entire poem; for more on ᶜAntarah and wine see Kennedy, *Wine Song*, 152–54. Also see Labīd's *Muᶜallaqah* for another example; al-Zawzanī, *al-Sabᶜ*, 109–10, verses 55–61, and Sell's translation of the ode, *Desert Tracings*, 32–44.

6. Quoted by Abū Tammām, *Sharḥ Dīwān*, 2:875–78.

7. See Th. Emil Homerin, "Echoes of a Thirsty Owl: Death and Afterlife in Pre-Islamic Arabic Poetry," *Journal of Near Eastern Studies* 44 (1985):165–84.

8. Ṭarafah ibn al-ᶜAbd, *Dīwān* (Beirut: Dār al-Ṣādir, 1961), 30–31, verses 47–51; for a translation of the complete poem see Michael Sells, "The Muᶜallaqa of Ṭarafa," *Journal of Arabic Literature* 17 (1986): 21–33. Concerning this poet see *EI2*, 10:219–20 (J.E. Montgomery), and *EAL*, 2:759 (T. Bauer). For more on wine and blood vengeance see S. P. Stetkevych, *Mute Immortals Speak*, 42–43, 55–118, 228, 282–83.

9. Abū Faraj al-Isfahānī, *Kitāb al-Āghānī* (Beirut: Dār al-Tawjīh al-Lubnānī, n.d.), 16:15. For more on the Arab courts see Nicholson, *Literary History*, 30–54, esp. 53 for his translation of this passage. Also see *EI2*, 4:998, 1002 (J.E. Bencheikh).

10. Quoted in Louis Cheikho, *Shuᶜarā' al-Naṣrānīyah baᶜd al-Islām* (Beirut: Imprimerie Catholique, 1924–27), 183. Concerning al-Akhtal see Cheikho, ibid, 170–91; al-Isfahānī, *al-Āghānī*, 7: 169–88; Hāwī, *al-Shiᶜr al-Khamrī*, who also cites this poem, 106–107, 97–128, 387–420; *EI2*, 1:331 (R. Blachère); *EI2*, 4:1002 (J.E. Bencheikh); *EAL* 1:67–68 (G.J.H. Van Gelder), and Kennedy, *Wine Song*, 94–100. For more on Christian poets and Christian influences on Arabic poetry see Cheikho, ibid.; his *Shuᶜarā' al-Naṣrnīyah*, 2nd ed. (Beirut: Dār al-Mashriq, 1967), and Shawqī Dayf, *Ta'rīkh al-Adab al-ᶜĀrabī* (Cairo: Dār al-Maᶜārif, 1982), 1:97–103.

11. Also see Hāwī's commentary, *al-Shiᶜr al-Khamrī*, 107–108.

12. Ibid., 140–46, 163–70; also see the extensive entry "*khamriyya*," *EI2*, 4:998–1009 (J. E. Bencheikh); "khamriyya" in *EAL*, 1:433–35 (G. Scholler/A. Giese), and Fuat Sezgin, *Geshichte des Arabischen Schrifttmus* (Leiden: E. J. Brill, 1975) 2: 326–27. For al-Uqayshir, see *EI2*, 4:1002–1003 (J.E. Bencheikh), and *EAL*, 2:795 (P.F. Kennedy).

13. *EI2*, 4:1003–1004, 1008 (J.E. Bencheikh), and Harb, "Wine Poetry," 224–26. For al-Walīd ibn Yazīd see *EI2*, 11:128–29 (H. Kennedy and Renate Jacobi); *EAL*, 2:803 (R. Jacobi); his *Dīwān*, ed. F. Gabrielli (Damascus: Maṭbaᶜat Ibn Zaydūn, 1937); Dieter Derenk, *Leben und Dichtung des Omayyaden Kalifen Al-Walīd Ibn Yazīd* (Freiburg: K. Schwarz, 1974), and Hāwī, *al-Shiᶜr al-Khamrī*, 120–28. For the Qur'ānic prohibitions and Islamic laws against wine see *EI2*, 4: 994–97 (A.J. Wensink and J. Sadan), and also see Ignaz Goldziher, *Muhammedanische Studien* (Halle, 1880–90), 1:19–33; translated by C. R. Barber and S. M. Stern in *Muslim Studies* (London: George Allen & Unwin, 1967), 1:27–38.

14. Abū Nuwās, *Dīwān*, ed. Ewald Wagner (Wiesbaden: Franz Steiner, 1988), 3:106. Also see Yaseen Noorani, "Heterotopia and the Wine Poem in Early Islamic Culture," *International Journal of Middle Eastern Studies* 36 (2004):345–66; Hamori, *Art*, 47–60, and the detailed studies of the poet by Philip F. Kennedy, *Wine Song*, esp., 194–244, and his *Abu Nuwas: A Genius of Poetry* (Oxford: Oneworld, 2005), esp. 57–78. Also see *EI2*, 4:1004–1005 (J.E. Bencheikh); *EAL*, 1:41–43 (G. Schoeler/A. Giese); Scholer, "Bashshār B. Burd," *CHALABL*, 290–95, Harb, "Wine Poetry," *CHALABL*, 227–31, and J. E.

Bencheikh, "Thèmes bachiques et personnages dans le dīwān d'Abū Nuwās," *Bulletin d'études orientales* 18 (1963–64):1–84.

15. Abū Nuwās, *Dīwān*, ed. Ewald Wagner, 3:106. Ahlwardt's reads *aliṭnī* ("to bugger") in place of *alṭinī* ("to cover, protect") in the final verse; *Dīwān des Abu Nowas*, ed. Wilhelm Ahlwardt (Greifwalt: C. A. Koch, 1861), 39.

16. Abū Nuwās, *Dīwān*, ed. Wagner, 3:61, verses 1–3, and see Hamori's translation, *Art*, 71–73. Also see Kennedy, *Wine Song*, 43, 86–148, and Noorani, "Heterotopia," 350–54.

17. Abū Nuwās, *Dīwān*, ed. Wagner, 3:280–81, and see Hāwī, *al-Shiʿr al-Khamrī*, 257–62; Hamori's translation, *Art*, 65–67, and Noorani, "Heterotopia," 354–61.

18. See Hāwī, who reads *mukhalliṣ* instead of *mukhallaṣ* (*al-Shiʿr al-Khamrī*, 257–62), and Hamori who also notes possible Manichean influences on this poem; *Art*, 66–67. Other verses ascribed to Abū Nuwās also refer to the primordial wine:

Leave the Bedouin to weep over wormwoods,
flatlands, and wastelands,
And turn aside to us whose morning drink is an aged wine
whose ancient era (*min qidmi-ʿahdihā*) reminds you (*tudhkiru*) of Noah.

See Ibrāhīm ibn al-Qāsim Raqīq al-Qayrawānī, *Quṭb al-Surūr fī Awṣāf al-Khamr*, ed. Aḥmad Jundī (Damascus: al-Muqaddamah, 1969), 563; Abū Nuwās, *Dīwān*, ed. Wagner, 3: 86, 96, 98, and Kennedy, *Wine Song*, 132–48, 177–80.

19. Regarding wine verse in the late Abbasid and Ayyubid periods see *EI2*, 4:1005–1006 (J.E. Bencheikh); M. K. Ḥusayn, *Dirāsāt*, 147–53; Rikābī, *La Poésie*, 250–52, Harb, "Wine Poetry," 231–32, and for an example see Bahā' al-Dīn Zuhayr, *Works*, 1:92–94 (tr. Palmer, 2: 109–10); for wine poetry from Andalusia, see Michael Sells, "Love," in Menocal, ed., *CHALLOA*, 134–140.

20. Regarding Maʿarrī, see Suzanne Stetkevych, "Intoxication and Immortality: Wine and Honey in al-Maʿarrī's Garden," in *Critical Pilgrimages: Studies in the Arabic Literary Tradition*, ed. Fedwa Multi-Douglas (Austin: University of Texas Press, 1990), 29–48.

21. Concerning the doctrines of intoxication and sobriety see al-Sarrāj, *al-Lumaʿ*, 415–17; al-Qushayrī, *Risālah*, 1:236–38 (tr. Sells, *Early Islamic Mysticism*, 124–26); al-Kalābādhī, *al-Taʿarruf*, 116–17 (tr. Arberry, *Doctrine*, 110–12); al-Hujwirī, *Kashf*, 230–35 (tr. Nicholson, *The Kashf*, 184–88), and Schimmel, *Dimensions*, 58–59. Also see chapter 5. For a general introduction to Sufi wine imagery see ʿAṭif Jawdah Naṣr, *al-Ramz al-Shiʿrī ʿinda al-Ṣūfīyah* (Beirut: Dār al-Andalus, 1978), 328–84, and *EI2*, 4: 1006 (J.E. Bencheikh).

22. Al-Kalābādhī, *al-Taʿarruf*, 117.

23. Al-Qushayrī, *Risālah*, 1:237.

24. Abū Nuwās, *Dīwān*, ed. Wagner, 3:107, verse 5, and see Homerin, "Tangled Words," 190–93. For a similar example in love poetry, see van Gelder, "Rābiʿa's Poem," 73–75.

25. Al-Ḥallāj, *Sharḥ Dīwān*, 1:251–52, also quoted by Schimmel, *Veil*, 33, and see Harb, "Wine Poetry," 232–34.

26. Al-Kātib al-Iṣfahānī, *Kharīdat*, 2:320.

27. Cornell, *Abū Madyan*, Arabic text 157, 159, my translation; Abū Madyan, *Dīwān*, 59–60. Also see Cornell's complete translation, 156, 158, and Naṣr, *al-Ramz* (359–66), who quotes and analyzes another wine ode said to have been composed by Abū Madyan, but not found in his *Dīwān*.

28. For further references to wine, recollection, and gnosis in verse ascribed to Abū Madyan, see his *Dīwān*, esp. 70–79; in one poem (66–67), wine is also a symbol for God's gift of prophecy to Adam, Noah, Abraham, Moses, Jesus, and Muhammad.

29. There are several versions of this poem. My translation is based on the text of Yāqūt, *Muᶜjam al-Udabā'* (Cairo: Dār al-Ma'mūn, 1936), 19:316–19, but with several variants found in Ibn Khallikān's, *Wafayāt*, 1:271–72 and Muḥammad ibn Maḥmūd al-Shāhrazūrī's, *Nuzhat al-Arwāḥ wa-Rawḍat al-Afrāḥ*, 233–35. Also see the Arabic edition of Otto Spies and S.K. Khattak in their *Three Treatises*, 103–105, and the English translation by S.H. Nadeem, *Critical Appreciation*, 124–32. For more on Yaḥyā al-Suhrawardī, see the introduction.

30. The divine light is a central feature of al-Suhrawardī's theosophical doctrines of illumination; see John Walbridge, *The Leaven of the Ancients: Suhrawardī and the Heritage of the Greeks* (Albany: State University of New York Press, 2000), and Schimmel, *Mystical Dimensions*, 259–63. The "Light Verse" had been interpreted mystically prior to al-Suhrawardī; see for example al-Ghazālī's *Mishkāt al-Anwār*.

31. Cf. al-Tusturī's earlier views on these matters in Böwering, *Mystical Vision*, 184–230.

32. Ibn al-Fāriḍ, *Dīwān*, 173, verses 1–7.

33. See Kennedy, *Wine Song*, esp. 19–85. Also see Stefan Sperl's translation and brief analysis of this poem in his "Qasida Form and Mystic Path in 13th Century Egypt: A Poem by Ibn al-Fāriḍ," in *Qasida Poetry*, ed. S. Sperl and C. Shackle, 1:70–74; 2:106–11, and see the conclusion.

34. See chapter 2. Arberry interprets the beloved of this ode as being the Spirit of Muhammad who prays as the "Great Imam"; *Mystical Poems*, 2:92–93, n. 8–9.

35. Ibn al-Fāriḍ, *Dīwān*, 173, verses 8–9.

36. *Dīwān Majnūn Laylā*, ed. ᶜAbd al-Sattār Ahmad Farrāj (Cairo: Maktabat Miṣr, 1963), 294, verses 37–38, also quoted by Khairallah, *Madness*, 100. Concerning the beloved as an object of ᶜUdhrī worship also see Djedidi, *Uḍrites*, 79–86, and Vadet, *L'Esprit*, 249–63. Also see Sperl, "Qasida Form," 68–71.

37. Al-Būrīnī *Sulṭān*, 2:122, and Arberry, *Mystical Poems*, 2:93, n. 8.

38. Al-Nābulusī, *Kashf al-Sirr*, 406a–407b, and see Arberry, *Mystical Poems*, 2:92, n. 8–9. Also see verses ascribed to Abū Bakr ibn ᶜAbd al-Raḥmān ibn al-Miswar ibn Mukhramah similarly invoking *labbayka* cited by Ibn Qutaybah, *al-Shiᶜr wa-l-Shuᶜarā'*, 355–56, and quoted by Khairallah, *Madness*, 136, and Sperl, "Qasida Form," 68.

39. Ibn al-Fāriḍ, *Dīwān*, 175, verses 10–26, and see al-Nābalusī's interpretation, *Kashf al-Sirr*, 407b–10a.

40. E.g., verses 11, 12: *qalb*/"heart"; verses 12, 15: *maᶜnā*/ "subtle sense," "essence"; verse 13: *baqā*, verse 21: *yubqi*, verse 22 *yubqa*/"stay," "abide"; "remain"; v.14: *wajd*/"rapture"; verse 18: *maqām*/ "station."

41. Ibn al-Fāriḍ, *Dīwān*, 175, verses 27–35.

42. Concerning this clichéd Arab portrayal of the beloved see Arberry, *Mystical Poems*, 2:94, n. 27, and al-Jāhiẓ, *Fī al-ᶜIshq wa-al-Nisā'*, in *Majmūᶜat Rasā'il al-Jāhiẓ*, ed. ᶜAbd al-Salīm Muḥammad Hārūn (Cairo: Maktabat al-Khānjī, 1964) 3:139–59; tr. Charles Pellat in the *Life and Works of Jāḥiẓ* (Berkeley: University of California Press, 1969), 258–59.

43. I follow Arberry's interpretation of *mulk* and *zamān* as "space and time"; *Mystical Poems*, 2:95, n. 35. Also see al-Nābulusī, *Kashf al-Sirr*, 411a–13b.

44. Ibn al-Fāriḍ, *Dīwān*, 158–61. For other translations see Martin Lings, *Sufi Poems* (Cambridge: Islamic Texts Society, 2004), 66–74; Arberry, *Mystical Poems*, 2:84–90; Nicholson, *Studies*, 184–88; A. Safi in *Bulletin of the School of Oriental and Asian Studies* 2:235–48; Emile Dermenghem, *L'Éloge du vin* (Paris: Les Éditions Véga, 1931), and L'Hôpital, *Poèmes mystiques*, 217–43.

45. Concerning the eight verses that are numbered 23–30 in many printed editions of the *Dīwān* and their dubious ascription to Ibn al-Fāriḍ, see Homerin, "Ibn al-Fāriḍ's Personal *Dīwān*," 240–42.

46. Hāwī, *al-Shiᶜr al-Khamrī*, 257–62; Hamori, *Art*, 66–67, and Kennedy, *Wine Song*, 43, 179.

47. For other examples of Ibn al-Fāriḍ's frequent use of the conditional, see Ṣādiq, *Shiᶜr Ibn al-Fāriḍ: Dirāsah Uslūbīyah*, 107–10. Also see Arberry, *Mystical Poems*, 2:84–90, and al-Yūsuf, "Baᶜḍ Yanābīᶜ," 99–104, who notes poetic antecedents for several of Ibn al-Fāriḍ's images. For more on many of these major wine themes and images, and their poetic relationships, see *EI2*, 4:998–1009 (J.E. Bencheikh), esp. 999–1001; al-Sarī ibn Aḥmad al-Rifā', *al-Muḥibb wa-al-Maḥbūb wa-al-Mashmūm wa-al-Mashrūb* (Damascus: Mājid Ḥasan al-Dhahabī, 1986), esp. vol. 4, and Kennedy, *Wine Song*.

48. Cited in Khairallah, *Madness*, 73 from *Ḳays b. al-Mulavvaḥ*, 96.

49. See Ḥāwī, *al-Shiᶜr al-Khamrī*, 150; *EI2*, 4:998–1009 (J.E. Bencheikh), esp. 1006, and Kennedy, *Wine Song*, 9, 15.

50. See Th. Emil Homerin, ed. and tr., *The Wine of Love and Life: Ibn al-Fāriḍ's al-Khamrīyah and al-Qayṣarī's Quest for Meaning* (Chicago: Center for Middle Eastern Studies, University of Chicago, 2005). Also see William Chittick, "The Five Presences: From al-Qunawī to al-Qaysarī," *Muslim World* 72 (1982):107–28, esp. 123–24.

51. Homerin, *Wine of Love*, 13–16. Al-Qayṣarī cites the Qur'ānic passages 76:5, 17–18, and 83:25–27, which describe the incomparable drink of Paradise. In some Sufi circles, the proper practice of *dhikr* was thought to return the rapt mystic momentarily to the Day of the Covenant; see for example, al-Kalābādhī, *al-Taᶜarruf*, 160–61, (tr. Arberry, *Doctrines*, 166–67), and see chapter 5.

52. Homerin, *Wine of Love*, 16–20. Al-Qayṣarī's equations crescent "moon" = ᶜAlī; "stars" = saints/gnostics are also supported by verses 625–27 of Ibn al-Fāriḍ's *al-Tā'īyah al-Kubrā*; see the following chapter. Qur'ān 16:16

points to the guiding stars as one of the many signs of God's bounty to humanity.

53. For more on these probable references to Muḥammad, see chapter 2.

54. Homerin, *Wine of Love*, 20–24.

55. Homerin, *Wine of Love*, 24–38. Also cf. verses 615, 627 of the *al-Tā'īyah al-Kubrā*, and see the following chapter.

56. In support of his interpretations, al-Qayṣarī cites the last half of Qur'ān 2:171: *summun bukmun ᶜummun fa-hum lā yaᶜqilun*, "Deaf, dumb, blind, so they are not intelligent." This verse refers to the unbelievers who refuse to follow God's guidance; Homerin, *Wine of Love*, 27. Most of the later commentators follow al-Qayṣarī's interpretation with slight variants.

57. Homerin, *Wine of Love*, 38–39; also see Yaḥyā al-Jīlānī, *Ḥall al-Muᶜḍilāt min Rumūz al-Mushkilāt*, microfilm of manuscript 4116 (3812), Yahuda Section, Garrett Collection, Princeton University, 21b, and During, *Musique*, 164–65.

58. Al-Qayṣarī (*Wine of Love*, 41) and al-Jīlānī (23b–24a) view the monks as Muslim gnostics. Nicholson, following al-Nābulusī (*Studies*, 186–87), interprets this passage more literally as portraying Christians whose religious experience, from a Muslim perspective, is incomplete; also see Harb, "Wine Poetry," 233–34. However, in context of Ibn al-Fāriḍ's *al-Khamrīyah* (esp. verses 1, 8–20) and other poems, this heavenly drink of immortality (= the beatific vision?) can not be tasted by erring mortals on earth, but only by the pure of heart who dwell in Paradise after the Judgment Day.

59. For al-Junayd's views on *fanā', balā'*, and *baqā'*, see chapter 5.

60. See Lings who interprets the beloved's saliva to be the *al-Ruḥ al-Muḥammadī*, and linked to the wine's mixing in verse 4; "Mystical Poetry," 256–57.

61. Homerin, *Wine of Love*, 40–43, and al-Jīlānī, *Ḥall al-Muᶜḍilāt*, fol. 25b. Also see chapter 2 and the following chapter concerning Ibn al-Fāriḍ's finding traces of the beloved in nature and in the Sufi *samāᶜ*.

62. Homerin, *Wine of Love*, 43–45.

Chapter 5: Poem of the Sufi Way in "T"—Major

1. Perhaps Ibn al-Fāriḍ was aware of narrative religious poems in Persian, such as those by Ṣanāᶜī and ᶜAṭṭār, although the moods, motifs, and meter of the *al-Tā'īyah al-Kubrā* are clearly those of Arabic poetry; see Carlo A. Nallino, "Il poema mistico arabo di Ibn al-Fāriḍ in una recente traduzione italiana," *Rivista degli studi orientali* 8 (1919–20):20–21.

2. Saᶜīd al-Dīn al-Farghānī, *Muntahā al-Madārik fī Sharḥ Tā'īyat Ibn al-Fāriḍ*, ed. ᶜĀṣim Ibrāhīm al-Kayyālī (Beirut: Dār al-Kutub al-ᶜIlmīyah, 2007); ᶜAfīf al-Dīn al-Tilimsānī, *Sharḥ Tā'īyat Ibn al-Fāriḍ al-Kubrā*, manuscript 1328 (Taṣawwuf Ṭalᶜat), Cairo: Dār al-Kutub al-Miṣrīyah; ᶜIzz al-Dīn al-Kāshānī, *Kashf al-Wujūh al-Ghurr li-Maᶜānī Naẓm al-Durr*, microfilm of manuscript 4106 (3979), Yahuda Section, Garrett Collection, Princeton University, and Dāwūd al-Qayṣarī, *Sharḥ Tā'īyat al-Sulūk*, microfilm of manuscript 4107 (4352), Yahuda Section, Garrett Collection, Princeton University. For more on these and later

commentators and their positions on Ibn al-Fāriḍ and his verse, see Homerin, *From Arab Poet*, esp. chapters 1 and 3, and Homerin, *Wine of Love*.

3. See ᶜAlī Sibṭ Ibn al-Fāriḍ's introduction to the *Dīwān*, 13–14 (tr. Homerin, *ᶜUmar Ibn al-Fāriḍ*, 313–14, and quoted above in chapter 1). Also see Homerin, *From Arab Poet*, chaps. 1–2, and Nicholson, *Studies*, 167–68.

4. See Homerin, *From Arab Poet*, chapters1–3, and chapter 4 for twentieth-century works on the poet and his *al-Tā'īyah al-Kubrā*, which include Nicholson's study and partial English translation in *Studies*, 162–95; A.J. Arberry's complete translation, *The Poem of the Way* (London: Emery Walker, 1952); C.A. Nallino, "Il poema mistico," 1–106; Nallino, "Ancora su Ibn al-Fāriḍ e sulla mistica musulmana," *Rivista degli studi orientali* 8 (1919–20):501–62, and works by M. Ḥilmī, especially his *Ibn al-Fāriḍ wa-al-Ḥubb al-Ilāhī*. These and more recent studies will be referred to throughout this chapter.

5. Cited by ᶜAlī Sibṭ Ibn al-Fāriḍ in *Dīwān*, 14–15(tr. Homerin, *ᶜUmar Ibn al-Fāriḍ*, 314).

6. Ibn al-Fāriḍ, *Dīwān*, 66–143 for the Arabic text to the complete poem, and Homerin, *ᶜUmar Ibn al-Fāriḍ*, 67–291 for an annotated English translation of the poem.

7. This is the reading by al-Kāshānī, *Kashf al-Wujūh*, 25a–b; al-Qayṣarī, *Sharḥ Tā'īyat al-Sulūk*, 17b–18a; Nicholson, *Studies*, 199 and Arberry, *Poem of the Way*, 9.

8. Concerning the "glance"/"gaze" in Arabic love lore, see Joseph N. Bell, *Love Theory in Later Hanbalite Islam* (Albany: State University of New York Press, 1979), 19–28. Al-Farghānī, *Muntahā*, 1:150, and al-Tilimsānī, *Sharḥ Tā'īyat Ibn al-Fāriḍ al-Kubrā*, 5a, interpret the glance as the cause of the poet's intoxication.

9. For Sufi opinions on this practice see Bell, *Love Theory*, 139–44, and Schimmel, *Mystical Dimensions*, 289–91.

10. Al-Farghānī, *Muntahā*, 1:150–55, and al-Tilimsānī, *Sharḥ Tā'īyat Ibn al-Fāriḍ al-Kubrā*, 5a.

11. Al-Farghānī, *Muntahā*, 1:161–63; al-Tilimsānī, *Sharḥ Tā'īyat Ibn al-Fāriḍ al-Kubrā*, 5b–7b; al-Kāshānī, *Kashf al-Wujūh*, 27a–28b, and al-Qayṣarī, *Sharḥ Tā'īyat al-Sulūk*, 19b–20b. Cf. al-Tusturī, in Böwering, *Mystical Vision*, 172.

12. Cf. Ibn al-Shahrazūrī, *al-Mawṣilīyah*, verse 27. Both poets probably allude to a divine saying in which God surrounds Paradise with *al-makārih*, "horrible things"; see Muḥyī al-Dīn Ibn al-ᶜArabī, *Divine Sayings: Mishkāt al-Anwār*, ed. tr. Hirtenstein and Notcutt, Arabic text, 7–8.

13. Al-Farghānī, *Muntahā*, 1:229–31; al-Tilimsānī, *Sharḥ Tā'īyat Ibn al-Fāriḍ al-Kubrā*, 9a-b; al-Kāshānī, *Kashf al-Wujūh*, 43a–b, and al-Qayṣarī, *Sharḥ Tā'īyat al-Sulūk*, 31a–b, who cites Qur'ān 5:1: "Oh you who believe, fulfill the bonds (*ᶜuqūd*)." Also see Nicholson, *Studies*, 206, n. 69.

14. Compare verse 55 of Ibn al-Fāriḍ's *al-Lāmīyah* in chapter 2, and also verse 14 of his wine poem beginning *adir dhikra man ahwa* cited in chapter 4. Also cf. al-Tusturī's similar views in Böwering, *Mystical Vision*, 185–230.

15. Al-Farghānī, *Muntahā*, 1:231–38; al-Tilimsānī, *Sharḥ Tā'īyat Ibn al-Fāriḍ al-Kubrā*, 9b–10a; al-Kāshānī, *Kashf al-Wujūh*, 43b–45a, and al-Qayṣarī, *Sharḥ Tā'īyat al-Sulūk*, 31b–32a. These three divine attributes are found together as

early as the third/ninth century; see Schimmel, *Mystical Dimensions*, 44, and Nicholson, *Studies*, 207, n. 71–73.

16. Al-Qayṣarī, *Sharḥ Tā'īyat al-Sulūk*, 31b, cites Qu'rān 95:4: "Indeed, We have created the human being in the best of stature (*aḥsana taqwīm*)." The Qu'rān also states in several places that God fashioned the human forms (*ṣuwar*) and made them good/lovely (*aḥsana*); see Qu'rān 40:64, and 64:3. Al-Kāshānī, *Kashf al-Wujūh*, 43b–44a, goes beyond the Qu'rān, citing the much debated *ḥadīth*, "God created Adam in His/his form" (*ʿalā ṣūratihu*); for this tradition, see Graham, *Divine Word*, 151–52.

17. See al-Farghānī, *Muntahā*, 1:241; al-Tilimsānī, *Sharḥ Tā'īyat Ibn al-Fāriḍ al-Kubrā*,, 9b-10a; al-Kāshānī, *Kashf al-Wujūh*, 44a–45b, and al-Qayṣarī, *Sharḥ Tā'īyat al-Sulūk*, 32a–b. Cf. al-Tusturī on the "secret of the soul" in Böwering, *Mystical Vision*, 194–207.

18. Verse 77 as found in most published editions of the *Dīwān* and beginning: *khalaʿtu ʿidhārī* . . . has long been considered spurious; see *Dīwān*, 73, n. 77, where ʿAlī Sibt Ibn al-Fāriḍ noted that a certain Shihāb al-Dīn al-Shiblī claimed to have received this verse from Ibn al-Fāriḍ in a dream; also see Nallino, "Il poema," 56–57. This verse is also missing from the commentaries by al-Farghānī, al-Tilimsānī, and al-Kāshānī, though the verse is to be found in al-Qayṣarī's commentary and in the Chester Beatty manuscript.

19. This dialogue with the beloved occurs at approximately the same place (v. 84 ff) as it does in the poet's *al-Yā'īyah* (v. 81 ff). However, the beloved's rebuke of the poet in the *al-Tā'īyah al-Kubrā* is longer and more developed than that in the *al-Yā'īyah*; this is normally the case for many images and motifs shared in common by the *al-Tā'īyah al-Kubrā* and the other poems of the *Dīwān*.

20. Al-Farghānī, *Muntahā*, 1:246–48.

21. See ibid., 1:260–64; al-Tilimsānī, *Sharḥ Tā'īyat Ibn al-Fāriḍ al-Kubrā*, 9b–10a; al-Kāshānī, *Kashf al-Wujūh*, 50a–b; al-Qayṣarī, *Sharḥ Tā'īyat al-Sulūk*, 37b–38a, and Nicholson, *Studies*, 210, n. 98–99. Cf. al-Tusturī's reflection on the God's statement (Q 2:41): "So fear you Me!" in Böwering, *Mystical Vision*, 183–84.

22. Qur'ān 10:62–64 asserts: "Indeed, the friends (*awliyā'*) of God, they have no fear, nor do they grieve. Those who believe and are mindful will have glad tidings in this life and the next . . ." Also see al-Tusturī's interpretation of these Qur'ānic verses in Böwering, *Mystical Vision*, 236–37.

23. See al-Farghānī, *Muntahā*, 1:302–305; al-Tilimsānī, *Sharḥ Tā'īyat Ibn al-Fāriḍ al-Kubrā*, 12a–13b; al-Kāshānī, *Kashf al-Wujūh*, 61b–62ab, and al-Qayṣarī, *Sharḥ Tā'īyat al-Sulūk*, 46b–47a.

24. See al-Farghānī, *Muntahā*, 1:305–11; al-Tilimsānī, *Sharḥ Tā'īyat Ibn al-Fāriḍ al-Kubrā*, 13a–b; al-Kāshānī, *Kashf al-Wujūh*, 62a–64a, and al-Qayṣarī, *Sharḥ Tā'īyat al-Sulūk*, 47b–49a, and Arberry, *Poem of the Way*, 79. For more on the human as a divine idea, see later in this chapter.

25. A-Kāshānī, *Kashf al-Wujūh*, 63b–64a, points out that the poet's use in verse 160 of contrasting prepositions is a sure sign of union.

26. A-Farghānī, *Muntahā*, 1:311–15; al-Tilimsānī, *Sharḥ Tā'īyat Ibn al-Fāriḍ al-Kubrā*, 13a-b; al-Kāshānī, *Kashf al-Wujūh*, 63a–64b; al-Qayṣarī, *Sharḥ Tā'īyat*

al-Sulūk, 48b–50b, and Nicholson, *Studies*, 214–15. In the course of their commentaries on this passage, both al-Farghānī and al-Qayṣarī cite the important Sufi *ḥadīth*: "He who knows himself (*nafs*), knows his Lord." For more on this tradition see Schimmel, *Mystical Dimensions*, 189–90. For Ibn al-Fāriḍ's use of the root *sh*h*d*, see later in this chapter.

27. For example see Ibn al-Fāriḍ's *al-Tā'īyah al-Ṣughrā* (103 vv.) and his *al-Yā'īyah* (151 vv.), and chapter 4.

28. Concerning the role of a mystical guide in Sufi verse also see A.S. Ḥusayn, *al-Adab al-Ṣūfīyah*, 242–43.

29. Ibn al-Fāriḍ refers yet again to God and the senses; see al-Farghānī, *Muntahā*, 1:323–41; al-Tilimsānī, *Sharḥ Tā'īyat Ibn al-Fāriḍ al-Kubrā*, 13a–14b; al-Kāshānī, *Kashf al-Wujūh*, 72b–73a, and al-Qayṣarī, *Sharḥ Tā'īyat al-Sulūk*, 57a–b.

30. Al-Farghānī, *Muntahā*, 1:341–48; al-Tilimsānī, *Sharḥ Tā'īyat Ibn al-Fāriḍ al-Kubrā*, 14a–b; al-Kāshānī, *Kashf al-Wujūh*, 73a–77b, and al-Qayṣarī, *Sharḥ Tā'īyat al-Sulūk*, 57b–61b, and Nicholson, *Studies*, 216–18.

31. Al-Farghānī, *Muntahā*, 1:354–59; al-Tilimsānī, *Sharḥ Tā'īyat Ibn al-Fāriḍ al-Kubrā*, 14b; al-Kāshānī, *Kashf al-Wujūh*, 73a–77b, and al-Qayṣarī, *Sharḥ Tā'īyat al-Sulūk*, 57b–61b. For more on the doctrinal underpinning of this and other sections of the poem, see later in this chapter.

32. Al-Farghānī, *Muntahā*, 1:359, quotes God as saying in the Qur'ān 2:186: "If my servants ask you about Me, lo, I am near!"

33. Ibid., 1:361–62.

34. Al-Farghānī, *Muntahā*, 1:362–72; al-Tilimsānī, *Sharḥ Tā'īyat Ibn al-Fāriḍ al-Kubrā*, 15a–b; al-Kāshānī, *Kashf al-Wujūh*, 77b–82b, and al-Qayṣarī, *Sharḥ Tā'īyat al-Sulūk*, 61b–65b.

35. Al-Farghānī, *Muntahā*, 1:372–73; al-Kāshānī, *Kashf al-Wujūh*, 82a–b, and al-Qayṣarī, *Sharḥ Tā'īyat al-Sulūk*, 65a–b; Nicholson, *Studies*, 219–22, and Nallino, "Il poema," 74.

36. For more on the form-shifting beloved/ghoul in classical Arabic poetry see Sells, *Desert Tracings*, 67–68, and his "Bānat Suᶜād," 142–43. For a comparable example of a Sufi reading of the ᶜUdhrī motif of one's beloved as the source of all other lovers see Ibn al-ᶜArabī's *Turjumān*, esp. 44, verse 16 (tr. Nicholson, *The Tarjumān*, 70–71). However, in contrast to Ibn al-Fāriḍ's reading of the ᶜUdhrī beloveds in general as limited manifestations of absolute beauty, Ibn al-ᶜArabī uses them as symbols for his earthly beloved and spiritual inspiration, Niẓām, and then subsequently interprets the name of each ᶜUdhrī beloved as referring to a specific station on the Sufi path; also see Henry Corbin, *Creative Imagination in the Ṣūfism of Ibn ᶜArabī* (Princeton: Princeton University Press, 1969), 136–38, 322, n. 4.

37. Qur'ān 6:163 states: *lā sharīka lahu* ("He has no peer/equal.")

38. Cf. Ibn al-Fāriḍ's *al-Tā'īyah al-Ṣughrā*, verse 21, and his *al-Yā'īyah*, verse 93.

39. In particular, see al-Farghānī, *Muntahā*, 1:384–85, and Böwering, *Mystical Vision*, 149–53.

40. See al-Farghānī, *Muntahā*, 1:373–89; al-Tilimsānī, *Sharḥ Tā'īyat Ibn al-Fāriḍ al-Kubrā*,, 15b–16b; al-Kāshānī, *Kashf al-Wujūh*, 82b–86a, and al-Qayṣarī, *Sharḥ Tā'īyat al-Sulūk*, 65b–69a. Also see Nicholson, *Studies*, 223–24. All of

the major commentators interpret the poet's claim to be the archetypal lover manifest throughout human history to be a result of Ibn al-Fāriḍ's ecstatic union with Muhammad's spiritual presence or light, and they cite various *ḥadīth* attesting to Muhammad's prophetic priority, including: "I was a prophet while Adam was still between water and clay!," that is to say, before Adam's creation.

41. For more on Diḥyah and similar traditions regarding the physical manifestation of divine realities, especially to the prophet Muḥammad, see al-Farghānī, *Muntahā*, 1:389–99; al-Tilimsānī, *Sharḥ Tā'īyat Ibn al-Fāriḍ al-Kubrā*, 16b–17a; al-Kāshānī, *Kashf al-Wujūh*, 86a–89b; al-Qayṣarī, *Sharḥ Tā'īyat al-Sulūk*, 69a–72b, and Aḥmad ibn Hanbal, *Musnad* (Beirut: Dār al-Ṣādir, 1969), 6:146. Also see Nicholson, *Studies*, 224–25; "Hulūl" in *EI2*, 3:570–71 (L. Massignin-G.C. Anawati); Massignon, *Passion*, tr. Herbert Mason, 3:303–304, and Ḥilmī, *al-Ḥubb al-Ilāhī*, 314–51.

42. Following al-Farghānī, *Muntahā*, 1:401–404, and see Nicholson, *Studies*, 226, n. 288–89.

43. Later in the poem (v. 625), Ibn al-Fāriḍ ascribes to ᶜAlī a special understanding of the Qur'ān. Al-Farghānī, *Muntahā*, 1:403–404, cites the well-known saying: "*lā fatā illā ᶜAlī*," "There is no hero save ᶜAlī," noted earlier in reference to al-Mutanabbī's *al-Dhālīah*; see "Dhū al-Fakār" (E. Mittwoch) in *EI2*, 2:233. Also see al-Tilimsānī, *Sharḥ Tā'īyat Ibn al-Fāriḍ al-Kubrā*, 17a, and al-Kāshānī, *Kashf al-Wujūh*, 86a–89b. Al-Qayṣarī, *Sharḥ Tā'īyat al-Sulūk*, 73a–b, equates the brave (*fatā*) in verse 290 with the realized mystic, though as we have seen in his commentary on the wine ode, al-Qayṣarī gives ᶜAlī a status second only to the prophet; see chapter 4, n. 54, and Homerin, *Wine of Love*, 17–18.

44. Following al-Kāshānī, *Kashf al-Wujūh*, 91b–93a, and al-Qayṣarī, *Sharḥ Tā'īyat al-Sulūk*, 73b–75b. However, al-Farghānī, *Muntahā*, 1:410–11, designates ᶜAlī as the "highest Gnostic," citing a *ḥadīth* in which Muhammad says: "I am the city of knowledge, and ᶜAlī is its door." Also see Nicholson, *Studies*, 227, n. 299.

45. Al-Farghānī, *Muntahā*, 1:411–22; al-Tilimsānī, *Sharḥ Tā'īyat Ibn al-Fāriḍ al-Kubrā*, 17a–18a; al-Kāshānī, *Kashf al-Wujūh*, 93a–99b; al-Qayṣarī, *Sharḥ Tā'īyat al-Sulūk*, 75b–80b, and Nicholson, *Studies*, 228–31.

46. Literally the gnostic holds fast to "Ṭā Hā." This is both the name for chapter 20 of the Qur'ān and, by extension, an epithet for Muhammad; it is with this latter sense that the commentators read verse 332 in context of earlier references to Muhammad's prophetic light and spirit; al-Farghānī, *Muntahā*, 1:422–44; al-Tilimsānī, *Sharḥ Tā'īyat Ibn al-Fāriḍ al-Kubrā*, 18b–19a; al-Kāshānī, *Kashf al-Wujūh*, 99b, and al-Qayṣarī, *Sharḥ Tā'īyat al-Sulūk*, 80b. Also see Schimmel, *And Muhammad is His Messenger*, 108–109, and Ḥilmī, *al-Ḥubb al-Ilāhī*, 359–64.

47. Cf. Ibn al-Fāriḍ's *al-Lamīyah*, verse 29 and his *al-Jīmīyah*, verses 8–9. Also see al-Farghānī, *Muntahā*, 1:445–70; al-Tilimsānī, *Sharḥ Tā'īyat Ibn al-Fāriḍ al-Kubrā*, 19a–20b; al-Kāshānī, *Kashf al-Wujūh*, 99b–109a, and al-Qayṣarī, *Sharḥ Tā'īyat al-Sulūk*, 80b–86b.

48. The commentator al-Farghānī, *Muntahā*, 1:446–72, treats these verses as a section "on the realization of the truth, unity, and gnosis attached to the presence of oneness in union." Also see Sperl's insightful comments on verses 381–87 in his "Qasida Form," 1:76–78.

49. See al-Farghānī, *Muntahā*, 1:474–79; 2:3–10; al-Tilimsānī, *Sharḥ Tā'īyat Ibn al-Fāriḍ al-Kubrā*, 20b–21b; al-Kāshānī, *Kashf al-Wujūh*, 109a–12a; al-Qayṣarī, *Sharḥ Tā'īyat al-Sulūk*, 86b–88b; Nicholson, *Studies*, 232–33, and Ḥilmī, *al-Ḥubb al-Ilāhī*, 253–64.

50. See al-Farghānī, *Muntahā*, 2:10–19; al-Tilimsānī, *Sharḥ Tā'īyat Ibn al-Fāriḍ al-Kubrā*, 21b–22a; al-Kāshānī, *Kashf al-Wujūh*, 112a–19a, and al-Qayṣarī, *Sharḥ Tā'īyat al-Sulūk*, 88b–94b. For more on *samā*ᶜ, see Hujwirī, *The Kashf*, tr. Nicholson,, 393–420; During, *Musique*, 155–68; Schimmel, *Mystical Dimension*, 178–86, and below.

51. Cf. Ibn al-Fāriḍ's *al-Jīmīyah*, verses 30–34, quoted in chapter 2.

52. Al-Farghānī, *Muntahā*, 2:19–21; al-Tilimsānī, *Sharḥ Tā'īyat Ibn al-Fāriḍ al-Kubrā*, 22b; al-Kāshānī, *Kashf al-Wujūh*, 119a–20b; al-Qayṣarī, *Sharḥ Tā'īyat al-Sulūk*, 94b–96b, and Nicholson, *Studies*, 235–36.

53. Al-Farghānī, *Muntahā*, 2:21–30; al-Tilimsānī, *Sharḥ Tā'īyat Ibn al-Fāriḍ al-Kubrā*, 22b; al-Kāshānī, *Kashf al-Wujūh*, 120b–23a; al-Qayṣarī, *Sharḥ Tā'īyat al-Sulūk*, 96b–98a; Nicholson, *Studies*, 237–38, and especially, Ḥilmī, *al-Ḥubb al-Ilāhī*, 211–15. Also see chapter 2 for comments by earlier Sufis regarding *dhikr* and the pre-eternal covenant.

54. Al-Farghānī, *Muntahā*, 2:30–40; al-Tilimsānī, *Sharḥ Tā'īyat Ibn al-Fāriḍ al-Kubrā*, 22b–23b; al-Kāshānī, *Kashf al-Wujūh*, 123a–30b, and al-Qayṣarī, *Sharḥ Tā'īyat al-Sulūk*, 98a–103b, all quote the *ḥadīth*: "I was a prophet when Adam was between water and clay." Also see Nicholson, *Studies*, 238–40, and Louis Massignon, *Essay on the Origins of the Technical Language of Islamic Mysticism* (Notre Dame: University of Notre Dame Press, 1997), 31, for various interpretations and uses of *lāhūt* and *nāsūt*.

55. Both al-Farghānī, *Muntahā*, 2:55, and al-Tilimsānī, *Sharḥ Tā'īyat Ibn al-Fāriḍ al-Kubrā*, 25a, cite from Qu'ran 6:9: "Had We sent an angel, We would have made him as a man to disguise (*labasnā*) him from them . . ."

56. For more on this pivotal verse, see later in this chapter. Also see al-Farghānī, *Muntahā*, 2:40–73; al-Tilimsānī, *Sharḥ Tā'īyat Ibn al-Fāriḍ al-Kubrā*, 23b–25b; al-Kāshānī, *Kashf al-Wujūh*, 130b–41b; al-Qayṣarī, *Sharḥ Tā'īyat al-Sulūk*, 103b–12a, and Nicholson, *Studies*, 242–45. Cf. al-Tusturī's linking of the two Days, in Böwering, *Mystical Vision*, 229.

57. Al-Tilimsānī, *Sharḥ Tā'īyat Ibn al-Fāriḍ al-Kubrā*, 26a, explicitly identifies this "pole of poles" as Muhammad forever. Also see Ḥilmī, *al-Ḥubb al-Ilāhī*, 352–55; Böwering, *Mystical Vision*, 236–37, and Schimmel, *Mystical Dimensions*, 199–204.

58. The three stages of certainty (*yaqīn*) were common in Sufi writings, though their precise meaning varied; see Nicholson, *Studies*, 247, n. 514, and Böwering, *Mystical Vision*, 207–16. Also see al-Farghānī, *Muntahā*, 2:73–91; al-Tilimsānī, *Sharḥ Tā'īyat Ibn al-Fāriḍ al-Kubrā*, 25b–26b; al-Kāshānī, *Kashf al-Wujūh*, 141b–48a, and al-Qayṣarī, *Sharḥ Tā'īyat al-Sulūk*, 112a–17a.

59. Al-Farghānī, *Muntahā,* 2:91–130; al-Tilimsānī, *Sharh Tā'īyat Ibn al-Fāriḍ al-Kubrā,* 26b–27b; al-Kāshānī, *Kashf al-Wujūh,* 148a–60b; al-Qayṣarī, *Sharḥ Tā'īyat al-Sulūk,* 117a–25b, and Nicholson, *Studies,* 250–51.

60. See Issa J. Boullata, "Verbal Arabesque," 152–69, esp. 160–66.

61. Ibid., 160–69. Building on observations by Nicholson, Ḥilmī, and Arberry, Boullata has attempted to relate the syntactical and morphological complexity of this passage to its metaphysical content: "Elements of order and harmony predominate in the style of this passage which speaks about order and harmony" (163). His astute grammatical analysis provides an informed and informative illustration of Ibn al-Fāriḍ's command of Arabic and its poetics. For translations of the entire passage see Arberry, *Poem of the Way,* 57–60, and Homerin, *ᶜUmar Ibn al-Fāriḍ,* 231–39.

62. In verses 557–64, Ibn al-Fāriḍ plays on the traditional threefold definition of a proper religious life and attitude: *islām, imān,* and *iḥsān;* see Nallino, "Il poema," 84–86 and Schimmel, *Mystical Dimensions,* 29.

63. Al-Farghānī, *Muntahā,* 2:130–66; al-Tilimsānī, *Sharḥ Tā'īyat Ibn al-Fāriḍ al-Kubrā,* 27b–28b; al-Kāshānī, *Kashf al-Wujūh,* 160b–71b; al-Qayṣarī, *Sharḥ Tā'īyat al-Sulūk,* 125b–32b, and Nicholson, *Studies,* 251. For more on these worlds and the divine names and attributes see S.H. Nasr, *An Introduction to Islamic Cosmological Doctrines,* rev. ed. (Albany: State University of New York Press, 1993); also compare Jaᶜfar al-Ṣādiq's four levels of Qur'ānic import in Nwyia, *Exégèse,* 167.

64. Al-Farghānī, *Muntahā,* 2:166–97; al-Tilimsānī, *Sharḥ Tā'īyat Ibn al-Fāriḍ al-Kubrā,* 28b–29b; al-Kāshānī, *Kashf al-Wujūh,* 171b–84a; al-Qayṣarī, *Sharḥ Tā'īyat al-Sulūk,* 132b–40a, and Nicolson, *Studies,* 252–54. Also compare Ibn al-Fāriḍ's reference to the "stars" in the second verse of his *al-Khamrīyah;* see chapter 4.

65. *Law laka mā khalaqtu al-aflāka.* The major commentators frequently cite this divine saying when commenting on this and similar passages in the poem. See al-Farghānī, *Muntahā,* 2:264, al-Tilimsānī, *Sharḥ Tā'īyat Ibn al-Fāriḍ al-Kubrā,* 30a, and Schimmel, *Mystical Dimensions,* 215; Nicholson, *Studies,* 255, Ḥilmī, *al-Ḥubb al-Ilāhī,* 364–81, and Böwering, *Mystical Vision,* 149–53.

66. In his commentary, *Studies,* 256, Nicholson cites Qur'ān 2:245: "God withholds and expands, and to Him you shall return."

67. Al-Farghānī, *Muntahā,* 2:197–214; al-Tilimsānī, *Sharḥ Tā'īyat Ibn al-Fāriḍ al-Kubrā,* 29b–30a; al-Kāshānī, *Kashf al-Wujūh,* 184a–89a, and al-Qayṣarī, *Sharḥ Tā'īyat al-Sulūk,* 140a–43a. Also see Nallino, "Il poema," 90–91, and Nicolson, *Studies,* 255–56.

68. On the *Maqāmāt* of al-Qāsim al-Ḥarīrī (446–516/1054–1122), to which Ibn al-Fāriḍ refers, see *EI2,* 3:221–22 (D.S. Margoliouth and Ch. Pellat) and *EAL,* 1:272–73 (R. Drory). Also see al-Farghānī, *Muntahā,* 2:223–24, and Böwering, *Mystical Vision,* 253–61.

69. Among Ibn al-Fāriḍ's notable predecessors to use the puppeteer-puppet analogy was the Arab philosopher Ibn Ḥazm, the Persian poet ᶜUmar Khayyām in his *Rubāᶜīyāt* and the Persian Sufi ᶜAṭṭār in his *Ushturnāmah;* see Nallino, "Ancora," 557–58, and Schimmenl, *Mystical Dimensions,* 278. Ghurayyib

conjectures that the military scenes in verses 691–95 may refer to the Battle of Damietta, which occurred during the poet's lifetime; *ᶜUmar Ibn al-Fāriḍ*, 17–19. Also see Nicholson, Studies, 189–91, and Nallino, "Il poema," 74, 104.

70. Al-Farghānī, *Muntahā*, 2:259 cites the *ḥadīth* in which Muhammad says: "God has seventy veils of light and darkness. Were He to raise them, the splendor of His face would consume whatever creature saw it."

71. Al-Farghānī, *Muntahā*, 2:248, refers the divine saying in which God declares: "I was a hidden treasure and loved to be known"; see Schimmel, *Mystical Dimensions*, 189, and William Chittick, *The Self-Disclosure of God* (Albany: State University of New York Press, 1998), 20–22.

72. Al-Farghānī, *Muntahā*, 2:224, notes that through this analogy between the *nafs'* disguise in the body and God's veiled presence in creation, the seeker can grasp what the prophet Muhammad meant when he said: "He who knows himself (*nafs*), knows his Lord." Also al-Farghānī, *Muntahā*, 2:224–67; al-Tilimsānī, *Sharḥ Tā'īyat Ibn al-Fāriḍ al-Kubrā*, 29b–32a; al-Kāshānī, *Kashf al-Wujūh*, 189a–201a; al-Qayṣarī, *Sharḥ Tā'īyat al-Sulūk*, 143b–50a, and Nicolson, *Studies*, 260–62. Al-Hujwirī quotes al-Bisṭāmī as saying "that human actions are metaphorical and that God is the real agent"; *The Kashf*, tr. Nicholson, 276.

73. Al-Farghānī, *Muntahā*, 2:278, quotes Qur'ān 19:93: "There is no one in the heavens and on earth save that he comes before the Merciful as a worshiper."

74. See al-Farghānī, *Muntahā*, 2:224–97; al-Tilimsānī, *Sharḥ Tā'īyat Ibn al-Fāriḍ al-Kubrā*, 29b–32a; al-Kāshānī, *Kashf al-Wujūh*, 201a–205b; al-Qayṣarī, *Sharḥ Tā'īyat al-Sulūk*, 150a–53; Nicholson, *Studies*, 262–65, and Ḥilmī, *al-Ḥubb al-Ilāhī*, 382–88.

75. This is certainly how the commentators interpret the figure; see al-Farghānī, *Muntahā*, 2:299; al-Tilimsānī, *Sharḥ Tā'īyat Ibn al-Fāriḍ al-Kubrā*, 34a; al-Kāshānī, *Kashf al-Wujūh*, 205a–206b; al-Qayṣarī, *Sharḥ Tā'īyat al-Sulūk*, 154a,and Nallino, "Il poema," 105. Also see Giuseppe Scattolin, "Realization of 'Self' (ANĀ) in Islamic Mysticism: the Mystical Experience of Umar Ibn al-Fāriḍ," *Mélanges de L'Université Saint-Joseph* LIV (1995–96):119–48, esp. 143.

76. Al-Farghānī, *Muntahā*, 2:299–310; al-Tilimsānī, *Sharḥ Tā'īyat Ibn al-Fāriḍ al-Kubrā*, 34a–b; al-Kāshānī, *Kashf al-Wujūh*, 206b–208a; al-Qayṣarī, *Sharḥ Tā'īyat al-Sulūk*, 154a–55b, and Nicholson, *Studies*, 265–66.

77. For a different division of the poem based on the mystical stages of separation (*farq*), identification (*ittiḥād*), and union (*jamᶜ*), see Scattolin, "Realization of Self," and the introduction to his edition of the *Dīwān*, 5–6, 11–12.

78. Concerning Ibn al-Fāriḍ's personal pride in his poetry, see chapter 2, and Ghurayyib, *ᶜUmar Ibn al-Fāriḍ*, 129–30, who compares Ibn al-Fāriḍ's mixing of lyrical verse with more rhetorical discourses to the works of Hugo and Lamartine.

79. See "*muzdawija*" in *EAL*, 2: 567–68 (W. Stoetzer), and "Didactic Poetry," *EAL*, 1:193–94 (G.J.H. Van Gelder). Even earlier, several Shīᶜī authors composed *daᶜwā* poems championing the Fatimid cause and praising their Imām, yet these differ substantially from the far more lyrical *al-Tā'īyah al-Kubrā*; see Qutbuddin, *al-Mu'ayyad al-Shīrāz*, esp. 235–56.

80. Nallino previously noted Ibn al-Fāriḍ's use of the guide form, "Il poema," 21. By contrast, Sperl views the *al-Tā'īyah al-Kubrā* as a unified *qaṣīdah* whose climax occurs mid-way through the poem with verses 381–87. Though his division of the poem into a beginning, middle, and end is simplistic, Sperl offers several insightful comments in his brief analysis of the poem; see his "Qasida Form," 74–81, and the conclusion.

81. See chapter 3.

82. Concerning al-Junayd's doctrine of intoxication (*sukr*) and sobriety (*ṣaḥw*) see Ali Hassan Abdel-Kader, *The Life, Personality and Writings of al-Junayd* (London: Luzac & Co., 1962), 88–95, and al-Hujwirī, *The Kashf* (tr. Nicholson), 184–89. In addition to Abdel-Kader's introduction to al-Junayd's thought (65–116), also see R.C. Zaehner, *Hindu and Muslim Mysticism* (New York: Schocken Books, 1969), 133–61; Roger Deladriere, *Junayd: Enseignement spirituel* (Paris: Sindbad, 1983), 31–38; M. Abdul Haq Ansari, "The Doctrine of One Actor: Junayd"s View of *Tawḥīd*," *Muslim World* 73 (1983):33–56; Andras Hamori, "A Sentence of Junayd's," in *Intellectual Studies on Islam*, ed. Michael Mazzaoui and Vera Moreen (Salt Lake City: University of Utah Press, 1990), 147–52, and Micheal A. Sells, "Junayd: On the Affirmation of Unity (Tawḥīd)" in his *Early Islamic Mysticism*, 251–65.

83. Al-Junayd, "*Kitāb al-Mīthāq*," in his *Rasā'il*, ed. Abdel-Kader in *Writings of al-Juanyd*, 40–43 (Arabic text). My translation differs from Abdel-Kader's (160–64) and Ansari's ("One Actor," 155–60); also see Deladriere's French translation in *Junayd*, 155–60.

84. Especially see the comments on this passage by Zaehner, *Hindu and Muslim Mysticism*, 139–48, and by Andras Hamori, "A Sentence of Junayd's," 147–52. Al-Junaid's contemporary al-Tusturī held similar views of this important event; see Böwering, *Mystical Vision*, 146–57.

85. Also cf. Ibn al-Fāriḍ, *al-Tā'īyah al-Kubrā*, verses 216, 382.

86. Al-Junayd, *Rasā'il*, 33, 42 (Arabic text).

87. Ibid., 32–38, 42–43 (Arabic text). For a similar spiritual psychology by al-Tustarī, see Böwering, *Mystical Vision*, 241–46.

88. Cf. Jaᶜfar al-Ṣādiq's (d. 148/765) earlier use of *shabah*. ("phantom") in a similar mystical context, cited by Nwyia, *Exégèse*, 179–82, and by Carl W. Ernst, *Words of Ecstasy in Sufism* (Albany: State University of New York Press, 1985), 10–11.

89. Al-Junayd, *Rasā'il*, 56–57 (Arabic text). Also see Ansari's translation, "One Actor," 50, and that of Sells, "Junayd," 256. Commenting on al-Junayd's doctrine of mystical union, al-Hujwirī explained the matter as follows (*Kashf*, 363–65; trans. Nicholson, *The Kashf*, 283): "All this means that the Unitarian in the will of God has no more a will of his own, and in the unity of God no regard for himself, so that he becomes like an atom as he was in the eternal past when the covenant of unification was made and God answered the question which He Himself asked, and that the atom was only the object of His speech." Also see Böwering, *Mystical Vision*, 205–207, 220–25 for al-Tustarī's related interpretation of *dhikr* as "remembrance of God by means of God," and that "[The Real] bears witness to Himself by Himself."

90. Al-Junayd and Ibn al-Fāriḍ consistently use *l*b*s* when dealing with the spirit's dwelling in creation. Far more frequent in Sufi literature is the use of derivatives of this root to refer to Satan's "deceptions." Also see al-Ḥallāj's infrequent use of this root in reference to the human being "clothed with divine attributes"; Massignon, *Essay*, 24, 31, and Ernst, *Ecstasy*, 20, 27, 39, 149.

91. E.g., al-Junayd, *Rasā'il*, 32–33, 41–42, 55–56 (Arabic text). Also see Ansari, "One Actor," 48–54; Böwering, *Mystical Vision*, 215–16, and Scattolin, "Realization of Self," 144–45.

92. Also see the *al-Tā'īyah al-Kubrā*, verses 210, 491, 517, 638, 649–50, 714; Scattolin, "Realization of Self," 144–45, and cf. al-Tusturī's struggle between the *nafs* and the *qalb*, in Böwering, *Mystical Vision*, 258–61.

93. Cf. al-Tusturī's views in Böwering, *Mystical Vision*, 175–85.

94. Thus, Ansari, "One Actor," 51–52, terms al-Junayd's doctrine of union *waḥdat al-fā'il* ("unity of one actor") to contrast it with the later doctrine of *waḥdat al-wujūd* ("unity of being"). Ansari's analysis of al-Junayd's beliefs and doctrines is quite sound. However, he was apparently unaware of Böwering's study of al-Junayd's contemporary al-Tustarī, and so Ansari may have overemphasized al-Junayd's originality on matters of mystical union (e.g., Böwering, *Mystical Vision*, 185–207).

95. Al-Junayd, *Rasā'il*, 33 (Arabic text), and see Sells, "Junayd," 259–65, for a translation of the entire epistle.

96. Al-Junayd, *Rasā'il*, 55–57 (Arabic text). Also see Ansari, "One Actor," 48–56; Abdel-Kader, *Life*, 68–75; Deladiere, *Junayd*, 131–33, and Sells, "Junayd," 251–65. Taking a similar position as al-Junayd was al-Tustarī; see Böwering, *Mystical Vision*, 220–25.

97. Muhammad al-Ghazālī, *Mishkāt al-Anwār*, ed. Abū ʿAlā al-ʿAfīfī (Cairo: Dār al-Qawmīyah lil-Ṭibaʿah wa-al-Nashr, 1964), 58; my translation. For a complete English translation of this work see W.H.T. Gairdner, *Al-Ghazzali's Mishkat al-Anwar* (London: Royal Asiatic Society, 1924).

98. Al-Ghazālī, *Mishkāt*, 55; my translation.

99. Ibid., 55–56; my translation.

100. Ibid., 51–52, 56–57, 76–77, and see Böwering, *Mystical Vision*, esp. 149–65, 218.

101. Al-Ghazālī, *Mishkāt*, 84–93. Nallino, "Il poema," 11–12, earlier drew attention to the similarity between al-Ghazālī and Ibn al-Fāriḍ.

102. This point has been glossed over by twentieth-century scholars who were, perhaps, interested in discovering a type of ecumenicist in the poet; e.g., Ḥilmī, *al-Ḥubb al-Ilāhī*, 382–405; A. Mahmūd, *Shiʿr Ibn al-Fāriḍ*, 39–40; A.J. Nasr, *Shiʿr ʿUmar Ibn al-Fāriḍ*, 217–20, and Sperl, "Qasida Form," 1:78–80.

103. Regarding this tradition see chapter 3, n. 49. Also see Ḥilmī, *al-Ḥubb al-Ilāhī*, 388–93.

104. See Nwyia, *Exégèse*, 93–94; Böwering, *Mystical Vision*, 145–265, and Nallino, "Ancora," 558, who draws attention to the similarity between verse 714 and al-Qushayrī's account of *mushāhadah*; *Risālah*, 1:245–47 (tr. Sells, *Early Islamic Mysticism*, 130–32). Again, this may not be a case of direct bor-

rowing but of common knowledge and a shared mystical tradition to which al-Qushayrī substantially contributed.

105. Scattolin attempts to explain Ibn al-Fāriḍ's mysticism in terms of Sufi notions of the "perfect man" (*al-insān al-kāmil*); see his "Realization of Self," and the introduction to his edition of the *Dīwān*, 8–11. Ibn al-Fāriḍ, however, does not use this term, whereas he clearly alludes to the Light of Muhammad as his mystical apotheosis, as Scattolin has acknowledged elsewhere; see his "L'Expérience Mystique de Ibn al-Fāriḍ a travers son poèma Al-Ta'iyyat Al-Kubrā," *MIDEO* 19 (1989):203–23, esp. 217, and his "The Mystical Experience of Umar Ibn al-Fāriḍ," *Muslim World* 82:3–4 (1992), 274–86, esp. 283–84.

106. Most recently see Waugh, *Memory*, 70–71; Ṣādiq, *Shiʿr ʿUmar*, 18, and A. Naṣr, *Shiʿr ʿUmar Ibn al-Fāriḍ*, 39. A rare exception was Nallino, who felt that Ibn al-Fāriḍ's mystical beliefs were closer to those of al-Ghazālī than to those of Ibn al-ʿArabī; see his "Il poema" and "Ancora," which refute the notion that Ibn al-Fāriḍ was an adherent of the Ibn al-ʿArabī school of Sufism. Also see, Ḥilmī, *al-Ḥubb al-Ilāhī*, 278–405, whose study is unfortunately marred by his misunderstanding of Ibn al-ʿArabī's complex and multilayered teachings as pantheism. Also see Homerin, *From Arab Poet*, especially, chapter 4, and the works of Scattolin.

107. Al-Maqqarī, *Nafḥ al-Ṭīb*, ed. Iḥsān ʿAbbās (Beirut: Dār Ṣādir, 1968), 2:166, who ascribes this account to the Egyptian historian al-Maqrīzī (d. 845/1441). The later Ottoman writer, Evliyā Çelebī also gave a version of this story in his *Seyāhetnāmesī* (Istanbul: Devlet Matbassi, 1938), 10:573. Also see Ḥilmī, *al-Ḥubb al-Ilāhī*, 337–40, who refutes the historicity of this correspondence.

108. For a concise overview of the work and influence of Ṣadr al-Dīn al-Qūnawī, see William Chittick, "Rūmī and *waḥdat al-wujūd*," in *Poetry and Mysticism in Islam: the Heritage of Rumi*, ed. A. Banani et al. (New York: Cambridge University Press, 1994), 70–111, esp. 77–79; also see *EI2*, 8:753–55 (W.C. Chittick).

109. Homerin, *From Arab Poet*, 29–30, 40–42, and Arberry, *Mystical Poems*, 8.

110. Ibn al-Fāriḍ, *al-Tā'īyah al-Kubrā*, verse 743.

111. ʿAlī Sibṭ Ibn al-Fāriḍ in *Dīwān*, 12–13 (tr. Homerin, *ʿUmar Ibn al-Fāriḍ*, 311–12).

112. See al-Farghānī's *Mashāriq al-Ḍarārī*, ed. Saʿīd Jalāl al-Dīn Āshtiyānī (Mashhad: Dānishghāh-i Firdawsī, 1980), 5–6, and *Muntahā*. Also see W.C. Chittick, "Spectrums of Islamic Thought: Saʿīd al-Dīn al-Farghānī on the Implication of Oneness and Manyness," in *The Heritage of Sufism*, ed. Leonard Lewisohn, (Oxford, 1999), 2:203–17, and Chittick, "Rūmī," 79–81.

113. Austin, *Ibn Al-'Arabi*, 7–11, and Homerin, *Arab Poet*, 3, 35–37, 47–49.

114. For al-Qūnawī's personal copy of the *Dīwān* of Ibn al-Fāriḍ, see G. Scattolin, "Oldest Text," 83–114; his "Towards a Critical Edition," 503–47, and Gerald Elmore, "Sadr al-Dīn al-Qūnawī's Personal Study-List of Books by Ibn al-ʿArabī," *Jouranl of Near Eastern Studies* 56:3 (July, 1997):161–81, esp. 181.

115. In particular see Nallino, "Il poema" and "Ancora," and more recently the work of Giuseppe Scattolin, including *L'esperienza mistica di*

Ibn al-Fāriḍ attraverso il suo poema Al-Tā'iyyat Al-Kubrā (Rome: PISAI, 1988); "L'expérience mystique"; "Al-Farghānī's Commentary on Ibn al-Fāriḍ's Mystical Poem *Al-Tā'iyyat Al-Kubrā*," *MIDEO* 21 (1993):331–83; "Mystical Experience," and "Realization of Self." Also see Ḥilmī, *al-Ḥubb al-Ilāhī*, 337–40.

116. Ibn al-ᶜArabī, *al-Futūḥāt al-Makkīyah* (Cairo, nd), 3:67.

117. See William C. Chittick, *Sufi Path*, 89, 133, 217, 284, 326.

118. Ibn al-ᶜArabī, *al-Futūḥāt al-Makkīyah*, 3:68. For another translation and a brief analysis of this passage see James Morris, "Rediscovering the 'Divine Comedy': Eschatology and Spiritual Realization in Ibn ᶜArabi," *Newsletter of the Muhyiddin Ibn ᶜArabi Society* 19 (Autumn, 2003):8–9. Also see Thomas W. Arnold, *Painting in Islam*, 14-15, who earlier drew attention to the use of the shadow play in the work of both men.

119. Regarding the shadow play in earlier Persian Sufi poetry, see Schimmel, *Dimensions*, 278–79. On *tajallī*, also see Ḥilmī, *al-Ḥubb al-Ilāhī*, 340–41; Böwering, *Mystical Vision*, 172–75, and al-Kalābādhī, *al-Taᶜarruf*, 121–23 (tr. Arberry, *Doctrine*, 117–19).

120. Ḥilmī, *al-Ḥubb al-Ilāhī*, 340–51.

Conclusion: The Poetry of Recollection

1. Al-Nābulusī, *Kashf al-Sirr al-Ghāmiḍ*, Ibrāhīm ed., 1:63–64, and see Th. Emil Homerin, "'On the Battleground:' al-Nābulusī's Encounters with a Poem by Ibn al-Fāriḍ," *Journal of Arabic Literature* 38 (2007):353–411; *From Arab Poet*, 24–28, 38–39, 76, and *EAL*, 1:12–13 (R.L. Nettler).

2. E.g., al-Farghānī, *Muntahā*, 1:315–16; 2:277, 299, 309; al-Tilimsānī, *Sharḥ Tā'īyat Ibn al-Fāriḍ al-Kubrā*, 19b–20a, 23a, 30a; al-Kāshānī, *Kashf al-Wujūh*, 62a–b, 64b–65a; Nicholson, *Studies*, 167–68; Nallino, "Il poema," 49–50 and his "Ancora," 503.

3. Scattolin, "Realization of Self," 140–41, and also see his introduction to his edition of Ibn al-Fāriḍ's *Dīwān*, 4–11.

4. E.g. al-Farghānī, *Muntahā*, 2:291, 301, and al-Tilimsānī, *Sharḥ Tā'īyat Ibn al-Fāriḍ al-Kubrā*, 23a, 30a.

5. See J. Stetkevych, "Arabic Literary Persona," 55–77; *The New Princeton Encyclopedia of Poetry and Poetics*, ed. Alexander Preminger et al. (Princeton: Princeton University Press, 1993), 900–902, and Homerin, *ᶜUmar Ibn al-Fāriḍ*, 35–36.

6. Ibn al-Fāriḍ, *Dīwān*, 149, verses 1–2, and cf. 152–53; for an English translation of the complete poem see Th. Emil Homerin, "Ibn al-Farid: Rubaᶜiyat, Ghazal, Qasida," in *Windows on the House of Islam*, ed. John Renard (Berkely: University of California Press, 1998), 194–201.

7. See chapter 3.

8. Ibn al-Fāriḍ, *Dīwān*, 92, verses 257–60.

9. Arberry, *Mystical Poems*, esp. 2:13–18; L'Hôpital "Le vocabulaire amoureux"; Ṣādiq, *Shiᶜr Ibn al-Fāriḍ: Dirāsah Uslūbīyah*; al-Yūsuf, "Baᶜḍ yanābīᶜ Ibn al-Fārid"; Boullata, "Verbal Arabesque," and S. Speral, "Qaida Form," discussed in more detail later.

10. Jalāl al-Dīn al-Suyūṭī, *al-Barq al-Wāmiḍ fī Sharḥ Yā'īyat Ibn al-Fāriḍ*, manuscript 881 (Shiʿr Taymūr), Cairo: Dār al-Kutub al-Miṣrīyah.

11. Al-Būrīnī, *Sulṭān*, 1:16, and see *EAL*, 1:163 (R.L. Nettler).

12. Al-Būrīnī, *Sulṭān*.

13. Ḥusayn, *al-Adab*, 370–75; Th. Emil Homerin, "Living Love: The Mystical Writings of ʿĀ'ishah al-Bāʿūnīyah," *Mamlūk Studies Review* 7 (2003):211–34, and ʿAbd al-Ghanī al-Nābulusī, *Dīwān al-Ḥaqā'iq wa-Majmūʿ al-Raqā'iq* (Beirut: Dār al-Jīl, 1986), 78–83.

14. Muhammad al-Būṣīrī, *Dīwān*, ed. Muhammad Sayyid Kīlānī, 2nd ed. (Cairo: Muṣṭafā al-Bāb al-Ḥalabī, 1973), 238–49, and Ibn al-Fāriḍ, *Dīwān*, 152–53. Also see *EAL*, 1:163 (C.E. Bosworth); Homerin, *From Arab Poet*, 22–24, 55–58; Mubārak, *al-Madā'iḥ al-Nabawīyah*, and Schimmel, *Muhammad*, 176–215.

15. Aḥmad Ibn Abī Ḥajalah, *Al-Ghayth al-ʿĀriḍ fī Muʿāraḍat Ibn al-Fāriḍ*, Microfilm 319 (Taṣawwuf) of manuscript 31 (Adab). Sūhāj, Egypt: Maktabat Sūhāj, Cairo: Arab League Manuscript Institute. Also see *EAL*, 1:303 (T. Seidensticker).

16. Sperl, "Qasida Form," 66–74; Ibn al-Fāriḍ, *Dīwān*, 173–76, and see chapter 4, for a complete translation of the poem.

17. Ibid., 73–74.

18. Ibid., 74–81. Sperl does not identify the poem beginning *adir dhikra* as a wine poem.

19. Ibn al-Fāriḍ, *Dīwān*, 50–54, and see chapter 1. Cf. Ibn al-Fāriḍ, *Dīwān*, 144–48, 152–53, 166–67.

20. J. Stetkevych, "Arabic Qaṣīdah," 778–781, and Sperl, "Qasida Form," 66–67.

21. Louis Martz, "Meditative Action and 'The Metaphysick Style,'" in his *The Poem of the Mind* (New York: Oxford University Press, 1966), 33–53, quote from 33.

22. Ibid., 43. Also see Louis Martz, *The Poetry of Meditation*, 2nd ed. (New Haven: Yale University Press, 1962), his *The Paradise Within* (New Haven: Yale University Press, 1964), and Arthur L. Clements, *Poetry of Contemplation* (Albany: State University of New York Press, 1990).

23. Martz, "Meditative Action," 44.

24. Ibn al-Fāriḍ, *Dīwān*, 107–108.

25. Ibn al-Fāriḍ, *Dīwān*, 108–10, verses 420–41 (tr. Homerin, *ʿUmar Ibn al-Fāriḍ*, 194–201).

26. E.g. Ibn al-Fārid, *Dīwān*, 43, verse 80; 65, verses 102–103; 146, verse 31; 150. verse 19; 164, verse 27; 167, verse 19; 172, verse 51; 173, verse 8; 180, verse 47, and 184, verse 37.

27. Homerin, "On the Battlefield," and *From Arab Poet*, 76–92. Also see Waugh, *Memory*, 65, 71–74, 80, 134–38, 164, 181, and his *The Munshidīn of Egypt* (Columbia: University of South Carolina Press, 1989), esp. 86–95, 104–116, 152–56, 188–207.

28. Ibn al-Fārid, *Dīwān*, 158–61, and see chapter 4.

Bibliography

Abdel-Kader, Ali Hassan Ed. and Tr. The Life, Personality and Writings of al-Junayd. London: Luzac & Co., 1962.

Abu Deeb, Kemal. "Towards a Structural Analysis of Pre-Islamic Poetry, Pt. I." *International Journal of Middle Eastern Studies* 6 (1975):148–184. Pt. II. *Edebiyat* 1 (1976):3–69.

Abū Madyan. *Dīwān*. Ed. al-ʿArabī ibn Muṣṭafā al-Shawwār al-Tilimsānī. Damascus: Maṭbaʿat al-Taraqqī, 1938.

Abū Nuwās. *Dīwān*, Ed. ʿAli Faʿūr. Beirut: Dār al-Kutub al-ʿIlmīyah, 1987.

———. *Dīwān*. Ed. Ewald Wagner. 4 vols. Wiesbaden: Franz Steiner, 1988.

———. *Dīwān Abī Nuwās*. Ed. Ahmad ʿAbd al-Majīd al-Ghazzālī. Cairo: Maṭbaʿat Miṣr, 1953.

———. *Dīwān des Abu Nowas*. Ed. Wilhelm Ahlwardt. Greifwalt: C. A. Koch, 1861.

Abū Tammām. *Sharh Dīwān al-Hamāsah* by Ahmad ibn Muhammad al-Marzūqī. 4 vols. Ed. Ahmad Amīn and ʿAbd al-Salām Hārūn. Cairo: Maṭbaʿat Lajnat al-Ta'līf wa-al-Tarjamah wa-al-Nashr, 1952.

ʿAlī Sibṭ Ibn al-Fāriḍ, *Dībājat Dīwān Ibn al-Fāriḍ*. In *Dīwān Ibn al-Fāriḍ*. Ed. Guiseppe Scattolin, 1–34. English translation by Homerin, *ʿUmar Ibn al-Fāriḍ*, 301–35.

Alavi, Mohd. Badruddin. "Some Aspects of the Literary and Poetical Activities of Avicenna." In *Avicenna Commemoration Volume*. Ed. V. Courtois. Calcutta: Iran Society, 1956, 65–72.

ʿAnkawi, ʿAbdullah. "The Pilgrimage to Mecca in Mamluk Times." *Arabian Studies* 1 (1974):146–70.

Ansari, M. Abdul Haq. "The Doctrine of One Actor: Junayd's View of *Tawḥīd*." *Muslim World* 73 (1983):33–56.

Arberry, A. J., ed. and tr. *The Mystical Poems of Ibn al-Fārid*. 2 vols. London: Emery Walker, 1952, 1956.

———, ed and tr. *The Poem of the Way*. London: Emery Walker, 1952.

Arnold, Thomas W. *Painting in Islam*. New York: Dover Press, 1965.

al-Aʿshā. *Dīwān*. Ed. Muḥammad Muḥammad Ḥusayn. Beirut: Mu'assasat al-Risālah, 1963.

Ashtiany, Julia, et al., eds. *Cambridge History of Arabic Literature ʿAbbasid Belles Lettres (CHALABL)*. Cambridge: Cambridge University Press, 1990.

ᶜAṭṭār, Farīd al-Dīn. *The Conference of the Birds*. English translation by Afkham Darbandi and Dick Davies. Penguin Books, 1984.

Badawī, Aḥmad Aḥmad. "From Primary to Secondary Qaṣīdas," *Journal of Arabic Literature* 11 (1980):1–31.

———. *Al-Ḥayāh al-Adabīyah fi ᶜAṣr al-Ḥurūb al-Ṣalibīyah fī Miṣr wa-al-Shām*. Cairo: Maktabat Nahḍat Miṣr, 1952.

Bahā' al-Dīn Zuhayr. *The Poetical Works of Behā-Ed-Dīn Zoheir*. Ed and English translation by E.H. Palmer. Cambridge: Cambridge University Press, 1876–78.

Baljon, J. M. S. "The 'Amr of God in the Koran." *Acta Orientalia* 23 (1958):7–18.

Bauer, Thomas and A.Neuwirth, eds. *Ghazal as World Literature I: Transformation of a Literary Genre*. Beirut: Orient-Institut Beirut, 2005.

———. "Ibn Ḥajar and the Arabic Ghazal of the Mamluk Age." In T. Bauer and A. Neuwirth, eds. *Ghazal*, 35–55.

———. *Liebe und Liebesdichtung in der Welt des 9. und 10. Jahrhunderts*. Wiesbaden: Harrassowitz, 1998.

Beeston, A.F.L., et al., eds. *The Cambridge History of Arabic Literature: Arabic Literature to the End of the Umayyad Period* (= *CHALUP*). Cambridge: Cambridge University Press, 1983.

Bell, Joseph Norment. *Love Theory in Later Hanabalite Islam*. Albany: State University of New York Press, 1979.

Ben Cheneb, Mohammad. *Tuhfat al-Adab fī Mīzān Ashᶜar al-ᶜArab*. Paris: Libraire D'amerique et orient, 1954.

Bencheikh, J. E. "Thèmes bachiques et personnages dans le dīwān d'Abū Nuwās." *Bulletin d'études orientales* 18 (1963–64):1–84.

Biesterfeidt, Hans Hinrich and Dimitri Gutas. "The Malady of Love." *Journal of the American Oriental Society* 104:1 (1984):21–55.

Blachere, R. *Abou T-Tayyib al-Motanabbī*. Paris: Adrien-Maisonneuve, 1935.

Bloch, Alfred. "Qasida." *Asiatisch Studien* 2 (1948):106–132.

Bly, Robert. *The Eight Stages of Translation*. Boston: Rowan Tree Press, 1983.

Bolle, Kees W. "Secrecy in Religon." In *Secrecy in Religion*. Ed. K.W. Bolle. Leiden: E.J. Brill, 1987, 1–24.

Bonebakker, S. A. *Some Early Definitions of the Tawryia and Safadī's Fadd al-Xitām ᶜan at-Tawrīya wa'l-Istixdām*. The Hague: Mouton & Co., 1966.

Boullata, Issa J. "Toward a Biography of Ibn al-Fāriḍ." *Arabica* 38(1981):38–56.

———. "Verbal Arabesque and Mystical Union: A Study of Ibn al-Fārid's al-Ta'iyya al-kubra," *Arab Studies Quarterly*, 3: no. 2 (Spring, 1981):152–69.

Böwering, Gerhard. *The Mystical Vision of Existence in Classical Islam*. Berlin: Walter De Gruyter, 1980.

Bruijn, J.T.P. de. *Of Piety and Poetry: the Interaction of Religion and Literature in the Life and Works of Hakīm Sanāᶜī of Ghazna*. Leiden: E.J. Brill, 1983.

Bürgel, J.C. "Love, Lust, and Longing: Eroticism in Early Islam as Reflected in Literary Sources." In *Society and the Sexes in Medieval Islam*. Ed. Afaf Lutfi Marsot. Malibu, CA: University of California Press, 1979, 96–101.

al-Būrīnī. *Sharḥ Dīwān Sulṭān al-Āshiqīn Sayyidī ᶜUmar Ibn al-Fāriḍ*. Ed. Rushayyid ibn Ghālib al-Daḥdāḥ. 2 vols. in 1. Cairo: al-Maṭbaᶜah al-ᶜĀmmah, 1888.

al-Būṣīrī, Muhammad. *Dīwān*. Ed. Muḥammad Sayyid Kīlānī. 2nd ed. Cairo: Muṣṭafā al-Bāb al-Ḥalabī, 1973.

Cheikho, Louis. *Shuᶜarā' al-Naṣrānīyah*. 2nd ed. Beirut: Dār al-Mashriq, 1967.

———. *Shuᶜarā' al-Naṣrānīyah baᶜd al-Islām*. Beirut: Imprimerie Catholique, 1924–27.

Chittick, William. "The Five Presences: From al-Qunawī to al-Qaysarī." *Muslim World* 72 (1982):107–28.

———. "Rūmī and *waḥdat al-wujūd*." In *Poetry and Mysticism in Islam: the Heritage of Rumi*. Ed. A. Banani, et al. New York: Cambridge University Press, 1994), 70-111.

———. "Spectrums of Islamic Thought: Saᶜīd al-Dīn al-Farghānī on the Implication of Oneness and Manyness." In *The Heritage of Sufism*. Ed. Leonard Lewisohn. Oxford, 1999, 2:203–17

———. *The Sufi Path of Knowledge*. Albany: State University of New York Press, 1989.

Clements, Arthur L. *Poetry of Contemplation*. Albany: State University of New York Press, 1990.

The Cloud of the Unknowing. Ed. Clifton Wolters. Penguin Books, 1974.

Coakly, Sarah, ed. *Religion and the Body*. Cambridge: Cambridge University Press, 1997.

Corbin, Henry. *Avicenna and the Visionary Recital*. English translation by Willard R. Task. New York: Pantheon Books, 1960.

———. *Creative Imagination in the Ṣūfism of Ibn ᶜArabī*. English translation by Ralph Manheim. Princeton: Princeton University Press, 1969.

———. *Sohrawardī d'Alep*. Paris: Libraire orientale et americane, 1939.

Cornell, Vincent. *The Way of Abū Madyan*. Cambridge: Islamic Texts Society, 1996.

Cousins, Ewert. *Bonaventure: The Soul's Journey to God; The Tree of Life; The Life of St. Francis*. New York: Paulist Press, 1978.

al-Damāsī, ᶜAbd al-Fattāḥ al-Sayyid Muḥammad. *Al-Ḥubb al-Ilāh fī Shiᶜr Muḥyī al-Dīn Ibn al-ᶜArabī*. Cairo: Dār al-Thaqāfah, 1983.

Dayf, Shawqī. *Ta'rīkh al-Adab al-ᶜArabī*. 9 vols. Cairo: Dār al-Maᶜārif, 1982.

al-Daylamī, Abū al-Ḥasan. *ᶜAṭf al-Alif al-Ma'lūf*. Ed. J.-C. Vadet. Cairo: Maktabat al-Maᶜhad al-ᶜIlmī al-Faransī lil-Āthār al-Sharqīyah, 1962. English translation by Joseph N. Bell and Hassan Mahmood Adbul Latif Al Shafie. *A Treatise on Mystical Love*. Edinburgh: Edingburgh University Press, 2005.

Deladriere, Roger, tr. *Junayd: Enseignement spiritual*. Paris: Sindbad, 1983.

Derenk, Dieter. *Leben und Dichtung des Omayyaden Kalifen Al-Walīd Ibn Yazīd*. Freiburg: K. Schwarz, 1974.

Derminghem Emile and Bachir Messilkh. *Ibn al-Faridh: 2 poemes mystique*. Montpelliar: La Licorne, 1952.

Dīwān Majnūn Laylā. Ed. ᶜAbd al-Sattār Ahmad Farrāj. Cairo: Maktabat Miṣr, 1963.

Djedidi, Tahar Labib. *La Poesie amoureuse des Arabes: le cas des ᶜUdhrites*. Algiers: Société Nationale d'Edition et de Diffusion, 1974.

During, Jean. *Musique et extase*. Paris: Albin Michel, 1988.

Elmore, Gerald. "Sadr al-Dīn al-Qūnawī's Personal Study-List of Books by Ibn al-ᶜArabī." *Jouranl of Near Eastern Studies* 56 (1997):161–81.

El Tayib, Abdulla "Pre-Islamic Poetry." In A.F.L. Beeston, et al., eds. *CHALUP*, 27–113.

Encyclopaedia of Islam, 2nd ed. (*EI2*). Ed. H.A.R. Gibb, et al. Leiden: E.J. Brill, 1954–2002.

Encyclopaedia of the Qur'ān (*EQ*). Ed. Jane Dammen McAuliffe. Leiden: E.J. Brill, 2001–2006.

Encyclopedia of Arabic Literature, (*EAL*). Ed. Julie Scott Meisami and Paul Starky. London: Routledge, 1998.

Ernst, Carl. *The Shambala Guide to Sufism*. Boston: Shambala Publications, 1997.

———. *Words of Ecstasy in Sufism*. Albany: State University of New York Press, 1985.

Evliyā Çelebī. *Seyāhetnāmesī*. 10 vols. Istanbul: Devlet Matbassi, 1938.

Ezz El-Din, Hassan El-Banna. " 'No Solace for the Heart:' The Motif of the Departing Women in the Pre-Islamic Battle Ode." In S.P. Stetkevych, ed., *Reorientations*, 165–79.

al-Farghānī, Saᶜīd al-Dīn. *Mashāriq al-Ḍarārī*. Ed. Saᶜīd Jalāl al-Dīn Āshtiyānī. Mashhad: Dānishghāh-i Firdawsī, 1980

———. *Muntahā al-Madārik fī Sharḥ Tā'īyat Ibn al-Fāriḍ*. Ed. ᶜĀṣim Ibrāhīm al-Kayyālī. 2 vols. Beirut: Dār al-Kutub al-ᶜIlmīyah, 2007.

Fish, Stanley E. *Self-Consuming Artifacts*. Berkeley: University of California Press, 1972.

Gaster, Theodor H. *Thespis: Ritual, Myth, and Drama in the Ancient Near East*. New York: Norton and Co., 1977.

Gelder, Geert Jan H. van. "Rābiᶜa's Poem on the Two Kinds of Love: A Mystification?" In *Verse and the Fair Sex*. Ed. Frederick De Jong. Utrecht: M.Th. Houtsma Stichting, 1993, 66–76.

al-Ghazālī, Muḥammad. *Iḥyā' ᶜUlūm al-Dīn*. 4 vols. Cairo: ᶜĪsā al-Bābī al-Ḥalabī, n.d.

———. *Mishkāt al-Anwār*. Ed. Abū ᶜAlā al-ᶜAfīfī. Cairo: Dār al-Qawmīyah lil-Ṭibaᶜah wa-al-Nashr, 1964. English translation by W.H.T. Gairdner. *Al-Ghazzali's Mishkat al-Anwar*. London: Royal Asiatic Society, 1924.

Ghurayyib, Mīshāl. *ᶜUmar Ibn al-Fāriḍ min khilal Shiᶜrihi*. Beirut: Dār Maktabat al-Ḥayāh, 1965.

Gibb, H. A. R. *Arabic Literature*. Oxford: The Clarendon Press, 1963.

Goldziher, Ignaz. "Die Gottsliebe in der Islamischen Theologie." *Der Islam* 9(1919):144–45.

———. *Muhammedanische Studien*. 2 vols. Halle, 1880–90. English translation by C. R. Barber and S. M. Stern. *Muslim Studies*. 2 vols. London: George Allen & Unwin, 1967.

Graham, William A. *Divine Word and Prophetic Word in Islam*. The Hague: Mouton, 1977.

Gruber, Christine Jacqueline. "The Prophet Muhammad's Ascension (*Mi'raj*) in Islamic Painting and Literature: Evidence from Cairo Collections." *Bulletin of the American Research Center in Egypt*, no. 185 (Summer, 2004):24–31.

Grunebaum, G. E. von. "Aspects of Urban Literature Mostly in the Ninth and Tenth Centuries." In *Themes In Medieval Arabic Literature*. Ed. Dunning S. Wilson. London: Variorum Reprints, 1981, IV:281–300.

———. *Muhammadan Festivals*. New York: Olive Branch Press, 1988.

———. "The Nature of the Arab Literary Effort." *Journal of Near Eastern Studies* 7 (1948):116–122.

———. "The Response to Nature in Arabic Poetry." In D.S. Wilson, ed. *Themes*, VII: 137–51.

al-Ḥallāj, Manṣūr. *Sharḥ Dīwān al-Ḥallāj*. Ed. Kāmil Muṣṭafā al-Shaybī. Beirut Maktabat al-Nahdah, 1974.

Hämeen-Anttila, Jaako. "Abū Nuwās and Ghazal as a Genre." In T. Bauer and A. Neuwirth, eds. *Ghazal*, 87–105.

Hamori, Andras. *The Art of Medieval Arabic Literature*. Princeton: Princeton University Press, 1974.

———. "Ascetic Poetry (*zuhdiyyāt*)." In J. Ashtiany, et al., eds. *Cambridge History of Arabic Literature ᶜAbbasid Belles Lettres*, 265–74.

———. "Love Poetry (*ghazal*)." In J. Ashtiany, et al., eds. *Cambridge History of Arabic Literature ᶜAbbasid Belles Lettres*, 202–18.

———. "Al-Mutanabbī." In J. Ashtiany, et al., eds. *Cambridge History of Arabic Literature ᶜAbbasid Belles Lettres*, 300–14.

———. "A Sentence of Junayd's." In *Intellectual Studies on Islam*. Ed. Michael Mazzaoui and Vera Moreen. Salt Lake City: University of Utah Press, 1990, 147–52.

Harb, F. "Wine Poetry (*Khamriyyāt*)." In J. Ashtiany, et al., eds. *CHALABL*, 219–30.

Hāwī, Īliyā. *Fann al-Shiᶜr al-Khamrī*. Beirut: Dār al-Thaqāfah, 1960.

Haydar, A. "The Mu'allaqa of Imru' al-Qays: Its Structure and Meaning." Pt. I. *Edebiyat* 2 (1977):227–261. Pt. II. *Edebiyat* 3 (1978):51–82.

Hilāl, Muḥammad Ghunaymī. *Laylā wa-al-Majnūn*. Beirut: Dār al-ᶜAwdah, 1980.

Ḥilmī, Muṣṭafā Maḥmūd. *Ibn al-Fāriḍ wa-al-Ḥubb al-Ilāhī*. 2nd. ed. Cairo: Maṭbᶜat Miṣr, 1971.

Homerin, Th. Emil. "A Bird Ascends the Night: Elegy and Immortality in Islam." *Journal of the American Academy of Religion* 58 (1991):541–73.

———. "Echoes of a Thirsty Owl: Death and Afterlife in Pre-Islamic Arabic Poetry." *Journal of Near Eastern Studies* 44 (1985):165–84.

———. *From Arab Poet to Muslim Saint: Ibn al-Fāriḍ, His Verse, and His Shrine*. 2nd rev. ed. Cairo: American University in Cairo Press, 2001.

———. "Ibn al-Fāriḍ's Personal *Dīwān*." In *The Development of Sufism in Mamluk Egypt*. Ed. Richard McGregor and Adam Sabra. Cairo: Institut français d'archéologie orientale, 2006, 233–43.

———. "Ibn al-Farid: Rubaᶜiyat, Ghazal, Qasida." In *Windows on the House of Islam* Ed. John Renard. Berkely: University of California Press, 1998, 194–201.

———. "In the Gardens of al-Zahrā': Love Echoes in a Poem by Ibn Zaydūn." In *The Shaping of an American Islamic Discourse*. Ed. E.H. Waugh and F. Denny. Atlanta: Scholars Press, 1998, 215–32.

———. "Living Love: The Mystical Writings of ᶜĀ'ishah al-Bāᶜūnīyah." *Mamlūk Studies Review* 7 (2003):211–34.

———. " 'On the Battleground:' al-Nābulusī's Encounters with a Poem by Ibn al-Fāriḍ *Journal of Arabic Literature* 38 (2007):353–411.

———. "Preaching Poetry: The Forgotten Verse of Ibn al-Shahrazūrī." *Arabica* 38 (1991):87–101.

———. "Saving Muslim Souls: The *Khānqāh* and the Sufi Duty in Mamluk Lands," *Mamlūk Studies Review* 3 (1999):59–83.

———. "Sufis and Their Detractors in Mamluk Egypt." In *Islamic Mysticism Contested*. Ed. Frederick de Jong and Bernd Radtke. Leiden: E.J. Brill, 1999, 225–47.

———. "Tangled Words: Toward a Stylistics of Arabic Mystical Verse." In S.P. Stetkevych, ed. *Reorientations*, 190–98.

———. *ᶜUmar Ibn al-Fāriḍ: Sufi Verse, Saintly Life*. New York: Paulist Press, 2001.

———, ed. and tr. *The Wine of Love and Life: Ibn al-Fāriḍ's al-Khamrīyah and al-Qayṣarī's Quest for Meaning*. Chicago: Center for Middle Eastern Studies, University of Chicago, 2005.

al-Hujwirī, Alī ibn Uthmān. *Kashf al-Maḥjūb*. Ed. Valentin Zhukovskii. Leningrad: Maṭbaᶜat Dār al-ᶜUlūm, 1926. English translation by R.A. Nicholson. *The Kashf al-Maḥjūb*. London: Luzac & Co., 1911. Reprint ed. 1959.

Ḥusayn, ᶜAlī Ṣāfī. *Al-Adab al-Ṣūfī fī Miṣr fī al-Qarn al-Sābiᶜ al-Hijrī*. Cairo: Dār al-Maᶜārif, 1964.

———. *Ibn al-Kīzānī: al-Shāᶜir al-Ṣūfī al-Miṣrī*. Cairo: Dār al-Maᶜārif, 1966.

Ḥusayn, Muḥammad Kāmil. *Dirāsāt fī al-Shiᶜr fī ᶜAṣr al-Ayyūbīyīn*. Cairo: Dār al-Fikr al-ᶜArabī, 1957.

Ḥusayn, Muḥammad Muḥammad. *Asālīb al-Ṣināᶜā fī Shiᶜr al-Khamr wa-al-Naqā bayn al-Aᶜshā wa-al-Jāhilīyīn*. Alexandria: Munsha'at al-Maᶜārif, 1960.

Hyde, John Dennis. "A Study of the Poetry of Maymun Ibn Qays al-Aᶜsha." Ph.D. diss. Princeton University, 1977.

Ibn Abī Ḥajalah, Aḥmad ibn Yaḥyā. *Al-Ghawth al-ᶜĀriḍ fī Muᶜāraḍat Ibn al-Fāriḍ*. Cairo: Arab League Manuscript Institute microfilm 319 (Taṣawwuf) of manuscript 31 (Adab) Maktabat Sūhāj, Sūhāj, Egypt.

Ibn Abī Rabīᶜah, ᶜUmar. *Dīwān*. 2nd ed. Beirut: Dār al-Andalus, 1983.

Ibn Abī Uṣaybiᶜah. *ᶜUyūn al-Anbā' fī Ṭabaqāt al-Aṭibbā'*. Cairo: al-Maṭbaᶜah al-Waḥḥabīyah, 1882.

Ibn al-Ahdal, al-Ḥusayn. *Kashf al-Ghitā'*. Tunis: Aḥmad Bakīr, 1964.

Ibn al-Aḥnaf, al-ᶜAbbās. *Dīwān*. Ed. ᶜĀtikah al-Khazrajī. Cairo: Dār al-Kutub al-Miṣrīyah, 1954.

Ibn al-ᶜArabī, Muḥyi al-Dīn. *Divine Sayings: The Mishkāt al-Anwār of Ibn ᶜArabī*. Ed. with English translation by Stephen Hirtenstein and Martin Notcutt. Oxford: Anqa Publishing, 2004.

———. *Dīwān*. Būlāq, 1855. Reprint edition, n.p., 1963.

———. *Fuṣūṣ al-Ḥikam*. Ed. A.A. ᶜAffifī. Cairo: ᶜIsā al-Bābī al-Ḥalabī, 1946. English translation by R.W.J Austin. *Ibn Al-'Arabi: The Bezels of Wisdom*. New York: Paulist Press, 1980.

———. *Al-Futūḥāt al-Makkīyah*. 4 vols. Cairo: Maktabat al-Thiqāfah al-Dīnīyah, nd.

———. *Turjumān al-Ashwāq*. Beirut: Dār Ṣādir, 1966. English translation by R.A. Nicholson. *The Tarjuman Al-Ashwaq*. London: Royal Asiatic Society, 1911. Partial translation by Michael Sells. *Stations of Desire*. Jerusalem: Ibis Editions, 2000.

Ibn al-Athīr, Diyā' al-Dīn. *Al-Mathāl al-Sā'ir*. Ed. Muḥammad Muḥyī al-Dīn ᶜAbd al-Ḥamīd. Cairo: Muṣṭfā al-Bābī al-Ḥalabī, 1939.

Ibn al-Fāriḍ, ᶜUmar. *Dīwān Ibn al-Fāriḍ*. Ed. Guiseppe Scattolin. Cairo: Institut français d'archéologie orientale, 2004. Partial English translation by Nicholson. *Studies in Islamic Mysticism*, 162-266. Arberry. *The Mystical Poems of Ibn al-Fārid* and his *The Poem of the Way*. Homerin. *ᶜUmar Ibn al-Fāriḍ*. Wheeler M. Thackston, Jr., "The *Jīmīyah*." In I. Lichtenstadler, ed. *Introduction*, 312–14. A. Safi in *Bulletin of the School of Oriental and Asian Studies* 2:235–48. Partial French translation by Derminghem and Messilkh. *Ibn al-Faridh*. L'Hôpital. *ᶜUmar b. al-Fārid: Poèmes mystiques*.

Ibn al-ᶜImād. *Shadharāt al-Dhahab fī Akhbār Man Dhahab*. 8 vols. Cairo: Maktabat al-Qudsī, 1931.

Ibn al-Muᶜtazz. *Kitāb al-Badīᶜ*. Ed. I. Kratchkovsky. London: Luzac & Co., 1935.

Ibn Ḥajar al-ᶜAsqalānī. *Kitāb Tahdhīb al-Tahdhīb*. 12 vols. Beirut: Dār Ṣādir, 1968.

Ibn Hanbal, Aḥmad. *Musnad*. 6 vols. Cario, 1895. Reprint ed. Beirut: Dār al-Ṣādir, 1969.

Ibn Jubayr. *Riḥlat Ibn Jubayr*. Beirut: Dār al-Ṣādir, 1964. Partially translated into English by R. J. C. Broadhurst. In L. Lichtenstadler, ed. *Introduction*, 376–92.

Ibn Khallikān. *Wafayāt al-Aᶜyān*. Ed. Iḥsān ᶜAbbās. 8 vols. Beirut: Dār al-Thaqāfah, English translation by B. Mac Guckin de Slane. *Ibn Khallikan's Biographical Dictionary*. 4 vols. Paris: Oriental Translation Fund of Great Britain and Ireland, 1842–1871.

Ibn Qutaybah. *Al-Shiᶜr wa-al-shuᶜarā'*. Ed. M.J. De Goeje. Leiden: E.J.Brill, 1904.

Ibn ᶜUnayn. *Dīwān*. Ed. Khalil Mardam. Beirut: Dār Ṣādir, 1974.

Ibn Zaydūn. *Dīwān Ibn Zaydūn wa-Risā'iluhu*. Ed. ᶜAlī ᶜAbd al-ᶜAẓīm. Cairo: Dār Nahḍat Miṣr, 1957.

Imrū' al-Qays. *Sharḥ Dīwān Imrū' al-Qays*. Beirut: Dār al-Ṣādir, n.d.

al-Iṣfahānī, Abū Faraj. *Kitāb al-Āghānī*. 20 vols. in 10. Beirut: Dār al-Tawjīh al-Lubnānī, n.d

al-Isfahānī, Abū Nuᶜaym. *Ḥilyāt al-Awliyā' wa-Ṭabaqāt al-Aṣfiyā'*. Cairo, 1932. Reprint ed. Beirut: Dār al-Kutub al-ᶜArabī, 1980.

Jacobi, Renate. "Abbasidische Dichtung." In *Grundris der arabischen Philologie*. Ed. H. Gatje. Wiesbaden: Ludwig Reichert, 1987, 2:41–64.

———. "The Camel Section of the Panegyrical Ode." *Jounal of Arabic Literature* 13 (1982):1–22.

———. "Die Anfänge der arabischen Ġazalpoesie." *Der Islam* 61 (1984):218–50.

———. "The Origins of the Qasida Form." In S. Sperl and C. Shackle, eds. *Qasida Poetry*, 1:21–34.

———. *Studien zur Poetik der altararabischen Qaside*. Wiesbaden: F. Steiner, 1971.

———. "Theme and Variation in Umayyad Ghazal Poetry," *Journal of Arabic Literature* 23 (1993):109–19.

———. "Time and Reality in *Nasīb* and *Ghazal*." *Journal of Arabic Literature* 16 (1988):1–17.

———. "Al-Walīd ibn Yazīd, the Last Ghazal Poet of the Umayyad Period." In T. Bauer and A. Neuwirth, eds., *Ghazal*, 131–47.

al-Jāhiẓ. "*Fī al-ᶜIshq wa-al-Nisā'*," In *Majmūᶜat Rasā'il al-Jāhiẓ*. Ed. ᶜAbd al-Salīm Muḥammad Hārūn. Cairo: Maktabat al-Khānjī, 1964, 3:139–59. English translation by D.M. Hawke from Charles Pellat, ed. *The Life and Works of Jāḥiẓ*. Berkeley: University of California Press, 1969, 258–59.

Jamīl. *Dīwān*. Beirut: Dār Ṣādir, 1966.

Jayyusi, Salma K. "Umayyad Poetry." In A.F.L. Beeston, et al., eds. *The Cambridge History of Arabic Literature: Arabic Literature to the End of the Umayyad Period*, 387–432.

al-Jīlānī, Yaḥyā. *Ḥall al-Muᶜḍilāt min Rumūz al-Mushkilāt*. Microfilm of manuscript 4116 (3812). Yahuda Section, Garrett Collection, Princeton University.

al-Jurjānī, ᶜAlī. *Kitāb al-Taᶜrīfāt*. Beirut: Dār al-Kutub al-ᶜIlmīyah, 1983.

al-Kalabādhī. *Al-Taᶜarruf li-Madhhab ahl al-Taṣawwuf*. Beirut: Dār al-Kutub al-ᶜIlmīyah, 1980. English translation by A.J. Arberry, *Doctrine of the Ṣūfīs*. Cambridge: Cambridge University Press, 1935. Reprint ed. 1977.

Karamustafa, Ahmet. *Sufism: The Formative Period*. Edinburgh: Edinburgh University Press, 2007.

al-Kāshānī, ᶜAbd al-Razzāq. *Iṣṭalāḥāt al-Ṣūfīyah*. Ed. A. ᶜAbd a-Khāliq. Minya, Egypt: Dār Ḥarā', 1980.

———. *Sharḥ ᶜalā Fuṣūṣ al-Ḥikam*. Cairo: n.p., 1891.

al-Kāshānī, ᶜIzz al-Dīn. *Kashf al-Wujūh al-Ghurr li-Maᶜānī Naẓm al-Durr*. Microfilm of manuscript 4106 (3979). Yahuda Section, Garrett Collection, Princeton University.

al-Kātib al-Iṣfahānī, ᶜImād al-Dīn. *Kharīdat al-Qaṣr wa-Jarīdat al-ᶜAṣr*. 3 vols. Damascus: al-Maṭbaᶜah al-Hāshmīyah, 1955.

Kays B. al-Mulavvaḥ ve-Dīwāni. Ed. by Sevkiye Inalcik. Ankara: Turk Tarih Kumuru Basimevi, 1967.

Kennedy, Philip F. *Abu Nuwas: A Genius of Poetry*. Oxford: Oneworld, 2005.

———. *The Wine Song in Classical Arabic Poetry*. Oxford: Clarendon Press, 1997.

Khairallah, A.E. *Love, Madness, and Poetry*. Beirut: Franz Steiner, 1980.

Khan, Ruqayya Yasmine. "On the Significance of Secrecy in the Medieval Arabic Romances." *Journal of Arabic Literature* 31 (2000):238-53.

Knysh, Alexander. *Ibn al-ᶜArabī in the Later Islamic Tradition*. Albany: State University of New York Press, 1999.

———. *Islamic Mysticsm: A Short History*. Leiden: E.J. Brill, 2000.

Kuntze, Simon. "Love and God: The Influence of Ghazal on Mystic Poetry." In T. Bauer and A. Neuwirth, eds. *Ghazal*, 157–79.

Lane, E.W. *Arabic–English Lexicon*. Cambridge: Islamic Text Society, 1984. 2 vol. Reprint of the 1877 Edinburgh: Williams and Norgate.

Lichtenstadler, Ilse, ed. *Introduction to Classical Arabic Literature*. New York: Shocken Books, 1976.

L'Hôpital, Jean-Yves. *ʿUmar b. al-Fārid: Poèmes mystiques*. Damascus: Institut Français d'Études Arabes de Damas, 2001.

———. "Le vocabulaire amoureux dans les poèmes de ʿUmar b. al-Fāriḍ." *Annales Islamologiques* 36 (2002):77–116.

Lings, Martin. "Mystical Poetry." In J. Ashtiany, et al., eds. *Cambridge History of Arabic Literature ʿAbbasid Belles*, 235–64.

———. *Sufi Poems*. Cambridge: Islamic Texts Society, 2004.

Lyall, Charles. "The Pictorial Aspects of Ancient Arabian Poetry." *Journal of the Royal Asiatic Society* (1912):133–152.

Maḥmūd, ʿAbd al-Khāliq. *Shiʿr Ibn al-Fāriḍ*. Cairo: Dār al-Maʿārif, 1984.

Martz, Louis L. *The Paradise Within*. New Haven: Yale University Press, 1964.

———. *The Poem of the Mind*. New York: Oxford University Press, 1966.

———. *The Poetry of Meditation*. New Haven: Yale University Press, 1954.

al-Maqqarī. Aḥmad ibn Muḥammad. *Nafḥ al-Ṭīb*. Ed. Iḥsān ʿAbbās. 8 vols. Beirut: Dār Ṣādir, 1968

Massignon, Louis. *Essay on the Origins of the Technical Language of Islamic Mysticism*. English translation by Benjamin Clark. Notre Dame: University of Notre Dame Press, 1997.

———. *The Passion of Hallāj*. 4 vols. English translation by Herbert Mason. Princeton: Princeton University Press, 1982.

Mauss, Marcel. *The Gift: Forms and Functions of Exchange in Archaic Societies*. English translation by Ian Cunnison. New York: Norton and Co., 1967.

Meir, Fritz. "The Dervish Dance." In *Essays on Islamic Piety and Mysticism*. Tr. John O'Kane. Leiden: E.J. Brill, 1999, 23–48.

Menocal, M.R., et al. *The Cambridge History of Arabic Literature: the Literature of al-Andalus*. Cambridge: Cambridge University Press, 2000.

Monroe, James T. "Hispano-Arabic Poetry During the Caliphate of Cordova: Theory and Practice." In *Arabic Poetry: Theory and Development*. Ed. G.E. Von Grunebaum. Wiesbaden: O. Harrassowitz, 1973, 125–54.

Mubārak, Zakī. *Al-Madā'iḥ al-Nabawīyah*. Cairo: Muṣṭafā al-Bābī al-Ḥalabī, 1943.

Al-Mufaḍḍalīyāt. Ed. Aḥmad Muḥammad Shākir and ʿAbd al-Salām Muḥammad Hārūn. Cairo: Dār al-Maʿārif, 1983. English translation by Charles Lyall. *The Mufaddalīyāt: an Anthology of Ancient Arabian Odes*. Oxford: Clarendon Press, 1918.

Morris, James. "Rediscovering the 'Divine Comedy': Eschatology and Spiritual Realization in Ibn ʿArabi." *Newsletter of the Muhyiddin Ibn ʿArabi Society* 19 (Autumn, 2003):8–9.

al-Mutanabbī. *Dīwān*. Ed. Muṣṭfā al-Shayqā et al. 4 vols. in 2. Cairo: Dār al-Maʿrifah, 1936.

al-Nābulusī, ʿAbd al-Ghānī. *Dīwān al-Ḥaqā'iq wa-Majmūʿ al-Raqā'iq*. Beirut: Dār al-Jīl, 1986.

———. *Kashf al-Sirr al-Ghāmiḍ fī Sharḥ Dīwān Ibn al-Fāriḍ*. Microfilm of manuscript 4104 (3223), Princeton: Yahuda Section, Garrett Collection, Princeton University.

Nadeem, S.H. *A Critical Appreciation of Arabic Mystical Poetry*. Lahore: Islamic Book Service, 1979.

Nallino, Carlo A. "Ancora su Ibn al-Fāriḍ e sulla mistica musulmana." *Rivista degli studi orientali* 8 (1919–20):501–62.

———. "Il poema mistico arabo di Ibn al-Fāriḍ in una recente traduzione italiana." *Rivista degli studi orientali* 8 (1919–20):20–21.

Naṣr, ᶜAṭif Jawdah. *Al-Ramz al-Shiᶜrī ᶜinda al-Ṣūfīyah*. Beirut: Dār al-Andalus, 1978.

———. *Shiᶜr ᶜUmar Ibn al-Fāriḍ*. Beirut: Dār al-Andalus, 1982.

Nasr, Sayyed Hossein. *An Introduction to Islamic Cosmological Doctrines*. Rev. ed. Albany: State University of New York Press, 1993.

———. *Three Muslim Sages*. Cambridge, MA: Harvard University Press, 1963.

al-Nawawī, Yaḥya. *Al-Arbaᶜīn al-Nawawīyah*. Ed. Ibrāhīm ibn Muḥammad. Tanta, Egypt: Maktabat al-Ṣaḥabah, 1986. English translation by Ezzedin Ibrahim and Denys Johnson-Davies. *An-Nawawi's Forty Hadith*. N.p., n.d.

Neuwirth, Angelika. "Victims Victorious: Violent Death in Classical and Modern Arabic Ghazal." In T. Bauer and A. Neuwirth, eds. *Ghazal*, 259–80.

Nicholson, Reynold A. *A Literary History of the Arabs*. Cambridge: Cambridge University Press, 1907.

———. *Studies in Islamic Mysticism*. Cambridge: Cambridge University Press, 1921. Reprint ed. 1967.

Noorani, Yaseen. "Heterotopia and the Wine Poem in Early Islamic Culture," *International Journal of Middle Eastern Studies* 36 (2004): 345–66.

Nwyia, Paul. *Exégèse coranique et language mystique*. Beirut: Dar al-Machriq, 1970.

Ohlander, Erik S. *Sufisn in the Age of Transition*. Leiden: E.J. Brill, 2008.

Preminger, Alexander, et al, eds. *The New Princeton Encyclopedia of Poetry and Poetics*. Princeton: Princeton University Press, 1993.

al-Qayṣarī, Dāwūd. *Sharḥ Tā'īyat al-Sulūk*. Microfilm of manuscript 4107 (4352). Yahuda Section, Garrett Collection, Princeton University.

Qutbuddin, Tahera. *Al-Mu'ayyad al-Shīrāzī and Fatimid Daᶜwa Poetry*. Leiden: E.J. Brill, 2005.

Al-Qushayrī, Abū al-Qāsim. *Al-Risālah al-Qushayrīyah*. 2 vols. Ed. ᶜAbd al-Ḥalīm Maḥmūd and Maḥmūd Ibn al-Sharīf. Cairo: Dār al-Kutub al-Ḥadīthah, 1972–74. English translation by Alexander Knysh. *Al-Qushayri's Epistle on Sufism*. Reading, UK: Garnett, 2007. Partial English translation by M. Sells. In *Early Islamic Mysticism*, 97–150.

Rahman, Fazlur. *Major Themes of the Qur'ān*. Chicago: Bibilotheca Islamica, 1980.

Raqīq al-Qayrawānī, Ibrāhīm ibn al-Qāsim. *Quṭb al-Surūr fī Awṣāf al-Khamr*. Ed. Aḥmad Jundī. Damascus: al-Muqaddamah, 1969.

al-Rifā', al-Sarī ibn Aḥmad. *Al-Muḥibb wa-al-Maḥbūb wa-al-Mashmūm wa-al-Mashrūb*. Damascus: Mājid Ḥasan al-Dhahabī, 1986.

Rikabi, Jawdat. *La Poesie profane sous les Ayyubides et ses principaux representants* Paris: G.-P. Masionneuve & Co., 1949.

Ritter, Hellmut. *Das Meer der Seele*. Leiden: E.J. Brill, 1955.

Rubin, Uri. "Pre-existence and Light: Aspects of the Concept of *Nūr Muhammad*," *Israel Oriental Studies* 5 (1975):62–119.

Ṣādiq, Ramaḍān. *Shi ᶜr Ibn al-Fāriḍ: Dirāsah Uslūbīyah*. Cairo: al-Hay'at al-Miṣrīyah al-ᶜĀmmah lil-Kitāb, 1998.

al-Ṣafadī, Ṣalāḥ al-Dīn Khalīl, *Al-Wāfī bi-al-Wafīyāt*. Ed. Sven Dedering et al. Wiesbaden: In Kommission bei Franz Steiner Verlag, 1959.
Salām, Maḥmūd Zaghlūl. *Al-Adab fī al-ᶜAsr al-Ayyūbī*. 2 vols. Cairo: Dār al-Maᶜārif, 1983.
al-Sarrāj al-Ṭūsī, Abū Naṣr. *Al-Lumaᶜ*. Ed. ᶜAbd al-Ḥalīm Maḥmūd and Tāhā ᶜAbd al-Bāqī Surūr. Cairo: Dār al-Kutub al-Ḥadīthah, 1960.
Scattolin, Giuseppe, ed. *Dīwān Ibn al-Fāriḍ*. Cairo: Institut français d'archéologie orientale, 2004.
———. *L'esperienza mistica di Ibn al-Fāriḍ attraverso il suo poema Al-Tā'iyyat Al-Kubrā*. Rome: PISAI, 1988.
———. "L'expérience mystique de Ibn al-Fāriḍ a travers son poèma Al-Ta'iyyat Al-Kubrā," *Mélanges de L'Institut Dominicain d'études orientales* (*MIDEO*) 19 (1989):203–23.
———. "Al-Farghānī's Commentary on Ibn al-Fārid's Mystical Poem *Al-Tā'iyyat Al-Kubrā*." *MIDEO* 21 (1993):331–83.
———. "The Mystical Experience of Umar Ibn al-Fāriḍ," *Muslim World* 82:3–4 (1992):274–86.
———. "The Oldest Text of Ibn al-Fāriḍ's *Dīwān*: A Manuscript of Konya." *MIDEO* 24 (2000):83–114.
———. "Realization of 'Self' (ANĀ) in Islamic Mysticism: the Mystical Experience of Umar Ibn al-Fāriḍ." *Mélanges de L'Université Saint-Joseph* LIV (1995–96):119–48.
———. "Towards a Critical Edition of Ibn al-Fāriḍ's Dīwān." *Annales Islamologique*. 35 (2001):503–47.
Schimmel, Annemarie. *And Muhammad is His Messenger*. Chapel Hill: University of North Carolina Press, 1985.
———. *As Through A Veil: Mystical Poetry in Islam*. New York: Columbia University Press, 1982.
———. " 'I Take off the dress of the body': Eros in Sufi Literature and Life." In S. Coakly. *Religion and the Body*. Cambridge: Cambridge University Press, 1997, 262–88.
———. *Mystical Dimensions of Islam*. Chapel Hill: University of North Carolina Press, 1975.
———. "Secrecy in Sufism." In *Secrecy in Religion*. Ed. K.W. Bolle. Leiden: E.J. Brill, 1987, 81–102.
Scholer, G. "Bashshār B. Burd, Abū 'L-Atahiyah and Abū Nuwās." In J. Ashtiany et al., eds. *Cambridge History of Arabic Literature ᶜAbbasid Belles*, 290–95.
Sells, Michael. "Bānat Suᶜād: translation and introduction." *Journal of Arabic Literature* 21 (1990):140–54.
———, "Bewildered Tongue: The Semantics of Mystical Union in Islam." In *Mystical Union in Judaism, Christianity, and Islam*. Ed. Moshe Idel and Bernard McGinn. New York: Continuum, 1996, 87–124.
———, ed. and tr. *Desert Tracings: Six Classical Odes by ᶜAlqama, Shanfara, Labid, Antara, Al-Aᶜsha, and Dhu ar-Rumma*. Middletown: Wesleyan University Press, 1993.

———. *Early Islamic Mysticism*. New York: Paulist Press, 1996.
———. "Love." In *The Cambridge History of Arabic Literature: The Literature of al-Andalus* (*CHALLOA*). Ed. María Rosa Menocal, et al., eds., Cambridge: Cambridge University Press, 2000, 126–58.
———. "The Muᶜallaqa of Ṭarafa," *Journal of Arabic Literature* 17 (1986):21–33.
Sezgin, Fuat. *Geshichte des Arabischen Schrifttmus*. 9 vols. Leiden: E. J. Brill, 1975.
al-Shahrazūrī, Muḥammad ibn Maḥmūd. *Kitāb Nuzhat al-Arwāḥ wa-Rawḍat al-Afrāḥ*. University of Chicago. Microfilm of manuscript 908, Istanbul: Yeni Cami.
al-Shaybī, Muṣṭafā. *Dīwān al-Dūbayt fī al-Shiᶜr al-ᶜArabī*. Tripoli: Manshūrāt al-Jamiᶜah al-Lībīyah, 1967.
Sibṭ al-Marṣafī. *Fatḥ al-Makkī al-Fā'iḍ Sharḥ Yā'īyat Ibn al-Fāriḍ*. Manuscript 1566 (Adab). Cairo: Dār al-Kutub al-Misrīyah.
Sperl, Stefan. *Mannerism in Arabic Poetry*. Cambridge: Cambridge University Press, 1989.
———. "Qasida Form and Mystic Path in 13th Century Egypt: A Poem by Ibn al-Fāriḍ." In S. Sperl and C. Shackle, eds. *Qasida Poetry*, 1:62–74; 2:106–11.
Sperl, Stefan and C. Shackle, eds. *Qasida Poetry in Islamic Asia and Africa*. 2 vols. Leiden: E.J. Brill, 1996.
Spies, Otto and S.K. Khattak. *Three Treatises on Mysticism*. Stutgart: W. Kohlhamer, 1935.
Stetkevych, Jaroslav. "The Arabic Lyrical Phenomenon in Context." *Journal of Arabic Literature* 6 (1975):55–77.
———. "The Arabic Qaṣīdah: From Form and Content to Mood and Meaning." *Harvard Ukrainian Studies* 3–4 (1979– 80):774–781.
———. "Name and Epithet: The Philology and Semiotics of Animal Nomenclature in Early Arabic Poetry." *Journal of Near Eastern Studies* 45 (1986):89–124.
———. "A *Qaṣīdah* by Ibn Muqbil." *Journal of Arabic Literature* 37 (2006):303–54.
———. "Some Observations on Arabic Poetry." *Journal of Near Eastern Studies*, 26 (1967):2–3.
———. "Toward an Arabic Elegiac Lexicon: the Seven Words of the *Nasīb*." In S.P. Stetkevych, ed. *Reorientations*, 58–129.
———. *The Zephrys of Najd*. Chicago: University of Chicago Press, 1993.
Stetkevych, Suzanne P. "Abbasid Panegyric and the Poetics of Political Allegiance: Two Poems of al-Mutanabbī on Kāfūr." In S. Sperl and C. Shackle, eds. *Qasida Poetry*, 1:35–63; 2:92–105, 421–22.
———. "The ᶜAbbasid Poet Interprets History: Three Qaṣīdahs by Abū Tammām." *Journal of Arabic Literature* 10 (1979):49–65.
———. *Abū Tammām & the Poetics of the ᶜAbbāsid Age*. Leiden: E.J. Brill, 1991.
———. "Intoxication and Immortality: Wine and Honey in al-Maᶜarrī's Garden." In *Critical Pilgrimages: Studies in the Arabic Literary Tradition*. Ed. Fedwa Multi-Douglas. Austin: University of Texas Press, 1990, 29–48.
———. *The Mute Immortals Speak*. Ithaca, NY: Cornell University Press, 1993.
———. *The Poetics of Islamic Legitimacy: Myth, Gender, and Ceremony in the Classical Arabic Ode*. Bloomington: University of Indiana Press, 2002.

———. "Pre-Islamic Panegyric and the Poetics of Redemption." In S.P. Stetkevych, ed. *Reorientations*, 1-49.

———, ed. *Reorientations/Arabic and Persian Poetry*. Bloomington: University of Indiana Press, 1994.

———. "Structuralist Interpretations of Pre-Islamic Poetry: Critique in New Directions," *Journal of Near Eastern Studies*, 42 (1983):85–107.

al-Suhrawardī, Yaḥyā. *The Mystical & Visionary Treaties of Suhrawardi*. English translation by W.M. Thackson, Jr. London: Octagon Press, 1982.

al-Sulamī, *Ṭabaqāt al-Ṣūfīyah*. Ed. Aḥmad al-Sharbasī. Cairo: al-Shaᶜb, 1962.

al-Suyūṭī, Jalāl al-Dīn. *Al-Barq al-Wāmiḍ fī Sharḥ Yā'īyat Ibn al-Fāriḍ*. Manuscript 881 (Shiᶜr Taymūr). Cairo: Dār al-Kutub al-Miṣrīyah.

———. *Al-Muzhir fī ᶜUlūm al-Lughah wa-Anwāᶜihā*. 3rd ed. Cairo: ᶜIṣā al-Bābī al-Ḥalabī, 1945.

Ṭarafah ibn al-ᶜAbd. *Dīwān*. Beirut: Dār al-Ṣādir, 1961.

al-Thaᶜālibī, ᶜAbd al-Malik ibn Muḥammad. *Yatīmat al-Dahr fī Shuᶜarā' al-ᶜAṣr*. 4 vols. in 2. Cairo: Maktabat al-Ḥusayn al-Tījārīyah, 1947.

al-Tilimsānī, ᶜAfīf al-Dīn. *Sharḥ Tā'īyat Ibn al-Fāriḍ al-Kubrā*. Manuscript 1328 (Taṣawwuf Ṭalᶜat). Cairo: Dār al-Kutub al-Miṣrīyah.

Turner, Victor. *The Ritual Process: Structure and Anti-Structure*. Ithaca, NY: Cornell University Press, 1977.

United States Board on Geographic Names. *Official Standard Names Gazetteer: Saudi Arabia*. Washington D. C., 1978.

Vadet, J-C. *L'Esprit courtois en orient*. Paris: G.-P. Maisonneuve et Larose, 1968.

Walbridge, John. *The Leaven of the Ancients: Suhrawardī and the Heritage of the Greeks*. Albany: State University of New York Press, 2000.

Walīd ibn Yazīd. *Dīwān*. Ed. F. Gabrielli. Damascus: Maṭbaᶜat Ibn Zaydūn, 1937.

Waugh, Earle H. *Memory, Music and Religion: Morocco's Mystical Chanters*. Columbia, SC: University of South Carolina Press, 2005.

———. *The Munshidīn of Egypt*. Columbia: University of South Carolina Press, 1989.

Wickens, G.M., ed. *Avicenna: Scientist and Philosopher*. London: Luzac & Co., 1952.

Yāfī, ᶜAbd al-Karīm. *Dirāsāt Fannīyah fī al-Abab al-ᶜArabī*. Damascus: Matbaᶜat Jamiᶜat Dimashq, 1972.

Yāqūt. *Muᶜjam al-Buldān*. 5 vols. Beirut: Dār Aḥyā' al-Turāth al-ᶜArabī, 1979.

———. *Muᶜjam al-Udabā'*. 20 vols. in 10. Cairo: Dār al-Ma'mūn, 1936.

al-Yūsuf, Yūsuf Sāmī. "Baᶜḍ yanābīᶜ Ibn al-Fāriḍ." *Al-Maᶜrifah* 350 (1992): 86–112.

al-Zawzanī, al-Ḥusayn ibn Aḥmad. *Sharḥ al-Muᶜallaqāt al-Sabᶜ*. Damascus: n.p., 1963.

Zaehner, R.C. *Hindu and Muslim Mysticism*. New York: Schocken Books, 1969.

Index

Abbasid period, 10–13, 15, 51, 67, 106–107, 115, 138, 149–50
ᶜAbd al-Raḥmān ibn ᶜUmar Ibn al-Fārid, 2
Abraham, 5, 26, 125, 130–31, 134, 137, 140, 181, 189, 191
Abū Aᶜlā al-Maᶜarrī author of *Risālat al-Ghufrān*, 152
Abū Madyan, 24–25, 154–56, 158
Abū Nuwās, 15, 67, 107, 149–53, 169
Abū Tammām, 10–11, 15
Adam, 7, 52, 78, 83, 125, 151, 198, 214, 219, 228, 231, 238, 242
affliction, 75, 79, 108–109, 124–25, 137–38, 161, 181–82, 187, 247
ᶜahd. See: pact
Aḥmad al-Rifāᶜī, 18
ᶜĀ'ishah al-Bāᶜūnīyah, 246
al-Akhṭal, 148–49
Aleppo, 23, 38, 54
Alexandria, 16
ᶜAlī ibn Abī Ṭālib, 39, 123, 202
ᶜAlī ibn al-Murshid ibn ᶜAlī, 1–2
ᶜAlī, Sibt Ibn al-Fārid, 2, 56, 240, 243, 245
 Dībājah ("The Adorned Proem"), 2
Amīr al-Saᶜīd, 16
amr. See: command
ᶜAmr ibn ᶜAbd Wudd, 123
ᶜAmr ibn Kulthūm, 144
ᶜAntarah, 145–46
antithesis (*ṭibāq*), 10, 26, 49–53, 63, 72, 76, 92–93, 120, 124–27, 131, 163, 170, 184, 196, 204, 208, 230
Arabia, 1, 47, 117, 121, 128–29, 152
ᶜArafāt, 130–35, 139, 197, 204
Arberry, A.J., 32, 46–47
al-Aᶜshā, 144–45, 150
ᶜAṭṭār, Farīd al-Dīn, 15, 230
audition. See: *samāᶜ*
Augustine, 250
Avicenna. *See:* Ibn Sīnā
al-Aykī, Shams al-Dīn, 240
ᶜayn (source, eye/self-I), 33, 36, 173, 215
Ayyubid period, 1, 3, 15–17, 27, 51, 54, 57, 152
ᶜAzzah, 198

badīᶜ poetry 9–16, 23, 26, 49–54, 60–61, 230
Badr, 79, 89, 96–98, 136
badr (full moon), 16–17, 79, 173. *Also see:* moon
Baghdad, 38, 43, 68, 231
Bahā' al-Dīn Zuhayr, 16, 57
Banī Yazdādh, 37, 39, 41, 46
baqā' (abiding), 6, 19, 24, 52, 91, 96, 125, 173, 175, 214
Baradā, 56
Basmallāh, 94
basṭ (exhilaration, expansion), 125, 180–81, 191–92, 201, 220
bāṭin (inner, esoteric), 8, 200, 210, 214
beloved, 46–47, 77–83, 123–25, 162–64, 186–87. Also see: *ḥabīb*
Bishr ibn Abī Khāzim, 105–106

blamer (*lā'im/lāhin/ᶜādhil*), 33, 40–41, 57, 73–74, 85, 93–94, 110, 122, 148, 154–55, 158–59, 162, 171, 191–92, 205, 207–208, 234, 244, 250
body, 11, 45, 48, 58, 73, 79, 90–91, 95, 107–108, 118, 123, 130, 136–37, 140, 143, 152, 161, 163–64, 166–67, 170, 174, 200, 204, 207–208, 210–12, 215, 217, 220–22, 225, 241–42, 247
Boullata, Issa, 51, 254
bridal chamber (*jalwah*), 179–81, 193–94
al-Buḥturī, 15, 32
al-Būrīnī, Ḥasan, 32, 81, 98, 160, 245–46
al-Būṣīrī, Muhammad, 246
Buthaynah, 198–99, 245

Cairo, 1–3, 15, 29, 56, 135, 138, 239–41
camel, 103–107, 109, 111, 116–17, 122, 129, 136, 138, 182, 223
caravan, 105, 109, 121–22, 128–30, 135–36, 138–39, 249
Christianity, 4–5, 148–49, 153, 226, 250–51
command (*amr*), 45, 71, 81–82, 125, 137, 163–64, 168, 190–91, 248
contemplation, 48, 133, 180. Also see: *shuhūd*
covenant (*mīthāq*) 7, 22–23, 35, 47–48, 52, 57, 76, 78, 82–84, 101, 120, 135, 139–41, 172–74, 183–85, 191, 200, 211–17, 219, 231–33, 250–51. *Also see:* Day of the Covenant; pact

dahr (time, fate), 100, 151–52, 169
Damascus, 1, 15, 25, 56
Day of the Covenant (*yawm al-mīthāq*), 7, 22, 173–74, 200, 214, 233, 251
Day of Judgment, 4, 9, 46, 58, 71, 83, 93, 141, 214
al-Daylamī, Abū al-Ḥasan, 83, 90
dhikr (recollection, meditation) 7, 9, 21–22, 36, 47, 72, 84, 94, 118, 122, 132–33, 156, 158–60, 165, 172–75, 209, 212, 247, 251. *Also see:* recollection
Dhū al-Faqār, 39, 123
Dhū al-Nūn al-Miṣrī, 8–9, 15, 18
Dhū al-Rummah, 15
Diḥyah al-Kalbī, 201
disguise (*labs, labasa, talabbus, talbīsāt*), 198, 200–201, 217, 232
divine presence, 7, 24, 96, 98, 157, 180, 194, 250
dīwān al-inshā' (ministry of documents), 15
Donne, John, 250
double entendre (*tawrīyah* or *īhām*), 50–53, 121, 177
dū bayt (rhymed couplet), 28, 30, 57. Also see: *rubāᶜīyāt*

Eden, 112, 117, 182, 198
emanation (*fayḍ*), 173, 203, 208, 214, 216, 218, 243
encounter (*liqā'*), 51, 58, 72–73, 83, 113, 130, 132–35, 155–56, 181
exhilaration, expansion. See: *basṭ*

fanā' (annihilation), 6, 19, 24, 52, 91, 96, 181, 214, 233
al-Farghānī, Saᶜīd al-Dīn, 177, 240–41
Farthest Mosque (al-Masjid al-Aqṣā), 140, 205
fire, 8, 12–13, 17, 44, 48, 67–68, 85, 89, 98–99, 109–19, 126, 138, 156, 167, 170, 181, 223–24, 226, 228, 237–38
Fish, Stanley, 102

Gabriel, 5, 29, 201, 228
Ghassānids, 147–48
ghazal, 1, 15, 22, 27, 32–33, 35–36, 47, 61–84, 90–92, 97, 101–102, 103, 106, 109–10, 113, 121–23,

130, 141, 154, 159–60, 162, 165, 171–72, 177, 180, 182, 184–85, 234, 244–46, 248, 251
al-Ghazālī, Muḥammad, 18, 64, 235–39, 242
Iḥyā' ᶜUlūm al-Dīn, 18
Mishkāt al-Anwār, 18, 235, 238
ghulām (young slave), 164
glance (*naẓrah*), 32–33, 42, 59, 84, 89–90, 112, 123, 132, 178–80, 188, 206
God, 3–9, 13–14, 21–36, 46–48, 52, 58, 63–71, 75, 77–79, 81–84, 87, 90–92, 94, 97–98, 100–102, 106, 108, 112–15, 117, 121, 123, 125–26, 132–41, 153–54, 156–60, 172–75, 178, 181, 184–86, 188, 190–93, 196–98, 200–207, 210–11, 214–20, 225–26, 228, 230–38, 241–42, 246, 249, 251
as creator, 13, 26–27, 58, 83, 184, 198, 210, 222, 226, 232
as hidden treasure, 26
as the Real (*al-ḥaqq*), 172, 232–33
divine names and attributes of, 25–27, 94, 184–85, 215–18, 220, 226, 230
essence (*al-dhāt*; *lāhūt*) of, 25, 173, 175, 194–95, 208, 213, 216, 236
face or countenance (*wajh*) of, 46, 123, 190, 236
self-revelation (*jallat*/*tajallī*) of, 122, 178, 194, 196, 200–201, 220–21, 232, 242
gnosis (*maᶜrifah*; *ᶜirfān*), 10, 81, 96, 111, 113, 121, 132, 135, 154–55, 173–74, 194, 202, 215, 226, 230
Gnosticism, 4

ḥabīb (beloved), 13, 20, 80–82, 158–59, 165, 172–73, 193, 247, 251. *Also see:* beloved
ḥadīth, 2, 5–6, 23–24, 26, 35, 52, 80–81, 97, 119–21, 158–59, 173, 177, 196, 201, 229, 235, 247
Tradition of Willing Devotions, 6, 27, 202, 210, 216, 220, 226, 234, 241–42, 251
ḥaḍrah, 7, 24, 98, 157, 180, 194, 250. *Also see:* divine presence
Hajj pilgrimage, 47–48, 87, 109, 117–18, 125–41, 159–60, 186–88, 191, 196–97, 204, 212, 249–50, 252
ḥāl/*aḥwāl*. *See:* mystical states
Ḥalīmah, 81
al-Ḥallāj, al-Ḥusayn ibn Manṣūr, 11–13, 15, 18, 23, 26, 153–54
ḥaqīqah (reality), 8, 77, 191
al-Ḥarīrī, author of the *al-Maqāmāt*, 29–30, 221
al-Ḥārith ibn Ḥillizah al-Yashkurī, 104
Hārūt, 41, 46
heart. See: *qalb*
Hell, 21, 67, 93, 100, 125, 133
Herbert, George, 102
hijā'. *See:* invective verse
Ḥijāz, 65, 128, 137
ḥimā (sacred precinct), 47, 108, 122
al-Hujwirī, 133
Ḥuyai ibn Akhṭab, 123

Ibn ᶜAbd Rabbih, 15
Ibn Abī Ḥajalah, 81, 246
Ibn Abī Rabīᶜah, ᶜUmar, 15, 32, 63, 65, 67–68
Ibn al-Ahdal, al-Ḥusayn, 65, 69
Ibn al-ᶜArabī, Muḥyī al-Dīn, 25–27, 64–64, 116–17, 172, 229, 239–42
Fuṣūṣ al-Ḥikam, 26
al-Futūḥāt al-Makkīyah, 26, 239, 241
Turjumān al-Ashwāq, 27, 64
Ibn al-ᶜArīf, 18, 117–18
Ibn al-ᶜAsākir, al-Qāsim ibn ᶜAlī, 2
Ibn Bassām, 15
Ibn Dāwūd, 69
Ibn al-Fārid, ᶜUmar,
al-Dālīyah, 136–41
al-Dhālīyah, 32, 36, 39–51, 65, 77–78, 90, 248

Ibn al-Fārid, ᶜUmar *(continued)*
Dīwān, 2, 29–30, 32, 51, 56, 70, 118, 178, 184–85, 204, 210, 216, 241, 245–46
al-Fā'īyah, 70, 79
al-Hamzīyah, 121
in the *Wafayāt al-Aᶜyān*, 27–30
al-Jīmīyah, 84–102
al-Kāfīyah, 78–79, 91
Khamrīyah, 1, 143, 157, 165–75, 184, 245, 248, 251
al-Lāmīyah, 32, 34–36, 47–49, 52–53, 65, 70, 72, 76–77
life, 1–3
lyrical persona, 48–49, 200, 202, 212–13, 215, 219, 221, 226, 228, 230, 244–45, 249–51
Naẓm al-Sulūk ("Poem of the Sufi Way" = *al-Tā'īyah al-Kubrā*), 3, 30–31, 51, 65, 157, 175, 177, 178–245, 248, 251
poem beginning: *adir dhikra man ahwā*, 158–65, 246–48
al-Tā'īyah al-Ṣughrā, 100, 119–21, 128, 132–33
trance, 2, 31–32, 61, 178, 243
al-Yā'īyah, 53, 123, 127
Ibn Ḥazm, 69
Ibn al-Jawzī, 64
Ibn Jubayr, 134–35
Ibn Khallikān, author of the *Wafayāt al-Aᶜyān*), 15–30, 115, 246
Ibn al-Kīzānī, Muḥammad, 20–23, 32, 115–16
Ibn Maṭrūḥ, 16–18
Ibn Qutaybah, 15, 106
Ibn Rashīq, 15
Ibn al-Rūmī, 64
Ibn Sanā' al-Mulk, 16
Ibn al-Shahrazūrī, al-Murṭaḍā, 18–20, 30, 108–17, 154
al-Mawṣlīyah, 20, 109–15, 117
Ibn Sīnā (Avicenna), 69, 107–108, 236
"Ode to the Soul," 107–108, 155
Ibn ᶜUnayn, 16–18
Ibn Zaydūn, 63, 69
Ignatius of Loyola, author of *Spiritual Exercises*, 250
Ikhwān al-Ṣafā', 69
Imru' al-Qays, 32, 144
intoxication, 46, 120, 123, 143, 149, 152–54, 179–82, 185, 195, 197, 209, 214, 249, 251
invective verse (*hijā'*), 93, 103, 105–106, 115
al-Iṣfahānī, Abū al-Faraj, 15
al-Iṣfahānī, Abū al-Nuᶜaym, 18
Ḥilyat al-Awliyā', 18
al-Iṣfahānī, ᶜImād al-Dīn, 15
ittiḥād (unification, union), 196, 202, 226, 234–35, 243. *Also see:* union

Jacob, 79, 81, 114, 181
Jaᶜfar al-Barmakī, 51
jamᶜ (union), 137, 139, 191, 193, 197, 202, 214, 217–18, 228, 232, 234, 238, 243–44. *Also see:* union
Jamīl ibn Maᶜmar, 63, 66, 83, 199, 245
Jerusalem (al-Quds), 5, 140, 204
Jesus, 5. 249
Jinās. *See:* paronomasia
Job, 79, 81, 181
Joseph, 79, 81, 114, 181
Judaism, 4
al-Junayd, 18, 133–34, 231–34, 236, 239, 242

Kaᶜbah, 125, 129–34, 140, 190, 197, 212
Kamāl-Dīn Muḥammad ibn ᶜUmar Ibn al-Fārid, 2
al-Kāshānī, ᶜIzz al-Dīn, 177
Kawthar, 56
khalwah (solitude), 29, 180–81, 193–94
khamrīyah (wine ode), 1, 143–57
khānqāh (Sufi chantry), 1, 15
khayāl (the beloved's phantom), 22, 57, 71, 110, 139, 158, 222
al-Khayf, 42, 47, 126, 137, 139
kull (each, every, all, whole), 91, 164, 206

Kuthayyir, 199, 245

labasa. *See:* disguise
Lakhmids, 148
Laylā, 67, 109–10, 119, 122, 126, 150, 171, 244
L'Hôpital, Jean-Yves, 245
lightning, 87, 95, 108, 110, 119, 131, 209–10, 244
love sickness, 72, 121, 155, 204, 229
Lubnā, 122–23, 198

Majnūn. *See:* Qays ibn al-Mulawwah
al-Malik al-ʿĀdil, 16
al-Malik al-Kāmil, 3
Mamluk Period, 81
maʿnā (meaning, subtle sense, essence), 12, 24, 42, 78, 80, 82, 88, 95, 160–61, 183, 185, 214, 220, 232
manifestations (*maẓāhir*), 35, 113, 115, 172, 198–200, 215, 217–18, 225–28
maqām/maqāmāt, see: mystical stations
al-Maqqarī, 239
maʿrifah. *See:* gnosis
martyrs of love, 13, 34–35, 47, 53, 66, 90, 94, 98, 125, 249
Martz, Louis, 249–51
Mecca, 2–3, 5, 26, 28, 47–48, 64, 79, 117–18, 121, 125–26, 129–32, 135, 137–41, 148, 204, 241
Medina, 81, 118, 121, 128–30, 135, 138, 204
meditative poetry, 249–51
messenger, 74, 81, 101, 113, 209, 211, 228. *Also see:* Muhammad as God's messenger (*rasūl*)
metaphor (*istiʿārah*), 10, 22, 33, 50, 53–54, 63, 105, 115, 126, 148, 152, 180, 203–204, 235, 242, 248
metathesis (*qalb*), 54–55
Mimshādh al-Dīnawarī, 48
Minā, 42, 47, 117–18, 126, 130, 133–34, 137, 139
moon, 33, 41, 46, 77–81, 123, 162, 164–65, 169, 183, 185, 227, 236. Also see: *badr*
Moses, 5, 214, 228
  Burning Bush, 5, 113, 202
  Siani, 5, 181
Muʿādh ibn Jabal, 46–48
mufīḍ al-jamʿ (one bestowing union), 228
Muḥammad, 2–6, 15, 29, 33, 39, 46–47, 59, 77–79, 81–82, 96–98, 100–102, 112–13, 118, 120–21, 128, 130, 135, 140, 148, 159, 173–74, 177, 200–203, 213–14, 217–19, 226, 228, 236, 244, 246, 251
  as "beloved of God" (*ḥabīb Allāh*), 81, 173
  as God's messenger (*rasūl*), 6, 33, 102, 113, 120, 214. *Also see:* messenger
  as guide, 29, 93, 121, 173, 202, 215, 228
  as seal of the prophets (*khātm al-nabīīn*), 174, 228
  at Badr, 79, 89, 96–98, 136
  Light/Reality of, 77–79, 81–82, 97, 159, 173, 202, 213–14, 218, 220, 22528, 244, 251
  mantle (*burdah*) of, 59, 141
  Night Journey and Heavenly Ascension (*al-isrāʾ wa-al-miʿrāj*) of, 5, 72, 98, 112, 140, 202, 213, 236
  standard (*liwāʾ*) of, 78, 174
Muqaṭṭam Hills, 2, 29
Musāwir ibn Muḥammad al-Rūmī, 36–37, 39, 41, 46, 48
al-Mutanabbī, 13–15, 32–49, 52, 67, 77, 107, 248
muwashshaḥ, 25, 27. 152
mystical states (*ḥāl/aḥwāl*), 6, 26, 31, 42, 44, 49–50, 73, 91, 96, 114, 117, 120, 138, 148, 152–54, 160, 179, 181, 184, 191, 195, 197, 201–202, 209–10, 215, 220–21, 235, 243

mystical stations (*maqām/maqāmāt*), 6, 111, 125, 130, 133–34, 137, 140, 158, 161, 189, 191, 193, 202, 204, 206

al-Nābulusī, ʿAbd al-Ghānī, 81, 90, 98, 100, 123, 138, 243–44, 246
nafs (selfishness, concupiscence), 6, 36, 58, 70–71, 114, 124–25, 163–64, 186–87, 190–91, 193, 197, 207–208, 216–17, 221, 225, 232–33, 242
Najd, 119–21, 126, 244
nasīb (elegiac prelude), 33, 47, 47, 63, 65–66, 76, 103, 105–12, 115, 118, 125, 135, 139–40, 144, 171
nāsūt (human nature), 213
Neuwirth, Angelika, 90
Night of Power, 204, 206
Noah, 181

oppression, spiritual desolation. See: *qabḍ*

pact (*ʿahd*), 48, 76, 83, 120, 140–41, 161, 183–84, 189, 191, 228, 247. *Also see:* covenant
panegyric (*madīḥ*), 3, 16–17, 32–33, 36, 39, 45–49, 67, 77, 81, 93, 103, 105, 107, 115, 130, 135, 141, 246, 248
Paradise, 13, 67, 71, 94, 108, 114, 125, 133, 135, 152, 157, 169, 172, 181, 188, 232
parallelism, 51, 91, 185, 196, 208, 215, 217, 230
paronomasia (*jinās, tajnīs*), 10–11, 49, 51, 60, 91, 180, 184, 204, 208, 230
pilgrimage. *See:* Hajj pilgrimage
pre-eternity, 7, 13, 35, 52, 67, 77–79, 83, 132, 141, 152, 169, 174, 184, 200, 215, 231–36
puppet theater, 221–26, 241–42

qabḍ (oppression, spiritual desolation), 124–25, 180–81, 202, 220
qalb (heart), 19, 36, 39, 67, 70, 72–74, 82, 109, 114, 119, 130, 160, 185, 190, 203, 209–10, 212, 248
qaṣīdah (ode), 1, 15, 20, 23, 27, 65, 103–108, 114–15, 118, 121, 125, 128, 130, 135–36, 138, 141, 143, 145–46, 162, 165, 169, 171, 182, 188, 204, 229, 244
qawm (folk, tribe, Sufis), 57, 154, 173
Qays ibn al-Mulawwah (known as Majnūn), 66, 68, 122, 126, 159–60, 171, 185, 198, 244
al-Qayṣarī, Dāwūd, 172–75, 177
  Sharḥ al-Qaṣīdah al-Khamrīyah, 172–75
al-Qūnawī, Ṣadr al-Dīn, 239–41
Qur'ān, 4–8, 13, 20, 22, 25, 27, 46–47, 52, 66, 71, 81, 83, 93–94, 97–98, 100–102, 106, 112–14, 117, 121, 123, 125, 148, 156–57, 159–60, 173, 175, 177, 181, 186, 190, 198, 201–203, 206, 209, 211, 213–14, 219, 228–29, 235–36, 238, 251
  Light Verse (24:25), 156, 235–39
  Surat al-Aʿrāf (7:172), 52, 83, 215, 231
  Sūrat al-Insān (76), 100
  Sūrat al-Isrā' (17), 100–101
qurb (proximity, nearness), 14, 132, 156, 233
al-Qushayrī, author of the *al-Risālah*, 18, 242

Rābiʿah al-ʿAdawīyah, 9, 18
raḥīl (journey, quest), 103, 105–109, 112, 115, 118, 135, 138, 146
raqīb (spy), 21–22, 44, 73–74, 163–64, 179–81, 205
recollection, 7, 9, 21–22, 36, 63, 65, 71, 82, 130–35, 139–40, 150, 155–56, 160, 172–73, 185, 192, 209, 212, 249–52. Also see: *dhikr*
riḍā (acceptance), 36, 58, 71, 125, 130, 156, 184
riddles (*alghāz*), 28, 54–56, 60–61, 246

*rubā*ᶜ*īyāt* (quatrains), 54, 56–61, 246. Also see: *dū bayt*
rūḥ (spirit) 6, 11, 58–59, 67, 70–71, 124–25, 151–54, 170, 174, 203, 207–208, 221, 232–33, 236, 241, 243
ruins (*ṭulūl*), 105, 108, 110–12, 115–16, 135
Rūmī, Jalāl al-Dīn, author of the *Mathnavī*, 230
Ruwaym, Abū Muḥammad, 84

ṣabr (patience), 23, 51–52, 72–73, 114–15
Ṣādiq, Ramaḍān, 51, 245
al-Ṣafā, 43, 47, 132–34, 213
al-Ṣafadī, 3
Sahl al-Tusturī, 231, 236, 239
ṣaḥw. *See:* sobriety
saints. See: *walī*
Ṣalāḥ al-Dīn (Saladin), 2, 23
*samā*ᶜ (audition), 155, 174–75, 208, 210, 212, 251
Ṣanāᶜī, 15
Sarī al-Saqaṭī, 68
al-Sarrāj, Abū Naṣr, 133
Satan, 31, 66
Sayf al-Dawlah, 13
Scattolin, Giuseppe, 243–44
secret. See: *sirr*
self-praise (*fakhr*), 47, 105, 107, 115
separation, 12–13, 22, 24, 48, 52, 57, 67, 71–72, 76, 84–85, 91, 105, 108, 118, 121, 137, 139, 141, 155–56, 159, 164, 195–96, 200, 203, 205, 247, 250
shadow play. *See:* puppet theater
*sharī*ᶜ*ah* (law), 8, 201–202, 213
shuhūd (contemplation, witnessing), 190–91, 193–94, 197, 207–209, 214, 217, 233–35. *Also see:* contemplation
slanderer (*wāshin*), 73–74, 163–64, 192, 205, 207–208, 233
Sibṭ al-Marṣafī, 135
sirr (secret, joy), 71–72, 75, 84, 156, 180, 185, 232, 242
siwāk (toothpick), 47, 78
sobriety (*ṣaḥw*), 152–53, 179–81, 194–95, 197, 201–202, 214, 218, 231
Sperl, Stefan, 245–48
Standing (*waqfah*). *See:* ᶜArafāt
Suᶜād, 138, 141
Sufi verse, 8–10, 15, 18–20, 103, 108, 154
Sufism, 2–8, 14, 30, 63
al-Suhrawardī, Abū Najīb, 18
al-Suhrawardī, ᶜUmar, author of the ᶜ*Āwarif al-Ma*ᶜ*ārif*, 18.
al-Suhrawardī, Yaḥyā, 23–24, 30, 32, 155–58, 239, 242
sukr. *See:* intoxication
sunnah (custom, custom of Muhammad), 185, 214
al-Suyūṭī, Jamāl al-Dīn, 125, 245
Syria, 13, 15, 25, 27, 43, 65, 137, 139

Ta'abbata Sharran, 90
takhmīs, 27
tanassuk (austerity, asceticism), 46, 74
ṭarīqah (path, a Sufi order), 8, 14, 64, 108, 193
Taṣawwuf. *See:* Sufism
taṣḥīf (substitutions of radicals), 54–55
tavern (*ḥān*), 144–45, 150, 157, 165–69, 172–73, 175, 179–80, 185
tawḥīd (oneness, monotheism), 7, 218, 233–35
al-Thaᶜālibī, 13–14, 64
al-Tilimsānī, ᶜAfīf al-Dīn, 177, 243–44, 246
Traherne, Thomas, 250

ᶜUdhrī tradition, 35, 63, 66–68, 72–73, 75, 77, 83, 102, 109–10, 121–22, 126, 128, 159–60, 164, 171, 184, 198, 200, 208, 229, 244
ᶜUmar Khayyām, 57
Umayyad period, 65–66, 105–106, 148–49
union, 1, 7–9, 11, 13, 22, 43, 47–48, 51–52, 57, 63, 66–68, 71–73,

union *(continued)*
75–76, 83–84, 91, 96, 100–103, 105, 111–12, 117, 120, 125, 127–29, 133–35, 237, 139–41, 143, 153–59, 162–65, 173, 175, 179–81, 185, 187–218, 221, 226–38, 243–50. Also see: *baqā,' ittiḥād, jamᶜ*, and *waṣl*
uns (intimacy), 24, 132–33, 140
unseen world (*ᶜālam al-ghayb*), 218
al-Uqayshir, 149

Vaughan, Henry, 250
visible world (*ᶜālami-sh-shahādati*), 218

waḥdat al-wujūd (the unity of being), 25
wajd (passion, rapture), 46, 50–52, 59, 72–73, 91, 98–99, 111, 122–23, 154, 161, 181, 197
wajh (face). *See:* God
walī/awliyā' (God's chosen friends; saints), 18, 136, 139, 173, 188, 201, 215, 219, 228, 236–37
al-Walīd ibn Yazīd, 149
Wallāda, 69
waṣl (union), 19–20, 54, 59, 124–25, 163–64, 180–81, 234. *Also see:* union
wind, 41, 111. 116, 119–21, 126, 161, 180, 209, 218
wine, 1, 10, 19–20, 23–25, 46, 53, 88, 91, 96, 103, 111, 117–18, 120–23, 143–76, 178–81, 185, 192, 194, 209–10, 229, 244, 246–51
as the beloved, 171–72
as blood, 146–47
wine ode. See: *khamrīyah*
World of the Command (*ᶜālam al-amr*), 190–91
World of Dominion (*ᶜālam al-malakūt*), 218
World of Omnipotence (*ᶜālam al-jabarūt*), 218
wujūd (existence, being), 25, 74, 194–96, 208, 217, 233, 236

al-Yūsuf, Yūsuf Sāmī, 32, 245

Ẓāfir al-Ḥaddād, 16
ẓāhir (outer, exoteric), 8, 23, 76–77, 200, 210, 217
zajal, 152
Zamzam, 47, 125, 140
zāwiyah (Sufi lodge), 15
Zoroastrianism, 4
zuhdīyāt (ascetic poetry), 8–9

www.ingramcontent.com/pod-product-compliance
Ingram Content Group UK Ltd.
Pitfield, Milton Keynes, MK11 3LW, UK
UKHW041923140426
5217IPUK00014B/288

9 781438 439006